THE CHURCH AND ECONOMIC ACTIVITY
IN THE MIDDLE AGES

GILCHRIST, John. **The Church and Economic Activity in the Middle Ages. St. Martin's, 1969. 328p tab bibl 69-13685. 10.00**
Covers less than its title implies. The book is restricted essentially to economic views of the church as expressed through the councils, defined in their most narrow sense. This interesting book might have been fascinating but it appears to have been published rather too hurriedly, so that it lacks stylistic polish. The translations of the conciliar canons which are given in the appendix are agreeably fluent while being sufficiently exact. Since they are not generally available in translation, they alone would make this a useful book. With careful reading, it is also a good reference book on medieval economic theory, the literature for which has been comprehensively incorporated and quoted in the extensive footnotes and bibliography. By comparison, the literature on the councils has been given only brief attention. The text as a whole is somewhat confusing in view of the quite straightforward argument presented in favor of a gradualistic view of medieval economic development. The basic argument is, however, sound. All in all, of interest only to an audience of special students and professionals.

CHOICE   APR. '70

History, Geography &
  Travel
Europe

The Church and Economic Activity in the Middle Ages

J. GILCHRIST Ph.D.

Professor of History
Trent University, Ontario

Macmillan
LONDON · MELBOURNE · TORONTO
St Martin's Press
NEW YORK
1969

© John Gilchrist 1969
First published 1969

Published by
MACMILLAN AND CO LTD
Little Essex Street London W C 2
and also at Bombay Calcutta and Madras
Macmillan South Africa (Publishers) Pty Ltd Johannesburg
The Macmillan Company of Australia Pty Ltd Melbourne
The Macmillan Company of Canada Ltd Toronto
St Martin's Press Inc New York

Library of Congress catalog card no. 69–13685

Printed in Great Britain by
R. & R. CLARK LTD
Edinburgh

Contents

Preface

THIS book grew out of a chance meeting with the late Dr Marcellus Kik at the Institute of Medieval Canon Law,* Washington, D.C., in February 1964. Dr Kik had come to the Institute in the hope of finding some reference work dealing with the economic legislation of the medieval Church. Our joint search had no success, and this prompted Dr Kik to suggest that I might write such a work. Having then no idea of the size of the task, and having just completed one research project, I proposed a monograph of 'some eighty pages or so, consisting largely of a translation of conciliar decrees with commentary'. For this scheme Dr Kik secured the generous financial support of J. Howard Pew of Philadelphia. I am thus grateful to both men for unwittingly plunging me into a task that subsequently turned out to be far more arduous, and equally more rewarding, than I had anticipated.

A preliminary survey of the source materials soon convinced me that the proposed monograph would never do. What was first needed was a general survey, which would take into account the great mass of secondary literature, especially the articles scattered throughout the various learned journals. Such a project would need to be more than just a history of the Church and economic activity in the Middle Ages — if such could be written — but also, and more importantly, a work that would set out the basic principles on which the historical account must surely rest. This would involve the fundamental concepts and interrelationship of several disciplines, namely, the historical, legal, theological and economic, which I thought could be combined in the one work without sacrificing the pre-eminence, in my case, of the historian's craft.

* Now located at Yale, New Haven, Conn.

The decision to undertake what seemed to me a major work of synthesis was soon followed by an equally important decision. It became increasingly obvious that this subject merited more than one volume. However, as I did not want at that time to commit myself to a multi-volume history, the solution that finally emerged was to produce over a number of years three related but separate studies. The first work, which is now offered, is basically a general study of the Church and its economic policies and influences in the Middle Ages, but a great deal of importance is given to the canons and consituations of the General Councils of the Church from the fourth to the early sixteenth century. The second work, at present in preparation, will examine in detail the economic and social ideas of the canonists and theologians in the period, approximately, 1141–1274, a period that opened with the publication of the *Decretum* of Gratian, the Father of the science of canon law, and closed with the second Council of Lyons, which marked the passing of the great era of papal supremacy. The third volume will discuss the effect of economic changes on the institutional organization of the Church in the late Middle Ages (approximately 1274–1500).

This first work is very much unlike what had been projected in the winter of 1964. It is not, in the strict sense of the word, a history of the medieval Church and economic activity, yet it employs historical method and is intended to be read by historians. What I have tried to show is, firstly, the need for the historian of the Middle Ages to give attention to the Church as an economic power, and, secondly, the remarkable complexity of the issues involved. To do this, I rejected any hope of strict chronological treatment; the many examples cited are intended primarily to illustrate principles rather than movements, ideas rather than politics. The main divisions — except for Chapter 2, which deals with the growth of canon and conciliar law — represent themes rather than chronological or 'cause and effect' type of history. Thus Chapter 3 deals largely with economic concepts and sanctions as they influenced (*a*) the external relations of clerics with the laity, and (*b*) the internal harmony and peace of the Church. Chapter 4 is intended to be the main core of the work. It details the economic doctrines of the canonists and theologians, using evidence largely drawn from the period of the twelfth and thirteenth centuries, but with some historical analysis. Despite the economic and social changes of the later Middle Ages these doctrines continued to hold

good (Chapter 5). By contrast, Chapter 6 examines the doctrines at
work and seeks to discover whether theory and reality conflicted in
the Middle Ages or were in agreement. The conclusion re-examines
the celebrated theses of Weber and Tawney, seeking a final answer
to the two major questions posed by this study, namely, whether the
Church exercised an influence in economic matters proportionate to its
wealth, and to what extent was there conflict or harmony between the
economic behaviour of Christians and the doctrines of the Church.
Although the final assessment of Weber and Tawney is that their conclusions have been seriously modified, no one would deny the great
benefit conferred upon historical interpretation by their still justly
celebrated theses.

The inclusion of a large appendix of canons and constitutions of
the general councils in translation serves two purposes. First, these
decrees have been hard of access to the general reader, for Schroeder's
edition* is long out of print. Second, and more importantly, the
texts can be considered within a chronological framework. The
general councils remind the reader that at certain points on the historical time-chart such and such were the economic problems that
concerned the Church. In translating the texts I have completely
reworked Schroeder's translation. However, I am most grateful to
the Herder Book Company, St Louis, Mo., for so generously allowing
me to treat the translation in this way.

The present approach to the medieval Church, its institutions and
values, may create the impression that I set at nothing its spiritual
aspirations and achievements. Such has not been my intention. I
trust I may say that the true spiritual ideals of the medieval Church
will always command my respect and high regard. But it seemed
proper to begin this work from the opposite end of the scale of values,
to assume that the outward or temporal institutional life of the Church
responds to economic pressures, which, in turn, enlightens us as to the
nature of the spiritual ideals themselves.

Before his death in 1965 Dr Kik read the first draft in manuscript.
I am deeply conscious of his early encouragement and support, and his
approval of that first version convinced me that I should go ahead. As
to the final text, my publisher's readers in Australia and England made
many helpful suggestions for improvements, and I should like to

* H. J. Schroeder, O.P., *The Disciplinary Decrees of the General Councils*
(St Louis, Mo., 1937).

record my thanks to Dr Marion Gibbs of the Department of History, University of Melbourne, for seeing so far ahead.

In this process I am deeply conscious of my debt to a great number of historians, former teachers, friends and colleagues whose scholarship and kindness over the years have helped to form whatever good there is in a work of this kind, but for whose blemishes I have only myself to blame. To John LePatourel of Leeds I owe my first taste for medieval history; Philip Jones and John Taylor, apart from allowing me to test their patience in my early post-graduate days, convinced me of the need for a good firm style. Several of my colleagues of the Institute of Medieval Canon Law will easily recognize the great part that their work plays in my own, but in particular I wish to record my gratitude to Giles Constable of Harvard, Brian Tierney of Cornell, John Baldwin of Johns Hopkins, and John T. Noonan, Jr, of the University of California, Berkeley, for the example they have so splendidly set in their own researches.

Without the help of the late Eugene Willging, Librarian of the Catholic University of America, and his staff, as well as the immense co-operation of the Librarian (I. D. Raymond) and staff of the Barr Smith Library at the University of Adelaide, this work could not have been completed. If the bibliography has any merit it is entirely the result of their co-operation, as well as the speedy responses of the staffs of various overseas libraries that supplied microfilms and photostats of various serial literature. I am also grateful to the Rector and members of Canisius College, Pymble, N.S.W., for so kindly allowing me the use of their library and for giving so much of their time to discussing points of detail. Also, I should like to record that this work was completed in manuscript while I was a member of the Department of History, the University of Adelaide, South Australia. Especial thanks must go to the University for its generous grant of research aids and study leave that enabled me to begin the project. With several of my colleagues I found it rewarding to discuss various aspects of the text. In this regard I owe especial thanks to Israel Getzler, now at La Trobe University. Thankfully, he did not always agree with my ideas, which encouraged me to sift them a little more and to put them onto reinforced, if not safer, foundations. I should also like to record my debt to my third- and fourth-year students at Adelaide, who provided challenge and response to many of the ideas in this work. I am especially grateful to my former honours student and now research scholar at the University of Melbourne, Miss Heather Phillips, for her work on the index and checking of proofs. I am indebted to Miss Pamela Hailes of the Department's secretarial staff, who capably handled the various drafts and revisions of the manuscript.

In this catalogue of debts the final acknowledgements are to the three people to whom I am most indebted. These are Walter Ullmann of Trinity College, Cambridge, and Stephan Kuttner of Yale, who helped to shape the course of study that will occupy my pen for some time to come. They will, I hope, accept this acknowledgement for what it is. Lastly, the dedication is a small token to my wife, who first encouraged me to undertake a work of this kind. Without her support it could not have been written.

MEDIEVAL MONEY

Throughout the present work numerous texts and authorities are cited that refer to a large variety of medieval coins and monies of account. These include, to name a few, examples of *Penny Coinage* (penny =denarius =denier), *Large Silver* (Grossus denarius =great coin =grosso =gros) and *Gold* (florin, fiorino d'oro, ducat, ducato d'oro); also such coins of account as the shilling (=solidus =sou =soldo) and pound (=libra =lira =livre) as well as the mark. The considerable variation in the relative value of medieval currency is well-enough known, and there seems little point to be served in attempting to evaluate the various figures given by the authorities. Knowledge of real values would not, in most cases, add to or detract from the arguments or main themes of the text that follows. For further reference the reader should consult *The Cambridge Economic History*, III 576–602, Appendix: 'Coinage and Currency', by P. Spufford.

J. G.

1 Introduction: The Paradox of Spiritual and Economic Well-being

DURING the last quarter-century or so the scope of the study of the Middle Ages has been greatly enlarged. No branch of learning, no field of systematic enquiry has escaped the critical examination of the professional historian or the specialist in related disciplines. The results of these researches have led to frequent and often revolutionary changes in generally accepted interpretations concerning medieval society. Economic developments are no exception.[1] The long prevailing interpretation, that the Middle Ages laboured under a stationary agricultural economic system, dominated by feudal lords and clerics, which inhibited material change and progress, is dead.[2] Along with it has gone the concept that capitalism arose from the ashes of medievalism, deriving its ethic and inspiration from the Protestant Reformers. The connection between religion and capital, as the conclusion (chapter 7) of this work will hope to show, is more complex, more difficult to discern and to delineate, than the Weber–Tawney theses, taking these only as representative of hitherto existing concepts, had seemed to envisage. Instead, the economic historian today refers to the development of capitalism, though not of course of a capitalist society, as a continuous process beginning *c.* 1000 and receiving its main impetus from the remarkable economic expansion that took place during the twelfth and thirteenth centuries. By contrast, the following two centuries (1300–1500) show first a levelling-off (1300–1348) and then a decline in economic production, with very few new technological inventions or much material progress being made.

These conclusions, which are becoming generally known and accepted, derive from the work of a number of medieval economic historians, both American and European. Their detailed researches (especially into municipal archives) have won the profound admiration of their colleagues, and of specialists in other disciplines, who find themselves involved in and much dependent on their work. Such historians as Sapori, Ghinato, Lane, Renouard, Luzzatto, Lopez, De

Roover, to name a few, deserve special recognition. My indebtedness is obvious in the constant use I have made of their researches, a list of which is given in the bibliography.

However, despite the amount of research being done and progress made, differences of opinion still exist and doubtless will continue. The task is endless. No sooner is one position debated and lost, or held, than a second arises to engage the attention. Sometimes the differences amount to contradiction. For example, J. M. W. Bean, in his article in the Economic History Review, xv (1963), dealing with the population of England in the fourteenth and fifteenth centuries, rejects the accepted view that the population continued to decline. But in the same volume G. A. Holmes, in a review article, writes: 'Thanks to Professors Postan, Beresford and others everyone knows that in the fourteenth and fifteenth centuries the population of England fell considerably.'[3] Individual historians can witness to conflict of this kind even in their own works, especially where a decade or more separates different editions.

Economic historians can also have blind spots. One of these led to the present study. On the whole the economists have concentrated on unearthing and interpreting the facts of the medieval economy. Quite rightly they have given a great deal of their time to the history of the merchant and capital expansion. Generally they have little time to spare for the Church, except indirectly, and certainly little opportunity for the task of trying to relate theological and canonical concepts to economic ones. However, in recent years a number of historians, economic or otherwise, have produced works that show the importance of this type of study, e.g. Noonan on usury, Baldwin on the just price and Tierney on the poor law.[4]

The present work aims at being a broad study of the relationship between the Church and economic activity in the Middle Ages. It is therefore largely a synthesis of what others have done, rather than a detailed examination of a particular theme or period. The great amount of literature produced in the last decade or so calls for a re-examination of traditionally accepted views. In examining this material the author gives special consideration to the work of the medieval canonists and to a class of documents — the canons and constitutions of the ecumenical councils — generally neglected by historians. Of course, a study of ecclesiastical legislation in depth would have to deal with local as well as national and general councils, also with the unpublished writings of the canonists and theologians. That is a task for some future date. For the present the legislation cited is simply the canons of the first eighteen general councils, from Nicaea I (an. 325) to Lateran V (1512–17). As the documents are not easily available in translation, a number of representative canons have been translated and included in the Appendix. (Others referred to but not translated are indicated by °, e.g. °Lyons I 2.) The councils themselves cover the period of medieval Christianity, beginning with Constantine the Great's official recognition of the Catholic Church as the religion of the empire in 313, and closing with Luther's 95 Theses in 1517.

A study of the Church and economic activity in the Middle Ages is, in contrast with the declining influence of Christianity today, highly relevant. It is true that the question of the Church's influence in economic affairs in our own time would not be highly relevant, except to the church historian. But in the Middle Ages the Church was a richly endowed corporation whose income made it the wealthiest of societies.[5] Through their revenues churchmen disposed of a great part of the liquid capital of the Western world.[6] The Church was also a spiritual body that exercised a tremendous influence over the peoples of Europe. Arising out of its spiritual mission, the Church evolved weighty and distinctive ideas in economic and social matters, so that it became 'important in every sphere of medieval social life' and consequently a regulator of other people's consumption and expenditure.[7] This argument is reinforced by recalling the simple but sometimes overlooked fact that the local church physically was often the centre of economic and social activity. Churches were places of business and meeting places, as well as places of worship. Merchant churches, such as those in the Baltic and Scandinavian regions from the eleventh century onwards, and possibly earlier, played a significant role in the formation of towns and in the expansion of trade. In such a church as St Peter's at Novgorod (built c. 1185) the merchants would keep their goods, documents and such 'tools of trade' as the weighing scales.[8] Even civil court cases might be settled within their precincts. They were also places of refuge, even for the Jews, and strongholds wherein to lay up one's treasure. In the disturbed conditions of 1266 in England the Jew Aaron of Sidingham entrusted goods to Alan and his wife of Sidingham, who carried them 'with chattels of their own to the church, that they might be safeguarded from the pillagers that were gathering for the siege of Rochester Castle'.[9] Indeed, churches were often used as storehouses, so even monarchs sought their protection. Thus in London the New Temple was used as a royal treasury in the thirteenth century.[10] Despite the injunction of Christ, who 'cast out the merchants from the Temple and overthrew the tables of the money-changers', and the frequent citing of this text in various authorities, the parish church continued as a visible sign of the relationship between the Church and the medieval economy. Spiritually some of these things were not desirable, as the evidence of the conciliar decrees of Lateran IV 19 and Lyons II 25 illustrate. But abuses were hard to eradicate and, in fact, continued throughout the Middle Ages.[11]

Two questions then must receive close consideration, and they do in fact form recurrent themes throughout our work. The first question is whether the Church exercised an influence on economic matters proportionate to its wealth and spiritual authority? The second is to what extent was there conflict or harmony between the economic behaviour of Christians and the teaching of the Church? In other words, to what extent did theory and practice coincide? These questions must be asked. Not to do so would, to draw an analogy, amount to denying *a priori* that contemporary government expenditure in the U.S.A. or U.K., or elsewhere for that matter, concerns or influences the pattern of economic growth, and from this to conclude that the question whether it does or does not do these things is irrelevant.

Using this approach little has been said or written. There are, of course, some notable works already in print that deal with the *general* theme of Christianity and economics in the Middle Ages. Some of these are classics, but with their conclusions now questioned, such as Weber and Troeltsch. Others are modern, but feeble, e.g. Hollis. Frequently their authors generalize too hastily.[12] Their main weakness is the way in which they write of the Church and its 'theories', or the manner in which they gloss over the endless variety of the Middle Ages in its every aspect, whether material or spiritual. Of course there were no economic theories as such in the Middle Ages— economic judgements and decisions, yes, but text-book theory, no; at least not until the thirteenth century when, according to Noonan, the 'scholastic theory of usury is an embryonic theory of economics and the first of such attempts known to the West'.[13] The absence of direct (i.e. specifically directed) teaching by the Church on economic matters must always be kept in mind. The Church never claimed to have *de iure* a direct voice in the economic affairs of others; its direct teaching authority extended only to dogma and morals.[14] Indirectly, and in practice, the opposite was often the case. This dichotomy and virtual contradiction became a source of confusion, which ultimately contributed to the dilemma in which most Christians found themselves when dealing with material wealth.

The dilemma is dealt with at length below (pp. 50–3). Here only the main issues need be stated. Throughout the Middle Ages theologians and canonists recognized the right of ownership of private property, and they based this right on natural and divine law. It applied to individuals and corporations. The Church was a corporation, claiming and exercising the right to ownership over its possessions. Unfortunately, a church was a significant income-producing unit. It had numerous revenues, which included 'burial dues, Mass offerings, Easter offerings, offerings accompanying the administration of some Sacraments, such as baptism and marriage, and tithes'.[15] These attracted lay cupidity. This evoked a clerical reaction and resistance to all attempts by laymen or by the state to interfere in ecclesiastical property rights. Against this is the fact that as a *spiritual* body the Church existed to preach the gospel of Christ. In some respects His message on economic matters was non-committal and His attitude primarily one of non-concern: 'Render to Caesar the things that are Caesar's.' But, if anything, Christ rejected the things of the world. He belonged to the poor rather than to the rich, and He certainly never sought wealth.[16]

The practice of the Church in the Middle Ages was often very different. The reason for this was simple; as a great economic unit the Church could not practise absolutely what it so eloquently preached. At best it could only compromise. One could cite numerous canonical (including conciliar) decrees in which the Church asserted the right to acquire, possess and administer temporal goods, especially property, for the attainment of its own end.[17] Let us make no mistake on this point. Property was wealth. The whole structure of society rested largely on respecting customary rights relating to property. The Church had to respect the customary rights of others, of the laity, otherwise its own economic foundations could easily be undermined.

Consequently, ownership by prescriptive right was also recognized, and for very much the same reason.[18]

Thus the Church followed a policy in which ownership of property was a basic premise.[19]   Characteristically this teaching is embodied in canon 1495 of the modern Code of the Roman Church. Most commentators upon the canon agree that the Church is merely restating a doctrine that has been held from the beginning of Christianity, i.e. the Church, in order to preach salvation for all men, must employ certain temporal means. Its ministers are entitled to support and to the 'tools' of their trade.[20] But this argument holds its dangers. Both in the Middle Ages and beyond, the corporate nature of the Church had to be safeguarded from being undermined by clerical individualism. A great deal of pressure had constantly to be brought to prevent clerics treating their 'benefice' as private and disposable at will. °Lateran III 15 decreed that goods accruing through a benefice could not be willed to others by the cleric who held the benefice. In his gloss the commentator observed that whatever a cleric acquires *intuitu ecclesiae* belongs to the Church.[21] Pressure against individual clerics acquiring sole rights over church property was inevitable, for the Church had commitments to others if it was to fulfil its obligations in charity. Opportunities to acquire property and revenues were never rejected, for the expansion of Christianity after the fourth century made the need, and its satisfaction, correspondingly larger.

Thus, if the spirit of Christianity urged all men to despise wealth, common sense and canon law compelled the clergy to retain and protect the property of the Church. This then was the dilemma of the Church in the Middle Ages; how to preach its message to the world, which involved a denial of the world, and at the same time to be part of the world, materially and economically at least. Short of a universal abnegation of wealth and an heroic confidence in the unforeseeable tomorrow, the clergy could not escape the paradox. Inevitably, conflict between theory and practice arose, and in it resides the history of Christianity and economic activity in the Middle Ages. This consisted largely of the attempt to bring theological and doctrinal solutions to the conflict of interest. The right solution was never really absent; one can discern the escape mechanism 'right to own' and 'right use' from the beginning of the Christian era. The full implications, however, were not realized or dealt with until the period beginning *c.* 1100. *Extreme* measures, motivated by the recurrent theme of apostolic poverty, were sometimes proposed. Thus Pope Paschal II in 1111 suggested that the Church divest itself of its temporal possessions.[22] Philip III revived the idea in 1273, and the Norman legist Pierre Dubois in his *Summaria* (*c.* 1300) suggested that the king of France should hold the papal states as a fief for which the pope would receive a pension equal to its temporal revenues.[23] In the fifteenth century a member of the Curia of Eugenius IV opposed the pope on the idea of territorial sovereignty. He suggested that the *Donation of Constantine* (an eighth- or ninth-century forgery, in fact) was false and that territorial power had ruined the papacy. Let the princes have the states of the Church.[24]

Proposals to surrender temporal goods and resources were patently unrealistic, if we consider the growing strain on ecclesiastical, especially papal, finances as the Middle Ages progressed (see p. 93). The work of Lunt, Waley and Partner has demonstrated the financial problems of the papacy, especially after 1378. Papal armies (largely mercenaries brought together to safeguard the diminishing sources of revenue, mostly coming from the papal patrimony) exhausted available ready cash. In turn, this forced the popes to adopt other unpopular and even less efficient methods.[25]

The preoccupation of the Church with conserving its resources need not thereby have discredited its reputation. The resources came from the prevailing system; they changed as often as it changed. This forced the Church constantly to examine and to modify its teaching on economic matters in the light of its experience. The degree of modification depended largely on the rate at which the socio-economic structure of Western Europe altered. This explains why, in the first thousand years of the Church's history, little progress was made in canonical thought on economic matters. For the background-economy remained substantially unaltered from that which had been inherited from the Graeco-Roman civilization. This was an agricultural economy organized for consumption rather than for the market. Against this background the early Fathers had developed the Church's doctrine on property, trade and wealth. But by 1100 the traditional complex was rapidly altering. Production on a capitalist basis was becoming the driving force of the European economy, which had entered a period of rapid increases in manufacture and trade, all of which reached a peak around 1300.[26] In the early stages this widened the gap between the Church's economic doctrines and current practices, which, in turn, presented to the canonist and theologians the need to re-examine those doctrines.

The fact that this economic revolution of the Middle Ages occurred before 1300, and not after, as was formerly held, is important in a number of ways. The economic movement ran parallel to the intellectual and cultural revolution of the same period. The merchant, his capital and economic organization began to penetrate society about the same time as the theologian, philosopher and jurist were attaining new heights in analysing the intellectual and spiritual bases of Western European thought. The procedure involved, firstly, a comprehensive collecting and amassing of all the texts, and, secondly, the process of sorting, analysing and commenting upon them. This method inevitably included all the ancient texts relevant to economic thought. Consequently this led to some interesting reflections by canonists and theologians upon the economic aspects of problems confronting the new society.

Two factors relevant to their deliberations must be kept in mind. The first of these is that the economic revolution was primarily one of method and organization rather than of large-scale production.[27] Just as the work of the intellectuals did not affect the masses *directly*, so it is doubtful how far the majority were influenced by the commercial revolution. Capitalist production was not mass-production. The gross national product of any country in the Middle Ages was slight in comparison with present-day figures.[28] Agriculture dominated the total economy throughout the period. Here there was change also, but the great leap forward came in the towns, which contained only a minority of the population, probably never more than 10 per cent of the whole.[29] However, some historians argue a compensatory factor: that this 10 per cent bore an influence out of proportion to its numbers. One excellent example is the part played by townspeople in the heretical and popular movements of the late eleventh century and onwards. Also, tension between urban and rural elements developed, and it will be interesting to note how far this was reflected in the Church's policies.[30]

The second factor is that in conceiving and executing its policies the medieval Church enjoyed a power it does not have today. Not merely was the Church in its own right a vital part of society as a consumer and producer: it was also a supra-national society, a political body on a level with the 'state', using that term in a very loose sense.

It had the sort of persuasive and legislative authority that we would speak of the modern state as having. The Church derived this position — theoretically lost at the Reformation, but, in practice, long before — from the combination of its spiritual authority and economic strength, with certain historical accidents that made it the only educative and civilizing force in the West for several centuries. The Church's unity and cohesiveness as an institution (after all allowance has been made for the many abuses that occurred), together with its power of appeal to the *apostolica auctoritas* and the possession of the sentence of excommunication as an effective means for enforcing its will, far surpassed any comparable secular institution in the Middle Ages (see p. 138).

By contrast with the situation today, the authority of the medieval Church was universal, for, apart from Jews and heretics and infidels, and even these belonged in a certain jurisdictional and theological sense, everybody was a member of the Church.[31] The Church made laws, had its own courts and exercised a jurisdiction parallel and often superior to secular authority. It claimed special and direct authority over the clergy (monks, priests and a host of clerics in minor orders) and the right to administer its own possessions (cf Lateran I 8).[32]

Lateran I 8 is the classic exposition of ecclesiastical condemnation of lay interference in its affairs. However, later decrees show a gradual modification of the rigorous doctrine from one of absolute prohibition to one of relative prohibition, that is, laymen could not be granted control of church property without proper authority (papal, declared °Lyons II 22).[33] Lay investiture gave way to lay patronage and the proprietary church as such had disappeared by the thirteenth century.[34] The Church also claimed special authority over the laity, whose role in the Middle Ages as evidenced by conciliar decrees was a subordinate one.[35] °Lateran IV 44 expressed the Church's attitude clearly: 'no power to dispose of ecclesiastical properties has been given to laymen, even though they be religious men, their duty being to obey, not to command . . .'

The authority was direct in spiritual matters and indirect in temporal. Through such devices as the claim to decide cases involving oaths and vows, the church courts supervised the probate of wills, matrimony, charitable bequests, contracts and so on (cf °Lateran IV 37). Ecclesiastical authority could use this power against obstinate or contumacious laymen. Thus, the right to make a will was denied

heretics (°Lateran IV 3) and usurers (Lyons II 27). Also, in the thirteenth century, the papacy, by extending the concept of interference
'by reason of sin' (*ratione peccati*), claimed to be able to intervene
in any corporate or individual affair. Of course the practice was
radically different. How far the Church succeeded in enforcing its
claims, how far it modified them to conform to the common-sense
suggestions of canonists will be examined below.

Our method of examining these things — i.e. largely through
decrees of the general councils — does not exclude consideration of
other equally important sources and means of determining the Church's
economic teaching. The reality of what the Church considered vital
economic issues of the day must be sought also in the working of the
courts, in synodal legislation, in the decisions of the canonists. Conciliar legislation by itself cannot do much to reveal that reality. It
may suggest it, but that is all. Often a general council was the product
rather than the cause of the sweeping change its canons seem to introduce. The canons became the peaks thrown up by a seething mass of
conflict and movement for reform from below. That is why the first
four general councils, a product of dogmatic conflict in the early
Church, and the first four Lateran councils, a product of the Hilde-
brandine or Gregorian Reform movement (*c.* 1049 onwards), acquire
a special significance. But *more* significant is that, although the
general councils constituted only a small part of the body of canon
law, individual canons could acquire an importance out of proportion
to their original meaning and context. This depended on how the
canonists interpreted them. Unfortunately, canon law as an interpretative science did not begin until the late eleventh century. Effective church law dates from about that time, and it reached a climax
towards 1300. Thus what we know of the interpretation of conciliar
canons, even of the ancient ones, is based largely on canonistic glosses
and commentaries of the period 1141–1300. This imposes another
limitation on our work. How serious the limitation is can be dis-
cerned only by attempting, at this stage, to outline the development
of the conciliar decrees and their historical significance.

2 The Medieval Church and its General Councils

A. THE GROWTH OF CANON LAW

ANY study of the decrees of general councils must be seen against the background of the canon law of the Church.[1] The development of the law fell neatly into two periods. The dividing line was the work of the Bolognese monk, Gratian, in 1141. The distinction between the ancient and classical periods of canon law — that is, pre-Gratian (*ius antiquum*) and post-Gratian (*ius novum*) — is an important one. Before Gratian, although plenty of 'laws' with economic significance may be found in the canonical collections, the means of precise interpretation is lacking.[2] To take a law or any statement by a theologian or canonist at its face value could lead to gross error of interpretation. There is also another danger: pre-Gratian collections do not usually present their texts in close order of precedence or authority. Uniform presentation of texts, the attempt to define 'authority', really began with the Gregorian Reform (*c.* 1049 onwards). One of the most significant contributions by these eleventh-century reformers consisted in inaugurating a more systematic study of texts as distinct from merely compiling collections.

In the early Church, canon law as a body of *written* law barely existed. Scriptural texts and a tradition of decisions derived from the 'acts' of local synods formed the basis of ecclesiastical jurisdiction, so long as the Church was illegal in the Roman Empire and thereby excluded from corporate action. From Constantine (*c.* 313) onwards the situation changed. Catholicism was officially sanctioned.[3] This made possible general councils and the making of law to cover the entire Church. Even so the participants in the general councils were largely Greek, concerned with problems in the Eastern Church, so that much of their legislation probably had little direct relevance to the Church in the West. Although the canons of Nicaea I and later councils were quickly translated from the Greek into Latin and acquired a special significance for the West, they did not fully suffice for the

Roman Church under the leadership of the papacy. So these popes issued their own decisions in the form of decretal letters that, together with conciliar canons, became the basis of Western canon law. From the fourth century onwards small 'primitive' collections were made, and by the late fifth century there was enough material to provide a separate, and much needed, collection of canon laws, in the true sense.[4]

Over the next five and a half centuries a number of such collections were produced, for example, the *Dionysiana* (*c.* 574),[5] the *Hispana* (*c.* 600), the *Dionysio-Hadriana* (774),[6] the collection of Pseudo-Isidore (*c.* 846–52)[7] and the *Decretum* of Burchard of Worms (*c.* 1008–12). Burchard's *Decretum* by its sheer volume influenced later collections, long after new compilations specially suited to the needs of the papal reform of the Church that commenced with Leo IX (1048–54) had appeared.[8] The latter were numerous indeed, the most important being the *Collection in 74 Titles* (1074–6), and the collections of Anselm of Lucca (1083), Deusdedit (1083–6), the anonymous *Collection in Four Books* (*c.* 1085), Bonizo of Sutri (1089–95), the *Polycarpus* (1109–13), the *Caesaraugustana* (1110–20) and, above all, the three collections attributed to Ivo of Chartres (*Decretum*, *Tripartita*, *Panormia*) (1094–5).[9]

Briefly, what these 'Gregorian' collections did was to rearrange the subject matter, to introduce new titles and divisions, and to begin to discriminate among the various texts cited as authorities. These preliminaries were essential to the work of Gratian.[10] As the source of law, the collections emphasized papal authority, which they linked with conciliar canons in the rubric that general councils may be held only with the consent of the pope, and that it was the authority of the pope that determined whether a council was general or not.[11] Today, when there is reasonable agreement on what constitutes a general council, the connection may seem an academic point, but not in the Middle Ages, for, as we shall subsequently see, many of the early councils were neither summoned specifically as ecumenical councils, nor were they always regarded as such.

With Gratian began the truly scientific study of canon law in the Middle Ages.[12] His *Concordia discordantium canonum* or *Decretum* is a monument of canon law and a witness to the intellectual renaissance of the day.[13] The *Decretum* was not an official compilation, but it had an extraordinary influence. It was the source for the new schools of canon law and for the work of the decretists. It was accepted for use in ecclesiastical courts, and its influence lasted down to the publication of the *Liber Extra* of Gregory IX in 1234, and even beyond.[14]

Gratian also commented on the texts in an attempt to sort out their contradictions. In doing this he evolved his method of 'explain, elaborate and interpret', which influenced canonical interpretation for the rest of the Middle Ages.[15] The church courts became extremely busy. Papal authority and canon law complemented one another. The study of canon law became a major discipline and the means to advancement.* Several of the great popes, e.g. Alexander III (1159–81), Innocent III (1198–1216) and Innocent IV (1234–54), were skilled canonists.[16] The Roman court became the final court of appeal, the highest court, as well as being a court of first instance, if the pope so decided. The papal decisions were usually embodied in decretals or letters. The text set forth the problem, argued points of law and finally gave a decision. Such decretals, which were issued in their thousands, were definitive, for they superseded all inferior courts' decisions.

The decretals dealt with the day-to-day affairs of the Church and of society in general. As has already been pointed out, a complete understanding of the Church's role in economic affairs would demand an exhaustive study of the decretals, as well as the commentaries upon them.[17] After Gratian the *corpus* of canon law was completed by a number of collections of papal and conciliar decisions, i.e. the *Liber Extra* of Gregory IX (1234),[18] the *Liber Sextus* of Boniface VIII (1298), the *Clementinae* of Clement V (published by his successor John XXII in 1317), the *Extravagantes* of John XXII and the *Extravagantes Communes*.[19] The six collections constituted what has come to be known as the *Corpus Iuris Canonici*.[20]

Although the decretals used the method of jurisprudential enquiry (in contrast to Gratian's dialectical approach) to solve queries put to the popes, there was still a need for further interpretation once the text had become part of the canonists' stock in trade.[21] Numerous glosses were produced. The *glossa ordinaria* to the *Decretals* was compiled by Bernard of Parma (c. 1241–66). Johannes Andreae was the author of the gloss to the *Liber Sextus* and to the *Clementines*. Zenzelinus de Cassanis glossed the *Extravagantes J. XXII* in 1325.[22]

The greatest of the twelfth-century decretists was Huguccio, whose

* Its preponderance aroused Dante's indignation (*Paradise* IX 133–5).

summa was completed *c.* 1190.[23]   Many of his views were incorporated into the *glossa ordinaria* of Johannes Teutonicus to Gratian's *Decretum* and these will interest us, e.g. on charity.[24]   The full flowering of the canonical development was reached with the work of Cardinal Hostiensis (d. 1271).   His genius as a canonist has been compared to that of Accursius and Odofredus in Roman Law and to that of Thomas Aquinas in theology.[25]   Canonists, civilians, philosophers and theologians alike scaled the heights of their respective disciplines, so that, in retrospect, the later period (fourteenth and fifteenth centuries) always seems to be one of decline.   Johannes Andreae (1270?–1348) was the last medieval canonist who was in any way comparable to Hostiensis or Huguccio.[26]

In these developments an interesting and relevant feature (from the point of view of economic practice) is the efforts of the canonists to adhere to the principles of Roman Law.   The rediscovery of Roman Law in the late eleventh century and the opening of the great law schools, beginning with the greatest of them all, Bologna, influenced profoundly the legal systems of medieval Europe.   A great deal of what we shall have to say on the relationship between canon law and economics depends very largely on recognizing that in the Middle Ages there was a definite place for the Roman Law in the law of the Church.

The contribution made by Roman Law to the systematization of the canon law has already been noticed.   But the relationship went deeper than this, to the point that where canon law was silent, Roman Law could speak provided it did not contradict Scripture or accepted doctrine.[27]   In fact, in economic matters, the canon law was often silent or deficient.[28]

The Church had always had a strong interest in upholding the civil law.   The decree of Milan in 313 had safeguarded the Church's rights and guaranteed their future recognition by the emperors.[29]   Centuries later, when Church 'liberty', including its property, was seriously threatened, some canonist aimed to give this decree a more substantial form and juristic scope.   He produced the *Donation of Constantine*, which became the basis of many appeals asserting the territorial independence of the Church, especially during the eleventh and early twelfth centuries.   Such an appeal to secular law strengthened the canonists' natural interest in the work of the Roman lawyers at Bologna.   For the next two centuries the two systems interacted closely; for example, the canonical concept and juristic expression of the inalienability of church property — obviously a fundamental one for the Church, if it was to safeguard its possessions — was drawn almost entirely from the Roman Law.[30]   Likewise, in testamentary legislation, and again in the discussion of fraud and sale, the canonists drew upon the Roman Law.   On the other hand, the canonists rejected Roman Law where this conflicted with accepted Christian ethics.   This may be illustrated by the Roman doctrine relating to agreements based on simple understanding between the parties. Roman Law rejected this *nudum pactum* as a basis for claims.   The canonists, and later the theologians, enforced such agreements, arguing that he who breaks his word is guilty of the sin of lying.   It is hardly necessary to stress the importance this concept of 'my word is my bond' had for the development of a free economy.[31]

B. CONCILIAR LEGISLATION

The foregoing justifies the assertion that any study of the Church's teaching on economic matters will have to concentrate on the period after 1141.   This applies especially to the councils, whose history also falls into two distinct periods with a dividing line at *c.* 1100.

Conciliar decrees constituted only a small part of the sources of canon law.[32]   The canons of the eighteen general councils, from Nicaea I (325) to Lateran V (1512–17), some of which are often cited in the course of our enquiry, covered a period of twelve hundred years.[33]   Viewed in isolation, they cannot have had much significance for the economic affairs of the Church or for the rest of society.[34]   But of course they ought not to be viewed in this fashion.   Their effectiveness must be judged against the background of other legislation, judicial actions and interpretative commentaries.[35]   This raises questions that must for the present remain unanswered.   How far were the canons incorporated into other collections?   To what extent did the metropolitans, bishops and prelates in their provincial and diocesan synods, and in their chapter meetings, apply the decrees of the councils? And for the post-Gratian period especially, what had the theologians and canonists to say about the contents of particular canons?[36]   To answer these questions demands a detailed survey of local and synodal decrees and their filiation with canons of the general council of a type that Cheney, Gibbs and Lang have done for the English Church in the thirteenth century. Two things are certain: many of the conciliar texts merely 'took over' decrees of provincial or national councils. Lateran II, for Hefele, contained 'nothing new'. Many of the canons came from the councils of Clermont and Reims.[37]   The second point to notice is that no decrees were taken over *en bloc* by a provincial council. Only relevant decrees, it seems, were published. Thus Hubert, Archbishop of Canterbury, at the Council of Westminster (c.5) repeated Lateran III on procurations.[38]   Some bishops intended to implement decrees, but failed to do so.[39]   Another element of uncertainty lies in the possibility that certain canons were taken over by one council from another, from synod to synod, without much regard for questions of relevance or suitability.[40]   Lateran III 12 condemned clerics holding secular office, which was common in a feudal society. The decree did not meet general application in England when, in 1179, three of the four chief justices appointed were bishops, namely Ely, Norwich and Winchester.[41]   Finally, in economic matters the laity and not the clergy had the dominant role, which was much larger obviously than any other role they had in medieval christendom. For once, the clergy were practically excluded by reason of the subject-matter, and economic decisions lay outside ecclesiastical authority. The Church naturally enunciated principles of action in order to guide the individual in the morality of his decisions, but the day-to-day business of estate management, labour, trade, commerce, buying and selling lay beyond the teaching authority of the Church.[42]   This raises the final question whether, even if it may be assumed the bishops and clergy fulfilled conciliar canons, the laity paid much attention? These, then, are the sort of questions raised in a work of this kind, and, whether answered or not, the author hopes they will serve to remind the reader of the as yet primitive state of our enquiry into their nature.

The form of the medieval councils poses another danger for the unwary reader. He must avoid, it seems, projecting back into the Middle Ages the modern image of a general council, such as the recent twenty-first (Vatican) council.[43]   The Code of the Roman Church (cc.222–9) closely defines a general council.[44]   It is an assembly of bishops and other specified persons invested with jurisdiction, convoked by the pope and presided over by him, for the purpose of formulating decisions on questions of the Christian faith or ecclesiastical discipline. These decisions require papal confirmation. Cardinals, patriarchs, archbishops, bishops and titular bishops if summoned by name, abbots primate and abbots general of the monastic congregations, superiors general of the exempt Orders and such abbots and prelates as exercise jurisdiction over a district of their own are entitled to attend. An ecumenical council does not require all bishops to be present, and here it should be noted that many of the medieval councils were very poorly attended. The modern definition would not cover many of the early councils, e.g. in the matter of being summoned and presided over by the pope. Thus there were no Latin bishops and no papal representatives at Constantinople I (381). Some 150 members attended. This was not intended to be a general council, and was only gradually accepted as such. The first three Lateran councils were not seen as ecumenical from the commencement, but became so by subsequent recognition of their decrees. However, Lateran IV was conceived as one from the outset.[45] Even the greatest of the Greek councils, Chalcedon (451), attended traditionally by 600 members, had only one papal legate and two African bishops.[46] The barbarian invasion of Attila the Hun had made it impossible for bishops from the West to attend. No pope was personally present at the first seven councils, nor did his representatives always preside. Some modern authors are at pains to deal with this point. Thus Corish states that the council is convoked by the pope, either formally or explicitly, or, as in the case of the first councils, by his recognizing it as ecumenical and associating himself with its acts, presiding in person or by his legates, and confirming its decrees.[47]

The medieval councils, certainly until Lateran IV (1215), lacked the clear-cut form of the modern council. If then contemporaries were confused, can the medieval conciliar decrees be dismissed as somewhat irrelevant? The answer is no. Each council represented some crisis when the Church had to depart from its ordinary teaching to deal with the emergency. The decrees demand attention, especially the canons of the later (Latin) councils, in which disciplinary, including economic, issues predominated.

The *work* of a council must be seen as a unity, that is the events leading up to, through and after the council, to the point where the decrees have become part of the tradition of the canon law. Sometimes it is the preliminaries that excite the most comment. Thus

Innocent III, in summoning Lateran IV, ordered the metropolitans 'personally and by discreet agents' to enquire into a large number of problems relating to the Church of the day. The results of the enquiry, in the case of the Irish Church, to cite one example, revealed that the outstanding problems were of a socio-economic nature, such as the problem of ecclesiastical lands and feudal tenure, the completion of the diocesan organization, reluctance to pay tithes, and hereditary succession to ecclesiastical benefices.[48]   Other decrees were significant because of their dual economic and constitutional importance, such as °Lateran IV 46, which, for England, by preventing clergy submitting to arbitrary taxation, reinforced the theme of Magna Carta.[49]   A council like Lyons II fulfilled its purpose, not by its so-called reforms, but by granting a sexennial tenth on the income of all clergy, with few exceptions.[50]   Again, the fifteenth-century councils may have been remarkably unsuccessful, but they nevertheless illustrate the problems as the Church of the day saw them, as well as the failure to cope with real issues.   Thus Basel, which had condemned papal exactions, had, on 8 February 1434, to resort to exactly similar measures by imposing a tenth on the whole Church.[51]   It also gave favoured treatment to members of the Curia and to religious, which helped to get the clergy to desert the council.[52]   Nor can one read the diaries of members of the councils, e.g. Fillastre's *Diary of Constance*,[53] or speeches made by participants, without being struck by the intense activity that led to so much failure.[54]

The councils as a whole did not form a unity.   The first eight councils — whose meeting became possible after Christianity got acceptance under Constantine the Great — were Greek, all held in the East, eastern Europe or Asia Minor.   The majority of the participants were from the same region.   They were summoned, and even presided over (e.g. at Nicaea I), by the emperor or his legates.[55]   The emperor approved the decisions of the councils and subsequently promulgated them as imperial laws.   Eastern predominance was therefore natural, for Asia and North Africa were the strongholds of early Christianity.[56]

With the breakdown of the unity of the Roman Empire — the division of the Mediterranean world into two parts with a wedge of barbarian settlers down the centre — Roman Christianity began to dominate the western part.   The tradition of the general council died out in the East, but passed over to the West.   Consequently, the remaining ten Councils were Latin, summoned by the popes, meeting in the West (Italy, France or Germany), and attended largely by bishops, abbots and other representatives of the Roman Church.[57] The two sets of councils differed also in subject-matter. The Greek councils had been primarily concerned with doctrinal issues, and their procedure was modelled on that of the ancient Roman Senate, e.g. Constantinople I (381) summoned by Theodosius to settle the protracted dispute between Catholic and Arian, or Ephesus (431) against the doctrinal errors of Nestorius.[58] Some of these councils dealt with disciplinary and economic matters, but not all.[59] For this reason we can exclude four of the first eight or Greek councils from our consideration, i.e. Constantinople I (381), Ephesus (431), Constantinople II (553) and III (680-1). Admittedly the Greek Church tried to remedy the last occasion by holding the *Concilium Quinisextum* (692), but this council is not recognized in the West.[60]

The Latin councils grew out of the reform synods of the eleventh century, held in various European countries under the presidency of the popes or their legates from *c.* 1049 onwards, and were mainly concerned with disciplinary issues and secular affairs. The change in content coincided with, and was part of, the cultural and economic supremacy that the West began to achieve from that time onwards.[61] The East, of course, was no longer in communion with Rome.[62] The concern of the papacy with discipline, organization and reform of the Church was reflected in the work of the councils it summoned, e.g. investiture (1123), papal schism (1139), papal elections (1179), crusade and reform of discipline (1215), excommunication of Frederick II (1245), aid for the Holy Land (1274), the weakness and decline of the Knights Templars (1311), schism and heresy (1414), reform of the Church in head and members (1431-43); schism, reform and crusade against the Turks (1512-17).[63] The decrees were largely regulative or directive. Their contents mirror most of the economic and social conditions of the time that were of interest to the Church — simony, pluralism, usury, tithes, provisions for the crusades, papal finances, the Jews, lay interference in church matters, especially the administration of its property. These are the questions that largely concern the present work, so the texts of the Latin councils are frequently cited (see p. 256 n 65).

The Latin councils fall into two distinct groups. The first four (Lateran I-IV) portray an ebullient and confident Church, led by the

B

papacy. They were inspired by the reform ideals of the Gregorian movement.[64] Lateran IV was the culmination of this process. It is a monument of law, unique in the history of ecumenical councils. Its statutes will merit close consideration in several parts of this study.[65]

After Lateran IV the church leaders became increasingly concerned with narrow issues, to the detriment of the Church at large. This may seem a rash generalization. But even the most ardent of supporters of the Roman Church in the Middle Ages will probably admit that *c.* 1215 was the peak period, followed by a levelling-off, then a falling-away and eventual decline in the last two centuries (1300–1500). The papacy became more and more enmeshed as a temporal power in a political struggle for survival. The manner in which the crusade ideal was gradually transformed into a mere political weapon exemplifies this decline. It came to replace the sentence of excommunication and interdict, being directed against other Christians, even individuals. The change is already noticeable in the crusade against Constantinople in 1204, but the full force came later and it was shown in the campaign against Frederick II and then against his son, Manfred, the latter accused of an *impium foedus* in collusion with the Saracens of southern Italy.[66] Economic factors entered this struggle, and the question may be asked whether there was a causal relationship between the general economic decline of Western Europe after *c.* 1300 and the subsequent collapse of the spiritual authority of the Church?[67]

The changes after 1215 are mirrored in the later councils, which present an anti-climax. Their canons show new external forces at work. The councils take on a political tinge corresponding to the concern of the popes in temporal affairs. Thus Lyons I excommunicated and deposed the Emperor Frederick II.[68] The decrees of Lyons II (1274) and Vienne (1311–12) were negative and insufficient, except in their length.[69] After Vienne other developments began to make themselves felt in Europe generally. The secular state slowly emerged. Strong feelings of anti-clericalism were manifested, humanism and conciliarism permeated the Church; economic progress slowed down, war and plague created social and economic distress (see p. 85). If the Church had hoped to keep its hold on society, it would have had to approach differently the problems of the time, e.g. the social problems of vagrancy and lay education. But nothing was done. The decrees of the councils both general and provincial, as well as canonistic teaching, reflect only the old issues

and the old solutions.   Not surprisingly these later councils were ineffective, and the last of them, Lateran V (1512–17), concluded its
work on the very eve of the Reformation.[70]

The fifteenth-century councils that failed to bring about the much
needed economic and social reform had probably been destined to
failure from the beginning.   The constant demand for 'Reform of the
Head' meant only one thing, a curtailment of papal exactions of
money.   A council such as Basel showed the great rift between pope
and cardinals, who with large households to maintain, and, in the case
of the pope, heavy expenses for the payment of mercenaries, em-
bassies and renewal of loans, could see no farther than successive
attempts to limit each other's functions.[71]   Basel as a council also
failed to have decrees directed against papal exactions accepted and
applied to diocesan revenues.[72]   Papal and curial corruption in the
fifteenth century was not new: what was new was the obvious failure
to agree on real remedies.

The canons of the eighteen councils vary enormously in length.
Lateran II 24: 'We decree further that no payment shall be demanded
for chrism, oil and burial' is brief and to the point.   Vienne [38]
occupies six printed pages, after abbreviation.   Some decrees were
of their nature trivial.   Lateran IV 19 prohibited the use of churches
as warehouses, a decree already discussed.   The abuse seems to have
been a common one, yet, for us, hardly a matter for a general council.
Perhaps the very location of the decree emphasizes the depth of the
abuse and the amount of feeling it roused at the time.[73]   This type of
decree serves another purpose.   It helps to determine the extent to
which one may speak of doctrinal authority in relation to these largely
disciplinary measures.   If Lateran IV 19 is not doctrinal, what of the
canons on usury?

Again there is much repetition from council to council.   The same
subject reappeared even in the one council in different guises, thereby
producing a reinforcing effect.   Some conciliar canons or even groups
of canons were clearly dependent on other provincial or local synods,
e.g. the decrees of Lateran I (1123) have been compared to the programme of the Irish council of Cashel in 1101.[74]   Twenty-three of
the thirty canons of Lateran II repeated earlier legislation.[75]   There
was nothing unique in these relationships; they merely signify that
the programme of the Gregorian Reform was bearing fruit.

One difficulty about the canons is that the official acts of the councils have not always survived (e.g. Lateran I), so our knowledge of the workings of some councils is not complete.[76]   Again, to the reader, it may seem that the contents of certain canons included in the translation are not immediately relevant, e.g. on simony; invariably the longer canons contain material that is irrelevant.[77]   The decision as to what to omit or include is a personal one that depends on the ultimate significance, to the author, of the material, which the present text will elucidate.   The translations therefore contain canons on simony and clerical incontinence because these weakened the Church's financial structure.   Such decrees could be motivated by temporal as well as by spiritual considerations (see p. 32).

The validity of this argument may be seen in the distribution of subject-matter among the provincial reform synods of the late eleventh and early twelfth century.   The Gregorian reformers, men of Peter Damiani's calibre, had to be astute in financial matters.   Papal reform depended on a secure income, so the finances had to be set in order if spiritual objectives were to be attained (see p. 32).   The provincial councils in question contained some 320 decrees; of these 151 were 'economic', i.e. directed at simony, clerical marriage and the abuse of temporal offices, especially to safeguard ecclesiastical lands and revenues. The decrees threatened vested (usually lay) interests.   Consequently, although some of the opposition to church reform may have been genuinely religious, a large part derived from concern over the implied threat to lay, and individual clerical, control of church property and income.[78]

3 Growth and Development of Economic Doctrines 1049–1350

Some Special Considerations

A priori there must be some degree of correspondence between the Church's economic teaching, and therefore its legislation, and the economic structure of society at large. Admittedly, moral principles are of their nature unchangeable and unchanged, but their practical application will vary according to the nature of the society in which they are applied. The reaction of the medieval Church to the injunction of Christ to despise the things *of* the world, yet, as reason dictated, to secure enough goods to carry on its mission *in* the world, was not always the same.[1] A change in economic circumstances usually led to a corresponding adjustment in the Church's teaching. The factor of economic change did not lie in the control of the Church, and this must be kept in mind when examining the nature of the Church's economic doctrines.

A. The Economic Background

The Middle Ages in terms of its economic development divides into two contrasting periods, with the transitional stage 900–1100.[2] An agrarian, subsistence economy dominated the first period. Land was practically the sole source of productive wealth. Admittedly, after the collapse of the Roman Empire, trade and commerce did not die out, but they decreased and had no great impact on the general economy of Western Europe.[3] Some historians argue that trade began to expand again about the time of the Carolingian Renaissance (c. 800).[4] There seems no doubt that continuous urban and regional development occurs from the tenth century onwards, despite the inroads of Vikings and Magyars.[5] In general, however, Europe did not

feel the full effects of these changes until the twelfth century.[6]   From
that time historians begin to speak of an economic revolution —
capitalist, commercial and agricultural.[7]

The economic revival — whose home was Italy — did not occur
throughout Europe simultaneously, but at different times and places,
and often in quite different ways.   It also had other than economic
effects.   In Italy it led to communes and emancipation from Imperial
and papal control.   In England it contributed to the development of
royal centralization.   Both cases presented the Church in each region
with a different set of problems.[8]

Italy had the leading role.   Here the commercial town proper,
which most historians regard as the essential feature of the revival, for
it created supply and demand, all season buying and selling, had appeared by the end of the tenth century and even earlier.[9]   Venice was
the first of these intensely active commercial centres, then came Pisa,
Genoa and Florence by the late eleventh century.   Capitalism was
born in such places.   Expressed simply, this consisted of bringing
labour and capital together in a more convenient form than provided
by the existing feudal relationships.[10]   In agriculture it meant a radical
change in organization, such as the rise of the *complantatio* and *colonia
partiaria*.[11]   Increasing demand for food and high prices gradually led
to an increase in demesne farming, which reached its height in the
thirteenth century.   In England, on the Cistercian estates, the period
1276–1322 was 'the high farming years'.[12]   Villages tended 'not to
be enucleated, open-field systems do not exist or are peculiar, lordship
is weak and freedom widespread among the peasants'.[13]   Land values
in Sherington (Leicestershire, England) rose from about 1·75*d* an
acre in 1140 to 8*d* an acre in 1300.   Correspondingly the price of
wheat per quarter moved from 1·89*d* to 7·01*d*.[14]   In London communal rents rose by 50 per cent between 1234 and 1307; food prices
lifted two-thirds between 1212 and 1280.[15]   In commerce there
emerged the partnership principle in various forms, e.g. the bilateral
commenda (*collegantia* in Venice, *societas* in Genoa) in which one partner
at home provided two-thirds of the capital and the one who took the
voyage one-third.   Liability was limited, and the partners divided the
profits half and half.   For land-based commerce there was the *com-
pagnia* or ordinary partnership, which was especially used by merchants
who crossed the Alps.   From these individual arrangements developed
large-scale businesses and enterprises, which made the period down

to the early fourteenth century one of great economic growth.[16]

The companies comprised large and small investors. For example, at Genoa in the period 1155–64 there were some 180 investors; of these 130 made only one or two investments. Thus, two priests engaged several factors to carry their investments while on their own business ventures. In all, some 72 per cent of the investors contributed only 16 per cent of the total invested capital. Some 6·6 per cent owned 40·4 per cent of the investments, that is, £23,170. The biggest investor was Ingo de Volta (£4035) and the busiest Bonusiohannes Malfilaster who invested in 44 different contracts with a total capital outlay of £2245. Together with the factors some 520 persons were concerned.[17] From such companies developed the great family businesses of the late thirteenth and early fourteenth centuries, where the name was a collective one, comprising a group of merchant investors, with a duration of many years, and involving numerous ventures with periodic renewal and reforming of the articles of association. Such were the great firms at Florence, the Scali who lasted more than a hundred years, the Bardi and Peruzzi for seventy years.

Trading privileges were acquired, often at a price, such as allowing one's ships to be used for protection and conveyance of the crusade armies.[18] Great fortunes were made. The total patrimony of Bartolo di Jacopo Bardi when he died around 1320 was 17,240 florins in movables and 8400 in property. Subsequently his sons increased the family fortune to 129,142 florins. Between 1310 and 1345 the Bardi company had 120 employees on its payroll, distributed among 25 branches (12 in Italy, 4 in the Levant, and 9 in France, the Low Countries, England, Spain and Tunis).[19] The economic failures in Italy around 1345 brought the era to its close. In all these things, especially the failure of the banks, the papacy had a part, as we shall see.[20]

Italy may have been pre-eminent in the economic revival, but there were other centres of trade and growth, notably Flanders, and later England, France and Germany.[21] Different regions or towns had their specialties: Gascony for wine, Milan for armour, Lucca for silk, Florence for its bankers.[22] But the dominant product was cloth, especially the export of fine cloths, which helped to keep the balance of trade with the East.[23]

Throughout, the cause of the growth seems to be related to the rise in population.[24] The period from about 1000 to 1348 saw a general increase in the population of Europe, especially in Northern Europe, e.g. the population of England more than tripled between 1086 and 1346;[25] in Italy it rose from 5 to 7 or 9 millions in the period 950 to 1300.[26]

In particular cases the growth rate can be calculated, e.g. for Taunton in Somerset, England, where the male population over twelve years of age *c.* 1209 was 612 persons, and in 1359 was 1448 persons. This was an accumulative annual rate of 0·85 per cent, i.e. almost twice the rate of population increase in England over the eighteenth century. In 1200 the population of London was 30,000, rising to 60,000 by 1340. In the Fenland the population density of the Wapentake of Elloe before the Black Death was 0·46 or 293 persons to the square mile. In 1951 it was 0·32 or 208 persons per square mile. Of the large cities, before the Black Death, the population of Paris was 80,000, Toulouse 24,000, Cologne 40,000, York and Bristol 10,000–14,000; Milan, Naples, Florence each over 50,000; Ghent 56,000, Bruges 35,000, Antwerp 18,000.[27]

Such increases created supply and demand for goods, led to migration of labour, the spread of new ideas and techniques, and the need for capital.[28] Inventions, such as the water-mill and water-wheel, the windmill (*c.* 1105), the system of levers, the horse-collar and whipple-tree, the rudder (1180), and later the clock, introduced a mechanical rhythm into a world once governed only by its natural rhythms. A simple tool like the hinged flail (*c.* 1000) speeded up the threshing of corn. In the thirteenth century large sailing vessels emerged, and the oared trader virtually disappeared.[29] The fulling mill also revolutionized the cloth-making industry.[30]

The growth of new towns and the movement of labour was especially important. The Germans were in demand as miners and metal workers, Flemish craftsmen for wood.[31] In 1300 some 450 foreign workmen were brought from Paris, Brussels, Brabant, Namur and Bruges to work in the English mints; 25 of these crossed over to Ireland to recoin money.[32] Such movements often cut across feudal barriers, but found sympathetic understanding from the canonists (see p. 86). With the growth of urban industry and trade there emerged the whole complex of a capitalist system, such as partnerships, joint liability, banking, double-entry bookkeeping, bills of exchange and letters of credit.[33] The whole process was intensely dynamic. The role of the merchant moved from being a predominantly itinerant function to that of the sedentary organizer of a network of intricate financial operations. This development coincided with, and was part of, the rise and subsequent decline of such institutions as the Champagne fairs.[34] These were held in a cycle from January to October at such places as Lagny, Bar-sur-Aube, Provins and Troyes, and lasted from sixteen to fifty days. As fairs they declined after 1260, except for their financial functions, which lasted until about 1320.[35]

In the towns of Europe the commercial expansion produced the new class of bourgeoisie, whose names matched those of the great feudal families that now ceded first place to them. Thus, in Venice, were the Balbi, Soranzo, Ziani and Mastropiero; in Siena, the Tolomei, Buonsignori and Salimbeni; in Florence, the Bardi, Peruzzi, Alberti, Acciaiuoli, Albizzi, Medici and Pazzi; in Genoa, the Spinola, Doria, Grimaldi, Fieschi, Uso di Mare, Gattilusio, Lomellini and Centurioni; in Douai, the Markiet, Le Bland, Boinebroke; in Ghent, the Uten Hove and Van der Meire; in Arras, the Stanfort, Crespin, Hucquedieu and d'Yser families. They concentrated wealth and power in their 'companies'. Such things not merely created for the Church an atmosphere alien to the traditional thought, and forced churchmen to consider their teaching on trade, capital and the merchant anew, but they also directly, and immediately, involved the Church and its clergy scattered throughout the society in which the changes occurred.[36] The legislation of council and synod reflect the reactions.

B. The Church Without — Alienation and Recovery of Economic Resources

The Church found its attitudes coloured by the fact of it being the dominant landholder in Europe.[37] This was no accident. In a religious age the Church received and encouraged gifts of land through the generosity of the faithful. During times of migration, and later of the Crusades, the clergy were well placed to benefit from those who needed cash in return for their property.[38] The Church was a permanent corporation.[39] Its lands were protected from 'internecine war and fratricidal ambition', which was one of the factors that created social mobility in the Middle Ages. During periods of war, wealthy members of the nobility often sought refuge for themselves and their lands with the monastic orders.   Many laity appreciated the advantages enjoyed by the Church in this respect.   There is, for example, the fascinating phenomenon of lay landholders turning themselves, their lands and their families, into 'monasteries', with the intention of avoiding certain common burdens that fell on lay but not church lands, such as occurred in England in the late seventh and eighth centuries.   The parallel with contemporary taxation practices is obvious.   In the later Middle Ages groups of merchants took minor vows as unbeneficed clergy for similar reasons.   In business matters, civil law was often more harsh than canon law, a point that is often overlooked when considering the relevance and influence of the latter.[40]

The growth of certain institutions in the Church had more than an ordinary impact upon general economic activity.   The most important was the development of the papacy and its finances.   Although the following description is taken mainly from the thirteenth and early fourteenth centuries, when the papal Camera became most highly organized, the observations apply generally to its finances throughout the Middle Ages.   The revenues came from spiritual and temporal sources.   The spiritual revenues included an income tax on the clergy (the tenths or *decimae*), various *servitia* paid by prelates on appointment to office, annates from priests collated to a benefice, certain payments such as the *visitationis tributum* by bishops on *ad limina* visits, various chancery fees and taxes on religious orders.   There was also the income from the preaching of indulgences and from gifts and legacies.[41]   Temporal revenues derived from three main sources: firstly, the income from the papal states, a large proportion of central Italy donated to the papacy by the Frankish kings in the eighth century, and added to by later popes; secondly, the *census* from papal monasteries, and churches that lay outside the patrimony; and, thirdly, Peter's Pence.[42]   In the period of economic growth the revenues were assured.   But as soon as depression hit particular churches or countries, outgoing or foreign payments were the first to suffer.

In the collection and organization of these revenues the papacy arranged for agents outside the Camera.   At first these were the Templars, later the Sienese and finally the Florentine bankers.   The Roman branch of such houses usually had moneys to lend as capital to other branches of the firm.[43]   Its manager held the office of Depository in the papal Camera, so that the two institutions became closely associated.[44]

Another institution that led to ecclesiastical accumulation of property was that of the religious orders — the black monks from the sixth century, the white monks from the twelfth, the friars from the thirteenth — with their self-imposed rules and highly regulated way of life. Their self-denying ordinance fostered a rapid growth in land and revenues.*

Finally, there was the tithe. This tax played a large part in the medieval economy; according to Constable, 'no tax in the history of Europe can compare with tithes in length of duration, extent of application, and weight of economic burden. Who paid and who received these tithes, is an important question for historians.'[45]

Theoretically, all this income was needed, for the Church was the only (if not the ideal) equivalent to the welfare state of today. If the Church was to fulfil its programme conscientiously, the revenues had to be safeguarded. Throughout the history of canonical and conciliar legislation strict attention was given to the conservation of ecclesiastical property (cf Chalcedon 26, Nicaea II 12). The canons make it clear that the initial motive was not self-interest — 'ecclesiastical revenue, which is decreed to be for the Church's own use or to provide food for the needy and sustenance for pilgrims' (°Constantinople IV 15) — and that church property existed for the good of Christendom at large. It was held as a sacred trust. Thus, if we consider Chalcedon 26 more closely, in conjunction with cc. 22 & °25, and with °Nicaea II 11, it becomes clear that the Church had also to be protected against the squandering of its patrimony by bishops as well as from depredatory laity.[46] Furthermore, the implications of Nicaea II 12 were that a bishop must not impose excessive burdens upon church property and income; if he founded a monastery, he could not endow it with more than 2 per cent of the possessions of his church, or bestow more than 1 per cent upon any church he wanted to reward.[47] The language of Lateran III 19 expresses this attitude very well, when it speaks of 'goods intended for the use of the churches, the clergy and Christ's poor'. These numerous restrictions (cf °Constantinople IV 15) do not indicate what actually happened, that is, widespread alienation, by *emphyteusis* especially, and that the canons were dead-letters until the important

* This is an exposition of growth in ownership, and not in the *de facto* poliation of the medieval church by 'pious' lay rulers.

canonical revival of the eleventh century gave them great importance, for example, °Constantinople IV 15 became the influential decree of Gratian C.12 q.2 c.13.

The stress upon preventing alienation becomes all the more understandable when it is realized how difficult it was to recover such property. Even the Church recognized the mutual advantages of some form of statutory limitation on recovery (see p. 100). In *emphyteusis*, which was a long-term contract of lease for rental, the initial grant had often been of uncultivated land to which the tenant had to make improvements. Title easily became obscured. Even where this did not happen, the canonists, when considering the decree of °Constantinople IV 15, specially provided for the rights of the tenant, e.g. he was entitled to compensation for improvements. The Church had first option on buying the improvements, but if it failed to exercise this right within two months, then they could be put on the open market. Only if the lessee failed to pay his rent for two or three years (cf Constantinople IV 20) could he be evicted and so lose the right to compensation for improvements. For such reasons the general councils insisted that the bishops and abbots appoint stewards (*economi*):[48] the task of the steward was 'to administer church property in accord with the instructions of the bishop, so that the administration of the church may not be unattested and thereby ecclesiastical property squandered and reproach brought upon the priesthood' (Chalcedon 26).

In the Eastern Church, lay as well as clerical stewards were used, but in the West only clerics were permitted (cf Lateran I 8; °II 25). The reason for this distinction — an important one for the contemporary problems of the laity in the Church — is historical. In the Greek Church there was a strong tradition of secular participation in church government. The imperial supervision of the early councils proves this easily enough (see p. 18). In the West the collapse of the Roman Empire left a vacuum that was eventually filled by the papacy. The papacy combined both the temporal authority of the emperors and its own spiritual functions as Christ's viceregent. Thus it resisted strongly all lay interference, which it regarded as unlawful. To be accurate, clerics were also forbidden to act as stewards of lay estates. In fact the opposite process to what the papacy intended happened.*[49]

* Different historical experiences leave their mark on the churches even today. The Roman Church will permit little lay control over its property. The

Ecclesiastical wealth attracted predators. It was not, as many imagine, simply a matter of *lay* invasion of church lands. Although this was the common feature, there were many cases of bishop against his clergy, monastery against monastery, religious against seculars. °Nicaea II 4 condemned oppression of clerics by bishops for the sake of gain. °Constantinople IV 19 sought to protect bishops from similar exactions by the metropolitans. Yet these things were slight in comparison with lay oppression. By the end of the tenth century the proprietary church system, in which the individual church, monastery or even bishopric was treated as a piece of private property, dominated the economic substructure of the Roman Church. The revenues of these churches provided a powerful incentive to those who sought to 'own' them.[50]

Historians have long disputed whether the proprietary church had its roots in Germanic Law and the Germanic spirit or in some inheritance of the former Roman Empire. The truth seems to be that it was a product of no special ideology, but of the social conditions of the time and place.[51] Land-owners who founded churches and monasteries on their estates usually treated these as personal property;[52] at the other end of the scale, bishops and abbots in times of unrest found it useful to enlist the protection of a lay lord. For this they had to pay a price. Part of the price was that control of elections and a large share of the income passed into lay hands. Lay control of canonical election aroused the greatest opposition. Several canons condemned it (cf Nicaea II 3, °Constantinople IV 12 and °Lateran IV 25), but the secular powers could never accept the alternatives offered at different times. For proprietary rights gave the secular powers an easy source of revenue and an assured means of rewarding clerics who had served the ruler well. In the case of episcopal elections, even when chapter and later papal control was substituted, the secular ruler still had influence. In England on the eve of the Reformation eight of the fifteen resident bishops were royal nominees, rewarded with rich sees for their services to the Crown. As a main cause of the English Reformation (likewise on the Continent) one could cite the evidence gathered by Elton and Hughes, who agree in their criticism of an episcopacy that no longer functioned primarily for the pastoral care of the Church.[53]

Greek Church until recently would, and many of the reformed Churches are almost entirely governed by lay councils in this respect.

The proprietary system differed fundamentally from the system envisaged in the conciliar canons, where the bishop directed and controlled the whole of diocesan finances. The effects of this dualism were disastrous in terms of both lay and clerical spirituality. For centuries popes and bishops 'solved' the problem by accepting the *fact* of lay control, but retaining the *theory* of the early canons. What was needed was a revision and compromise between the two. The opportunity did not come until the eleventh century, when a powerful papacy set the pattern for reform.

The need for reform and revision was great. The loss of property and revenue already referred to had reached its climax. The loss consisted mainly of lay appropriation of tithes and offerings and ecclesiastical estates; fraudulent sale, leasing and enfeoffing by administrators to laymen; usurpations and depredations. Gerbert, later Pope Sylvester II (999–1003), complained on being chosen Abbot of Bobbio that 'the entire monastic patrimony had been granted away'. Nothing was left under his control: the Bishop of Pavia, like many feudal prelates, was even using church property to reward his knights. Fortunately, Gerbert persuaded the Emperor Otto III to cancel all grants made by the abbots of Bobbio in the previous fifteen years.[54] Elsewhere the position was worse. In one of the most damning documents of the time, the *Libri tres adversus simoniacos* (1054–8), the author, Cardinal Humbert of Silva Candida, paints a very black picture of the economic ruin of the Church in Italy. He attributed the cause to simony and clerical greed. There are, in fact, numerous documents of this period that witness the alienation of estates, loss of revenues and the consequent decline of churches and monasteries.[55] It is not surprising then that the Gregorian reformers attacked simony and clerical marriage as both spiritual and economic evils.[56]

For this reason the translation lists the canons condemning simony (cf Lateran I 1). During the first three centuries there was little simony in the Church.[57] But the rapid growth in church property from the period of Constantine onwards made clerical office a source of wealth as well as of power. Eventually the purchase of spiritual office and benefits became so widespread that it seemed to threaten the continuity of the Church as such. The opponents of simony condemned it in stringent terms, even, in some cases, to the extent of treating it as a heresy. The most violent debate on simony occurred in the period from about 1000 to 1150. For some time it was debated whether simoniacal orders were valid or not. By the twelfth century the matter was settled, but not the abuse itself.[58]

Similarly, clerical marriage was condemned (cf Lateran I 21) primarily for the moral principle involved, but also for the practical consequences on ecclesiastical society. Children of such marriages had to be provided for, and, as Herlihy argues, the way to do this was to get them some church property.[59] The success of the reformers in eliminating this particular abuse may be seen in the decline in the use of matronymics to disguise such transactions. The decline began about the middle of the eleventh century, and with it the number of associated land exchanges. In return, provisions for a celibate clergy had to be made. This was done by introducing the concept of the benefice, together with a large-scale movement to recover churches, their lands and tithes. The tithe income was vital. If recovery had been wholly successful, it would have made the clergy financially independent and no longer forced to survive by simony.[60] But this was not to be.

The strict theological tradition was that everyone paid tithes to the church where he received the sacraments.[61] In reality, by the eleventh century either the majority of the 'parish' churches had passed into or were part of the proprietary system, held by laymen and monks, largely, who appropriated the tithes to their own use, or among those churches that were still canonically under episcopal control, the whole or a large part of the tithe-income had been lost to others (*via* usurpation, episcopal grant and sale). In this case the tithe had become another feudal due that could be bought, sold, inherited and divided.[62]

The Cluniac and early Gregorian Reform programmes in alliance with powerful financial interests who gambled on the outcome, such as Matilda of Tuscany and the family Pierleoni, urged the laity to give up their control and interest in proprietary churches and their tithes. The laity responded, but not in a way that would have helped bishops and secular clergy. Lay restorations usually went to the monasteries. Thus the bishop did not recover his ancient control of diocesan finance.[63] The relationship between the restoration of churches and the reform movement may be seen in the case of the monastery of Saint-Vincent du Mans, for which Chédeville has compiled a chart of restoration. The movement began about 1040 and lasted until *c.* 1140, with the peak period 1080-1100.[64]

It is possible that the moral life of such 'restored' churches improved under monastic supervision.   But the danger was that the monastery became tempted to usurp all the income and appoint some poorly paid incumbent to do the work.[65]   It certainly detracted from the authority of the bishops, who frequently complained of the imbalance between monastery and diocese.   Constable comments, 'as time went on the reformers increasingly emphasized the canonical principles of division and of episcopal control over tithes', but to no avail, for 'by the early twelfth century there were no effective barriers to monastic acquisition of tithes, and the consent of the bishops had become, in spite of occasional difficulties, almost a formality'.[66]   The papacy, in fact, had the council legislate against such abuses.   Several decrees (e.g. Lateran I 18) tried to ensure that the *whole* of the lay tithe was restored to the secular clergy, and that the monasteries fulfilled their obligation concerning appropriated parish churches by appointing suitable priests. The decrees insisted on some episcopal control over clergy who served in these churches.   But these were mostly exhortatory, for no practical remedy was provided for their infringement.[67]

Custom as well as lay and monastic obstinacy opposed the papal attempt to conciliate the bishops of the Church.   In the end the papacy abandoned its attempt to recover the whole of the tithe.   Instead it insisted that the patrons surrender the fourth part, the *quartese*, which would normally belong to the parish church.   Sometimes it was a third.   Lateran IV 32 embodied this practical solution and frankly departed from the policy of some hundred years or so: 'we decree that, notwithstanding any custom on the part of a bishop, patron, or anyone else, priests must receive a fair share of the income'.   The parish priest must reside, except where the church is annexed, then a suitable vicar is to be appointed and given a proper stipend.   This part of the decree was directed against monastic appropriations.   Appointment of perpetual vicars was certainly not new.   In England perpetual vicars had been usual in the twelfth century.   Before 1215 there are records of some two to three hundred such vicarages.[68]   After 1215 the bishops strove to get the decree generally implemented, but not always successfully.   It was another hundred years before they recovered proper control over churches formerly owned or served by monks.   Vienne [18] allowed the bishop to allot a proper share of the revenues to the parish priest after suitable interval of time.[69]

As Lateran IV 32 insisted on a sufficient share of the income (*portio sufficiens*), the question naturally arises, what was considered a sufficient income for a parish priest in the thirteenth century? In the *glossa ordinaria* to this decree in the *Decretals* of Gregory IX, Bernard of Parma designates it as the amount necessary for the quality of life, to support dependants and to provide hospitality.[70]   The median income of a parish priest in England was about £10 p.a.   But the minimum salary of a vicar was fixed at only 5 marks.   A labourer earned 2*d* per day; a craftsman 4*d*.   Relatively, then, the parish priest was well provided for, but not his deputies.[71]

Finally, payment of tithes did not in the Middle Ages constitute as grave a source of grievance as some modern historians would have it.[72] Attempts to avoid payment were not very common, although there is some evidence that towards the end of the period the number increased.[73]   Where lands had fallen into the hands of the Jews, the latter had to pay compensation for loss of the tithes (Lateran IV 67).[74] As for those individuals who tried to diminish the amount owing by making prior deductions for expenses and taxes, the canonists asserted that predial tithes must be paid before such deductions, although these were allowable against personal tithes.[75]   Such abuses were never fully eradicated.   As in modern taxation laws there was always a way round the legislation.   In fact some of the conciliar decrees provide a striking commentary on the methods employed.   Vienne [11] sought to prohibit the practice by which certain religious allowed their servants to graze their flocks (which were not exempt from tithe) with those of the monastery (which were).   Tithes, of course, had to be paid on animal produce, except from animals owned by lepers (cf Lateran III 24).   On the whole the laity paid their tithe and remained satisfied with its incidence.[76]   Whatever disagreement existed over tithes was largely a clerical affair, which at times created violent conflict between monks and the secular clergy, and even within the ranks of the religious Orders themselves.

Despite the papacy's failure to wrest complete control of churches and tithes from lay hands, the partial gains were impressive enough. Canonical legislation contributed to the successes.   It is a fact that the canonical collections as well as synodal legislation show a very large increase in the number of texts relating to recovery of church lands. The increase was necessary because the canonists had to build a case for recovery on weak foundations.   Earlier collections contained scattered texts condemning lay invasion, but in practice the ecclesiastical authorities had long tacitly condoned many of the so-called abuses. A body of customary law and prescriptive rights supported existing economic arrangements, against which the canon law said little or had failed to act. Hence new law had to be made to appear as old law, and custom, not canon law, as the innovator.[77] It is not true to say that custom was given short shrift. The papacy never rejected it as such, but only when it appeared to militate against the good of the whole Church. °Lateran III 16 condemned only 'customs that are contrary to reason and in conflict with the sacred canons'.

Recognition of the need to turn papal innovation into a 'traditional' canonical right resulted in a large number of texts drawn from early Christian and Roman Law sources being widely published in the new canonical collections — some for the first time. Many of these texts came *via* the ninth-century collection of Pseudo-Isidore. As for the Roman Law texts, these dealt largely with the inalienability of church property. The general principle of Roman Law was to forbid all forms of alienation. The canon law simply adopted this principle and applied it to all church property, i.e. lands, permanent fixtures, buildings, churches, hospitals, and even annuities left by will. Some exceptions were permitted, e.g. alienations to pay debts. In these cases the guiding principle was 'necessity — utility'.[78]

An analysis of the number of such texts in the various collections may illustrate this development. At the beginning of the eleventh century, before the reform got under way, Burchard of Worms' collection had 131 texts touching on church temporalities. The majority of these texts were scattered throughout the twenty books. By contrast, Deusdedit's collection in 1085 had 315 texts, mostly in one group (book III had 289 texts). Burchard accepted the principle of lay control and wanted only to reform it.[79] Deusdedit, Anselm of Lucca and other canonists rejected the principle itself. The evidence of the new collections suggests that the restoration of church lands dominated a great deal of the thinking of the reformers.

These changes lead to the interesting question whether the newly found importance of the property rights of the Church created a better understanding of the laity's need to secure economic goods and the wherewithal for a living? Is there in the Church's practical attitude towards lay property and wealth an equivalent transformation from the eleventh century onwards?

The answer to this, apart from what the canonists and theologians

— the economic theorists — have to say, is that after *c.* 1100 no one could be unmindful of the economic ties that helped to bind society together. This applies especially to the mass of the clergy, who, again paradoxically, were more immersed in secular affairs — even to the point of having to earn a living by the 'trade' so despised — than at any other time in the history of the Church.[80]

The reformed papacy, the monastic houses, the bishops, the cathedral chapters, individual churchmen, students, travellers, even the pious pilgrim who would put aside the things of the world, often needed the aid of the money-changers and later the bankers.[81] The close relationship that existed between high ecclesiastical officials and the financial interests led to charges of extortion and bribery. Such accusations — not entirely without foundation — became part of the polemical struggle. Peter Damiani described the anti-pope Cadalus as 'a wicked money-dealer'; Gregory VII's opponents denounced him as a puppet of the financiers.[82] However much the reformers sought to escape the dilemma of their position, the fact is that the Church was the most efficient economic instrument and policy-maker during the Middle Ages. Moreover, because it had such a supply of talent, it became increasingly better equipped to deal with financial matters. By the time of the Avignonese papacy the Curia was staffed largely by men who were themselves sons of merchants.[83]

The crusades provide an example of the extent to which spiritual and material motives became inextricably involved.[84] Several of the conciliar decrees, both in length and in detail, spiritual and financial, show how far the papacy would go in trying to ensure the success of the crusade.[85] Thus the crusaders' property was protected at home (Lateran I 10); they were exempt from taxes, and interest payments were suspended (Lateran IV [71]).[86] Trade with the East was interdicted for four years in order to provide shipping-space for the crusaders, and Christians were forbidden to supply war-materials to the Saracens, especially wood and iron that were in short supply (Lateran III 24; IV [71]).[87] The crusades led to profits all round, not, as many think, derived largely from war booty, but from the grant of commercial privileges that followed the setting up of Christian kingdoms in the East.[88] The towns of Venice and Amalfi, and later Genoa and Pisa, grew rich on these profits.[89] Preparations for the crusades stimulated commerce and industrial crafts. The shipbuilding industry especially benefited by such undertakings as that of Venice,

which in 1201 contracted to supply a large fleet.[90]   The papacy also
sanctioned special taxes to pay for the expenses of the war, e.g. a tax
of one-twentieth for three years on all ecclesiastical revenues (Lateran
IV [71]) or one-tenth for six years (°Lyons II [1a]).[91]   This was the
first income tax imposed on the clergy, and it set a precedent in both
ecclesiastical and secular administrations.[92]   Also fines for blasphemy,
contributions by penitents, bequests in wills, special levies by secular
rulers were imposed.[93]   Such actions seemed to many contemporaries
far removed from the work of Christ in driving the buyers and sellers
from the temple.[94]

As for the heretic, he was treated somewhat more harshly than the
infidel, largely, of course, because being in a minority and living within
the Christian community of the Roman Church, he could be reached.[95]
The heretic with his rigorous abstinence, renunciation of family and
property, and simple dress, embarrassed Church and State, especially
by the insistent call for the suppression of all privileges and temporal
possessions.[96]   His punishment was the more severe.   Employers
were forbidden to hire heretics, their contracts were cancelled, possessions confiscated, and their persons reduced to slavery.[97]   The gloss
of Damasus on °Lateran IV 3 (*occupandam*) reads: 'And so Catholics
can seize the property of heretics, which act is not against the precept
of the ten commandments, "Do not covet they neighbour's goods."'
The heretic could not make a will, but he must honour his agreements
where demanded; yet all communication with heretics was forbidden.[98]   By way of contrast, consider the decrees of Basel Session
XIX (7 September 1434) on the convert, who is allowed to retain his
property and may even keep usurious profits of the *incerta* kind.   They
also enjoy the same privileges 'as others of native origin enjoy'.   As
a final measure neophytes who apostatized were treated as heretics.
Those who remained in their error, e.g. the Jews, were treated harshly,
but sometimes more generously by the Church than by the secular
authorities, e.g. the Jews in England in the thirteenth century.[99]

The Church's secular interests constituted a large part of the economic expansion of the time.[100]   During the vital period of growth
the Church did not impede but fostered economic progress.   Several
conciliar decrees (Lateran I 14; II 11; III 22) specifically protected the
merchant — among others — while going about his business.   The
same decrees forbade the imposition of new tolls or duties by un-
authorized persons.   In addition there were the substantial adjust-

ments made by the canonists and theologians to certain aspects of the merchants' world, e.g. in usury, the just price, duty towards the poor, the uses of wealth, all of which will be examined in detail below (see pp. 48-82). After *c.* 1350 the position changed, admittedly. However, accusations that may justly be levelled against ecclesiastical restrictions in the later Middle Ages, when any chance of effective interference had gone, can hardly be used to support a charge of impeding a process of expansion that, according to many historians, had come to an end.

What medieval churchmen can be charged with, is failing to temper legalism with charity and to recognize the extent to which economic motives lay behind numerous pious movements, e.g. the support for the crusades, especially when used against fellow Christians, albeit allegedly heretics (see p. 174). Numerous financial scandals became associated with the crusades, e.g. in 1239 the papal legate Stephen of Anagni used usurers to help in the levy in England, and in the mid-century the papacy redeemed crusade vows for cash.[101] Even women and young children could take the cross, only to redeem it immediately. The money that was raised was used to finance the papacy's European wars against Christians. In the end the unity of christendom was weakened by such tactics.[102]

C. The Church Within — Monks, Tithes and the Secular Clergy

A major factor responsible for the ultimate collapse of the medieval Church's universal acceptance by society may be found in the failure of the Church to settle its own internal disputes, in which economic matters played a substantial part. The very means inaugurated by the reformed papacy from the eleventh century onwards to resolve the conflict between the lay and ecclesiastical authorities, ultimately led to problems within the ranks of the clergy that were insoluble. What is in mind here is the special position that religious Orders had in the Church, which often gave rise to the disputes between themselves and the secular clergy over tithes and other sources of income.

In terms of the spiritual life the contribution of the medieval religious Orders was a great and positive one. But while we acknowledge and acclaim that contribution, our concern is with the economic aspect of medieval monasticism, where the picture is somewhat different.[103]

Historically, in its inception, monasticism was a lay movement and monks were subject to the authority of the bishop. However, despite injunctions against monks who destroyed church stability and order (°Chalcedon 4 and °23), especially those who wandered from monastery to monastery (°Nicaea II 21) or who, because they were laymen, lacked a title and therefore a source of income (Chalcedon 6), and despite the occasional reminder of the right of episcopal control and visitation, the councils failed to prevent the gradual weakening of that authority. In the Western or Roman Church development of Benedictine monasticism according to a well-defined 'rule' resisted such control. Also, the proprietary church system weakened the authority of the bishops themselves, and from the seventh century onwards more and more monasteries became exempt from episcopal supervision and were placed under papal jurisdiction.[104] Such exemptions roused the hostility of the secular clergy, and this situation continued throughout the Middle Ages despite the reassertion of episcopal authority from the twelfth century onwards. Much of the opposition had an economic basis and was felt by the monks as well as by the secular clergy.[105]

How far this dissension restricted the work of the religious Orders remains to be seen, but first let us examine the nature of their contribution to the economic well-being of society. Not surprisingly there are some very mixed views among historians today concerning this influence. The following illustrates one view:

It is perhaps a fact worthy of notice that the modern use of profit, expansion from retained earnings, arose and was systematised in the monasteries . . . the saintly men . . . are the true original of the non-consuming, ascetic type of capitalist. And Berdyaev has truly observed that Christian ascetism played a capital part in the development of capitalism; it is a condition of re-investment.

Other writers agree on this matter, and they point to such examples as the monasteries being the chief lenders to nobles going on crusades.[107] Nevertheless one may question de Jouvenel's view of such monks as 'saintly men'.

Such a view assumes too easily that monasteries and monks rose or could rise above the economic limitations of their time. The process of land accumulation, which the monasteries did well, often harmed laity and secular clergy. Quite early in the main economic revival of the period 1000-1300 the monks showed themselves capable and even ruthless exploiters of economic situations. The Cistercians carried out large-scale works of land reclamation in England, Belgium, Poland and other continental countries.[108] But, as the history of Canterbury cathedral priory shows, the Benedictine monks could be as well organized and developed. During this period the priory, under such capable administrators as Henry of Eastry (1285-1331), developed all the forms of competitive farming: consolidation of estates, re-leases of land at high rent, competitive leasehold rents, commutation of labour services for rent, and the retention of some services under a sort of dual system by which they could be commuted or restored at the option of the prior, so as to have the best of both worlds. The chief crop was cereals, in which the monks did a thriving business at home and abroad.[109]

The monks were also 'well aware of the vital importance of money in that dawn of economic revival'. From the seventh century onwards the names of a number of churches and monasteries are found on issued coins, e.g. 29 names for the period c. 625-650; 27 for the Carolingian period.[110] From the end of the tenth century several churches claim the privilege of the right to mint money, many of which claims were false.[111] The chartularies of Cluny and other monasteries show that the monks acquired a number of feudal mints throughout France.[112] At the same time (c. 1100) Cluny turned from a demesne economy to a monetary one, and in doing so it acted as a sort of forcing house of the money economy in regions intimately associated with it.[113] Subsequently this forced a crisis in the abbey because prices of goods increased and income had lagged behind. In 1125 the monks had to cut down on their standard of living.[114] Again, the monasteries accepted the proprietary churches returned by laymen and did not surrender them to the bishop. The increasing number of ordained monks led to the penetration of the pastoral life of the Church, especially, of course, by the friars in the thirteenth century. By contrast, monks and monasteries did not scruple to have dealings with the Jews when it suited them.[115] Consider the following extract from the *Calendar of the Plea Rolls of the Exchequer of the Jews* (1220) Essex: Abbot of Waltham Holy Cross had to show how he came to hold lands belonging to 'Simon Le Bret in Wrengel and Wormel.

The Abbot alleges that he holds the land in Wrengel by fine with King John for 25 marks, which he paid in discharge of Simon's debt in Jewish account . . .'[116]

These developments presented a bewildering picture of the religious life to their contemporaries, and they certainly created some ill-feeling. The main source, however, of opposition to the economic activities of the monks was the matter of tithe-exemption. This exemption brought the religious Orders into conflict with the secular clergy, and even led to discord in their own ranks. It became a major cause of concern for the popes.[117] The general councils mirror that concern and, incidentally, the inability of the papacy to solve the problem to everybody's satisfaction (see p. 100).

Monastic exemption from paying tithes consisted of a deliberate act by the popes, which set aside the common law of the Church according to which monks as well as laymen were supposed to pay tithes to the parish church in whose district the monastic lands were situated.[118] This innovation was really the work of two popes, Paschal II (1099–1118) and Innocent II (1130–43). Paschal II formulated the doctrine, and Innocent II first applied it on a large scale for the benefit not only of individual monasteries, but also of entire congregations.[119] The common exemption was for lands farmed by the monks themselves *sane laborum*.

Among the various religious Orders who enjoyed tithe-exemption, the Cistercians (founded 1098) were especially at fault in the way they used the privilege to build up large estates. The original privilege given to individual Cistercian abbeys and their dependants by Innocent II had restricted exemption to 'produce by your own hands'. But this was extended to virtually complete tithe-exemption, that is, from paying tithe on all their lands, whether farmed by themselves or leased out, or on produce for themselves or for outside trade.[120] By 1200 this Order, which had originally presented an aspect of apostolic poverty, had come to monopolize the wool trade and had become deeply immersed in what was after all a commercial enterprise.[121] The general European expansion of the cloth trade increased the demand for wool and hence for more land for sheep-rearing.[122] Every expansion of Cistercian property into existing tithe-lands meant a corresponding diminution in the income of the parish clergy through loss of tithes.[123] The establishment of granges often brought about a complete change in the place and its people to fit them for the economic needs of the abbey.[124] Despoliation and destruction of existing settlements sometimes followed. For example, the establishment of Revesby abbey in Lincolnshire, granted to Rievaulx in 1142, led to the disappearance of Thoresby and Sythersby villages. Thirty-one men refused to be resettled and were allowed to leave.[125] Other of the Cistercian business-methods also brought them into disrepute. The monasteries would often advance cash to individuals in order to get hold of their land for the production of wool. They became suppliers of credit, fulfilling the function of a rural bank.[126] Despite a prohibition by the General Chapter in 1189, the Cistercians continued these loan transactions.[127] The same Chapter tried to reduce the secular clergy's opposition over tithes by ordering that no lands were to be acquired other than by gift[128]—again with little success. Finally, Lateran IV 55 decreed that the Cistercians must pay tithe on all future acquisitions, except for noval land. They also retained exemption on all land acquired before 1215, provided they cultivated it themselves and for their own use.[129] The good effects of this decree were partly vitiated in the thirteenth century by the popes protecting Cistercian tithes and rented lands with further exemptions, which were also extended to other religious Orders.[130]

Neither the decree nor the exemptions could save the Cistercian Order from its mistakes.[131] To exist, the monks needed secular support, for which they had to pay in cash. Although no organized system of state taxation of the Church had been worked out, none of the clergy could escape frequent and heavy demands made upon them, especially from the thirteenth century onwards.[132] Thus, King John of England received a total of 24,027½ marks from the Cistercians and £100,000 from the rest of the clergy.[133] The English Cistercian houses were often in debt or near bankruptcy. The Crown encouraged the Order to undertake elaborate building programmes that forced them into debt contracts with the Jews and Italian bankers. An excellent illustration of this was the activity of Aaron of Lincoln, who lent the money to build nine Cistercian abbeys, as well as the cathedrals of Lincoln and Peterborough.[134] Several of the Jewish usurers employed royal capital.[135] The Crown in turn regularly deprived the Jews of their profits, so that the bankruptcy of the Cistercian Order in England at the end of the thirteenth century was largely due to this form of indirect taxation by the Crown.[136]

Excessive business confidence also played its part. The forward sale of wool to Italian merchants put the abbeys into debt.   Thus in 1275 Hubert, abbot of Wothney in County Limerick, Ireland, pledged the church of Thurles and chapels of Codach and Caprach as security for £1000 owed by him to merchants of Lucca.   They later foreclosed on the mortgage.[137]   In England, flourishing abbeys were often in debt; in 1290 the debt of Fountains Abbey was £1293, in 1301 Kirkstall's was £160.[138]   Deficit financing became a common feature during the fourteenth century.[139]

The extent of the Cistercian difficulties may be judged by the fact that at least eighteen times during Edward I's reign royal commissioners had to be appointed for their houses because of non-payment of debts.   Consequently there were numerous complaints about the Order at the end of the century.[140]   Nowhere in the Church was the contrast so striking between what one writer has called 'the principles and the reality'.[141]

Not only the Cistercians were at fault, but other Orders, e.g. the Knights Templars and the Knights Hospitallers.   The latter had acquired many privileges from 1113 onwards, such as tithe-exemption, burial rights and the right to serve as alms-collectors.[142]   This brought them some ill-fame, but the most serious accusations were kept for the Knights Templars. As a powerful banking institution they roused a great deal of hostility and cupidity, especially from the secular rulers. They were finally suppressed in 1312.[143]

The Orders roused public opinion against them by the manner in which they gained exemption from other common burdens, even those imposed by the papacy, e.g. from the financial provisions of Lateran I 10, IV [71], and °Lyons II [1a] for the crusade, despite express prohibition of such exemption.   The Cistercians paid 100,000 pounds Tours; the Templars, Knights of St John, and the enclosed nuns of the Order of St Augustine followed suit.[144]

Conflict between religious and secular over tithes was not, however, the fundamental issue.   Fundamentally it was a question of Orders who professed poverty in imitation of Christ, yet grew rich as corporations.[145]   Whereas the secular clergy professed no such poverty, yet remained poor.   One of the strongest manifestations of this conflict occurred at the University of Paris from 1253 onwards between the seculars and the mendicants.[146]

The cause of this dispute lay in the interpretation of the Franciscan and Dominican Rules concerning poverty.   Exactly what St Francis

had had in mind is doubtful, but it seems to have included the renunciation of the use of goods as such, and not merely their ownership.
The various prohibitions against money, even the touching of it, or
accepting payments in kind and other substitutes, beyond the barest
necessities for day-to-day living, convinces one that St Francis sought
to withdraw his friars from all dealings in property and cash.[147]
Similarly the General Chapter of the Dominicans in 1220 had 'pledged
the order to absolute, mendicant poverty'.[148]   In practice, absolute
poverty was impossible, especially when the Orders entered the universities or had to undertake the building of convents in the new towns.
A distinction arose between ownership and use of money and property,
which was helped by such decrees as *Quo elongati* (1230), which set up
a *nuntius*, and *Ordinem vestrum* (November 1245), which gave consent
for the use of intermediaries in financial matters.   The papacy assumed
'ownership' of Franciscan property.[149]

Against this background the secular masters at Paris, who suffered
loss of stipends and fees on the rise of the friars to prominence, denied
that the latter imitated the poverty of Christ as long as they retained
even the use of goods.   Numerous defences were put forward by the
friars, but the classic defence was Bonaventure's *Apologia pauperum*
(1269), which became the official doctrine of the friars and eventually
of the papacy.[150]   However, the matter was not settled there, for
among the Franciscans existed two parties of the Spirituals (total
poverty) and Conventuals (relative poverty).   Vienne [38] showed
the casuistry involved in the arguments of the Conventuals, which
were ultimately accepted by John XXII, in the bull *Quorumdam exigit*.
This bull determined that Christ and his disciples had not totally re-
nounced property rights, and it thereby constituted an important
element in the development of the doctrine of the *usus pauperum*.[151]

The secular clergy and the mendicants also came into conflict outside the universities over the encroachment of the friars upon traditional sources of clerical income, especially burial dues and mass fees
and legacies.[152]   Several canons in the councils deal with this problem.
Vienne [10] shows how insoluble the problem became.   Complaints
by bishops that the friars lured the faithful away from the parish
services by preaching and holding services at the same hour were
frequent and bitter.[153]   Originally, despite it being opposed to the
Dominican and Franciscan Rules, the friars had been granted privileges
of preaching and hearing confessions and burial rights by the papacy,

who saw them as suitable instruments of its policy.   Innocent IV had withdrawn the privileges on 21 November 1254, but Alexander IV restored them and Martin IV extended them in 1281.   The result was a fresh outbreak of opposition among the clergy, especially in France.[154] This lasted until Boniface VIII issued the constitution *Super cathedram* of 18 February 1300.   In turn Benedict XI abrogated the bull (17 February 1304), which Clement in the decree of Vienne [38] *Exivi de paradiso* merely restored.[155]   This satisfied neither party.   If anything, after the Council of Vienne the attitude of the seculars became more severe towards the mendicants.   For example, A. M. Burg in his work on the diocese of Strasbourg shows that grants to mendicants in the parishes of St Stephen (Strasbourg) and St Georges (Haguenau) in 1329 were more restricted than they had been in 1298.[156]   Nor should it be forgotten that the religious often had just complaints against the secular clergy, as Vienne [30] shows.   Unfortunately, none of the issues was finally settled.   They recurred throughout the fourteenth and fifteenth centuries, and Lateran V echoes them, although it too failed to accomplish anything.

In the face of general opposition from the secular clergy the religious Orders might have been expected to present a united front.   This was hardly the case.   The Orders disputed almost as much among themselves as with the seculars.   Tithe disputes led especially to conflict between the old established Orders of black monks, and the newer Orders of white monks.   Here the most famous case is that of the Cistercian Abbey of Le Miroir that refused to pay tithes on lands to the Cluniac priory of Gigny.   Bernard of Clairvaux championed the cause of Le Miroir, Peter the Venerable that of Gigny.   With two such opposing champions the issues became deep ones; in fact the dispute lasted from about 1137 to 1155, when it ended in favour of Gigny.[157]   Such disputes remind us of the need to understand the complexity and variety of medieval society and Church before calculating the contribution made by the Church solely in terms of a conflict between the clergy, on the one hand, and the laity, on the other.

In making these points, the Church has been portrayed as a body whose actions were determined largely by economic factors, a society where retention of existing assets and further acquisition were the main considerations.   To leave the matter there creates an impression of the medieval Church and economic activity as false as that presented by ardent historians who treat the medieval Church as an ideal society in whose ranks social justice reigned and whose idealism was shattered solely by the Reformation.   Medieval society, in which the average expectancy of life was thirty-three years, and in which the majority lived at subsistence level, could never be termed ideal.[158]   Men could act violently and irrationally in face of hatred; hence they would often burn crops, buildings and even churches (cf Lateran II 18).[159] Others resorted to reprisals, that is, the seizing of men, animals or goods until satisfaction was made (Lyons II 28).[160]   Such violence may have reflected the frustration inherent in a restricted economy. This was especially so in the early period.   Until the eleventh century society was so organized that luxuries — the surplus production of a virtually subsistence economy — went to the few.   International trade consisted largely of luxury goods and war supplies.[161]   The masses, despite recent attempts to reassess their position in a more favourable light, were subject to lay and ecclesiastical authority.   Successful pressure from below, as against concessions from the top, did not begin until the economic revolution got under way by 1000.   In the next three hundred years there were striking technological and economic advances.   The period was also one of a marked widening of the human spirit, with notable advances in theological, philosophical and canonical speculation.[162]   The Church may appear to have been concerned only for itself, but there is a different aspect, now to be presented, which is shown in the attempt by theologians and canonists to adjust the Church's teaching based on universal moral principles to the changing social and economic circumstances of the Western world.

4 The Economic Doctrines of the Canonists and Theologians

A. The Two Forums and the General Nature of the Church's Doctrine

IT has already been suggested that the decrees of general or provincial councils do not by themselves sufficiently indicate the relationship between Christianity and economics in the Middle Ages (see p. 15). For this we must — although this is not the only subject of our study — examine the overlapping interpretative commentaries of the canonists and theologians, which were particularly expressive during the intellectual renaissance of the twelfth and thirteenth centuries. Often there was conflict of opinion between the two disciplines, but usually they reached the same conclusions. They started from different premises — the canonists dealing with the external forum of church law, the theologians with the internal forum of conscience — but the distinction was often blurred, e.g. in the writings of the Paris School, dominated by the circle of Peter the Chanter c. 1200.[1] The distinction could be equally sharp. Thus, concerning usury, the canonists, faced with a bewildering mass of material and exceptions to the strict law, ended by concentrating on manifest or public usurers, who were mostly the petty pawnbrokers. They could not get at occult usurers, which included the great merchants, and their profits, for they claimed, and on paper proved, that they took no interest. Canon law, like any other system of civil law, could not judge mere intention. There was, indeed, a juridical concept of fraud with canonical penalties. An excellent example occurs in the gloss in the *Clementines* on Vienne [29]:

by their statutes they force debtors to pay usury indirectly, that is, when they know that they cannot recover money from the debtors, they hand over money on these terms: I hereby lend you freely a hundred for ten years. You at the end will return me the hundred. You will also at the same time make me a loan of a hundred. In this way one is obligated to 100 per cent interest, which is a greater burden for debtors than if they were to pay interest.[2]

In many instances the only difference between an ostensibly legal act and a fraudulent one lay in the intention of the lender. Here the canonist had little authority, and it fell to the theologian to treat the matter. In moral theology intention was what mattered. Thus there could be sin where there was no crime.

The two forums clearly represented two different standpoints of the Church in relation to the faithful. The external forum 'represented the right of the Church to judge her members in relation to the social body of christendom . . . The internal forum was the right of the Church to judge members in their relationship to God.' Usually the two jurisdictions were complementary. But — and this distinction is often missed by modern commentators — only because rigid principles had been adhered to in both cases.[3]

From this follows the important conclusion that when the medieval Church is charged with countenancing seemingly illicit commercial practices, more thought would show that the canonists were applying the high standard of jurisprudence often praised in the then contemporary civil systems of law. There is some evidence that those who escaped the canon law because there was no appropriate remedy did not escape the penalty of the confessional.[4] This, however, is a difficult matter to determine, for the argument is mainly speculative, as follows.

There was in the Middle Ages a strong tradition in the writings of the theologians, manuals for confessors and the preaching of such practical moralists as Bernardino of Siena against immoral business- and trade-practices.[5] One would suppose the confessors applied such teachings in the confessional. Merchants went to confession. They were certainly concerned with saving their souls, if their wills are anything to go by. Also they did in fact, as we shall see, go some way towards restoring usurious profits. Restitution of ill-gotten gains was commonly regarded as a condition, in the internal forum, of true penitence.[6] This was allied with the fear of death without having been absolved from sin and the denial of Christian burial. The councils themselves made great use of this pious fear; e.g. against money-lenders (Lateran II 13, III 25, Lyons II 27) and laity who retained tithes (°Lateran III 14); thus Lyons II 27:

No one may witness the wills of notorious usurers, and no one may hear their confession or give them absolution, unless they make full restitution or give a satisfactory pledge to that effect, in so far as their resources permit.

Wills of notorious usurers that make no reference to this point are *ipso jure* invalid.[7]

Doubtless these things suggest a relationship between moral and economic actions. Unfortunately, we have no direct indication of what the merchant thought. He was not a moralist and he did not write moral treatises. Nor did the confessor assess the effects of his work quantitatively. The connection doubtless was there, but the historian has no means of accurately charting it.[8]

Even in the external forum it is difficult to determine the extent and effectiveness with which legal obligations influenced the policy and actions of merchants. Did the merchant regard the law as something to be exploited to his own advantage, if possible, rather like some modern taxation and company Acts? Or did he find it reasonable and therefore a guide to good business as well as good morals? That depends on the nature of the doctrine, which we shall now examine in some detail.

First it is necessary to repeat a warning given at the beginning of this work (see p. 4). The Church was not directly interested in or concerned with economic theories. Therefore the basis of our reconstruction of motives and theories consists mainly of the *ad hoc* pronouncements of popes, councils, canonists and theologians. Only for the sake of convenience and some logical order are the pronouncements presented as a *continuous* development of ideas and principles. A great deal of the argument is therefore based on the impressions gained by examining these piecemeal assertions against the general social and religious background of the Middle Ages.[9]

The most striking feature of the medieval Church's approach to material well-being is its dualism. This created the self-destructive paradox alluded to already (see p. 5). On the one hand were many scriptural texts that urged men to despise riches: the Sermon on the Mount (Matt. 6:19–34); the lesson of Mark 19:20–5 that it is difficult for the rich to be saved; James 5:1–6, which condemned the rich who defrauded the poor; Paul 'The love of money is the root of all evil' 1 Tim. 6:10; also 1 Thess. 4:6 'that no man overreach nor circumvent his brother in any matter'; and Luke 16:19–31, the parable of the rich man and Lazarus.[10] On the other hand there existed texts, fewer in number, certainly, but individually just as persuasive, that encouraged thrift (e.g. Luke 20:9–10), hard work and profit-making such as the parable of the talents (Luke 19:12–26), and which did not frown on feasting (John 2:1–10) or even waste (the anointing of Christ's feet with rare oils, John 12:3–8).[11] But of all the texts, for and against, the most powerful was the description of Christ driving the buyers and sellers from the temple (Matt. 21:12) (see p. 52). Medieval scriptural exegesis could be obtuse, and a literal interpretation was often used in the early centuries. Among early Christians, who were socially a mixed society, and to all of whom the gospel injunction applied equally, to rich and poor, farmer and merchant, the hardest hit by the general principles derived from these texts were the merchant classes.[12]

In the writings of the early Fathers it seems that trade was singled out for condemnation, not ownership of property as such, nor the rural pursuits. Tertullian spoke of trade as avarice; St John Chrysostom considered merchants to be men who 'wish to become rich at any price. They wish to be rich without limits. They wish to be rich quickly.' Jerome treated trade as fraud; for Augustine it was a pursuit that turned men's minds away from true rest.[13] Gregory Nazianzus, however, thought well of sea-trade.[14] Leo I's conclusion that 'it is difficult for buyers and sellers not to fall into sin' became common opinion in the Church and set the stage, for the theory, that is, for the next six centuries.[15]

Thus in Scripture and among the Fathers the rural pursuits came off well, despite the fact that their economic basis in the period of the Roman Empire, and even beyond, was slavery. Many gross inequalities — although the specific example, slavery, did not survive in serious numbers beyond the eleventh century — typified the medieval world, but basically it was a matter of land distribution.[16] No one ever suggested a radical solution, such as the redistribution of property or popular rule, certainly not until towards the end of the Middle Ages. The Church was not, nor could it be expected to be, immune from these social attitudes. Several factors encouraged it to adopt its ambivalent attitude towards trade and commerce on the one hand and agriculture on the other. First, trade constituted only a small part of the economy, therefore the same pressure could not be brought upon churchmen. But, on the other hand, commerce could for the individual yield the greater profits and was therefore open to most temptations, hence it was to be avoided. Second, the Church's wealth lay in land. Trade was alien to the clerical vocation: the same

C

could not be said of estate management. The Church had to support a system of ownership and wealth in which it was *directly* interested. Third, the theologians, it seems, insisted on the nobility of manual labour from the example of Adam. Man must labour by the sweat of his brow.[17] Labour is a sign of virtue, idleness a sign of vice. But the labour had to be honest, which gave another reason why trade and commerce were stigmatized as unsavoury. In the Roman Empire *negotiatio* was often treated as synonymous with lying and cheating.[18] Fourth, government was hierarchical in Church and State. Trade and commerce cut across the base and threatened this form of government. This tended to keep the papacy within the conservative camp of landed wealth and property.

The Church's support of private property was not unqualified. Nor could it be, for in strict theology property had come into existence as a consequence of Man's Fall. Before the Fall, property was not essential.[19] The fruits of the earth, however, had been given to all men. Putting these two ideas together, it follows that a man may have absolute right of ownership, but not absolute use. Theologian and canonist proclaimed the 'Communis usus omnium quae sunt in hoc mundo'.[20] Ownership carries obligations. Use must be for the common good. For this reason, perhaps, the Church did not frown on state enterprise and price control in the interests of the common good. If anything, it actively encouraged it. There was plenty of free enterprise in the Middle Ages, especially in the twelfth century, but in some cities state regulations closely controlled or even monopolized the important 'export-trade', e.g. at Venice.[21]

The distinction between acceptance of property rights and a critical or even hostile aversion to certain trades and professions appears in the early canonical collections. The *Canons of the Apostolic Tradition* (third century) give a list of prohibited trades, which later canonists and theologians repeated and amplified over the centuries. These were pander, actor, teacher of young children (allowed if necessary for one's living), charioteer who races, gladiator and official in charge, soldier, civil magistrate, harlot, eunuch, magician, juggler.[22] Merchants were generally frowned on, an attitude eventually enshrined in Gratian. During the eleventh century the text of Matthew 21:12 was widely cited. The *Decretum* incorporated the text *Eiciens* as a *palea* (D.88 c.11), whence it passed into the normal decretal collections. Did this text, so typical of many others, mean that Gratian's doctrine on trade and its profits, which he condemned absolutely and without any attempt to distinguish between unjust and just profits, or even between the profits of trade and those of money-lending, would become the general canonical doctrine of the twelfth and thirteenth centuries?[23] Or was the merchant and his profits destined to become respectable, despite Gratian? The next section will examine this question.

B. The Merchant and his Profits

In the *Decretum* the position of the merchant is hardly a complimentary one. All commercial profits seem to be condemned, and the charge of usury is brought against certain forms of investment and partnership, that is, the loan involved in the contract of *commenda* or *societas*.[24] However, let it be said at once that subsequent canonical theory did not sustain Gratian. Even in his own time one of the early commentators on the *Decretum*, Rufinus, in his *Summa* (1157-9), emphasized the factors of expense and labour as a basis for profit-making. Later canonists and theologians refined and elaborated on the distinction between just and unjust profits, so that, as Dr Baldwin concludes: 'According to the best judgement of canonists and theologians of the twelfth and thirteenth centuries, if the merchant was careful and wise he could live with honour in medieval society.'[25]

The achievement of the canonists, whose teachings softened the rigours of the earlier doctrine, may be judged by considering the canonistic doctrine of buying and selling, especially in the writings of Huguccio and, later, Cardinal Hostiensis, where the analysis of sale reached its fullest development.[26]

By this time the canonists, despite individual differences of opinion, had come to consider buying and selling in three main categories.[27] The first category was that of forced sale, where certain goods bought for personal use or consumption had later to be sold. This was permitted to both laity and clergy, and profit could be made. The second class comprised the labour of craftsmen, who obviously increased the value of the goods they bought by the work put into the finished product. Here again trade and profit (the 'just price' we shall consider later) were permitted without restriction to the laity, and even to clerics in certain circumstances. This permission to clerics is not commonly known. Although the teaching of the Church on clerics and trade had long ago been expressed in Chalcedon 3 (as well as in earlier provincial decrees, e.g. Carthage in 397), and although this canon became general usage in the twelfth century (see Lateran IV 16), exceptions had to be and were made,[28] for three reasons. First, for the Church's own estates and business affairs; second, to protect the interests of 'minors, orphans and widows'; and, third, in cases of necessity.[29] Not all clerics were beneficed. Today, minor Orders constitute formal steps to the major Order of priesthood. All clergy have a title, which means, among other things, a source of income. But in the Middle Ages there were many in minor Orders who had taken the tonsure as a means of preferment. Often they were married and had no benefice, or the benefice was insufficient. Even so they enjoyed clerical privileges and restrictions, as here. Such unbeneficed clerics had to earn or supplement their living in secular pursuits. Clearly, the possession or lack of a benefice — stressed frequently by conciliar decrees — would have a significant effect on the clerics' role in society. And what of the suspended clerics? They too had to live.[30] Many of them, it seems, had no difficulty. As Celestine III complained, 'they hasten to laymen's pursuits', and, posing as merchants, they 'get involved in base pursuits and dealings with laity of their own kind'.[31] But what of the honest clerics? For them certain jobs were permissible and quite acceptable, e.g. teaching (cf. °Nicaea II 10), royal administration, certain forms of farming and animal husbandry, some crafts. But buying and selling, the practice of law and medicine for gain [cf Lateran II 9], as well as disreputable jobs such as being a butcher or an innkeeper (Vienne [8]) were forbidden. Such 'trades' were often held in disdain by laity as well as churchmen.[32] However, applying the prohibition proved difficult.

Various synodal decrees interpreted the *inhonesta mercimonia* in different ways — no doubt a result of local variation. The synod of Arras (c. 1275) stated that clerics could not be fullers, weavers, tanners, dyers or shoemakers. The 1298 Liège statutes forbade the craft of fuller, shoemaker, weaver, miller and perfumer. The 1366 Tournai synod allowed shoemaker and smith.[33] Generally, the Church stressed stability of beneficed clergy and prohibited 'wandering clergy' (cf °Chalcedon 5 & 6 and Lateran III 5) and ruled that monks could not live outside their monasteries (°Chalcedon 4).[34] Obviously clerics could not satisfactorily follow a trade without breaking canon laws, with exceptions. The canonists disputed among themselves the nature and scope of the exceptions. Thus, was the rearing of young animals in this category? Or did it fall into the third class, next to be discussed? Huguccio condemned such an occupation, Hispanus was doubtful, and the others recommended it as suitable for clerics.[35]

In practice, clerics had engaged in secular pursuits from the time of the early Church onwards, and gradually, in theory, the canonists came to apply one criterion, i.e. of motive, whether such work was undertaken from a genuine need (*necessitas*) or selfish gain (*turpe lucrum*).[36] Notice too that monks were treated as clerics in this respect, that is, although many of them were laymen, to engage in a trade was inconsistent with their vocation. But canon law could be less rigorous than the civil law, and this proved a source of abuse, for many laity took the tonsure in order to be exempt from the civil law. In this way they carried on their trade and business activities, immune from secular justice. Vienne [8] left it to the discretion of the ordinary to restrain such clerics.[37]

Finally, there was the merchant class proper, who bought with the motive of selling dear without any further addition to the goods or improvement. This was the *negotiatio* of the texts.[38] It was forbidden to the clergy (cf Gratian C.14 q.4 c.3). Traditionally it had been allowed to the laity, as a sort of evil necessity, but in the period of canonical reform of the eleventh and twelfth centuries, especially in Gratian's *Decretum*, it began to be submerged in the general class of usurious profits (cf C.14, q.4 c.9). If Gratian's indecision on this matter had been allowed to stand, there would have arisen a very serious inconsistency between medieval Church doctrine and general economic practice. Fortunately the decretists did not allow the bald condemnation to hold sway. They introduced a double distinction into the nature of profits made from buying cheap and selling dear. First, they distinguished the profits of sale from those of usury. In this respect Gratian's doctrine may be regarded as a mere interlude in the general history of the Church's doctrine concerning sale. Second, the canonists distinguished between profits made without and those made with some expenditure of time and labour and money. Where no expenditure was involved, the gain was the *turpe lucrum* of the traditional teaching. But, of course, in most business ventures the merchant invested his labour and capital. This gain was *honestus questus.*[39]   Most medieval trade fell within this category.   And if we consider the earning rate on capital employed, e.g. the estimate for the Florentine wool trade is 7–15 per cent, and 6–10 per cent for the merchant bankers, then this was very moderate gain.[40]   Thus a very interesting distinction had been introduced — one, indeed, that emancipates the merchant from the 'unequivocal accusations of the Church Fathers' — by asking: 'What are the merchant's motives?'[41] Did he, for example, intend his trade as a means of livelihood for himself and his family?   Then his work was justified.   Did he intend profit for the sake of profit?   Did he seek a monopoly with one end only — to fix the market?   The profit was illicit — a distinction not far removed from contemporary Christian teaching.[42]   In practice, most merchants pursued profit for its own sake and made restitution for the good of their souls in their wills.   This we shall examine below (p. 108).

This decretist teaching became commonly accepted in the thirteenth century.   The idea that a merchant's intention — whether or not he intended to use the profits for an honest living — should be the principal determinant of the rightness of his calling is a far cry from the notions that had held sway for the period down to and including Gratian.   Once this doctrine had been enunciated by the canonists, it was taken up by the theologians and substantially expanded.[43]

Of the partnership, the canonists and theologians generally approved. It was a way of raising money in three ways.   Firstly, capital hires the merchant, i.e. a service partnership;   secondly, the merchant hires the capital, i.e. finance partnership;   thirdly, all parties contribute capital and service, which was the type of the great merchant associations of the thirteenth century.   The second class was obviously close to the ordinary loan.   However, the element of risk involved and the canon law doctrine that usury is a crime committed only by individuals tended to bring it out of the canonists' hands.[44]   In the more obvious type of loan partnership, e.g. the loans *mutui ad negotiandum* of the Venetian nobility, the promise of interest was made, but the amount was left to the borrower to fix.[45]

The decrees of the general councils exemplify most of the foregoing developments.   In the first eight 'Eastern' councils, merchants as such are not mentioned.   'Secular pursuits' are, but usually to prohibit them to clerics.   But in the Latin councils several decrees deal with merchants, i.e. Lateran I 14;   II 11;   III 22 and 24;   IV [71];   °Lyons I

[5], °II [1c]. The occasions are not many, but the surprising thing about them is the favourable way in which they treat the merchants. Merchants are to go about their business unmolested and free of unjust taxes and tolls — a common method of exploitation where customs and tolls varied from region to region. Some thought will show that, whatever the theory dictated, practical interests encouraged the papacy to protect the merchant. Thus Gregory VII ordered Philip I, king of France, to restore goods that he had confiscated from Italian merchants. Manuals of confessors listed merchants among those who could be dispensed from observing the law of fasting and sabbath rest. Likewise the expansion of the institution of *Treuga Dei* favoured the merchant.[46] Admittedly, traders who supplied war materials to the Saracens were punished, but trade in other goods was allowed and continued throughout the Middle Ages and after the fall of Constantinople in 1453.[47] One of the notorious aspects of this trade was the supply of slaves by Christian merchants to Islamic countries, especially Muslim Spain.[48] Fortunately the greater part of the trade was in commodities. Honest merchants were specifically protected against attacks by pirates. Nowhere do the decrees treat merchants as inferior Christians, and this helps to disprove the assertion by Troeltsch, cited below, that merchants were regarded in the Middle Ages as inferior, second-class citizens.[49] Judging by the education available to merchants — in Italy there were very few who were illiterate — they were a literate and respectable class of a status higher than that of the civilian lay lawyers.[50] Again, it is worth noting that after the decree of Lateran IV 68, enjoining the Jews and Saracens to wear distinctive dress, exemption was granted to use Christian dress when travelling, for the Church consistently sought to protect persons, i.e. merchants and pilgrims, in transit (cf Lateran I 14).[51] Self-interest — the desire to maintain free access to and from Rome and the Holy Places for clergy and the faithful as well as to safeguard the transportation of revenues — may have been among the motives, but this does not lessen the debt owed to the Church.[52]

Finally, although the conciliar decrees do not put any special significance or mark of inferiority on the merchant, could it not be argued that certain parts of the Church's doctrine, especially the doctrine of the just price and the canons prohibiting usury, effectively denied the merchant the means of pursuing his calling, that is, free competition and access to a supply of capital, which would hinder the growth of

partnerships and large-scale trade?   The following section will examine these two themes.

C. The Just Price

Changes in the attitude towards the merchant's status are reflected in
the canonistic approach to profits through the idea of the just price.
Until recently a great deal of misunderstanding has existed about the
just price, based on a misconception of what it was.[53]   The modern
error that it was a labour theory of value goes back to Henry of
Langenstein (1325–97), whose teaching on the just price had only a
limited application in his own work and, even as a 'general' theory,
represented only a minority tradition in the Middle Ages.   Nevertheless it was Langenstein's theory that was put into circulation in the
nineteenth century and became the commonly held one by latter-day
historians.[54]   Thus, Troeltsch canonized the false notion that:

In theological theory, therefore, trade was considered the most reactionary
form of earning a living, ethically lower in the scale than agriculture and
manual labour, and it was safeguarded by the precautionary regulation that in
fixing the price all that might be asked was the cost of production plus the
additional amount necessary for a moderate profit.[55]

Henry of Langenstein had declared that the producer may charge
enough to keep up his station in life, so this helps to fix what a moderate profit would be.
Some Christian apologists for the Middle Ages saw this form of
price-fixing as a protection of the poor against the rich, a safeguard
against over-charging and, equally, a protection for the producer
against a fall in the market.   They compared it with the assumed
disastrous effects of *laissez-faire* economics.[56]   On the other hand their
opponents have charged that such a doctrine impeded progress, for it
prevented competition and protected the inefficient producer.[57]
In holding such views without questioning their origin, both parties
demonstrated their willingness to reject the validity of certain economic
principles when applied to the Middle Ages and also their eager attri-
bution of an inordinate economic influence to the medieval Church.
Unfortunately their premises were faulty, so that under the sustained
weight of the attack by several scholars, especially by Baldwin and

De Roover,[58] the traditional concept of the just price has been radically revised.[59] The following pages present the conclusions of these historians.

The just price as a canonical concept belongs to the later Middle Ages (c. 1100 onwards).[60] The early canonists do not mention it, nor do any of the general councils. It derived in fact from the revived Roman Law of the twelfth century, and its adoption by the canonists illustrates what was said earlier about the connection between the two systems of law.[61]

On the doctrines of sale and price medieval Roman Law enunciated two important principles. The first was the principle of *laesio enormis*. In classical Roman Law this was a remedy in a particular case (*fundus*) for the seller, enabling him to sue for recovery where the price received was *less than half* the just price. The medieval glossators extended the application from *fundus* to *res*, thus turning it into a general concept. They also opened it as a remedy for the buyer as well as the seller. Within these limits there was plenty of room for the second principle to operate, namely, the traditional Roman concept of free bargaining between buyer and seller: *Licet contrahentibus invicem se naturaliter circumvenire*, that is, parties to a contract are free to get the better of one another.[62] Free bargaining helped to determine the just price, which was in fact no more than the ruling market price produced by economic fluctuations in supply and demand. It could also be the price fixed by competent authority, i.e. the state or municipality.[63] The civil courts would only interfere, on the grounds of *laesio enormis*, where the just price was severely abused. This would be where fraud or misrepresentation or advantage was used. Otherwise the buyer had to look out for himself.

This doctrine of the Roman lawyers provided the canonists with the term *justum pretium*. In adopting the term, did they reject the civilists' sense and apply it to the 'cost of production plus . . . a moderate profit' notion as asserted by Troeltsch and others? They did not. Baldwin thoroughly investigated the use of the term by the canonists. He concluded that the canonical just price was simply the current price fixed in the free market or by the State, together with the principle of *laesio enormis*.[64] A decretal of Alexander III allows a seller who receives less than half the just price either to cancel the contract or to receive a supplement bringing the price to the 50 per cent mark. The canonists, too, extended the principle to the buyer.[65]

C 2

This new interpretation had immediate application to other theories about the profits of the medieval merchant. It could be used to justify a much greater range of price variation than the revised usury doctrine.[66]   For example, it enabled the merchant to charge interest for goods bought on credit. He could claim that the credit price was the just price, whereas a lower cash price was a discount.[67]

As in usury, the majority of the theologians followed the canonists in their conclusions about the just price, with one distinction — they refused to allow for error in price-charging. They thus rejected the principle of *laesio enormis*.[68]   The theologians began from a different set of principles, arguing that the value of a thing depended not on its intrinsic merit, but upon its utility, i.e. its capacity to satisfy needs.[69] This explains why they insisted that goods should be sold only at the proper market price and that restitution should be made in case of error.[70]   This utility means social utility, not the utility peculiar to each individual buyer.[71]   However, by accepting the market price they thereby agreed that the just price could fluctuate. Aquinas himself argued that 'the early high price and later low price were equally just and lawful'.[72]   The now widely cited example of Aquinas's teaching proves that he did not enunciate a labour theory of value.[73] Aquinas considered the question of a merchant with a load of grain to sell in a famine-stricken area. Prices are high. The question is whether the merchant is obliged to inform his customers that ample supplies are on their way, which will lower the price. If he tells them this, they will probably cease to buy and his profit will fall. Thomas answers that he is not obliged to tell, although a virtuous merchant would probably do so.[74]   This was the view of the majority of the theologians.[75]

This conception of the just price frees the medieval Church from many of the charges brought against it. Economic growth was not impeded by bad teaching or price regulation. Utility and need were the fundamental determinants of price.[76]   The system did not protect the inefficient merchant or craftsman: he sold at a loss, or not at all. The efficient producer was not penalized. Nor did membership of a guild 'ensure the individual craftsman a non-competitive local market'.[77]   There was always foreign competition, substitute goods and materials, and, in the last resort, consumer resistance.[78]

Baldwin's reinterpretation has won general acceptance. Bartell wanted to modify it so as to incorporate the best of both theories.

He argued that 'the prudent recognition of just value determined market price'. He thus tried to reintroduce by the back door the 'cost of production plus reasonable profit' view.[79] The economic producer may have acted thus and sold his goods, but what about the uneconomic producer? In the case of a common commodity with a number of producers and wide sale the law of supply and demand had to operate rather than individual price-fixing. Bartell held that the theological approval of the right of buyer and seller flexibly and freely to decide exchange price belonged to the later scholastics, namely, San Bernardino and San Antonino (1389–1459), archbishop of Florence, who in turn attributed the opinion to Duns Scotus.[80] However, according to de Roover, San Bernardino followed Aquinas on the just price, which was the market price *secundum aestimationem fori occurrentis*.[81]

Does this mean that there was no such thing as an unjust price? Was the impoverished buyer or seller at the mercy of the other? He was not. The canonists did have a doctrine on unjust price, for which they used the term *pretium affectionis*, i.e. price discrimination.[82] The unjust price took advantage of some 'weakness' or necessity on the part of buyer or seller, or it was a figure fixed outside market fluctuations. Artificially fixed prices, brought about by base business methods, such as monopoly or price agreement, forestalling, regrating and engrossing, were considered unjust.[83] Profits of monopoly* were illicit (cf Gratian C.14 q.4 c.9). Here again the canonists were largely indebted to the Roman Law, which condemned monopoly, treating it as intentional fraud. *Unintentional* fraud did not affect a contract of sale unless *laesio enormis* entered.[84] Nor did the canonists prohibit all price fixing.[85] They clearly approved of those state or municipal statutes that repeated or enforced doctrines similar to their own.[86]

Finally, for luxury goods or items that had no clear market price, the canonists disagreed on the exact method of how to charge for them. Some believed that experts should fix a price, but others thought that anyone who could afford to buy luxuries or works of art must be prepared to pay whatever price the seller could persuade him to pay.[87]

Buttressed, some would say hedged, by these concepts the average

* This includes monopsony, oligopoly.

medieval merchant by the thirteenth century had no difficulty in carrying on his business. So wide were the variations permitted by the canon law that the whole question of the merchant's conduct was virtually removed from the external forum of canon law to the internal forum of conscience. The moral theologian and not the canonist became the obstacle to profits, if there was any.[88]

D. USURY[89]

The history of the medieval Church's teaching on usury provides a good example of the different application of basic moral principles to varying social and economic conditions. This history is a compli-cated one. However, the reader will find the issues easier to grasp if he keeps in mind the following four conditions. First, medieval canonists and theologians had little regard for the historical develop-ment of doctrine. Second, they had great respect for the writings of the ancient Fathers and canons of the early general councils, which appeared in a socio-economic system of largely subsistence farming for the masses, with production of a few luxury goods for the minority ruling classes. Third, the doctrine on usury found in those writings and canons did not undergo any significant change from the fourth to the eleventh century, for what need was there? The European economy — despite the break-up of the Roman Empire — remained tied to the soil, capitalism had not yet emerged, credit demand was low; most loans were for consumption purposes, usually made out of 'idle' money or goods — all of which would have brought the loan under the usury laws.[90] By definition the *mutuum* excluded interest. Fourth, when the canonists did tackle the problem of reviewing the doctrine they had to deal with (a) a bewildering variety of new methods of raising loans and making profits that had emerged during and since the late tenth century,[91] and (b) the knowledge that Gratian, whose *Decretum* with *paleae* provided the starting-point of their own work, tended to equate all profits with usury.[92] It should be added that from a theological standpoint the interpretation of a doubtful doctrine may legitimately be examined against the practice of the Church, which, in our case, is the Roman Church.[93]

If the twelfth-century canonists had been able to examine the texts, which were their starting-point, in their historical setting, they would have found their task much easier. Despite the texts of Deuteronomy 23:19–20, Exodus 22:25, Leviticus 25:35–7 and Luke 6:34–5 — commonly cited as the scriptural basis for condemning usury — the early canons of provincial councils provide evidence that the prohibition applied only to clerics, e.g. Elvira c.20 (an. 306?), Carthage c.12 (345), Aix-la-Chapelle (789) and Paris (829).[94] Among the canons of the first eight general councils there is only one text on usury, Nicaea I 17, and it refers explicitly to clerics. Did it implicitly include laymen? Noonan thinks it did, but this is doubtful, especially as loans at interest were legal according to civil law in Byzantium.[95] Nicaea I 17 went into the *Dionysiana* and likewise the *Hispana*. Both versions occur in Gratian D.47 c.2 and C.14 q.4 c.7.[96] After the *Hispana* there are no other significant texts until the *Hadriana*. This contained the text *Nec hoc quoque* of Leo I (=Gratian C.14 q.4 c.8), which became the basis of a great deal of later legislation, but it does not contradict the present argument.[97]

After 800 the prohibition of usury was gradually extended by decrees of provincial councils to include the laity.[98] Secular prohibitions were also introduced, and in 806 came the first medieval definition of usury: 'where more is asked than is given'.[99] But the clerical class remained the only really suspect class. Indeed no such thing as a formulated doctrine emerges until the later period.[100] The significant change came in the eleventh century, when usury began to be regarded as a sin against justice.[101] Finally, Lateran II 13 in 1139 extended the prohibition to the whole Church. Doubtless this was associated with the increase in money-lending under the impact of the economic revolution of the time. Some historians even imply that it was entirely a selfish motive that led the Church to tighten the prohibition.[102] But this is inconsistent with two obvious features of the change: first, the clergy were already excluded from usurious transactions, therefore no new legislation was necessary, and, second, it would have been easier for the Church to sanction limited forms of usury.[103] Most of the clergy used some form of deficit financing, and the overall cost of avoiding open infringement of the prohibition was probably greater than borrowing on a free market. Instead the prohibition can be seen as a genuine attempt, somewhat misplaced when applied by rigorists to *all* profits of commercial enterprise, to protect consumer credit in an age when there were few opportunities to save for emergencies provoked by illness, disease, fire, war, alien seizure of one's goods or property, all of which deprived the peasant or artisan of his means of livelihood and forced him into the hands of the money-lender or pawnbroker.[104]   Several conciliar texts, e.g Lateran II 13 and III 25, illustrate the importance of this problem in the later period.

Historians who criticize the continued and increasingly severe nature of the medieval Church's usury laws, seeing these as a misguided attempt to prohibit economic expansion, make the double mistake of, first, overlooking the fact that the commercial revolution did not strengthen the economic security of the masses, but weakened it, which called for an even greater attention to laws that prohibited such abuses as usury; and, second, assuming too easily that text-book definitions of usury such as are found in Gratian's *Decretum* were generally applied without discretion (see p. 66).   Of course the texts lend themselves at any time to a rigorist interpretation, which will never be absent throughout the Middle Ages, and which will, in fact, re-emerge and become increasingly common sometime after 1350, but generally the texts became favourably interpreted, so that in practice usury came to be treated as the lending of money at exorbitant rates of interest.[105]

Gratian's *Decretum* was the starting-point of this development. Thus C.14 q.3 c.3 states that 'whatever is added to the principal is usury', and this applies to all forms of loan whether of money or goods.   Other chapters condemn usury 'unequivocally'.[106]   What were the decretists to make of this?   In practice they knew that lending at interest was common and necessary.   In the medieval business world one can in fact distinguish two types of borrower and creditor, and correspondingly two median levels of interest rates.   First, there was distress-borrowing, usually consumption loans in an emergency. Here, resort was had to the money-lender or pawnbroker for a loan on security of land or personal possessions.   The greater the risk, the higher the rate of interest.   Throughout the Middle Ages a rate of 2*d*. per pound per week (=43 per cent p.a.) was common for such loans.[107] Even where the 'mortgage' system was used, i.e. the lender taking the usufruct of the security, 20 or 25 per cent interest was often charged.[108] This includes Christian as well as Jewish lenders, so that in fact the median rate of interest represents what must have been an economic rate for loans of this type.[109]   Moreover, lending at interest continued quite openly in such cities as Venice and Toulouse, and the municipal or state authorities, e.g. in the Low Countries, usually licensed or protected the public usurers.[110] Distress-borrowing, because of the high rate of interest and the knowledge that, as usual, the poor suffered the most because they had least security and therefore were committed to exorbitant rates of interest, which accordingly worsened their economic position, specifically came within the usury prohibition (see p. 121). The second class of loan, however, consisted of commercial borrowing or production loans by and from merchants from the Italian banking companies; here, where the risk was minimal, e.g. lending to citizens of the same town, the interest rate could be as low as 7–15 per cent.[111] Even where the commercial risk was high, the loan was often treated as an investment, that is, for a share in the profits. In the end, commercial loans through banking became transformed or disguised and were removed from the usury prohibition.[112] Loans to secular rulers were mostly high-risk, but they carried different rewards, such as the securing of trading rights and privileges.[113]

The canonists must have viewed the seeming gulf between Gratian's rigorist condemnation of all profits and the commercial practice of the twelfth century with some dismay. But they solved the difficulty of bringing the two into line by introducing a double distinction, firstly, between commercial profits and 'usurious' transactions, and secondly by gradually narrowing the meaning of usury until for all practical purposes it meant an exorbitant, i.e. an unjust charge, for lending money, which was a serious sin, as it has continued to be down to the present day.[114] In this approach the underlying principle consisted of developing and extending the concept that there should be compensation or damages for overdue and risk-inducing loans.[115]

The method of the canonists and theologians consisted of making exceptions to the 'law' of usury, and this system came to dominate the later medieval doctrine. This, of course, is fairly typical of all medieval canon law and theology, and it is the failure of modern historians to understand this that leads them to make such bald, unqualified statements as the taking of interest was forbidden in the Middle Ages or that the Church came later to change its doctrine. Without asking what was meant by 'interest' or was there ever such a thing as a 'doctrine' of usury, which people today usually take to mean a sort of infallibly defined teaching, however wrong they may be, then only confusion and misunderstanding result.

Nor was the method of exceptions a new one. Such exceptions occur even among the early Fathers of the Church. Thus the text of Ambrose 'where there is right of war, there is right of usury' seems a particular case of the general principle derived from the Deuteronomy text, which introduced the notion of the double standard and was thereby often adduced as the scriptural authority by which loans between Christian and Jew, Saracen and Christian were permitted.[116] It is often forgotten that the principle was not a one-way one, that is, justifying only Jewish usuries to Christians, but operated in reverse equally well.[117] In dealing with the Jews, heretics and infidels, several canonists urged the right to take usury because it contributed to diminishing the wealth of the enemies of the Church.[118] Negatively, the working of this particular exception may be seen by examining the question whether one could make usurious loans for the redemption of Saracen captives held to ransom or not. Some canonists sanctioned them, but, on the basis of Lateran II 13, Alexander III (1159–81) declared that no dispensations could be granted.[119] Here he followed the theologians.

From this example it may be argued that the 'doctrine' was only being elucidated and defined by the twelfth century, so that there was less excuse for the canonists making exceptions in this period, and beyond, than there had been previously. The text of Lateran III 25 proves how wrong this assumption is. It appears to repeat the main terms of Lateran II 13, but actually it introduced an important distinction by confining the canon to *notorious* usurers (*usurarii manifesti*).[120] Although the term did not acquire precise meaning until Lyons II in 1274,[121] a great deal came to depend on the implied distinction between open and concealed usury. The manifest usurers were those who could be shown to be such beyond a doubt, and this applied mainly to one class — the pawnbrokers — who publicly set themselves up as usurers, were licensed by the municipal authority or even by the Church, and whose transactions were recorded.[122] Indeed they became the only group who contravened the usury laws by demanding back more (*usura*) than what was given (the *mutuum*). The money-changer, the merchant-banker and the occult usurer avoided the drastic penalties of the laws passed from 1139 to 1311–12.[123] Only in conscience, and therefore in the forum of the confessional, could such men be held guilty.[124]

The foregoing illustrates the background against which the canonists and theologians had to work when they sought to bring some coherency and consistency into the mass of texts and divergent practices relating to usury. Their achievement by the mid-thirteenth century may be seen by detailing the exceptions found in the work of Hostiensis. He lists thirteen such cases. They are as follows: (1) *feuda*, i.e. where the fief is returned to the donor as a security for a loan, the donor may take the fruits without deducting them from the capital loaned; (2) *fidejussor*, i.e. a guarantor forced to contract a loan at interest because of his obligation may demand payment of the interest from the party concerned; (3) *pro dote*, i.e. if a dowry cannot be produced and a gage is given instead, the husband may take the fruits of the gage until such time as the dowry is paid; (4) *stipendia cleri*, i.e. if a layman holding a benefice belonging to the Church gives it to the Church as security for debt, the income does not diminish the debt; (5) *venditio fructus*, i.e. sale of the revenues of a piece of land is equivalent to a rent charge and constitutes a contract of sale; (6) *cui velle jure nocere*, i.e. usury may be demanded of an enemy; (7) *vendens sub dubio*, i.e. sale at a higher than the prevailing price for credit terms provided the future price of the commodity is in doubt; (8) *pretium post tempora solvens*, i.e. payment of damages where debtor who has bought goods fails to pay on the agreed date; (9) *poena nec in fraudem* (also known as the *poena conventionalis*), i.e. a penalty clause written into a loan contract that provides for compensation if the debtor fails to repay the principal on the agreed date; (10) *lex commissoria*, i.e. the contract allows the seller to recover his property within a fixed term, then the buyer retains the profits of his period of use; (11) *gratis dans*, i.e. a gift by the debtor; (12) *socii pompa*, i.e. where an article is lent to another for purposes of show, the lender may take payment, for the article is not consumed; and (13) *labor*, i.e. a creditor may take payment for his work.[125]

Of course parties to a loan often resorted to one or other of these forms in order to avoid the charge of usury. Gratuitous loans were the most common. Notaries in the Middle Ages presented innumerable loans of money or goods as gratuitous, which they were certainly not.[126] A true gift by a borrower to his creditor was of course lawful.[127] This made it very difficult to prove a charge of usury, for it was the intention and not the form of the act that constituted the difference between an illicit and licit transaction. However, some methods were more obviously fraudulent and could possibly be proved to be such in the ecclesiastical court. These constituted the charge *in fraudem usurarum*. The common methods were (1) the contract often specified as *racione amicabilis mutui* by which A borrows 60 from B and signs the contract for 80, (2) purchase of the gage or security with right of repurchase within a certain time, the 'purchaser' meanwhile drawing income from the property, (3) deliberate use of the penalty *poena conventionalis*.[128] The use of the bill of exchange, which underlies medieval banking, constitutes a major exception that is dealt with below (see p. 74).

A doctrine based on numerous exceptions was a cumbersome approach and left the way open to deceits and abuses. There was a need to simplify, to find a basic approach to all usury. The simplest solution would have been if the canonists and theologians could have recognized that in every loan there was an intrinsic value of time that the borrower gained and the lender lost, and that for this the lender should have compensation — our modern interest — that accrued from the beginning of the loan.[129] Unfortunately the very term used for the loan, *mutuum*, excluded the idea that the borrower should 'pay' something over and above the capital sum. Thus the writers were saddled with their premise that intrinsically the loan was gratuitous. However, from about the middle of the thirteenth century such canonists as Hostiensis and Innocent IV began to ignore the old arguments based on the intrinsic injustice of usury; they prohibited it solely because of its harmful consequences.[130] Then, logically, the next step was to have more concern for the lender. Did he not lose in the transaction? Might not a merchant asked for a loan by someone in need be put to some loss by his charitable act? From this and other usages it came about that what had been denied by intrinsic title was acquired through extrinsic ones. Three main titles emerged from the mass of exceptions, that is, *damnum emergens* (loss occurring), *lucrum cessans* (profit ceasing) and *periculum sortis* (risk of loss of principal).[131] These three concepts may be regarded as a single case of 'compensation' for loss arising for reasons extraneous to the loan itself, and the term *interesse* was used to denote them.[132] In its strict Roman Law sense, from which the canonists originally adopted the term, *interesse* meant damages arising from non-payment of a loan at the stipulated time and place. This form of 'interest' became operative only on the day the loan period expired, and did not, in theory at least, apply retrospectively. In fact the 'damages' was usually a fixed sum or percentage that became payable however short the delay in repaying the loan as agreed. This was the *poena conventionalis* already referred to, which was also an excellent means of avoiding usury charges (see p. 67). However, the new application of *interesse* gave 'a lawful reason for charging beyond the principal even though ... [the] debtor is in no way at fault'.[133] Moreover, it was due from the start of the loan. It was the first indication of a doctrine of interest in the modern sense. Hostiensis recognized *lucrum cessans* fully.[134] Motive was what mattered. Thus a merchant who forgoes a chance to make a profit because he makes a charitable loan can reasonably take interest. Provided his intention was honest and he was not accustomed to make such loans.[135]

It may be argued that 'motive' was beyond the competence of the courts to determine. That is so, but what they substituted as a rough guide was the rate of interest charged. The professional money-lender had high overheads and had to charge a correspondingly high rate of interest. The casual or charitable loan was compensated by a rate of somewhere between 5 and 12 per cent (see p. 113).

Although the first theologian to admit interest was Astesanus (*c.* 1312), it should be stressed that the scholastic theologians of the thirteenth century developed their doctrine out of the canonistic teaching. Like the canonists, the theologians did not oppose profits as such, but only interest on borrowed money. Ultimately they permitted the distinction between usury (sinful) and interest (in certain circumstances).[136] Robert of Courçon (d. 1219) was among the first theologians to discuss usury. From him there was a continuous line of development to St Thomas Aquinas (?1225–74).[137] Some theologians, e.g. Peter Cantor and his circle were fierce opponents of usury in the most absolute sense. They opposed taking the lawful *poena nec in fraudem*, i.e. damages for non-repayment of the loan at the time stipulated, on the grounds that this amounted to selling time, 'which is by nature a common possession and therefore non-vendible'.[138]

This objection, which was based on a concept falsely attributed to Aristotle that money is sterile, was commonly raised by theologians against all classes of loans. Consequently they were initially more hampered than the canonists, whose theories were reasonably pragmatic in application.[139] The theologians treated money as a fungible good, like wine, whose use cannot be sold or leased as distinct from its possession, for it is destroyed by its use. Therefore money can only be sold, not lent, and the cost cannot be more than a return of a like sum or of equivalent value. By contrast, non-fungible goods, such as a house or a plough or property, have a use that can be sold distinct from their possession.[140] The canonists agreed with this doctrine, which, fundamentally, is correct — here modern commentators have mostly missed the point — when applied to modest charitable loans made to a friend or neighbour for consumption purposes.[141] Equally so the medieval writer failed to perceive that the pawnbroker deserved compensation for his function in enabling individuals to anticipate earnings.[142]

At first the more strict position of the theologians, based on the question of intention, made them refuse several of the canonistic concessions because they felt that the intention behind them was usurious, and they tried to get at the merchant-bankers, whose usury was occult, usually, and therefore fell outside the canon law. The doctrine of intention could, however, lead to an amelioration of the strict law, for it was not difficult to move from judging a loan as usurious by the mere fact of interest being charged, to asking whether, when interest was charged, the loan was in fact usurious. By the same reasoning the theologians eventually arrived at the quite different notion that there is no real distinction between monetary and real capital. San Bernardino of Siena, who may be reckoned one of the outstanding economists of the Middle Ages, and who applied the teaching as a practical moral theologian, had crossed this boundary, when he said, 'Money has not simply the character of money; but it has beyond this a productive character, which we commonly call capital.'[143] Future money could then be sold at a price, a just price, of course, but nonetheless one justifying interest.[144]

E. THE SUPPLIERS OF CREDIT — PAWNBROKERS, AND MERCHANT-BANKERS*

Having surveyed the process by which canonist and theologian released the merchant and his profits from the major restraints to free action, it seems appropriate to examine the suppliers of credit, who, if we take medieval Bruges as an example, consisted of three different

* See p. 27.

classes, i.e. pawnbrokers (often referred to as *lombardi*), money-changers and merchant-bankers.[145] Every large-scale institution had some dealing with one or all of the three groups. The Church was no exception. As a temporal society it consisted of a number of diverse institutions, highly dependent on revenues, investments, loans and credit. From the papacy downwards by 1200 elaborate financial systems had emerged that were deeply involved in the money-market.[146] The complex relationship that existed between the various groups — e.g. between the pope and the great banking-houses of Italy in the thirteenth century — had its roots in the distant past of the Church's history. Lopez comments:

Ever since the fifth century the moneyers had been increasing their influence and prestige. They handled investments of the church institutions, sat at the side of the imperial judges and built up extensive estates of their own. Money, of course, was their business. Then as the economic and political tide began to turn, the moneyers had to take sides. Some of them cast their lot with the religious reformers and occupied leading positions in the emerging communes, others forsook their origins to merge with the diehard feudal nobility. The decline of the moneyers closely followed upon the revival of the money-economy.[147]

Before the rise of the Italian bankers the Jews filled the vacuum caused by the decline of the moneyers. They had the advantage of the Deuteronomy double provision by which they could charge usury and so fulfil the needs of their Christian clients.[148] The decrees of the councils, now supported by an increasing number of regional or individual studies, show that, on the whole, the Jews had a favourable position in canon law and in society until the fourth Lateran Council (1215). For a century or so (*c.* 1050–1200) the Jews, often in co-operation with monasteries and other emerging Christian capitalists, were regarded as indispensable, especially for the two major occupations of the Middle Ages — building and warfare.[149] The canonists generally treated them as lying outside the strict provisions of church law, except in certain matters, e.g. they could not have Christian servants (cf Lateran III 26), nor could they take sacred objects in pawn.[150] Jews were tolerated by the early Church, no attempt at forced conversion being made, for conversion was a privilege not to be lightly treated (cf Nicaea II 8).

Unfortunately the rise of the Jews to financial predominance (*c.* 1000 onwards) eventually brought them into a clash with their Christian rivals. The advent of the crusades, which they helped to finance, laid the Jews open to pillage by marauding armies and even to loss of capital by the declaration of a moratorium on all interest payments by crusaders.[151]

Lateran IV (1215) marked the turning-point in the general position of the Jew in Christian society. His conversion became desirable, even if force had to be used (cf Lateran IV 70), and financial inducements were offered to converts, e.g. by guaranteeing their rights of inheritance (Lateran III 26) or even, as late as the fifteenth century, retention of part of their usurious profits.[152]

Although the language of the councils from Lateran IV onwards indicates that commercial and business dealings between Christians and Jews continued (cf Lateran IV 67)[153] the fact is that the Jews gradually ceased to play a large part in international commerce and finance and became confined to pawnbroking.[154] Even here they faced competition from Christian rivals, such as the Cahorsins and the Lombards or Tuscans.[155] These regarded the Jews as rivals to be put out of business. This forced the Jews to depend for their continued existence on royal or municipal licence, so that, e.g. in England, their fate became delicately balanced between political and economic pressures until their expulsion in 1290.[156] As long as they fulfilled the function of a financial milch cow, a means of indirect taxation for rulers hampered by feudal restrictions, the Jews were protected, but, in the end, economic pressure by Christian merchants and moneylenders, as well as the emergence of more efficient methods of royal taxation, made the Jews a political nuisance. And no longer did they have much protection from the Church.[157]

Some commentators assume that the Jews brought their fate upon themselves because they charged exorbitant interest. In fact Jewish rates were not excessive, comparatively speaking. The Christian money-lenders charged the same rate from locality to locality. A pledge rate of 30–43 per cent appears high, but not when one considers the expenses involved.[158] And these were many, e.g. the cost of licence to act as a pawnbroker, return upon capital invested, payment for the pawnbroker's own labours, provision of house and strongroom, storage charges on pledges, hired assistants, sale and losses on unredeemed pledges; in this way the net return was reduced to about 8–10 per cent. Present-day legal rates are notably higher.[159] However, the Jews could operate profitably at a lower rate of interest.

Thus in 1430 the *Signoria* of Florence invited the Jews to return to the city as pawnbrokers subject to a maximum limit of 20 per cent interest and social restrictions, but with a monopoly of money-lending.[160] Despite the restrictions, the Jewish community had increased its wealth to 50 million florins by 1495.[161] A detailed study of medieval Jewish money-lending, based on the Perpignan records, is that it was reasonably conducted.[162]

Jewish money-lending and pawnbroking never compared in volume to the transactions of the medieval bankers, who were descended from the earlier money-changers.[163] Medieval Europe had a great variety of coinages, thus the money-changers supplied the need generated by the expanding money economy. They took their profit from the fluctuations in the prices of the different currencies. These were frequent and unpredictable, so the changers ran a certain 'risk'.[164] International centres such as the fairs and meeting-places for general councils or the papal palace at Avignon attracted the money-changers. In 1327–8 there were some forty-three money-changers in Avignon.[165]

Some of these 'exchangers' began to accept money on deposit and to finance various enterprises either as true partners or merely putting up the money as a loan. The Genoese bankers *c.* 1200 paid 10 per cent on term deposits and charged 20 per cent on the *mutua*.[166] Deposits for payment on demand earned no interest, only convenience for their owners. But this varied.[167] Out of these small beginnings developed many of the procedures of modern banking between then and the fourteenth century. By the mid-thirteenth century there were about 80 banking-houses in Florence alone, not counting those in Lucca, Siena, Genoa and other Lombard towns. In England in 1231 there were some 69 Italian banking-houses operating.[168] The capital was huge. At the height of the banking boom the Bardi on 1 July 1318 had one company with a total capital of 875,638 florins, whose relative value may be determined by the fact that Clement VI in 1348 bought Avignon for 80,000 florins.[169] Most of the instructions given by depositors were oral ones, which explains many of the puzzling features about the early records of banking.[170] The banks also invested in business ventures, which probably accounts for the high failure rate of merchant-bankers in the Middle Ages.[171] Thus the Salimbeni bank failed in 1260 as a result of non-payment of a loan of 22,000 florins to Siena.[172] When Edward I died he owed the

Italian firms £118,000 and the customs and other revenues had been assigned to the Frescobaldi. Edward II brought the debt to £400,000, and in the process ruined the Frescobaldi Company in 1315. His successor, Edward III, was the greatest villain of them all — he had 1,365,000 gold florins from the banks and did not repay in 1339.[173] This left the main banks under-capitalized, hence the failures in 1345–6, when three of the most important Florentine companies — the Acciaiuoli, Peruzzi and Bardi — went bankrupt.[174] They had over-extended their credit. Their collapse affected the rest of the European financial and commercial structure.[175] The Alberti, Strozzi and Medici in turn took them over, but their operations were never as big; the era of large-scale banking in Italy had, for a time, ended.[176]

The chief depositors in these companies were Italian nobles, clerics and businessmen, all of whom were anxious to profit from the banks' trading activities.[177] What then of the charge of usury? Usually this was avoided because the loans were treated as investments with a flexible rate of interest or dividend being paid. In Florence this was by way of a gift *discrezione*, which thereby evaded the usury charge. Such 'gifts' usually amounted to 7–8 per cent or 10 per cent on the loan, but as there was no contract the banker was not obliged to pay. However, consistent failure to pay the *discrezione* would lead to his depositors going elsewhere with their funds. This system was a development of the canonical exception *gratis dans* listed above.[178] Another method was to treat the interest as compensation for delay in repayment of the term deposits.[179] As for the bankers' lending activities, the practically universal means of avoiding usury accusation was to conceal the loan in an exchange transaction (*cambium per litteras*) or bills of exchange. The borrower purchased a bill payable at another time and place, usually, and the rate of exchange concealed, of course, interest. De Roover adds:

Although the presence of concealed interest is undeniable, the merchants argued — and most of the theologians accepted these views — that an exchange transaction was not a loan (*cambium non est mutuum*) but either a commutation of moneys (*permutatio*) or a buying and selling of foreign currency (*emptio venditio*) . . . The practical consequence was to tie banking to exchange, be it manual exchange or exchange by bills.[180]

Such a transaction involved four persons. First, the remitter or bank supplying the loan; second, the taker or drawer of the money;

third, the factor of the creditor in the city on which the money will be repaid, known as the payee or beneficiary; and, finally, the correspondent of the debtor, who will pay the bill. For example:

20 July in Venice

[Ducats] 500

Pay at usuance to G. Canigiani 500 ducats in sterling 47 per ducats by Medici & Company.

Signed Bartolomew Zorzi & I. Michiel

[On the back] F. Giorgio and Petro Morozino

In Venice the Medici Company lend Zorzi & Michiel 500 ducats. This sum must be repaid in London in sterling at the rate of 47 pence per ducat, i.e. £97 18s. 4d. at usuance. Usuance (the period allowed for movement of bills between cities) was three months for Venice to London. Therefore repayment will be 20 October. Giorgio & Morozino will repay the money to Canigiani. In practice, payment is not made, but the bill is protested and therefore sent back to the place of issue to be repaid by the borrower. Canigiani rewrites the bill for £97 18s. 4d. plus his fee of 4s. On 20 October the rate of exchange is 44 pence to the ducat. The return bill is 535 ducats, again payable at usuance of three months. Therefore on 20 January the Medici Company can collect 535 ducats from Zorzi & Michiel. This gives a per annum rate of interest of 14 per cent. If the rate of exchange in the period of six months had fluctuated violently for some reason, then either party stood to gain or lose by the transaction. Where the bankers remitted a bill free, e.g. in the case of the papal monies, the cost of the service was borne by the transmission of someone else's money in the reverse direction, the papal monies simply being used to supply the 'loan' in the city of origin.[181]

Variations of genuine exchange developed to cut the cost of the operation and to eliminate the element of risk. As early as 1188 there is recorded at Genoa a form that became common and was known as 'dry exchange' (*cambium seccum*). This involved only two parties, and no bills were transmitted. It was still speculative because the parties did not know the rate of re-exchange.[182] Fictitious exchange, in which 'the rates were artificially fixed so the banker knew his profit in advance were condemned by the theologians because the risk element was missing'.[183]

More important, because usually overlooked, is the fact that many merchants also found fictitious exchange wrong because it could easily upset the normal money-market.[184]   Where the exchange was associated with the sale or purchase of goods, the canonists regarded with suspicion excessively low or high prices alleged to have been paid.   They were evidence of usurious fraud.   However, in practice, many ecclesiastical institutions, from the papacy downwards, indulged in these negotiations.   Morally they evaded the spirit of the law; economically such exceptions contributed to the emergence of the medieval system of banking.[185]   That the total effect would have been different had open interest charges been permitted is doubtful. Certainly banking would not have been tied to exchange and the presumed hampering effect of the latter would have been removed.   But equally it may be argued that exchange fostered *international* banking and commercial transactions that otherwise would not have occurred. In either case it is difficult to describe the church doctrine unequivocally as either harmful or beneficial.

Among the ecclesiastical institutions that have been often accused of doing most to thwart the spirit of the laws condemning usury, the Order of Templars deserves special mention.   It was largely the growth of the Order as a wealthy banking organization that brought about its downfall in 1312.[186]   As an Order the Templars had special privileges granted by the pope and, e.g. in England, by the king. They were exempt from secular taxes and feudal dues, payments of tolls and customs, and from seizure of their agricultural produce in time of war.[187]   Internationally their banking activities were widespread: they even had Muslim clients.[188]   There is, however, some evidence that they abstained from usurious acts.   The interest they received was for 'damages' for non-repayment on time.[189]   The final abolition of the Order was due to royal greed, and none of the charges of secret worship or evil and unnatural vice brought against them was ever proved.[190]

F. The Uses of Wealth — Charity and the Poor

Modern discussions of the relationship between economic progress and the problem of the alleviation of poverty, the extent of 'obligation', of the haves towards the have-nots, were not missing from the Middle

Ages. In the early Church the proletariat had by the second century already lost its purchasing power. The State seemed helpless to cope with the problem, which gradually fell to the Church.[191] Numerous documents attest the concern of Christianity throughout its history for the well-being of certain classes — widows, orphans, exiles, the workless, lepers, prisoners, captives, the sick, travellers, the plague-stricken. These are the 'poor' for whom the Church has always sought special treatment. Lateran III 18 puts the general principle: 'The Church of God as a devoted mother is bound to provide for those in need, both in the things that pertain to the body and also in those that pertain to the good of soul.' How then did the medieval Church fulfil this duty? What relationship was there to the institution and use of wealth?[192]

Again we come up against the dilemma that faced Christians and the Church's teaching authority. On the one hand, from the ancient world the Church had inherited some of the Stoic tradition relating to the community of property. Elements of this are found in the writings of Saints Cyprian, Ambrose, Zeno of Verona, Basil and Jerome; later these texts went into Gratian (cf C.12. q.1. c.2). Together with scriptural exhortations concerning the virtues of poverty and the burden of the rich, and which pointed to the second greatest commandment as 'Love thy neighbour' (Matt. 25:34–40; Mark 12:30–1; Luke 6:31, 38; Rom. 12:5), they created the ideal that those who wished to follow Christ (by definition all Christians) must renounce private wealth and property.[193] But there were texts that treated private property as part of the normal social order. In fact private possession dominated the social and economic order of the Middle Ages and therefore the thinking of most canonists and theologians.[194]

How was the conflict resolved? The canonists, in commenting on the appropriate texts in the *Decretum*, developed the ancient concept of a distinction between 'right to own' and 'right use', a notion that 'became a fundamental tenet of medieval sociology'.[195] The theologian took this a step further by stressing that, although the divine natural law had originally established a community of property, the human law had 'added private ownership as a useful corrective to man's neglect of this ideal situation'.[196] This justification of private wealth did not signify unlimited dominion over one's goods. Nor could one seek wordly goods beyond one's needs,[197] for, in that case, all Christians became morally obliged to give what was superfluous to their needs to the poor.[198] °Constantinople IV 15 expressed this when it ordered that Church property could not be alienated, for this would harm 'ecclesiastical revenue, which is decreed to be for the Church's own use or to provide food for the needy and sustenance for pilgrims'.[199] Likewise Hostiensis: 'Pope and churches hold the goods they have not as their own, but as common possessions, that thence they may help all men suffering want.'[200] Thus not even the pope could do as he pleased with his property.[201]

In practice the early Church as a body, and Christians individually, recognized their obligation to provide for the poor. The bishops did so by allocating part of the diocesan income — one-third or one-quarter — for this purpose.[202] Here the obligation was a juridical one (with individuals, only a matter of conscience) imposed by canon law (cf °Chalcedon 8).[203] In a mainly agricultural economy such arrangements seem to have sufficed. This is borne out by the fact that the decrees of general councils relating to the poor belong mostly to the Latin and not to the Greek period. Increasing reference to the poor indicates, most likely, a change in their needs rather than in the attitude of the Church. The economic revolution of the twelfth and thirteenth centuries created new problems, involving proportionately larger numbers than previously. Also, and this fact is often overlooked, the early Church's provision for poor-relief had been radically upset. The ancient system no longer held. The proprietary church system, including large-scale monastic appropriation of parish churches and tithes, had deprived the bishops of control over diocesan funds.[204] The papacy circumvented the problem in terms of ecclesiastical administration by encouraging the parish system, and it used the same foundation to provide poor-relief during the rest of the Middle Ages.[205] In addition there was the charitable work of the various monastic orders and houses and of the religious guilds who tithed their income for that purpose.[206] A useful source of income came from the restitution of ill-gotten gains, the *incerta* of the usurer, as well as of excessive profits made from trade. These various sources of income meant that the thirteenth century had solved the problem of its poor. Nor was this type of relief regarded by the recipient as charity; instead he treated it in the way that we treat state maintenance today.[207]

The Latin decrees refer, in passing, to what was done. Almshouses, leper-houses (with special tithe-exemption, cf Lateran III 23) and pilgrim centres (Vienne [17]);[208] special provisions for education (Lateran III 18 and °IV 11); the establishing of monastic hospitals (Vienne [30]; Lateran V Sess. IX Bull of the Reform [5]) are signposts to a vast system of medieval poor-relief. We are only just beginning to understand and to mark out its precise nature and extent.[209]

Some striking examples exist to show how strong was the obligation to give alms in the Middle Ages and how far removed from the present-day conception of charity.[210] King John of England was not noted for his good will towards the clergy. He was also constantly in debt. Yet he paid alms from his revenues.[211] The recipients? Mostly religious houses. In the fourth year of his reign the Pipe Rolls record an income of £24,000, and donations of £1450 to charities: approximately 6 per cent. And the king gave to other charities as well, e.g. thirty-four hospitals received royal alms. The payments were impersonal, for they were unaffected by John's quarrel with the papacy. More significant, perhaps, was the Cistercian example. In 1210 they refused to make any grants-in-aid to John, who, in turn, took from them some 25,000–30,000 marks, nevertheless the king gave the Order the usual allowances for charity.[212] The majority of individuals honoured their obligation, possibly because the Church regarded property rights and ownership as lawful *once* the duty of charity had been fulfilled.[213]

If the laity were subject to such pressures to ensure 'right use' of their wealth, how much more so were the clergy, both individually and collectively? On this matter a great deal has been written in recent years, especially dealing with the problem of the extent to which the monasteries continued to fulfil their obligations. The conclusion of these studies is that throughout the Middle Ages the percentage of monastic income given to charitable purposes remained constant at about 5 per cent.[214] Various factors operated to retain this figure, which applied to most ecclesiastical alms-giving. Even public opinion played a part, for if the clergy failed to set the example, what hope was there for the rest? Such attitudes lay behind what may be termed the sumptuary legislation of the councils. Condemnation of extravagance in clerical dress is a recurrent theme in conciliar decrees (cf Lateran IV 16). However, this legislation ran counter to the medieval tradition, probably a continuation of the Roman, that men of authority should be distinguished by their dress.[215] Nor is there much evidence that either clerics or laity obeyed the injunctions. It is interesting to reflect on what effect a successful prohibition would have had. As most of the import trade of the early Middle Ages consisted in luxury goods, 'costly textiles and robes . . . seasonings, medicinals, and colouring mediums . . . precious stones and plate and metal work',[216] it could be argued that this diverted limited capital resources from more essential purposes. But it might equally be argued that this expenditure kept commerce alive and encouraged expansion where otherwise there would have been none.

But what of the poor themselves? Various interesting speculations have been made to account both for their number and their degree of poverty in the Middle Ages. These range from an idealistic but somewhat confused portrayal of poverty as a desirable state that fitted in with Christ's Sermon on the Mount and which was alleviated by the Church so that there was a sort of golden age in the twelfth and thirteenth centuries, to the view that the Church, especially by its system of tithes, produced much of the poverty.[217] Others treat the economic expansion of these two centuries in Malthusian terms, that is, the expanding population outstripped the increasing food supply; in this view the Black Death, by its disastrous wiping-out of nearly a third of Europe's population, was a blessing in disguise.[218] And when all this has been said, lest any loophole be left by which the Church might escape the charge of impeding progress, its system of charity is accused of being wasteful and haphazard. Thus in England the standard comment about the so-called 'new' poor-law system introduced by the Tudors is that it eliminated the idler and the malingerer from the system.[219] Recently Professor Brian Tierney has published two studies on what the medieval canonists had to say on these matters. What follows draws largely on his conclusions, which point to the existence in the Middle Ages of a discriminatory theory more developed and more humane (poverty was not a crime) than anything for the next six hundred years.[220] It was also the forerunner of the later, but much emasculated, Tudor 'innovation'.

Firstly, there is the evidence of Huguccio. Dealing with the question of whether the stranger should be discriminated against, the canonist said he was to be helped without discrimination, i.e. examination, unless he claimed to be a priest. As for the local poor, they are all to be helped except where this would do harm. Who are the exceptions? 'This is to be understood wherever anyone can work and earn his living by his labour, but instead refuses to do so, preferring to spend his time in gambling and dicing.'[221]   The idler, the waster, who would be merely encouraged in idleness by charity, was to get nothing.   There is plenty of evidence that the monasteries acted on this principle, e.g. the account-book of the English Cistercian abbey of Beaulieu records that in harvest time the able-bodied had to do a share of work in the field for their food.[222]   But discrimination on religious or moral grounds was out.   The infidel and excommunicate were to be cared for, and persons who had erred in the past were not excluded.[223]   Johannes Teutonicus put the principle in these cases: 'In case of doubt it is better to do too much than to do nothing at all.'   The parable of the good Samaritan was after all a potent example to Christians.[224]

On these foundations a widespread and reasonably efficient system was built up in the twelfth and thirteenth centuries.[225]   An increasing number of studies of the spread of hospitals (a misleading term in translation, for it covers leprosaries, orphanages, maternity homes and homes for the aged and infirm) confirms this view.[226]   In canon law, hospitals enjoyed special immunities and consideration in the Middle Ages.   Some even had the right of asylum.   Mundy gives the figures for mid-thirteenth century Toulouse, which, with a population of about 25,000, had twelve hospitals, seven leprosaries and other services, e.g. local monasteries with their infirmaries.   L'Isle Jourdain had one leprosary and two hospitals.   Narbonne two leprosaries and five or six hospitals.   Montpellier one leprosary and seven hospitals.[227]   In England by the middle of the fourteenth century there were 600 hospitals, ranging from large houses such as St Leonard's of York, which cared for 200 poor men, to very small ones.[228]   In Florence, for 1336–1338, the following extract from the chronicle of Villani illustrates the close relationship between the spiritual and temporal functions of the Church:

We find that the churches then in Florence and in the suburbs, including the abbeys and the churches of friars, were 110, among which were 57 parishes with congregations, 5 abbeys with two priors and some 80 monks each, 24 nunneries with some 500 women, 10 orders of friars, *30 hospitals with more than 1000 beds to receive the poor and the sick*, and from 250 to 300 chaplain priests. [My italics.][229]

Throughout Europe there were similar foundations in the towns and cities.   Most of the care was non-specialized and crude by modern standards.[230]   In times of distress great cruelty often took the place of charity, e.g. the massacre of lepers and confiscation of their goods at Périgueux on 27 April 1321. The lepers were blamed for the epidemic of plague that had broken out.[231]   However, the cruelties of the late Middle Ages do not affect the correctness of Dr Tierney's judgement that the poor were better looked after in the thirteenth century than in any subsequent century until the present one.[232]

5 The Period of Transition: Fourteenth and Fifteenth Centuries

So far the discussion has concentrated on the twelfth and thirteenth centuries. Ecclesiastical writers — practical moralists as well as canonists and theologians — had shown themselves aware of contemporary social and economic problems. They had seen the need to re-examine conclusions drawn from unchangeable principles, which underlay all the Church's teaching, in the light of the ever-changing aspects of society. The development in doctrine that ensued was consistent and necessary. The Church remained the main voice on social and economic as well as on directly spiritual affairs.

How different was the period that followed. It was one of relative decline in those disciplines — law, philosophy and theology — that had in the previous period contributed so much to medieval thought.[1] New social, economic and political patterns and problems emerged. To these changes the Church was not immune, but it failed to respond positively. It failed to propose new solutions to the problems that the transitional period presented. It was also confronted with new philosophic speculations, notably of the Ockhamist school, that affected its status in society.[2] The combination of the two factors produced an outlook increasingly conservative and introspective. The gulf between the Church's spiritual ideals and its members' failure to fulfil them in their daily lives grew ever more paradoxical. What, for example, are we to make of the fact that in Bruges, during this later period, the Collegiate Church of St Donatian licensed several pawnshops on its property? These numbered fourteen in 1380 and they were run, not by Lombards, but by Flemings and Walloons. Because of the ecclesiastical licence, they were free of municipal supervision.[3] Or of the loans by Pope Clement V to Edward II (169,000 florins) for a mortgage on the revenues of Gascony?[4] Or of Nicholas V, who granted the great French merchant Jacques Cœur (1393–1456) a wide licence to trade with the infidels?[5]

The increasing gap between the Church's practice and its Christian

teaching did not go uncriticized. Gerard Groote, ascetic and reformer (1340–84), founder of the Brothers and Sisters of the Common
Life, attacked both lay and clerical morals. Of the senators of Deventer he said that not a single man had been admitted to heaven
because they had invaded church lands.[6]   But the monasteries themselves had brought about such treatment by the manner in which they
had departed from the common life, lowered their standards of ad-
mission, and given dispensations concerning the vow of poverty.[7]
It is typical of the age that Gerard's opponents included not only lay,
but clerical, opponents, especially the mendicants.[8]   It was not all a
matter of moral 'decline'.   At Orvieto during the second half of the
fifteenth century the sacred drama of the theatre was considerably expanded, and the groups took on a look of orderly but studied withdrawal from material pursuits, a return to prayer and penance, and the
practice of poverty.[9]

Whether these changes are to be described as moral 'decline' or not
is irrelevant to our purposes. What they do is to present a different
picture of the age. It is the fact of radical reformers such as we find
in the early fifteenth century, with their dreams of liberty and of a
world where taxes and duties do not exist, whose efforts encouraged
the Fathers at the Councils of Constance and Basel to attack papal
fiscalism.[10]   Or there is the example of Pius II, of all fifteenth-century
Renaissance popes surely the most secular, with his judgement of the
Florentines 'as traders and a sordid populace who can be persuaded to
nothing noble'.[11]

The conciliar decrees as well as canonical writings exemplify these
processes; they continue to deal with the by then arid questions of the
previous century, they seem unaware of the changing nature of society.
Simony was condemned (°Constance Sess. XLIII [4]), taxes on the clergy
restricted (ibid. [6]), clerical dress governed (ibid. °[7]), provisions
made for converting the Jews (Basel Sess. XIX).   Lateran V admittedly
recognized the problem of the papal *curia* and of the cardinals and issued
decrees for reform of both, but the decrees were only intended to make
the existing system more workable. The only new thing in the
councils of the fifteenth century is the extraordinary attention given
to financial matters. Basel seems to have made it its main business to
deprive the pope of his financial powers, without any provision for
the future. The length of the decrees and the excessive legal terminology in which they were couched express the need for revolutionary

reform more than the contents themselves. Of the social problems of the day they say little or nothing.[12]

The theologians and canonists continued to express a social and economic ethic, but in a context removed from real problems. This was possibly both a symptom and a cause of the growing rift between religion and society at large.

The rise of the national state created a new entity, a political organism that felt it had duties of a social and economic nature as well as the Church. For this as well as for the conduct of wars that national rivalry gave rise to, the states needed money. Unfortunately, in a period of inflation and rising prices, the secular powers suffered from a chronic shortage of cash. Thus in England the Crown's expenses increased from between £40,000 to £70,000 in c. 1300 to an average of roughly £200,000 in the 1320s.[13] The Hundred Years War created financial crisis on crisis. In all, the war cost England a million pounds, mostly paid for out of the cloth and wool exports, which created a balance of payments problem.[14] France faced similar difficulties in the same period. In Italy, rivalry among the states absorbed a great part of the gross income of the communes. Thus Florence was involved in four wars in the early part of the fifteenth century.[15] In the first war against Milan in 1424 the military expenditure reached 70,000 florins monthly. Numerous forced loans were levied and a number of business firms went bankrupt.[16] Society became virtually organized for war, so that the State emerged as the supreme economic power, a corporation sole without rival.

To help finance the wars the various states made increasing demands on clerical property and income. The clergy usually paid up, but only after much argument and dispute. Such opposition did not improve the Church's image. A partial solution would have been for the Church to carry more of its share of national taxation, on an agreed rather than a 'forced' or 'voluntary' basis.[17] This was a complex problem that ought at least to have been examined by the canonists. In fact the traditional attitude that sought to exclude laymen from ecclesiastical affairs was upheld and made even more severe. Lateran III 19 had permitted lay taxation of clerics provided the bishop agreed.[18] °Lateran IV 46 further laid down that the papacy must be consulted. Boniface VIII reaffirmed these provisions, and at the very end of our period Lateran V [8] on reform of the Curia applied it rigorously.[19] Thus, in an age of increasing cupidity, the Church tended all the more to assert its rights; yet a closer analysis of the problem might have suggested a solution to the advantage of both sides, for the middle man (the collector and agent and money-lender) was often the chief person to benefit under the existing system.[20]   The clergy were, in effect, taxed by the secular powers, especially when matters came to a crisis, e.g. in France in 1296–7 when Boniface VIII, despite the prohibitions of *Clericis laicos* (24 February 1296), had to issue the bull *Etsi de statu regni* that the French clergy could make a grant when they thought necessary (31 July 1297).[21]   Even so, clergy tended to abuse their existing privileges, such as carrying lay persons' goods as their own in order to exempt them from various tolls and taxes.   Despite the papacy's general condemnation of such practices (cf Vienne [21]), the abuses continued.   Not surprisingly the secular powers became increasingly violent towards such clergy.

Numerous problems that existed in this later period related to the question of employment of the peasant and urban proletariat.   For example, cheap food imports from East German lands forced agricultural prices down and caused the peasants to move to the cities and look for work.[22]   The decline in the Flemish textile industry also forced workers to migrate.   Leaving aside the question of the average *per capita* income, there is no doubt that the percentage of poor increased.   In Basel 25 per cent of the citizens in 1424 did not have the minimum taxable income of 10 florins; in 1453 it was 32 per cent.[23] Increase in the number of unproductive poor pressed upon the fixed and even diminishing resources.   The social upheaval produced problems that were beyond the capacity of the canonists and theologians to solve.   Although the canonist had much to say about the payment of tithes by migratory workers,[24] he could not cope with such matters as depopulation, especially the problem of the returned soldier, vagrancy, plague and famine;[25] the growth of guild restrictions in trade and commerce and the restriction of workers' 'unions';[26] the growing use of unskilled labour, especially of women; the 'putting out' system in industry;[27] the problem of consumer credit (see p. 115); nor with the chaotic state of the Church's finances, dubious methods of fund-raising (e.g. indulgences), growth of personal extravagance among laity and clergy, and competition among the mendicant orders for a limited amount of alms.[28]   All ranks and classes of society were affected: even the wealthy, so that what one writer has called 'noble gangsterism' (cf the Wars of the Roses in England) came from the fall in real value of their rents and a corresponding failure to achieve economic reorganization of their estates.[29]

Price fluctuations became more frequent and extreme than in the previous 200 years. In a good year (1287) in England wheat sold at 20d a quarter, barley at 26d, and oats at 24d. In the famine years 1315–27 prices were multiplied by more than ten; wheat reached 24s, barley 16s, and oats 20s.[30] A century later, Landucci's diary for the period 1450–1516 in Florence shows a rapid price movement within a short period of time, e.g. wheat on 6 May 1497 was 3 lire a bushel, 31 May 5 lire, 24 June 3 lire, which affected the purchasing power of the wage earner.[31] Peasants committed suicide on failing to buy bread at the price fixed by the commune.[32]

Speculators and powerful economic interests did not have to suffer. Thus the two centuries present a picture of an ever-widening gap between rich and poor. With increasing competition between ecclesiastical and secular authorities for a relatively fixed amount of credit, it was the poor who paid the bill. Usury legislation only aggravated the position, for it increased the costs of borrowing and forced the poor to resort to the unlicensed money-lenders.[33] Not until the creation of the *montes pietatis* was a beginning made to remedy the situation. Unfortunately the *montes* were often inefficient, so that their interest rates became equally burdensome.[34]

This view may appear at variance with that sometimes held of the Renaissance period as one of unprecedented expenditure on art, building, literature, courtly magnificence and self-indulgence by the upper classes.[35] Such display surely depended on a flourishing and expanding economy? In one sense this was so. Take the example of Florence under the Medici. Lorenzo the Magnificent calculated that his family had spent 663,755 florins between 1434 and 1471 on buildings, charity and taxes.[36] Expenditure of such large sums provided some labour and commercial activity. However, other evidence suggests that the Medici expenditure was in inverse proportion to the declining fortunes of the business. Also, much of the wealth of the family came from sources 'that were not an index of Florentine commerce and industry', i.e. agriculture, real estate, war loans at high interest and banking.[37] Ploughing the profits back into commercial and industrial activities, which had been a feature of Florentine business in the early fourteenth century, had been replaced by going into real estate, both urban and rural, and lavish spending of accrued profits.[38]

This process was not special to the fifteenth century. What was new was that there was no corresponding influx of new capital into commerce and industry. The oligarchical control of the state by the Medici enabled them to concentrate much of the wealth into its own hands.[39]

Such a development in one place raises the general question of the overall economic decline after 1350. To such a decline, if indeed there was one, historians attribute the causes of much of the social and economic distress of the late Middle Ages. The exact nature and cause of the economic change is still debated by the experts. The pages that follow will attempt to present the problem and summarize the evidence in the debate.

If one were to count heads, the proponents of the 'decline' theory would win the day. To them must be added those who prefer the term 'economic stabilization' or even 'stagnation', but who deny that there was regression.[40] Lopez puts the general position when he says that 'no serious historian, I believe, will regard the Renaissance as a period of universal, unrelieved, and sharp economic decay. None, I hope, will envisage it as an age of unruffled, unqualified, and steep economic growth.'[41] Few historians, in fact, do dispute Lopez's argument directly. Instead they resort to what may be called the 'Malthusian — *per capita*' type of response. Thus Kosminsky: 'si nous évaluons le nombre des biens produits par tête d'habitants.... La majorité des savants y admettent plutôt une expansion.'[42] Kosminsky also appeals to the uncertainty about time, place and extent of the economic depression, and makes the telling point that 'sometimes it was a question of movement from one centre to a newer one, from town to country, nation to nation'.[43] Kosminsky goes further than this. He lifts the argument into a category that is really beyond the ability of the historian to explore. The fourteenth and fifteenth centuries brought about 'la liquidation de l'économie seigneuriale, la commutation et la diminution de la rente féodale qui ont amené à l'amélioration de la situation des paysans'.[44] The lot of the peasant may have temporarily worsened, but it must have been better because it was a necessary stage to the future revolution of the proletariat.

Most of Kosminsky's research was based on England. His conclusions do not appear conclusive for that region and certainly not for the main centre of the medieval economy, Italy. Lopez, for example, pointed out that a slight recession in a giant may nullify *pro rata* in-

creases in a small country. England's woollen industry expanded in
the later Middle Ages. In 1392 it exported 43,000 pieces of cloth.
In the meantime Florence, the great textile capital, had begun its
decline. By 1378 its production had shrunk by at least 55,000 pieces.[45]

What then is the evidence for decline? This may be examined
under the headings of country, industry, town and institution. For
countries there is obviously a great deal of uncertainty. Increasing
quantities of statistics after 1450 have too easily led historians to confuse
these with evidence of increasing production. For France the general
agreement is one of decline. The year 1300 marked the limit of
progress until the eighteenth century.[46] In Italy the main centres
declined, except that Lombardy enjoyed a long period of agricultural
expansion, with a partial decline c. 1400–30.[47] Brittany from c. 1370
began to enjoy a period of expansion in its salt trade, but this must be
set against corresponding decline of the older medieval centres in the
Low Countries, England and Germany.[48] Burgundy, with territories
stretching into the Low Countries, had a steady growth in the period
of the Grand Dukes; there was a busy port at Auxerre, Châtillon
produced cloth like any Flemish town, the Saône ports expanded and
wine exports from the Côte d'Or were made. But meanwhile
Bruges in maritime Flanders slowly declined; and in the Dutch
towns there was decay, except for Amsterdam, which began to show
signs of activity in the late fifteenth century. The size of the population of these new towns, which were the future sixteenth- and seventeenth-century centres of trade, must be taken into account when
making comparisons.[49] Normandy had reached its maximum in
1350. Between 1150 and 1350 Rouen had enlarged its walls three
times, and not thereafter. The turn in the economy and population
growth came in the fifteenth century, but not enough to fill the empty
spaces within the fourteenth-century walls, certainly not until the
eighteenth century.[50] In England, despite the modifications produced
by some historians, the general impression seems to be one of ex-
pansionist activity before 1300 and after 1450. The contraction beginning about 1300–20 saw the rise of some industries, e.g. cloth
manufacture, and decline in others.[51] For Poland Malowist writes
of 'une période de développement économique rapide' in the twelfth
and thirteenth centuries. This led to 'le remplacement graduel des
anciennes prestations paysannes en nature et en travail par la rente en
argent'.[52] The fourteenth century saw a decline, but in the fifteenth

the nobles began to exploit their estates. This led to expansion of the mineral and cloth industries, but, and we cite this example at some length to recall the arguments of Kosminsky, at the cost of peasant freedom. The nobles brought economic pressure on the peasants, and political upon the diets, to ensure that the labour remained tied to their lands. As well, the policy of the diets undermined urban development.[53]

From regions to industries the same tale must be told. Certain lesser but vital industries became re-located. Salt production is a good example. The Bourgneuf Bay industry in Brittany gained at the expense of Lincolnshire and Norfolk in England, Lüneburg in Germany, and the Low Countries. These regions ceased to export salt in the late fourteenth century.[54] In a major production centre, such as the Gascon wine industry, the effects of war, plague and famine may be seen throughout this period. In 1300 the export was 90,000 tons annually. In 1348–9 it was 6000. Thereafter frequent fluctuations occurred, which affected the English cloth industry, for Gascony was a main market for English exports. The market fluctuated according to the state of the war. In 1399 exports were 37,000 tons.[55] But the true barometer of the medieval economy was the cloth industry. In England this prospered, but the total production of wool seems to have diminished. Citing the evidence of individual estates, e.g. those of Canterbury cathedral priory, the period *c.* 1322 was the peak of wool production. The profit was £157. Drought and sea-floods in the years 1324–6 killed 4585 sheep.[56] By 1330–1 profit had fallen to £88 12s 0d.

In Italy, where the main producing centres were, production figures and profits fell considerably from about 1322 onwards. Kosminsky has argued that the losses were only temporary and that the fifteenth century was

L'époque d'un nouvel épanouissement de son économie . . . dans le domaine de l'industrie textile nous ne voyons point de déclin, il n'y a qu'un partiel déplacement de l'industrie dans la campagne, le passage à la production d'autre tissus; d'autres branches de l'industrie textile (les soieries) se développent par endroits. Au xv siècle de nouveaux progrès sont à constater dans le domaine banquaire. Le capital monétaire italien stimule le progrès de l'économie dans d'autres pays, en particulier dans les pays de la Péninsule.[57]

The answer to this lies in the following figures given by Lopez and Miskimin for Florentine cloth production: 88,000 pieces in 1338;

26,000 in 1378; 14,000 in 1600; 8000 in 1627. At Marseilles the export taxes for the period 1400–80 are well below the average for the years 1250–1350.[58] In banking De Roover's book on the Medici bank (1397–1494) emphasizes that the Medici firm, 'the greatest single economic force in Italy during the fifteenth century' did not equal either in amount of capital employed or number of agents or activities the greatest of the pre-1345 banking houses, that is, the Bardi.[59] In Italy as a whole no medieval firm, with the lone exception of the Medici, even remotely 'approached the size of the big three' of the pre-1345 period, that is, the Bardi, Peruzzi and Acciaiuoli.[60] At Venice, Bruges and Florence business contracted during the fifteenth century, until, in the end, 'deposit banking was nearly destroyed until it was revived around 1575 with the creation of public banks in Palermo, Naples, Venice, Genoa, and other trading centres.'[61]

The towns provide the clearest evidence of the economic decline. Most historians comment on the collapse of prosperity, and rise of a narrow, oligarchical form of government, and guild restrictions, in the middling-sized towns. Thus Toulouse from 1410 to 1443 experienced six severe famines, six plagues, eight great fires and floods, twenty years of warfare and banditry, and two important social revolts. Of four bridges in the town at the end of the thirteenth century, only one remained. Suburbs vanished, population sank by a full third.[62] Small villages vanished for good.[63] Large cities, such as Venice, London, Paris, Milan, Florence and Genoa, succeeded in adapting themselves to general decline by monopolizing the trade of the region.[64] In Italian cities the oligarchies took control, so that the towns became again 'what they had been in the late Antiquity ... hungry parasites feeding on the tribute of half-starved peasants'.[65] The causes of the decline were numerous, and they varied from region to region, town to town, but most writers refer to the factors of the plague cycle, famine cycle, the rise of such non-Western powers as the Ottoman Turks, offensive wars, a series of revolutions and social troubles, the saturation of resources, population and climatic changes.[66]

The consensus of opinion is that the Middle Ages had spent itself in the achievements of the previous two centuries. The inventive and creative genius either transferred itself to other media or disappeared altogether. The rate of technological invention slowed down considerably.[67] For the Church the changes created not only economic but also spiritual problems, typified by the Great Schism, the growth

D 2

of heresies such as Hussitism and Wyclifism, and the conciliar movement.[68]

In this decline the Black Death of 1348 was particularly disastrous in
its demographic effects, for there was a sudden and immediate fall of
something like one-third of Europe's population.[69]   Many cities lost
50 per cent of their people.   In meridional France the population
figures for Albi (10,700), Castres (9500), and Millau (7340) before the
Black Death had fallen respectively to 4800, 4200 and 3332 some time
after.[70]   Nor were country areas better off.   Whatborough and
Elmesthorpe (Leicestershire, England) lost some 44–45 per cent of their
population.[71]   In Siena the woollen industry closed down, trade was
at a halt, and for a time the town government failed to respond to the
need for action.[72]   However, the Sienese economy quickly recovered,
and by 1353 the position prior to the Black Death had been reached.
Elsewhere, e.g. in Florence, the situation was not so fortunate.[73]
Successive outbreaks of plague, e.g. at Orvieto in 1348, 1363, 1374 and
1383, struck successive age groups, so that recovery became impossible.[74]

Population decline may have begun as early as about 1300 when,
according to some historians, 'demographic and economic developments began to reach an equilibrium and thus began to provoke a
decline in productivity and a growing difficulty in maintaining the
level of subsistence'.[75]   Basic crops such as cereals were early affected,
and their shortage created price fluctuations and famine conditions
beyond the capacity of governments of the day to remedy.[76]   This
produced a Malthusian situation that the Black Death corrected rather
than provoked.   In turn the sudden decline of population in 1348–50
meant that *per capita* a greater supply of money became available,
and that a shortage of labour forced up wages, so that, for a time, the
post-plague economy was better than before.   But this part of the
argument ignores the effect of decline to and beyond the point at
which efficient production became impossible.   It also ignores the
qualitative effects of the disasters.[77]   Nor does the argument account
for continued decline in production after the period of population
recovery in the fifteenth century.[78]   Tragically, the Church benefited
temporarily by the increased number of bequests left the clergy by
plague victims.[79]   Complaints were common that the clergy enriched themselves.[80]

There were, as already stated, some exceptions to the economic
decline.   Lombardy was one of these.   In the later medieval period

it enjoyed an economic boom that lasted till around 1620. The cause
was a political and economic transformation of the basis of land-
owning. The abbeys and monasteries were short of cash, a situation
exploited by the secular dukes. The latter, using a variety of fiscal
methods, caused the ownership of lands to pass from the Church. By
the mid-sixteenth century the Church owned only 10–15 per cent of
land in Lombardy compared to 65–70 per cent in southern Italy.[81]
Elsewhere, however, royal fiscal measures tended to unsettle agricultural interests, e.g. in England.[82] In France, Germany, Italy and
Spain money grants had to be paid for by concessions. The guilds
became overbearing, oligarchical and unco-operative. Such attitudes
might appear to have militated against even the maintenance of pre-
1348 *per capita* level of production. However, even if, as some historians assert, *per capita* production was maintained in some areas, this
did not apply to international trade.[83]

The various economic fluctuations of the fourteenth and fifteenth
centuries created difficulties for the Church, which, with the papacy
at the centre, became increasingly immersed in, and concerned with,
financial problems.[84] Some of these difficulties arose from factors
beyond the Church's control. For example, English monasteries
were heavily burdened by their patrons and other influential nobles.
Frequently they had to go as surety for their patron's debts, or the
provision of a few nights' lodging for the king and his retinue could
put the monastery in debt for the rest of the year.[85] At the same time
the monasteries experienced an increasing demand upon their charitable
services for the poor.[86] Among the Benedictine monasteries, Saint-
Martin-de-Tournai provides a good example of the change in fortunes
that could be experienced from 1300 onwards. In 1290 Saint-Martin-
de-Tournai was a flourishing institution, yet, forty years later, the
number of its monks had declined and it had lost many of its lands, so
that the religious life was seriously impaired.[87]

The papacy as a temporal power was also affected, for by virtue of
its large Italian patrimony it had to maintain a complex administrative
system. In addition there was the burden of its spiritual administration of the Church.[88] Money was short, and, for various reasons,
acquisitions of new lands (a process that usually offset rising costs)
ceased in the fourteenth century. Thus there began a period of
spiralling costs and diminishing returns.[89] The disastrous policy of
Boniface VIII in advancing the fortunes of the Gaetani family and

reducing their Colonna rivals initially caused the papacy to be transferred to Avignon in 1309, and, in the long run, contributed to the
financial disorder of the papal state.[90]   The popes were forced into
war to protect their Italian lands, and the cost of hiring mercenaries
added to their burden.[91]   John XXII (1316–34) during his pontificate
had a total income of 4,100,000 florins.[92]   Of this he had to spend
over three-fifths in the attempt to recover control of the papal state.
During the Schism both pope and anti-pope spent large sums in an
effort to secure the papal states.   Clement VII (anti-pope) spent
500,000 florins between 1385 and 1393 in his attempt to re-establish
his power in the south.[93]

The changes that set in with the transfer of the popes to Avignon do
not mean that the Avignonese popes were poor financiers, but rather
the opposite.   John XXII managed to keep the papacy solvent, for
he was an extremely good administrator and his pontificate set the
pattern for the rest of the period of the Avignonese captivity.[94]   Its
banking facilities (*via* the Italian houses) became noted throughout
Europe, the efficiency of which may be judged by the fact that the cost
of transmitting moneys to Avignon was kept to an average of between
1 and 5 per cent of the total.[95]

However, when the papacy returned to Rome, the Great Schism
destroyed all the good work of the Avignonese popes.[96]   Rival popes
seeking support of the secular rulers had to make concessions.   Clement VII gave the French King commendatory rights to several bishoprics and 750 other benefices.[97]   These grants, in turn, encouraged a
regional and national spirit among the clergy, who saw Rome no
longer as a protector, but as a destroyer of their liberties and rights.[98]
Thus the popes gradually failed to have clerical support in their
efforts to impose the direct tax — the tenth — on clergy outside
Italy.[99]   After a Statute of 1388 in England, the popes could make no
more levies on the English clergy.[100]

When the Schism ended, there was urgent need to restore papal
finances, yet the councils, affected by the spirit of the conciliar movement, did little or nothing.   The Council of Constance (1414–18),
although it actually ended the Schism, failed to provide the needed
reforms.   It even surrendered revenues by cancelling the right of the
popes to levy procurations, revenues of vacant sees and tenths.[101]   If
consented to, it would have made the papacy unworkable.[102]   Later,
Basel forbade the payment of annates.[103]   In all, the papacy's spiritual

revenue fell by two-thirds between 1378 and 1429.[104]

The papacy, deprived of its foreign income, resorted to temporary and unpopular expedients, such as the preaching of indulgences,[105] the exploitation of lawsuits appealed to Rome, and the sale of offices.[106] Boniface IX (1389–1404) appears to have been the first pope to sell offices, which later popes enlarged and exploited. Sixtus IV (1471–84) created three new colleges of officials, one of which, that of solicitors, had 100 members. By 1486 most of the offices in the chancery, penitentiary and camera were venal. By the time of Lateran V the income from the sale of posts amounted to one-sixth of the total budget.[107] Such methods brought loud complaints against the Curia for its financial exactions, and increased the disrepute into which papal authority had fallen.[108] Worse still, the papacy was suspected of selling church lands, an act that drew the full censure of canonical authority. Boniface VIII was accused of this, and John XXIII at the Council of Constance.[109] Anyway, not much of the money reached the papal exchequer, for officials along the way siphoned off the most part.[110] These expedients, as Partner and others have shown, produced little revenue. Taking this into account, together with the fact that spiritual revenue continued to diminish, the papacy had to rely increasingly on the income from the papal states.[111] This draws much of the fire from the contemporary accusations of papal exploitation of the Church abroad, but it forced the papacy into even greater imitation of its secular rivals.

The effect of the financial crises was damaging to the papacy. Rightly or wrongly, a great deal of the criticism directed at the papacy by the heretics, and later by the Protestant reformers, is that it paid lip-service to spiritual values opposed to capitalism, yet was itself deeply immersed in, and concerned with, its fate as a shareholder in capitalism.[112] Or again, if the papacy organized its financial affairs properly, it did so with the aid of the bankers, and in return it protected them by threatening excommunication and interdict.[113] The weapon was used against laity and churchmen alike, but it did not make the papacy any more respected.[114]

The reformers, both Catholic such as Gerard de Groote and heretic as Wyclif, failed to perceive that the papacy as a temporal and spiritual lord was as much committed to prevailing economic trends and measures as any lay prince. There is nothing very different in the papacy's response to fourteenth- and fifteenth-century changes in its finances. The fall in income was not matched by any corresponding decrease in expenditure, namely, for the upkeep of the Curia, the defence of papal states, maintenance of legations abroad, and for the lavish display that entered with the Renaissance. In these circumstances the cost of borrowing money rose. Other Italian states became rivals to papal hegemony in central Italy and helped to force up the interest rates.[115] These factors may help to explain why the papacy, in the later Middle Ages, became increasingly rigorous in its condemnation of usury and why it failed to accommodate itself any longer to the economic policies of the city states.[116]

Just as papal leadership during the earlier period had contributed to the success of reform, now the process was reversed. Without a lead from the popes the rest of the Church seemed to follow into disruption. Lay piety, instead of bestowing land and income upon the religious and secular clergy, began to express itself by the lavish founding of colleges and chantries. It had little thought for the parish clergy, whose income, worse still, tended to decline in real money terms. In London, in the smaller parishes, the incumbent's income was only about 10 marks a year. Gross inequalities existed, so that fifteen parish priests had income ranging from £2 7s 0d to £34.[117] In the Low Countries, Gerard de Groote bitterly attacked vicars who hired lowly paid curates or leased their churches for rent.[118] Total reform was needed, but this too was prevented by the more immediate and attractive solution of plural holdings of benefices.[119] Consequently pluralism became common, and the distribution of the income within the clergy more and more inequable. In England in 1366 there were 450 pluralists. Of these only 245 resided in parishes. William de Wykeham, keeper of the Privy seal, held the archdeaconry of Lincoln and ten prebends. With an income of £873 6s 8d he was the worst offender.[120] Disparities among episcopal incomes were even more pronounced. In England at the close of the fifteenth century Canterbury, Durham and Winchester had about £3000 each; Rochester had barely £450. Most of the pluralists and at least half the bishops were hardly pastors of souls. They owed their promotion to royal favour. They were in fact civil servants, whom the king rewarded at low cost to himself by securing church benefices for them.[121] The abuses of patronage and reservations became widespread. Most higher posts went by provisions, the smaller prebends by patronage, usually to friends or relations. These conditions made the formation of a properly trained clergy impossible.[122]

Unedifying events occurred. 'Crusades' against Christians continued. Thus in 1324 John XXII issued an indulgence for those who would go to war against the Visconti of Milan. Among those who bought the indulgence were merchants who had traded with the Saracens against ecclesiastical prohibition.[123] On the other hand the rising states took strong action against 'foreign' clerics. In 1337 the English crown confiscated the property of alien religious Orders and then released the property to the monks at an annual rent.[124] The religious Orders themselves often presented an unchristian image or adopted dubious methods. In Spain the Hospitaller Fernandez de Heredia spent most of fifty years (c. 1329–79) enriching himself, his illegitimate children and his relatives at the expense of the Order.[125] The Carmelite Order in the fifteenth century tried to remedy its financial difficulties by unscrupulous means. Bequests to the Order had fallen off. The Order took advantage of the anticlerical feeling to preach a campaign of Christian and apostolic poverty. They hoped to win popular favour and offerings.[126] No wonder the secular clergy opposed them and their entry into the parishes. Then there was the rivalry between the Dominicans and the Franciscans over the *montes pietatis*, mentioned above. Informers were encouraged to cite blasphemers, among others, with a promise of one-third of the fine as a reward.[127]

Paradoxically, by the end of the Middle Ages papal 'money-grabbing' was at its lowest point. The Protestant reformers had little case to argue when they accused the papacy of destroying the Church for its own ends. They would have done better to have examined the extent to which secular rulers had appropriated Church revenues.[128]

The economic decline of the Church can be exaggerated. A notable instance is that of monastic finances.[129] Using England as an example, there is no need today to cite the platitudes of a Gasquet or the vituperisms of a Coulton. The recent work of David Knowles and Hugh Evenett suggests that the problem of monastic finances has been mis-stated.[130] Individual monasteries' incomes fluctuated, but overall did not seem to worsen too drastically. The following figures for Christ Church, Canterbury, illustrate both trends:[131]

1292	£2062 16s 11¾d
1331	£2540
1411	£4100 10s 9¾d

$$1434 \quad £2381 \ 18s \ 0\tfrac{3}{4}d$$
$$1454 \quad £2115 \ 10s \ 8d$$
$$1468 \quad £1828 \ 0s \ 7d$$
$$1473 \quad £2841 \ 3s \ 3d$$
$$1536 \quad £2349 \ 8s \ 5\tfrac{3}{4}d$$

The total income of all the monasteries was about £200,000 (somewhat larger than the royal income) and out of this the monasteries had no difficulty in meeting expenses. As most monasteries worked on a system of deficit financing, the existence of debts did not necessarily mean insolvency. In any case the lender was usually too astute to advance credit to a poor monastery, and there seems to have been no lack of creditors anxious to advance money.

The monasteries did not suffer from lack of income, but rather from impositions and wasteful use of their resources. There are signs, e.g. at Christ Church, that from about 1375 onwards the financial system began to break down, thus in 1384 the treasurers ceased to enrol their accounts in the whitebook for public scrutiny. These changes did not mean a collapse in the economy of the priory, indeed it recovered its prosperity in the fifteenth century, so that by 1473 its debts came to only £264 13s 0¾d. What it did do was often to prevent reform and to encourage further abuses. The monks with their crowds of servants and luxury of diet and dress hardly observed the Rule.[132] Leicester Abbey had a similar history, but without the economic recovery in the fifteenth century.[133]

On many monastic estates in the later Middle Ages lay stewards were in charge of the manors. Even in exceptional cases, where monk wardens were appointed, e.g. Christ Church, Ely and Bec, lay stewards were their assistants. The crowds of hangers-on of both groups absorbed much of the monastic finances.[134] Inevitably, charitable works suffered. Knowles has calculated that altogether 10 per cent of the monastic income went to charity, but others consider this figure is too high.[135] In any case, although it was enough to maintain the former level of monastic charitable works, it was insufficient to cope with additional burdens imposed by the increase of poverty in the fifteenth century. The same applies to the parish system of relief. In short, the problem of poverty had outstripped the resources and ingenuity of the medieval Church.[136] Imperceptibly the Church began to cede to the secular state and to the laity the authority and influence it had so long wielded in economic matters.

6 The Doctrines at Work

In trying to estimate the influence of the Church in economic matters, especially the success or failure of its teachings, the changes in the medieval economy, with periods of transition *c.* 950–1050 and again from *c.* 1300–50, have to be kept in mind (see p. 23).

Of the first period, from the fourth to the tenth century, not much need be said. The general councils show some concern for economic activity, but not a great deal. Meanwhile the Church became extensively feudalized. This created many problems for the second period, one of great economic growth, whose opening coincided with the movement for ecclesiastical reform known as the Gregorian Reform (*c.* 1049–1122). From that time to about 1300 a positive correlation exists between the doctrines and the economy at large.

This chapter will examine that relationship under four main headings:

    A. Church Property and Organization
    B. Profit and Usury
    C. The Just Price
    D. Charity and the Poor

These divisions generally correspond to the sequence of the doctrines outlined in an earlier chapter. But this time it is the practice, rather than the theory, that is under scrutiny.

A. Church Property and Organization

The most noteworthy feature of the reformed canon law of the eleventh century onwards, as far as economic matters are concerned, is the stress put upon the preservation of ecclesiastical property. All in all, according to Herlihy, there was *c.* 1050–1120 an 80 per cent decrease in land transfers, a process especially marked in Italy, Spain and France.[1]

The concept of the inalienability of ecclesiastical lands was connected with a moral aim to eliminate priest-marriage and to abolish simony.[2] Special provision had to be made for a celibate clergy, and lands that had been lost to lay relatives and to secular powers had to be recovered and retained. Consequently the Church began to hold on to its land, a policy emulated by laymen, who bought up scattered pieces and consolidated them into large estates. In an interesting study Herlihy attributes the influence of the Church in raising the status of married women as one reason why eleventh-century women became prominent as landholders (see p. 33). This policy of buying also stimulated the money-market. There was a need for cash. High interest rates were offered. Money and treasure that had been hoarded came out in response. Herlihy gives an excellent example of this stimulation of the money-market in the case of Italy, where 40 per cent of contracts for land purchase involved payment of substitute money — gold ornaments, jewellery, furs, swords and armour. The peak of the movement was about 1038–70, but it lasted for another fifty years.[3]

An interesting aspect of the Church's land-buying policy is that it created surplus labour.[4] This was especially noticeable on Cistercian estates during the twelfth century. At the beginning the impetus was healthy. Redundant labour had to re-locate itself, thus supplying a work force for the new towns and contributing to the demand for goods, which were decisive factors in the economic expansion of the time.[5]

The demand for goods came both from a rising standard of living, and from the population increases from c. 1000 onwards. This raises the question of how far the Church's teaching on marriage favoured the increase. Russell's view is that 'ecclesiastical policies favoured increasing population'.[6] Ecclesiastical authors wrote against abortion and infanticide. They also stressed the positive injunction 'increase and multiply'. From these developments came also the disappearance of slavery in Catholic Europe.[7]

More especially, the impact of legislation of the Church in relation to its own economy may be judged by examining its success in reclaiming tithes.[8] After an unsuccessful period of trying to recover the whole of the tithes that had been lost to the Church, the popes adopted a more realistic approach. Lateran IV 32 recognized that only a portion of the tithe could be recovered — the parish priest's. In parts of Europe the Church successfully implemented this decree. In northern Italy it was almost universally successful. It ensured a minimum revenue for the parish clergy, some independence from lay influence, and also met with the approval of laymen who 'saw not only justice but also advantage in a reform that still left three-quarters in their own hands'.[9]

In the later Middle Ages, however, the collection of tithes became difficult. Already many predial tithes had been commuted for money. Lay persons and religious had got control of others, and the friars often encouraged the faithful not to pay their tithe to their ill-educated priest, but to give it to charity or to the friars themselves.[10] The wills of London citizens testify to this evasion of tithe-payment. Many wills (some seven out of ten) open with a bequest to the testator's parish church 'in payment of tithes and offerings withheld'. The sums restored range from a few pence by workers to the £10 or £20 of the wealthy capitalist.[11]

A similar success attended the papacy's attempt to persuade the religious Orders to appoint perpetual vicars to churches held by them (cf °Vienne [4]). The records of the Abbey of Saint-Vincent-du-Mans provide a specific example of restoration of sequestrated parish-church revenues to the parish priest. The process began with the cure of Sables in 1220 and then extended to churches of Beton, Doucelles, Saint-Ouen de Ballon, Saint-Croneille and Saint-Patrice-du-Désert et-Marolettes.[12]

This type of compromise was a realistic appraisal of the possible. Three centuries later Lateran V, instead of attempting a similar compromise on matters affecting Church and State, pursued the extremist line of clerical independence.[13] This happened on the eve of the Reformation. Yet churchmen were not entirely to blame. If the canonists had failed to evolve new financial teachings to cater for the needs of the secular states, the latter had not suffered any serious loss of income. Recent work by Partner and Lunt, among others, has shown that from the fourteenth century the princes forced the papacy to grant them an ever-increasing share of church revenues.[14] The odium of exacting these sums fell on the Church and its agents, which became a further weapon with which the secular powers could undermine papal authority. In the period of the Reformation, denunciation by the Protestant reformers of papal exactions was common, but propaganda glossed over the part that the princes had played in maintaining and fostering those same ideas.

These facts do not constitute a defence of papal policy and action in the later Middle Ages. The Renaissance popes, like other Renaissance princes, proved their efficiency by exploiting all possible sources of revenue, by transforming, in the fifteenth century, the once free communes of the papal states into units of authoritarian papal rule.[15] To

their aid they brought the spiritual weapon of excommunication, even
to force debtors to repay their loans, as Pius II in his *Commentaries* shows
on a few occasions.[16]   Like any Renaissance prince the pope monopolized the sale of such basic commodities as salt.   He was also quick
to seize the advantages of the discovery of alum on papal lands at
Tolfa in 1460.   Having entered a partnership with the Medici for its
production, the papacy then tried to remove the competition of imported Turkish alum.[17]   To pay its hired soldiers it sometimes granted
assignments of the tallage of its towns with right to pillage if the
town defaulted.[18]   For that day and age these procedures ranked as
acceptable business methods, for a later age they have become sources
of accusation and sometimes scorn.

In general the critics of the medieval Church fasten too easily upon
the later events and failures.   They overlook, for example, the way
in which the Church nurtured the growth of civil liberties 'in a large
number of towns from Worms to Tournai' in the tenth century, and
that these became the basis for the municipal liberties of the twelfth
century.[19]   Out of the constant conflict between Church and State,
even at the economic level, was born that sense of constitutionalism
that came to be part of the medieval heritage.   Also, the papacy introduced new methods of taxation, especially as part of its programme to
help finance the crusades, which showed the national states how to
tax income and goods as well as land.[20]   Nor should it be forgotten
that, in the thirteenth century, in land-holding the Church contributed to the development of the life-lease in contrast to perpetual
leases.   This avoided the constant danger of loss of lands and gave
some hope of future reversion.[21]

Passing from the papacy to the monasteries, the most important, and
still much debated, question concerns the influence of the monastic
economy within the various European states, especially of the Cistercian Order.   The latter has been heavily criticized in recent years,
but this criticism is directed against their business dealings in the later
period.   These, thanks to the work of scholars such as Donkin, are
today commonly known and documented.[22]   The later abuses tend
to overshadow the benefits conferred during the early years, which
should not be forgotten.[23]   For example, in England, many of the
seventy-seven abbeys were founded in underdeveloped or neglected,
but potentially fertile, regions such as north-east Yorkshire, which was
'waste' and bog, and which had been depopulated after the Norman

Conquest.[24] The Order preferred such areas because there were no feudal dues, tithes to pay or other financial burdens. Also the laity were more likely to grant 'waste' lands than existing profitable estates.[25] Using the system of the monastic grange, largely run by lay brothers, the monks furthered the development of these areas. Consequently they were in the forefront of, and some would say they began, large-scale wool production in England as others did elsewhere.[26] By sponsoring the fulling mill they contributed to the English cloth trade, although they themselves did not reap the benefits of these things.[27] Later, things were different. Depopulation of estates, conversion of arable to pasture, tithe disputes with the secular clergy and the Benedictine monasteries led to bitter wrangling that needed conciliar legislation to settle (cf Lateran IV 55).[28] The economic prosperity of the Order led them to such abuse of their privileges as the marketing of non-monastic wool.[29] In 1262 the Crown issued royal mandates warning the Cistercian abbots in Lincolnshire about putting other men's wool with their own to avoid payment of customs. Similar injunctions of 1275 accused the Cistercians of Louth Park, Kirkstead and Revesby of having bought up wool and other produce over a period of fifteen years in order to sell to foreign merchants. As a result Lincoln had lost 100 marks of customs dues. The monks obviously disregarded the warning, for in 1302 the Commons of Lincolnshire complained that 'men of religion drove a wool trade, not only in produce of their own sheep, but by sending men out to buy cheap in order to sell dear'.[30] The action of the Cistercians is equally explicable on economic grounds, for, as Graves suggests, the occurrence of the scab among sheep from 1277 onwards caught the monks with no means of fulfilling long-term contracts for supply of wool. They had to buy from outside sources. Nor did they make much profit. They had to buy short on borrowed money, and so began the circle of debt and yet more debt.[31]

Monastic, especially Cistercian, involvement in large-scale business activities was a sorry affair. The methods they used were often reprehensible, even to laymen. In particular one may remark on the large-scale recruitment of the *conversi* and hired labour. Proportionately these *conversi* and hired labourers were the mainstay of the Order. The Cistercian abbey of Beaulieu in the thirteenth century had some 58 professed monks and about 150 lay brothers as well as the hired labour.[32] In the fourteenth century, Canterbury cathedral priory had 25 obedientiaries, many with their own household, and by 1400 there were twice as many servants as monks at the abbey.[33] Maintenance of such large numbers, as well as the monks' expensive tastes, such as imported best Flemish cloth for their dress,[34] created serious financial problems for the abbey. Moreover, many of the monastic commercial practices antagonized the rest of the countryside as well as the merchants. They smacked of those monopolies forbidden by the canonists.[35] Then there is some evidence, in England at least, that the abbeys acquired cheaply lands that had been given as security to the Jewish money-lenders, hence the presence of the Jews could be an advantage as much as a disadvantage.[36] Again the Cistercians used their privilege of exemption from paying customs duties and tolls to transport the goods of other merchants.[37] Such exploitation of their economic strength left the religious Orders without defenders during the later Middle Ages.

A last question about the monks is the degree to which they influenced farming methods. The cumulative impression left by the study of a number of individual monasteries is that we may have underestimated the monastic example. Canterbury cathedral priory had several manuals of husbandry for its use in the late thirteenth century, including four manuscripts of the celebrated treatise by Walter of Henley. The registers contain frequent references to it. The financial administrators, the *seniores ad scaccarium*, especially under the priorate of Henry of Eastry (1285–1331), project an image of careful management of resources; they give attention to such problems as the sale of corn, care of sheep and cattle, marling of land, and the purchase of seed grain from other parts rather than using less productive strains of their own growth.[38]

Negatively, the business acumen of the monks may have helped to undermine objections the laity may have had to adopting a loose interpretation of the Church's teaching. In other words, clerical and monastic example proved more powerful than doctrine.

B. PROFIT AND USURY

One area in which the ecclesiastical economy did not have much *direct* effect was in the establishment of its own monetary institutions.[39] Despite the emergence of the Order of Templars as an international banking organization, the Church authorities relied mainly on lay banks.[40] The papacy, especially, preferred Italian merchants and bankers. Until the crash of 1345–6 they used the Peruzzi, Bardi, Bonaccorsi and Acciaiuoli;[41] next the Alberti until 1376, then the Guinigi of Lucca, and between 1401 and 1494 the Medici.[42] Merchant-bankers were frequently charged with the task of collecting the crusade tenths as well as other dues from princes, laity and clergy.[43] They also acted as 'supply merchants, money-changers, postal agents, agents of information' and even as unofficial legates.[44] In these matters the papacy showed itself extremely businesslike. For example, whenever it thought a clerical escort would provide a cheaper method than bank transfer for moving money, e.g. from France to Lombardy, an escort was used.

Lesser institutions and individuals also preferred lay money-lenders and bankers. No special distinction was made between Jew and Christian, foreign and local, until the later Middle Ages. In 1213 Canterbury cathedral priory negotiated a number of loans for long terms and at high rates of interest. The creditors included Jews of the town as well as Italian merchants of various cities of origin, such as Rome, Siena, Bologna, Florence and Pistoia. The rate of interest varied from 15 to 20 per cent.[45] Eventually, by the time of the priorate of Henry of Eastry (1285–1331), Jew had given way to Christian and foreign to local capital.[46] Cluny, under Peter the Venerable c. 1125, resorted to Jewish usurers at Mâcon, and gave, contrary to canon law, church ornaments as a pawn. In 1149 the abbey owed 2000 marks of silver and preferred to borrow from the Christian merchants.[47] The abbey of Bury St Edmunds in the time of Abbot Hugh used Jewish usuries at a rate of interest by which 'a debt of forty marks increased to one hundred pounds'.[48] The Jew Aaron of Lincoln had among his debtors the Abbot of Westminster, the Prior of the Hospitallers, the bishops of Lincoln and Bangor, and the archdeacons of Colchester and Carlisle. The debts ranged from the Archbishop of Canterbury's 100 marks to John, priest of St Margaret's, debt of 4s.[49]

Upon the lay banking-companies the Church exerted a great deal of power and influence.[50] But this was surpassed by the effect of its usury doctrine of which De Roover writes:

Since the bankers, in this regard, tried as much as possible to comply with religious precepts, they had to operate without incurring the censure of the

theologians. As a result, banking in the Middle Ages and even much later
— on the continent until far into the eighteenth century — was quite different
from what it is today. It would be erroneous to believe that the usury doctrine was simply disregarded and had scarcely any effect on banking practices.[51]

On usury in the narrow sense of the word the effectiveness of
canonist doctrine depended on the willing support of the bishops and
clergy and the secular authorities.[52] °Lateran IV 6 recognized the
importance of provincial and diocesan synods by having bishops in
their assembly read the decrees of the council.[53]   From the examples
of France and England, where the basic research has already been done,
it is clear that in the thirteenth century the decrees of local synods
largely followed those of the general council; thus the canons on
usury were repeated in France at the local councils of Avignon 1209
and 1282, Saint-Quentin 1231, Château-Gontier 1232, Albi 1254, Sens
1269, Pont-Audemer 1279, Tours 1282, Bourges 1286.[54]   The council
of Pont-Audemer ordered the usury canon (cf Lyons II 26, 27) to be
read in parish churches every Sunday.[55]   The crusade provisions of
Lateran IV [71], °Lyons [5], and °Lyons II [1c], were ordered to be read
in the coastal towns on Sundays and feast days.

The 'success' and 'failure' of this policy can be seen in several
regions.   Toulouse provides a prime example.   Here there was a
long history of concealed usury, from the second half of the tenth
century onwards.[56]   The commonest form was the *mortgage*, which
lasted from the tenth to the twelfth century.[57]   About the middle of
the twelfth century, the system changed.   In 1163 came the first
instance of an open loan in which the interest is clearly a charge on
the debt.   From 1184 there are plenty of examples of such loans, and
the next three or four decades have been called the golden age of
usurers at Toulouse.[58]   But this 'golden age' began to change with
the advent of Fulk as Bishop of Toulouse (1205–31).[59]   He found the
episcopal lands deep in debt or pledged to the creditors.   Quite
rightly, he attributed some of these happenings to the lax usury laws.
As a remedy he created a special tribunal of two judges 'to hear
complaints and charges of usury', and this tribunal forced the usurers
to make restitution.   Under pressure of this sort, interest agreements
tended to disappear, certainly from the notarial records.[60]   Usurers,
when they applied to the courts to have repayment of a debt enforced,
claimed compensation for damages caused by delay in repayment,
with the clause added *preter usuram*.[61]   In practice, usury continued at

Toulouse. The merchants tried to avoid open usury and instead resorted to fictitious deals, e.g. loans of wheat (in fact, only money changed hands) made at a lower than market price and repaid later (again in money) at the current price. Similar transactions are recorded at Brussels.[62]

In the matter of usury, appeasement of conscience became easier as one ascended the social scale, for consumption loans were less common. Better security was available, and most loans could be concealed in one form or another, or even genuinely made by reason of the risk element. For despite the great learning and polished exposition of the canonists and theologians, the fact remains that the Church from the twelfth to the sixteenth century, from the lowest clergy to the papacy, existed by some form of credit financing. One can only cite examples. Hubert, Bishop of Limerick (1223–50), borrowed 166 marks from the Roman firm of Manetti. He repaid 60 marks on 20 February 1229, but having failed to pay the balance he was excommunicated and forced to make 'a new agreement before the papal judge'. In 1237 he repaid not the 106 marks owing, but 160 marks, that is, 54 marks interest over eight years.[63] The Irish clergy, in order to pay the huge aids and subsidies levied on them, resorted to the Italian bankers, and they usually had papal consent to contract the loans. Consequently the sees of Armagh and Cashel were in debt during the second half of the thirteenth century.[64] In 1324 in London a group of city merchants appear as creditors of abbeys and priories throughout England. The institutions repaid their debts by granting annuities, thus the Prior of the Order of St John gave annuities to the families of Oxford and Rothing.[65] John of Oxford, as well as being a successful wine merchant, was creditor of twenty-one religious houses. For London in the period 1324–44 recognizances of some twenty houses had a total value of £8000.[66] In France the Avignonese papacy had frequent dealings with its bankers, not merely for exchange purposes, but also as a creditor and sometimes as a debtor. In theory the papal Curia did not pay interest on its loans.[67] The bulls speak of loans made *gratuite et amicabiliter*. The reality was different. Vague terms such as *cum cambio* were used to disguise the fact of interest.[68] There was probably no real difficulty here, for the majority of canonists held that it was not unlawful to pay interest in case of necessity.[69] At Cologne in 1388 the Lombards lent the archbishop money with the tax revenues as a pledge. In other words, they became tax-farmers. One Ambrosius paid a weekly sum of 250 marks to farm the *Mahlpfennig*.[70]

The evidence of Lyons I [1] suggests that usury *had* become a problem that seriously affected the clergy.[71]   The latter, instead of paying off debts and running their parishes economically, had plunged into debt (especially over lavish building programmes) and taken out mortgages on property.[72]   Several decrees prohibit the pawning of sacred objects, which in itself exemplifies the actions of the clergy.[73] To prevent this, Lyons I [1] revived or rather enforced more strictly the ancient rule that an inventory should be made, on assuming office, of property, furnishings and debts, and immediate provision made to pay off the debts, especially those that were 'usurious or burdensome'.   No debts were to be contracted in future, except with consent.   In any case no debts were to be contracted on the open market — presumably, that is, with manifest usurers — to avoid excessive rates and public scandal.   Annual accounts were to be rendered.

Despite the deep involvement of churchmen in borrowing and lending, the laws as far as the laity were concerned were not allowed to remain dead letters.   Research into restitutions made by usurers gives some interesting conclusions.   Firstly, the canonists distinguished between restoring usurious gains that were *certa*, that is, to the borrowers or their families who were known, and *incerta*, which would go to the Church for charitable purposes.[74]   With public or manifest usurers there was no problem.   They could be, and were, taken before church courts and forced to make restitution unless, as often happened, the secular authority protected them, e.g. by licence.[75]   The comparative ease with which the ecclesiastical courts could deal with this class of usurer tended to make them overlook the occult usurer and the large-scale investor, who in any case by 1350 and onwards were well covered by the doctrine of exceptions and the concept of *lucrum cessans* and *damnum emergens*.[76]

In the end the various conciliar and local synodal decrees caught mostly only the pawnbrokers.   In the case of the merchant *élite*, who during their life at least seemed to escape the penalties of usury laws, the one saving condition is that they too lived in an age of religious belief, in which to save one's soul was the ultimate reality.   Men could acquire riches and great wealth, but they could not escape the mute accusation of having broken some law.   These men the Church could reach through fear of the final judgement.[77]   An outstanding example of this is the Merchant of Prato, for whom 'with old age came the last and worst anxiety: overwhelming fear of what would happen to him in a future life. Pilgrimages and periods of fasting, gifts of pictures to churches and of lands to convents, and, finally, the bestowal of all his great fortune to charitable works — none of these sufficed to dispel the haunting sense of guilt that darkened his last years — a gnawing anguish, a perpetual *maninconia* [*sic*].'[78] In merchant-banker wills of the twelfth to the early fourteenth centuries there are many and significant examples of restitution, mostly of the *certa* type.[79] An excellent example of restitution is the following document dated Lucca, 13 March 1220:

Ugolino and Arduino, brothers, [sons] of the late Ildebrandino, feeling weighed down by usuries which Genovese, [recently] deceased, had extracted from them, therefore appealed to the Supreme Pontiff, [asking] that Filippo, priest [and] rector of the Church of S. Pietro Somaldi, must not bury him before they are satisfied in regard to the usuries which they had asked him to return. This was done in Lucca, in the court of S. Pietro Somaldi, in the portico, in the presence of Gaiascone, [son] of the late Orlando Guasone, and of Guido, [son] of the late Orlandino, 1220, the third [day] before the Ides of March. [I], Benedetto, judge and notary of the lord emperor, took part in this entire [transaction] and I wrote this as a record.[80]

The merchants who made such loans were mainly Italian, their debtors, who mostly benefited from the last pangs of conscience, were usually from across the Alps. They included a variety of individuals, bishop as well as knight, and corporations, monastic or cathedral chapter and local guilds. In one of his bulls John XXII 'refers to two brothers of Asti, who are obligated to restore 60,000 gold florins for usuries abroad'.[81] Lyons II 27 admitted the right of the ordinary to fix the amount owing in restitution, but the popes often intervened in the case of prominent usurers, especially their own creditors. The *incerta* could be granted where the bishop or pope wished. So this provided a useful source of additional income. Not surprisingly, the proportion of *certa* to *incerta* tended to decrease in this period.[82]

The paradox of the Church as a viable, corporate society, subject to the reality of economic problems as any other secular body, and as a divinely instituted society, is seen in the history of Lyons II 26 and 27.[83] These two decrees originally formed a single text, which provides a curious document on usury and makes it worthy of comment at length.[84]

This legislation on usury is generally accepted as 'of far-reaching importance ... in the history of the later Middle Ages'.[85]   By showing the changes that the text underwent between the time of promulgation by the council and publication by the pope, it is possible to learn a great deal about the then contemporary attitude towards usury. The two main changes are very significant.   First, the draft version found in MS Washington 183 (Catholic University of America) prohibited usurers *in general* from hiring or leasing suitable business premises.   The published text, however, added a qualifying clause 'alienigenas et alios non oriundos de terris ipsorum', which means, in effect, that only foreign usurers were expressly denied right of carrying on their business.[86]   The second point is that the published version increased the penalties for public usurers by adding the clause 'Testamenta quoque manifestorum usurariorum aliter facta non valeant, sed sint irrita ipso iure' (Wills of notorious usurers that make no reference to this point are *ipso iure* invalid).[87]

These changes mean that the *foreign* and public usurer was regarded as the main culprit.   Guillelmus Durandus (*c.* 1230–96) in fact 'explained that the canon was not meant to extend to occult usurers or to native practitioners, even though public, but to the foreign manifest usurers like the Sienese and Florentines in England, and those who were called *prestatores, cahorsins* and *renovatores* in Italy, France and Provence respectively'.[88]   Confirmation comes from the report of Franciscus de Albano on the Lyons council.   The report informs us that the council had been 'asked specifically to curb the activities of the travelling merchants from Florence, Siena, Pistoia, Lucca and Asti', who went about the various regions exacting quite exorbitant rates of interest.[89]   Of course, it has to be kept in mind that foreign usurers and merchants roused hostile feelings because they stood for competition and sometimes financial loss.   In 1284 the citizens of Lincoln complained that foreign merchants displayed their wares in near-by places and deprived the city of revenues.[90]

The *glossa ordinaria* (on Lyons II 26) added that native usurers were open to other forms of punishment, but in any case they never did as much harm as foreigners.[91]   But mainly, I think, the legislation was aimed at the Lombards, the pawnbrokers.   In practice a Venetian prohibition of 1281 against foreigners carrying on money-lending activities in the state points to this conclusion, for, as we shall see, moderate interest on loans by local citizens was favourably regarded.[92]

As for the punishment of usurers, the papacy's action in adding the clause invalidating the wills of those who refused to provide for restitution later caused a great deal of controversy.[93]   Admittedly the clergy could refuse to attend or witness the drawing-up of a will, but by what authority could the Church invalidate it?   Gregory X had a precedent — a canon of the council of Paris in 1212 — and, as mentioned above, a powerful reason, but the clause created further tension between lay and clerical authorities.[94]   And it was also put to profit, for, despite the provision of Vienne [29] denouncing states that licensed (for a price) usurers,[95] the latter could always purchase papal exemption from the sentence of excommunication.[96]

The question of restitution by Jews was a more difficult one.   Initially the Deuteronomy provision had protected their position as the leading pawnbrokers in a Christian society.   But in the thirteenth century some theologians had questioned Jewish exemption from the general scriptural prohibition of usury.   This, no doubt, is why the records of Jewish usurers at Perpignan include appeals by Christians to the courts for restitution.[97]   Against this, the lay power's interest lay in protecting the Jew against such suits.

In some countries Jewish usurers disappeared altogether after the thirteenth century, but in traditional areas, such as Italy, they preserved their position.   Several communes made agreements with the Jews to open loan banks (*banchi di pegno*).   They first appeared in the duchy of Mantua in 1380 and lasted until 1808.   In the sixteenth century the duchy had forty such 'banks'.[98]   At Orvieto the Jews had privileges dating from a special statute in 1312, which made them true citizens, gave them rights of seizure of their debtors' goods, if necessary, and imprisonment until the debt was paid.   For these privileges the Jews paid heavily.   An individual Jew could pay an annual tax of between 10 and 100 livres at a time when the biggest guild paid only 50 livres.   After the Black Death the Jews felt secure enough to sue for recovery of debts from heirs of their now defunct debtors. The commune granted one-quarter of such debts to be collected, and prevented subsequent abuses by Orvietans,[99] but rather than get involved, the Jewish money-lenders were often willing to settle out of court.[100]   Vienne [29] is said to have implicitly condemned the Jewish claim that the double standard of Deuteronomy permitted them to exact usury from Christians, together with the secular authorities who enforced their claims against debtors.[101]   Against this is the papal

dispensation that sanctioned Jewish money-lending in Christian communities, e.g. Nicholas V in 1452, granted Lucca the right to have
'unum, vel plures Iudeum seu Iudeos feneratores' to provide consumer
credit.[102]

From around 1350 the number of explicit restitutions of usuries
in the wills of prominent merchants, whether of *certa* or *incerta*, declined absolutely. This indicates a change in the authority of the
Church and in the attitude of the merchant classes.[103]   As long as the
Church and municipal authorities had been in accord, the latter supported the jurisdiction of the church courts.   In Florence, before the
outbreak in 1345–6 of hostilities between the papacy and the Republic,
the secular tribunals accepted ecclesiastical verdicts without reservation.[104]   Then came the financial crash.   In 1343 the great Florentine
banks were on the verge of bankruptcy (see p. 74).   The Avignonese
papacy, instead of helping them, abandoned them.   The papal inquisitor Piero dell'Aquila also had arrested Salvestro Baroncelli, a
partner in the Acciaiuoli Company,[105] who owed money to the Church,
and he fined heavily those citizens who had lent money usuriously or
who had tried to justify this practice.[106]   No wonder then that in the
change of government 1345–6 the new *Signoria* legislated against this
form of inquisition.[107]   The Republic ceased to prosecute for usury
and passed hostile measures such as the suspension of the just price
regulations.[108]   Moreover, when it funded the public debt at 5 per
cent, it did so without any provision, as in the past, for the usury
regulations.[109]   For the next thirty years or so the government continued to grant its citizens immunity from ecclesiastical courts, and,
during the second wave of anti-papalism (this time war had actually
broken out) in 1375, the officials of the *monte* 'replaced the Church as
executors of the wills of manifest usurers'.[110]   Further restrictions on
usurers were removed.   Jewish money-lenders were licensed.   Communal sanctions against money-lending, which had made interest
recoverable at law, were lifted.[111]   In the fifteenth century the Jews
enjoyed a virtual monopoly of licensed pawnshops or *banchi di pegno*
in Florence.   From 1437 licences were granted only to Jews.   These
were the manifest usurers of the councils.   They still had some competition, however, from the *banchi a minuto* who made loans secured
by jewellery.[112]   Much of this was motivated by self-interest.   The
Florentines had to pay for the cost of the war with the papacy some-
how.   It had cost them about 2,500,000 gold florins.[113]   Wars with

the Visconti added another 5,000,000 to the debt. Is it then surprising that here and in Venice (in the War of Chioggia forced loans of 5,000,000 gold ducats had to be raised) and elsewhere in the north, by the early fifteenth century, the application of the Church's legislation on usury was often a matter of political expediency? San Bernardino's comment was short and to the point: 'You are all usurers' he told the Florentines.[114] This was not the judgement of a bigoted churchman. Bernardino has been called 'the best economist of the Middle Ages' and one who 'ranks among the greatest economists of all times'.[115] It is true he opposed the foundation of the *Monte delle Doti* at Florence in 1425, by which money was lent to the state and received back fifteen years later with interest as a dowry. On the other hand, in line with the theological principle involved, he supported the receiving of interest on forced loans and he made several exceptions to the strict letter of the law on the ground of *intention*. To the merchants, however, such decisions had become academic ones.[116]

The following example illustrates the operation of the usury laws in the fifteenth century. The account books (*c.* 1415) of Lazzaro Bracci, an Aretine merchant resident in Florence, show that he speculated on the exchange with Venice. He dealt in a large number of loans, but all of a business kind, the borrowers being other bankers and manufacturers. The method used was a type of 'dry exchange' known as *cambium ad Venetias*. No bills were transmitted to Venice, but the risk of a change in the market rate beyond the foresight of the lender or borrower was present. The average yield of Bracci's investments was 6·6 per cent.[117] Bracci also had some interest-bearing deposits with the Medici Company, the Medici received from him 300 florins *a discrezione* at 8 per cent.[118] San Antonino (1389–1459) and San Bernardino (1380–1444) had condemned *cambium ad Venetias*, but others, such as Lorenzo di Antonio Ridolfi (1360–1442),[119] approved it with some reservations.

Elsewhere the position was often more openly, if anything, usurious. At Venice loans at 20 per cent against security of land had long been the custom.[120] Luzzatto, in an interesting study, has shown that loans at moderate interest (between 5 and 12 per cent) were regarded as lawful and just, even by the clergy, while the usury laws were directed against immoderate rates.[121] Here usury applied to loans above 12 per cent or loans made with professional usurers outside the state, e.g. with the Tuscan money-lenders at Mestre, and also to concealed contracts, because this could mean excessive rates.[122] Luzzatto's final example was a notarial deed of 9 February 1400, when the struggle against usury was very strong. Giorgio Foscarini says he has received from his dear friend Andrea 200 gold ducats *causa amoris*, and that he will repay *de lucro sive de prode* 5% *in anno*. Thus 5 per cent is regarded as the minimum in such a case of a charitable loan. Luzzatto concludes that 'usury can be regarded as the pathological degeneration of a phenomenon of which interest at a variable rate of 5 to 12 per cent was the normal manifestation'.[123]

Bruges provides a similar example. The municipal records of the fourteenth and fifteenth centuries list numerous fines collected from persons found guilty of usury in the city court.[124] However, the conditions attaching to the grant of pawnbrokers' licences (for an annual fee) differed in the earlier and later periods. Around 1300 they specifically excluded 'manifest' usury and limited the interest to a low figure. But in the fifteenth century false pretences were cast aside and the Lombards were allowed straight usury, 'money for money'.[125] In Pistoia there had been passed in 1296 the statute 'That no public usurer be allowed in the state or diocese of Pistoia', but this, in effect, remained a dead letter.[126] In London, from 1363 onwards, prosecution for usury belonged to the jurisdiction of the mayor and aldermen of the city.[127] In the fifteenth century a special 'court of orphanage' had charge of children's portions in estate. From these funds the court formed trust funds from which to lend money at 10 per cent to merchants with sound security. Other companies did the same.[128]

Some commentators have seen in the increasing number of 'frauds' proof that the Church's influence on usury was negligible. According to Luzzatto the effect of the teaching was slight.[129] This may be true, but the very fact of the fraud proves that the general principle of usury still swayed men's consciences. In the earlier period Gregory IX's decretal *Naviganti*, which condemned sea-loans as usurious, presented a good example of the effect of papal teaching. After 1250 the sea-loan lost favour to the method known as 'sea-exchange'.[130] Moreover, Luzzatto's criticism neglects to acknowledge the great advances made in the doctrine by the canonists and theologians by restricting the categories to which 'usury' applied. These writers had brought the Church's teaching to the point where the taking of moderate interest was regarded as reasonable. The distinction between interest and usury (exorbitant, i.e. unjust, interest) was clear in practice, and it was acted upon, for most of the prosecutions in the later period were for what we would term usury.[131] It is true, neither canonist nor theologian could bring himself to depart radically from the traditional approach that involved such a mass of exemptions and distinctions. This was because they never quite grasped the proper significance of the time-factor in making a loan.[132] As next best, their doctrine of *lucrum cessans, damnum emergens* and *periculum sortis* achieved just that *implicitly*. As to the effect in occult usury, the reader is reminded of what was said earlier on the importance of the confessional.[133] It is doubtful whether exact elucidation of its importance is possible. But that it had *some* importance was seen by the fact that the general councils tried to enlist the confessional as an instrument of persuasion (cf Lyons II 27).

In the fifteenth century the creation of the *montes pietatis*, a sort of municipal, clerical pawnshop 'founded for the purpose of relieving the needs of the poor by loans of this kind and thus protecting them against the avarice of usurers', indicates the extent to which the doctrine and practice of usury had changed since the time of Gratian.[134] Ostensibly the *montes* were religious, charitable institutions introduced by the Franciscans in Perugia and Orvieto in 1462.[135] The *montes* collected funds to provide loans to the poor. The subscribers earned no interest, but were offered spiritual rewards. Eventually, to cover 'expenses', the poor had to pay interest.[136] Such charges, argued the Dominicans, were usurious because they were levied from the beginning of the loan and were exacted from those who needed the money for the necessities of life. By 1509, despite the conflict of opinion about the lawfulness of interest charged by the *montes*, there were some eighty-seven such institutions in Italy alone.[137] The Dominicans lost their case. Lateran V in the decree *Inter multiplices* sanctioned the *montes* and approved interest with a definition of usury that is qualified and much removed from the simple definition formerly attributed to the Fathers and to Gratian: 'Usury means nothing else than gain or profit drawn from the use of a thing that is by its nature sterile, *a profit that is acquired without labour, cost, or risk.*'[138] These institutions brought about the virtual disappearance of the public or licensed pawnshops. But occult and unlicensed pawnbrokers continued to thrive, for people often preferred to deal with them rather than with the *montes*.[139]

E

C. THE JUST PRICE

A like conclusion must be drawn about the just price doctrine in theory and practice. The doctrine from its inception in the twelfth century merely stated that the open or market price was the just one. It allowed the state to regulate prices for the public good.[140]   De Roover stressed that success of price controls depended on the municipal authorities: 'In the middle ages the implementation of economic policy rested to a large extent, if not exclusively, with the municipal authorities of cities, towns and boroughs.'[141]   This was especially true of the Italian city states and of the German imperial free cities.[142] Even in England and France the town was the main force in determining economic policy at large.   The evidence of municipal records is that the towns tried to impose standards and regulate sale; for example, they encouraged direct sale from producer to consumer to eliminate the middleman and to keep prices down.   They took action against individuals and groups who tried to monopolize the market or undercut competitors.   Such profits were treated as dishonest and had to be restored.[143]   In this way municipal actions reflected the prevailing teaching on the just price (see p. 59).

Direct secular intervention to fix prices occurred, especially in times of severe shortage or for staple products such as wheat, bread, wine, beer, or even to regulate certain types of trade completely.   Enactments by the Count of Toulouse in 1181 and 1182 regulated the 'practices, prices and wages of butchers, fishmongers, masons and lumber-merchants'.[144]   Douai had assizes for a number of basic commodities such as wood, peat, beer, hay, lime and even coffins; the authorities also fixed maximum prices.   Some towns introduced 'a crude form of rationing', e.g. fixing the price of the loaf, but varying the size.   This occurred in France and Germany in the twelfth century. Augsburg varied its 'standard loaf' from month to month with the price of wheat.[145]   The Spanish theologians advocated free competition as the best means of keeping price control, for price regulation in times of stress seemed ineffective.   What it usually led to was a total disappearance of the commodity in question.[146]   Maximum price edicts in France and England, in response to the famine of 1315–17, which fixed the price of grain at one-third the then current price, led to a complete withdrawal of grain from the open market.   In the end the edicts too were withdrawn.   There were, of course, some notable exceptions where state control was highly successful, e.g. the Venetian monopoly of shipping, already cited.[147]   In normal times, city authorities could usually fix a 'market' price for standard goods. The Mayor of London in the fourteenth century had the duty of setting prices for 'ale, beer, red wine, and, after inspection of supplies in the market, for meat and poultry; in the case of fish he [the Mayor] was supposed to inspect each shipload'.[148]   At certain times the controls were relaxed, e.g. at harvest time, to allow bakers to work without restriction.   At other times they were tightened up.   After the great storm of 1367 London forbade increases in building trades' wages and prices.[149]

The commonly held belief that the guilds had the *right* to fix the price of their members' products is a fallacy.   In fact, and through collusion, they succeeded in doing this, but the doctrine of the just price had been directed at that sort of thing.   The municipal authorities legislated to prevent the guilds from usurping this right.   Florence in 1293 passed the ordinances of justice and outlawed all price fixing by guilds.   Heavy penalties were decreed, but there is no evidence of their being imposed.   On the other hand severe fines against workers' guilds or unions were imposed.[150]   Scholastic writers and canonists rarely mentioned the guilds, and when they did so, it was to censure them for their monopolistic practices.   Unfortunately the scholastic doctrine on monopolies, which was intended to protect the consumer, 'led to the paradoxical result of favouring the strong at the expense of the weak and of depriving the masses of workers of all means of collective action'.[151]   The history of the Italian communes, notably of Venice and Florence, illustrates this very well.   In both cities before the 1330s the State prevented any one group of capitalists and merchants from gaining supreme control.   Subsequently, as in the case of Venice, the State's 'military needs, its colonial empire, its shipping and naval industry' led to a breakdown in the balance of interests.   Oligarchy eventually came to control the economic and political power in its own interests.[152]   Legislation against restrictive guild and trade practices came to smack heavily of political and economic discrimination.   In Florence the *Signoria* passed laws in the 1340s and 1350s against the lower guilds, e.g. against the meat-sellers, but sought to extend its own monopolies.[153]   In the fifteenth century, state ordinances, such as that of 1440 compelling small farmers to plant five mulberry trees annually for the next decade, served the sectional interests of the silk guild.   Nor was it mere coincidence that the leaders of the guild, such as Neri Capponi and Giovanni Guicciardini, took the lead in waging the war against Florence's rival silk producer, Lucca.[154]   Caught between the clash of interests, the lowest-paid workers suffered most.   San Antonino accused the Florentine clothiers of paying their employees in kind or in debased coin.   But generally the State did nothing to prevent the abuses.[155]   Becker even concludes that the anti-union attitude of Western Europe and U.S.A. had its origin not in Adam Smith's liberalism and eighteenth-century rationalism, but in medieval scholastic doctrine and statutes of the Italian communes.[156]

By the end of the Middle Ages, canonistic teaching on monopolies and just price had little practical effect.   The doctrines did, however, perform a useful function by standing for those ideals that have constantly 'to be recalled to the minds of men because they have not been fulfilled'.[157]   The clergy no longer had much influence in municipal affairs.   Self-interest occasionally worked wonders: Richental's *Chronicle of Constance* describes how 'envoys of the Pope, the King and other lords appeared before the town council of Constance, and said they were paying too dear for lodgings and that the price of all victuals was unfairly reckoned.   So the council appointed delegates to meet with them, and they made the following ordinance . . .'   This fixed prices until, with normal supplies available, 'the prices of everything diminished'.[158]   But these incidents were exceptions.   The growth of municipal government led to a policy of exclusion of clerics from public office and from the affairs of the communes.[159]   In Germany, which in the thirteenth century saw the rise of 400 new towns, the municipalities took control of appointing their own priests and also of church property.   With these changes there passed also responsibility and control of charitable works, as we shall see.[160]

D. CHARITY AND THE POOR

With the question of the medieval teaching on charity and the poor we are on surer ground.   In the primitive Church episcopal and private charity sufficed.   The early Christians even widened the scope of relief to include non-Christians and the able-bodied.   There were limits, of course.   Thus the able-bodied had to earn their keep after

two or three days' free aid.[161]   The seeds of the later discriminatory
theory of the canonists were being sown.[162]   With the economic
revolution of the tenth century onwards, there emerged an organized
system of parochial relief, which, down to about 1300, was effective
and usually sufficient.   After 1300 its effectiveness declined only
slightly, but it was no longer sufficient.[163]   The canonistic teaching on
charity and the uses of wealth developed a highly sophisticated theory
of responsibility towards the poor.   Especially, the able-bodied were
not encouraged to be idle.   Secular legislation and general practice
reflected the canonistic doctrine.   In England the Statute of Cambridge of 1388 introduced the distinction between the able-bodied
and the sick.   London merchants, according to Sylvia Thrupp,
seemed to feel 'reluctant to oppress the poor . . . Pity, however, was
only for the industrious poor, not for the astute hangers-on.'[164]
Unfortunately, by this time, the medieval poor law had become in-
adequate and frustrated.   The new social and economic factors produced
large numbers of vagrant, unemployed and able-bodied workers.[165]
Increasingly the gap between rich and poor widened, and, correspondingly, the sense of responsibility of one class towards the other lessened.[166]

Florence provides a good example of the unequal distribution of
wealth from about 1350 onwards.   The *Signoria* financed its wars by
special forced loans that earned interest at a nominal 5 per cent, but
in fact at 15 per cent.   Payment of the interest was usually met by a
tax on consumables, which therefore fell disproportionately on the
lesser guildsmen and workers.   The attractive rate of interest offered
by the *monte* created further economic difficulties, for some investors
withdrew from commercial enterprises and put their money into war
loans.[167]   This affected industrial development.

Amidst poverty, reigned plenty.   The following text from Pius II's
Commentaries needs no comment:

Francesco Sforza . . . sent the Pope three very fat steers which had been fed on
turnips and were used to being washed with warm water, combed every day,
and bedded on clean straw. . . . All liked the meat so much that they vowed
they had never tasted anything sweeter, but it was not bought cheaply, for
those who brought the oxen were presented with 100 gold ducats.[168]

Gradually there emerged a different attitude towards poverty.   It
ceased to be a misfortune, a blessing of Providence, a virtue extolled
by Christ in the Sermon on the Mount.   It took on a more modern
aspect of a crime, 'an assault by the poor upon society itself'.[169]   The

poor found refuge in heresies and obscurantist movements that only caused the church authorities to apply the law more strictly.[170]   They also found refuge in periodic uprisings that demonstrated social and political inarticulateness.   For the workers, although they carried heavy tax burdens, were without guilds and therefore without real access to the then accepted means of political expression and social reform.[171]   For these needs the canonists did nothing, although their doctrines continued into the sixteenth century to serve as a basis for systems of poor relief.   Thus in England the State replaced the Church as the directing body, but the medieval parish organization on which the poor law was based lasted till the nineteenth century.

Monastic charity played no great part in these developments.   In the early Church the problem of relief of the poor, e.g. at Rome, fell to the *diaconiae*, a kind of charitable centre, which existed apart from the monasteries.[172]   Eventually, when the *diaconiae* lost their original charitable functions in the ninth century, there succeeded the efforts of the bishop and diocesan clergy.[173]   Neither the black nor the white monks were so located that they could attend to the needs of the new poor that came with the economic expansion.   The lay religious Orders in their inception from Robert de Arbrisselles (d. 1117) to Francis of Assisi (d. 1226) had a great sympathy with the poor, but they too became institutionalized and involved in the struggle to compete with other religious and secular clergy.[174]

Studies of individual monasteries confirm that, generally, the monks were not over-liberal in their alms-giving.   In the later Middle Ages the allocations virtually ceased.   An analysis of the account-books of Canterbury cathedral priory for the period 1284–1373 shows that only 0·52 per cent of the almoner's income went to the poor, plus some gifts of food and clothing.   Most of the revenue went to the upkeep of the almoner's own large household or to maintain the *pauperes Dei*, i.e. fellow monks.[175]   Benedictine abbeys were not intended as hospitals for the sick.   A General Chapter held at Lérins in 1351 decreed that 'no sick, no lame or weakly constituted, no bastard or non-Catholics shall enter without the express consent of the abbot, and never younger than fourteen'.[176]

Contrasted with the monks, popes, princes and other secular and spiritual leaders spent a good percentage of their income on alms. King John of England, as already mentioned, spent about 6 per cent of his income on charity; Pope John XXII's gifts represented 7·16 per cent of his total expenditure.[177]   Eugenius IV, when he put the Hospital of the Holy Spirit in Rome back into repair, revived the arch-confraternity that supported it and promised an annual gift.   His cardinals followed suit.   There are over thirty extant bulls of Eugenius IV in which he aided French hospitals.[178]   Most communes contributed to the support of the city's hospitals and other charitable institutions.   Orvieto exempted church property from taxation and gave varying sums of money to the hospitals.[179]

One matter, however, in which the friars displayed initiative was in the provision of the *montes pietatis*.   This did something to solve one of the gravest social problems of the Middle Ages, namely, the lack of consumer credit for the workers.   But, unwittingly, the theorists had done much to create and aggravate that problem.   They failed to realize that 'charitable' loans were not a satisfactory solution to the problem of consumer credit.   The rise of the pawnbroker and petty money-lender in the earlier period at least reflected the need for their services.   But the Church in seeking to prevent high rates of interest by concentrating on the manifest usurers — the pawnbrokers, in effect — and driving them out of business, only succeeded in making such loans more risky and therefore subject to an even higher rate of interest.   The canonists and theologians overlooked the fact that the lender temporarily transferred his purchasing power to the borrower, and hence his capacity to enjoy the fruits of his labour.   The debtors were thereby enabled to anticipate future earnings, even if they did so by consuming the loan.   The professional pawnbrokers performed a service that called for a proper recognition.   Here alone is where the Church's usury laws had their greatest effect, and it was a moral and social rather than an economic disaster that resulted.   For the masses blamed the Church for their plight, and the *montes pietatis* came too late to save the Church in regions other than in Italy and Spain, where they were most widespread.

In general, the Church's influence on economic activity both as a temporal power and as a spiritual body with teaching powers was a positive one during the period of economic expansion *c.* 1000–*c.* 1300. In the subsequent economic decline the Church was too divided by internal schism and dissension, and challenged externally by the rising national states, to keep pace with the changing form of society. Lateran V illustrates the poverty of reform ideas on the eve of the Reformation.[180] The Reformation came and the initiative passed to the State.

7 Conclusion:
The Weber–Tawney Theses
in Retrospect

THIS work began by posing two questions. These were, first, whether the Church in the Middle Ages exercised an influence in economic matters proportionate to its wealth; and, second, to what extent was there conflict or harmony between the economic behaviour of Christians and the teachings of the Church (see p. 4). These two questions were constantly in mind during the subsequent treatment of the main issues involving the Church and economic activity. Briefly, the issues dealt with were the Church's attitude towards wealth and the use of its resources, the economic relationship between the various religious Orders and the secular clergy, and between the clergy and the laity, the merchant and his profits, the just price, usury, banking, charity and poverty. These themes were treated against the fluctuating economic pattern of the Middle Ages, which produced an economic revolution in the twelfth and thirteenth centuries, followed by a partial decline in the fourteenth and fifteenth centuries. Finally, some attempt was made to show the doctrines at work.

In some ways this treatment is disappointing, for it leaves the questions unanswered. But it stresses the complexity of the issues involved, a complexity that most historians have hitherto overlooked. Some historians — notably Weber and Tawney — have tackled the same themes and seemingly produced more convincing answers.[1] An attempt to examine their theses in the light of the present researches will, it is hoped, provide a fitting conclusion to the present study.

Weber's noted thesis dealing with religion and capitalist ethic in Western society was only part of a much broader enquiry, 'to ascertain whether and to what extent religious forces have taken part in the qualitative formation and the quantitative expansion of that spirit over the world'. He rejected the idea that only through the Reformation could capitalism have arisen, but nevertheless he found in one brand of Protestantism, Calvinism, especially as interpreted by the seventeenth-century Puritan divines in England, a powerful force that helped to create 'the ethos of the rational organisation of capital and labour'. Puritanism produced an ascetism that 'turned with all its force against one thing: the spontaneous enjoyment of life and all' that it had to offer'. Weber saw in Calvinism a doctrine that man was only the 'trustee of the goods which have come to him through God's grace'. He did not deny that such a doctrine had medieval roots, but 'it was in the ethic of ascetic Protestantism that it first found a consistent ethical foundation. Its significance for the development of capitalism is obvious.'[2] The self-imposed limitation of consumption and denial of creature comforts, allied with a doctrine that 'good works', notably of an acquisitive character, were a sign of God's grace to man, that he belonged to the predestined to be saved, led to an accumulation of capital and ultimately to the general notion that making money was good in itself. Such ideas provided a secure basis of capitalist society.[3]

By contrast, Tawney's magisterial *Religion and the Rise of Capitalism* had a more modest and ultimately more enduring approach than Weber's. He was concerned with the breakdown of the relationship between religion and capital, using this latter term to include political and social as well as economic attitudes towards wealth.[4] The emergence of modern social theory involved two related processes: firstly, the gradual relinquishing by the Church of its claim 'to maintain rules of good conscience in economic affairs'; and, secondly, the naturalistic concept of society in which the world of human affairs is regarded as self-contained and in need of no supernaturalistic explanation.[5] For Tawney these vital changes occurred in Holland and England of the sixteenth and seventeenth centuries. Tawney, unlike Weber, saw Christian doctrines of this crucial period as more alike than disparate; he stressed their medieval roots and their survival into the seventeenth century, until they became gradually eroded with the development of new economic forces. Unlike Weber, Tawney treated religion as a force in conflict with economic forces, rather than, in one special form of Calvinism, as a force that furthered its development.

Weber and Tawney dealt basically with much the same material and period of the sixteenth and seventeenth centuries. Both were prepared to look back at the Middle Ages for comparable experience and doctrines, which, on the whole, they did by taking examples from the time of Thomas Aquinas onwards. They recognized the Church as 'an immense vested interest, implicated to the hilt in the economic fabric, especially on the side of agriculture and land tenure', for the Church was 'itself the greatest of landowners . . .'[6] This was also my conclusion (see p. 27). Tawney acknowledged, too, the relevance of the canonists in determining the doctrines, but generally he did not develop this evidence.[7]

The basic criticism of Weber came from Tawney's pen. Weber had underestimated the amount of pre-Calvinist capitalist signs.[8] Weber took most of his texts and examples from seventeenth-century Puritanism. He had also ignored intellectual movements that favoured the growth of capitalism and which had nothing to do with religion, e.g. the political thought of the Renaissance, and speculation on money, prices and foreign exchange.[9] Moreover, Weber appeared 'greatly to over-simplify Calvinism itself'. The Calvinism of the seventeenth-century English Puritans was not that of Calvin and his immediate followers, who held to a rigorous discipline in which the individualism of the later form would have had no place. Weber, in effect, ignored the more interesting question as to why one form of Calvinism won out, and not another of the equally powerful alternatives that were less amenable to a capitalist spirit.[10]

Tawney seems right, and often is, especially when he makes numerous qualifications arising from the medieval background of the ideas he saw emerging in full force during the sixteenth and seventeenth centuries. But this should not blind us to the fact that Tawney also could not have been fully aware of the complexity of the issues involved. He overlooked, for example, what I tried to show, namely, the many differing traditions and changes that took place in the doctrines of the medieval canonists and theologians. At the beginning of the Christian era, Chrysostom (347–407) had with remarkable insight foreseen the fate of the medieval Church. He deplored the laxity of those persons whose selfishness forced the Church to deal in temporal works so that 'instead of praying and teaching, we must mingle with the crowd of those who sell wine and corn . . . and receive, in place of the glorious titles fixed by the apostles, names appropriated only to those engaged in secular life. Occupied with harvests, vintages, sales and purchases, we cannot walk in the footsteps of the lord . . .'[11] Of course clerical aversion to wealth and property never quite disappeared in the Middle Ages. It found expression in the writings of several ascetics and reformers as that of the ascetic Gerard Groote, whose *Sermo de paupertate infesto palmarum* was directed against

private property of religious.[12]   But this was very much a minority
tradition. In effect, the majority of churchmen accepted the fate
foreseen for them by St Chrysostom.   In this respect the secularization
of human affairs was not an innovation of the later Middle Ages, but
an expansion of something basic in Christian economic activity, and
not merely in antipathy to it.

The monasteries provide an excellent example of this process.
They became noted for their adherence to economic well-being
rather than the reverse.   Thus, the system of granges established by
monasteries, especially by Cistercian abbeys, became in some regions,
e.g. north-east Yorkshire, 'a principal widespread and effective instrument of economic policy'.   The granges were sited in extremely
good — often the best — geographical areas, those that gave easy
access to markets, communication and ports, and which had good soil
fertility, meadows, water table and relief.[13]   The economic achievements of the Cistercians have already been sufficiently dealt with, but
it is important to notice that monasteries of every kind of religious
Order pursued similar economic objectives.   For example, Leicester
abbey (Augustinian) or Christ Church, Canterbury (Benedictine) so
prospered that by the thirteenth century they had become not merely
producers of wool for export, but also middlemen, i.e. they bought
wool from others, who were less able to afford transport, in order to
sell it abroad.   Similar dealings in grain are also noted.[14]   Smith, in
his admirable study of the estates of Canterbury cathedral priory,
which we have cited on several occasions, described the lands of the
abbey, at the close of the thirteenth century, as resembling 'other large
estates of the period by being a capitalist concern, a federated grain
factory, producing largely for sale'.[15]   In this manner the abbeys
became economically and socially progressive institutions.   It is for
this, not for their alms and hospitality, that they should be remem-
bered, and it was this aspect of monasticism that the early Reformers
recalled, showing them as grasping institutions failing to live up to
their spiritual ideals.[16]

As another example of secularization among the clergy, the importance of the connection between the bankers and such apparently
spiritual functions as the holding of general councils has been stressed.
The Medici opened temporary offices at Constance (1414–18) and
Basel (1413–43) for the duration of the councils.   The Rome branch
of the bank was always the most profitable, supplying surplus profits

to other branches, and it reached its peak in 1439, when the profits came to almost 14,400 cameral florins. This was the year of the unity talks at the general council of Florence.[17]

The Weber–Tawney theses, by way of contrasting the pre- and post-Reformation periods, rightly concentrated on the period from the fourteenth century onwards; and the latter part of the Middle Ages, as we have noted, experienced a slowing down of economic expansion by contrast with the rapid growth of the previous two centuries (see p. 88). Thus the reaction of the Church in this later period, which included a tightening up of previously relaxed teachings, cannot be taken as typical of the whole. Nor can the examples of economic prosperity often cited by Tawney of the Medici in Florence or the emergence of Antwerp be taken only as forerunners of an economic revolution, but must also be seen as the aftermath of a revolution that had spent its force prior to the Black Death. These earlier changes Weber and Tawney hardly took into account. The free economy of the twelfth and thirteenth centuries has no mention. The Black Death does not appear in the two works except for passing references. There is then no indication that either author envisaged an economic growth other than linear and progressive.[18] Weber and Tawney thus projected back the fifteenth-century evidence to give them a view of the economy of the twelfth and thirteenth centuries as even more rudimentary and primitive than that of the later period. For Tawney and Weber the guild and the State must have always played an autocratic, overbearing role.[19] The economic individualism and speculative character of trade of the later sixteenth and seventeenth centuries came then to be associated with the religious changes.[20]

Speaking of sixteenth-century England, Tawney argued that 'With the commercial revolution which followed the Discoveries, a new age began'. Also 'as manufactures developed, cloth displaced wool as the principal export'.[21] These statements would have been perfectly applicable to the fourteenth century. Again, the rise of Antwerp prompted Tawney to reflect on the distinction between 'the medieval middle class, intent on the conservation of corporate and local privileges, with that of the new plutocracy of the sixteenth century, with its international ramifications, independence of merely local interests, its triumphant vindication of the power of the capitalist to dispense with the artificial protection of gild and borough and to carve his own career'.[22] In this development Tawney considered that the Bourse of

Antwerp played a leading role for it encouraged the 'flow of capital' and created 'the growth of an international banking system'.[23] Tawney wrote of international money and bills of exchange in almost the same terms for the sixteenth century as De Roover later did for the late thirteenth and fourteenth centuries. The many researches of De Roover compel us to antedate Tawney's accurate description by some 200 years or so (see p. 73). Techniques such as banking, bills of exchange, cheques, double-entry book-keeping and joint stock companies we now know to have originated at the height of the medieval economic revolution, and not later in response to some new ethos associated by Weber and Tawney with the religious changes of the sixteenth century. Basically Tawney was correct to associate a decline in the Church's teaching with an 'outburst of commercial activity and of economic speculation', but over-confident to locate this change in the sixteenth century.[24]

Weber and Tawney considered that medieval society was 'interpreted in short, not as the expression of economic self-interest, but as held together by a system of mutual, though varying, obligations'.[25] They readily admitted that 'in the great commercial centres there was sometimes . . . a capitalism as inhuman as any which the world has seen, and from time to time ferocious class wars between artisans and merchants', but outside these, 'pecuniary transactions were a fringe on a world of natural economy. There was little mobility or competition, there was very little large-scale organization.'[26] This concept of a natural economy prevailing throughout the Middle Ages has been sufficiently challenged, and we cited the very pertinent example of Gascony, which, specializing in viticulture, 'looked to other countries for the supply of those basic food-stuffs which she could no longer produce in sufficient abundance for her own people'.[27]

Having somewhat erred in viewing the medieval economy as evolutionary progressive, with the sixteenth century more productive than the fifteenth, and the fifteenth more than the fourteenth, and so on, it is not strange to find that parts of the Tawney thesis rest on the notion of a gradual evolution of English agriculture from a system of a 'natural economy' to one of 'money economy'.[28] From our evidence of the practices at such monasteries as Cluny in northern France and Christ Church, Canterbury, we saw that the matter of labour *versus* money services was largely a question of good economics.[29] In the latter half of the twelfth century there developed at Christ

Church the practice of letting to tenants at the rate of 1s. per acre *in perpetuum*, which aided the disintegrating tendencies of the time. It needed the stimulus of high corn and stock prices to persuade the monks to return to farming their own estates, which they did during the late thirteenth century; and even then it was largely wage labour that was used. By 1314 the economy of the Kentish estates of Canterbury cathedral priory 'rested almost entirely on a money-rent and wage labour basis'.[30] Then economic disasters reversed the trend so that some attempt was made to retain labour services.[31] Finally, in the late Middle Ages, a return to leasehold farming recommenced. Such fluctuations could hardly have been considered by Weber and Tawney, for they have, of course, become known to us through the various local studies by Hoskins, Beresford, Harvey and others. These studies present a picture 'of very considerable stability, economic and social, up to the time of the Black Death, and of the sharp break with the past that followed that catastrophe'.[32]

Tawney's inability to grant more than minimal flexibility to the medieval economy doubtless affected his ideas on themes dealt with in our own work. A largely natural economy dominated by the Church would argue for a highly regulated form of society.

In a natural economy of barter and exchange the middleman has little place, so we find both Weber and Tawney suggesting that in the Middle Ages the lot of the merchant was a sorry one. Thus Weber:

The dogma *Deo placere vix potest* which was incorporated into the canon law and applied to the activities of the merchant, and which at that time (like the passage in the gospel about interest) was considered genuine, as well as St Thomas's characterization of the desire for gain as *turpitudo* (which term even included unavoidable and hence ethically justified profit-making), already contained a high degree of concession on the part of the Catholic doctrine to the financial powers with which the Church had such intimate political relations in the Italian cities. . . . But even where the doctrine was still better accommodated to the facts, as for instance with Anthony of Florence, the feeling was never quite overcome, that activity directed to acquisition for its own sake was at bottom a *pudendum* which was to be tolerated only because of the unalterable necessities of life in this world.[33]

Likewise Tawney: 'The merchant pure and simple . . . enjoyed the double unpopularity of an alien and a parasite.'[34] Such conclusions are not supported by the present researches. For one thing, Weber and Tawney expressed matters in terms of extremes, whereas more recent historians appreciate the infinite variety of attitudes towards the merchants over the thousand years or so of the Middle Ages (see p. 57). Nor were the medieval attitudes 'dogmas' in any accepted sense. The evidence of the general councils was that merchants were protected and respected by the canonists. Certainly there is no evidence for the opposite opinion. In canon law and at the very heart of the Church, the papacy, the merchants, especially the great merchant bankers of the late thirteenth and early fourteenth centuries, were protected and encouraged. Of the many merchants of whom we have more than a cursory account — such as the merchant of Prato, Francesco da Datini — there is no evidence that they had other than respectable positions. As we shall presently see, the sons of medieval merchants entered the Church and achieved high positions. Their background seems to have been no bar to advancement.

If Weber and Tawney were to rewrite their works today they would probably modify the argument that Calvinism was 'perhaps the first systematic body of religious teaching which can be said to recognise and applaud the economic virtues'.[35] Not only had Calvin's concept of usury been anticipated long before Major, as Tawney rightly suggested,[36] but also it was a too dogmatic generalization that in the Middle Ages the profit motive was decried any more than in, say, seventeenth-century England.

Admittedly, Weber did not deny the existence of 'the impulse to acquisition, pursuit of gain, of money' before the Calvinist movement. Indeed, for Weber, 'unlimited greed for gain is not in the least identical with capitalism', and he suggested that in the Middle Ages there was plenty of rapacious greed, predatory enterprise and speculative activity. Weber rather saw 'capitalism [as] identical with the pursuit of profit, and forever renewed profit, by means of continuous, rational, capitalistic enterprise'. He suggested, of course, that this form was missing in the Middle Ages.[37]

Against this view we have cited a great deal of evidence, some of which came from the pen of De Roover. We may perhaps let his words sum up those findings. He is writing specifically of the Medici family, but his words apply more so to the even greater families of the period of the height of Italy's economic expansion, a century earlier:

The results of this investigation belie the Max Weber thesis, according to which the capitalistic spirit is supposed to be a product of the Calvinist Reformation. The Medici antedated the reform movement by several decades, but to deny that they were capitalists engaged in the pursuit of wealth would be doing them more than slight injustice.[38]

In the fifteenth century, for example, the education given in the church schools of London for merchants' children was 'focused upon the need of making what was considered prudent use of money'. But, in this case, it did not seem to have generated a gospel of hard work among the merchant class of London.[39] Things were different in Italy. The great burden of state taxes as well as the still superior economic position of the city states created a tremendous stress on money and its capacity to cure all ills. At Florence, among a set of directives for merchants going to distant lands, we find the following: 'Remember that money is all the help you have. It is your defense, honor, profit, and adornment.'[40] Benedetto Cotrugli of Ragusa, author of a fifteenth-century tract on *Commerce and the Ideal Merchant*, described 'the work of merchants as ordained in respect of the salvation of humanity'.[41]

The medieval merchant may have felt obliged to confess his sins and at the end of his life to make some form of restitution of ill-gotten gains (two matters considered above, although necessarily only in general terms because of the absence of suitable evidence for the historian), but these did not prevent great fortunes being made and inherited.[42] The type of sins that the merchant had to confess seems very like the errors that adherents to Calvin's theocracy had to avoid. Sharp business practices, such as monopolies, forestalling, price cutting, cheating and so on were forbidden in the correct medieval doctrine of the just price, but also in the seventeenth-century Puritan circles. The need to keep a reputation for private and business morality — as, for example, occurs in the twentieth Rule of the Guild of St Peter at the Church of St Peter, Cornhill, in London, which was the guild of fishmongers — is found equally strongly among the later Calvinists.[43] Some of the examples, especially Benjamin Franklin, frequently cited by Weber have a moral and economic background remarkably like that of a medieval merchant.[44] According to De Roover, several of the medieval economic doctrines, e.g. the teaching on the just price, were taken to the New World by the Puritans.[45]

On the doctrine of the just price Tawney argued that the dominant conception of Aquinas — that prices 'should correspond with the labour and costs of the producer, as the proper basis of the *communis extimatio*' — was the normal approach in the Middle Ages. And,

once again some two centuries too late in his calculation, Tawney
attributed to San Antonino the idea of the *laesio enormis* or margin of
50 per cent over price, with the interesting commentary that 'This
conclusion, with its recognition of the impersonal forces of the market,
was the natural outcome of the intense economic activity of the later
Middle Ages, and evidently contained the seeds of an intellectual
revolution.' But, Tawney continued, the characteristic doctrine of
the time was different, at which point he cited large extracts from
Langenstein as given by Schreiber.[46] Our treatment of the just price
showed that the long accepted view, based on the fourteenth-century
Langenstein, was mistaken. Tawney and others were mistaken about
Aquinas and wrong about equating the doctrine of just price with a
labour theory of value. As for the *laesio enormis*, this originated not
with San Antonino, but from the Roman Law in the twelfth century
(see pp. 59, 277 n 68). The deceptive attractiveness of Tawney's
aphorism, where he suggests that 'the medieval consumer is like a
traveller condemned to spend his life at a station hotel. He occupies
a tied house and is at the mercy of the local baker and brewer' should
not blind us to its great inaccuracy. It presumes a lack of competition
and the existence of a guild monopoly and control, neither of which
was true of the high Middle Ages.[47]

On usury, Tawney correctly analysed the medieval condemnation
of usury made largely for consumption. But as he leaned to a view
of the Middle Ages in which commercial activity was low and confined to a few centres, such as Florence, he tended to conclude that
most loans continued to be for consumption, not for production.[48]
The evidence of intense and widespread commercial activity of the
thirteenth and early fourteenth centuries was not available to him. In
consequence, he exaggerated the canonistic concept of usury inherited
by the sixteenth century by suggesting that it included almost all
profits (as Gratian had done, but four hundred years previously), and
then he projected this new 'concept' back as the typical teaching of
the medieval Church. He cited the thirteenth-century Raymond of
Peñaforte, but his reference hardly bore out his statement.[49] Tawney
knew of the activities of the fourteenth-century Italian bankers, and
he was very aware of the achievements of the Medici, but he treated
the international money-market as an escape from the ban on usury
rather than as a legitimately developed separate kind of institution.[50]
Also the Medici hardly improved on their predecessors. De Roover

concludes: 'The Medici Bank contributed little to economic growth and its funds, instead of being invested productively, were mainly used to finance either conspicuous consumption of royal courts, or military campaigns from the War of the Roses to the exploits of Italian condottieri, such as Sforza.'[51]   During the period 1422–70 the number of international banks fell from 72 to 33.   By 1494 only 6 were left.   What Weber and Tawney took to be the first beginnings of an entirely new economic expansion was, in effect, the renewal of a light long extinguished.[52]

As for the attitude of Calvin and his followers towards usury, a number of recent studies have substantially altered the traditional view expounded by Weber.   Thus, the church ordinance of 1541 at Geneva declared usury to be one 'of the crimes completely intolerable in a minister'.   The maximum allowable rate of interest was 5 per cent; any return in excess was usury.   An ordinance in 1557 raised the maximum rate to 6·7 per cent.   The distinction, and the permissible rates of interest, are identical with the much earlier practice already noted in Venice and elsewhere.[53]   According to Stein, Calvin brought the Protestant teaching into line with the already developed practice of the Roman Church.   'The sharp eye of Farissol detected the internal economic adjustments of the Catholic Church which took place before the Reformation, and particularly before Calvin broke with the traditional interpretation of Deuteronomic Law.'[54]   The exposition of Calvin's teaching on usury given by Lilley is completely in line with the medieval doctrine.   Lilley's conclusions are no longer valid in the light of what is known today of medieval commerce.[55]

The reader will recall that the events of the last two centuries of the Middle Ages were treated as a period of contraction of available resources, with increased competition between the Church and State for their share of that wealth.   This struggle created a tightening of the doctrines and gave a twist to the economy, and therefore to the Church's reaction, that were certainly not typical of the earlier period. For one thing the economic crises of the time limited commercial horizons, so that accumulated capital tended to move away from commercial investments into 'safer' forms, such as land or buildings[56] or municipal bonds.   Gentlemanly farming often became preferable to commerce.   The returns were lower, but safer.   Thus, the proportion of invested (commercial) capital fell rapidly in the fourteenth and fifteenth centuries.[57]   When Weber entered the debate, he did so at a point economically lower than it had been before the Black Death. Weber, looking, for example, at Florence *c.* 1480, would have seen a financial oligarchy controlling the public debt, the *Monte Comune*, and reaping the profits. Such a structure of the State in the later Middle Ages 'effectively prevented capital accumulation among those classes who were most directly interested in increasing production'.[58] Weber, faced with this evidence, but lacking in knowledge of the antecedents, described it as capitalist enterprise, but of a transitory, robber type. He then took this as the typical form of the Middle Ages.[59]

Both Weber and Tawney stressed the emergence of the concepts of work as a virtue, and idleness, with its concomitant characteristic of poverty, as a vice, as two main features that marked off the modern from the medieval period. To the Puritans Weber attributed the notion of work as a vocation, which, if it produces wealth, does so for the glory of God, thus such wealth must be safeguarded and properly used. This was the concept of the stewardship of wealth. Those then who lacked wealth were in some way judged by God.[60] The cure for poverty was not indiscriminate alms, as supposedly happened in the Middle Ages, but putting the able-bodied to work. Tawney may have disagreed with Weber on the broad theme of Calvinism and capitalism, but he agreed on this point and he speaks of the 'new attitude' of the Elizabethan system of putting the poor to work.[61]

Several modifications to this view have already been suggested. The evidence of medieval wills, e.g. for London merchants of the fifteenth century, exemplify the attitude that wealth was a gift of God, that God approved of capital accumulation so long as it was honestly won. Abuse of the poor or resort to such dubious methods as misrepresentation, giving short measure, and monopolies were condemned.[62] Similar restrictions were imposed by the seventeenth-century Puritan divines on the means of earning wealth. It had to be honestly acquired. Moreover, the papers of individual merchants, such as those left by John Lawney, a broker of the early fifteenth century, display *c.* 1430 'the mixed spirit of piety, pride and acquisitiveness in which the accumulation of property was pursued'.[63] And the guilds, at least in their early days, reveal the close connection between trade and religion; good work was essentially a religious duty.[64] As for the doctrines of discriminatory charity, both Tawney and Weber may be excused for mistaking the breakdown of the system of parish relief in the Middle Ages because they had no idea that the canonists had by the thirteenth century elaborated the doctrine of discrimination (see p. 80).

Another criticism of Weber and Tawney, and, indeed, of most historians, is that neither distinguished very clearly as to what is meant by the Church, a term they use throughout in a loose, often meaningless, sense. I have tried to emphasize the complexity of the problem. The infinite spread of income and wealth among the body of the clergy, especially among the secular clergy, means it is impossible to speak of the clergy as clearly distinct from the masses of the peasantry and urban workers. For example, in 1381 in England there were some 1360 clergy in the diocese of Exeter with a total income of less than £6000, whereas in the Winchester diocese were 1287 clergy with a total income of £19,000. The richer livings were usually in the gift of religious houses and collegiate churches, e.g. Beaulieu abbey held the church of St Keerne in Cornwall valued at £22 13s 4d.[65] With disparity of income came disparity of social status. Economically, many of the lower clergy had more in common with their peasant parishioners than with the higher prelates and laity.

Many of these economic and spiritual ills were the product not of deliberate intent, but of historical accident. The papacy, as we saw, was not immune to the changes, indeed its economic fortunes progressively declined during the fourteenth and fifteenth centuries. Well-meaning councils for reform failed to provide stable conditions for future development. From the Council of Lyons I onwards (1245) the work of the councils had become increasingly retrospective and therefore hardly durable (see p. 20). In the fifteenth century these developments reached their climax in the manner in which the Council of Florence nullified the work of Basel, and in the long and elaborate conditions laid down by Lateran V (1512–17) for reform of the papal Curia.[66]

Weber and Tawney ought, perhaps, to have considered more carefully the complex arrangements that tied the papacy to outmoded systems and theories. Tawney said of the papacy that 'as its financial system was elaborated, things became not better, but worse. The abuses which were a trickle in the thirteenth century were a torrent in the fifteenth.'[67] However, seen through the eyes of the papacy, these events take on a different interpretation:

All things have been tried.   No one has answered our prayers . . . We imposed tithes on the clergy, they set the pernicious precedent of appealing to a future council.   We ordered indulgences to be proclaimed.   They said this was a trap to extort money and a scheme of the greedy Curia.   On every single thing we do, the people put the worst interpretation.   We are in the position of insolvent bankers.   We have no credit.   The priesthood is an object of scorn.   People say we live in luxury, amass wealth, are slaves to ambition . . . And they are not entirely wrong.   There are many among the cardinals and the other members of the Curia who do these things and, if we are willing to tell the truth, the luxury and pride of our Curia is excessive. This makes us so hateful to the people that we are not listened to even when we speak the truth.[68]

As Partner has shown, the papacy derived less money from abroad during the fifteenth century than it had at the time of the Avignonese period (see p. 97).

We may end by considering the basic assumption in Tawney's work, which raises the question of the extent to which the Church of the Middle Ages succeeded in coming to terms with the economic forces that it encountered.   Tawney wrote: 'Compromise is as impossible between the Church of Christ and the idolatry of wealth, which is the practical religion of capitalist societies, as it was between the Church and the State idolatry of the Roman Empire.'[69]

Tawney expressed the concept in extreme terms, but the general idea is clear enough.   It is not our function to take issue on theological concepts, but it may be well to point to some aspects of the problem in the Middle Ages that enabled the Church to pass from its compromise with feudalism to a compromise with capitalism.   This involves the problem of the social origin of the Church's clergy.   If it can be shown that a due proportion of merchants' sons entered the ranks of the clergy and joined the religious Orders then we have a bridge, as it were, across which compromise could flow.   A general study of the social origins of clerics is still to be done.   Thus only indications can be given here.   There are sufficient, however, to justify a tentative conclusion and to make worthwhile further researches.

A number of studies suggest that the clergy at all times reflect the general social order.   We are familiar enough with the feudalization of the Church to realize this.   Thus, Smith on the monks of Christ Church, Canterbury, comments that 'socially, prior was a baron and monks a squirearchy' whose 'standard of living differed in no essential respect from that of their compeers in the feudal hierarchy'.[70] The monks had a high standard of living with a great variety in food and dress. By the thirteenth century the prior had his own officials and servants, also his own revenues and guest-houses. In 1287 his household had some twenty-four persons, whose clothes bill alone came to £13 6s 5d.[71] And so it was with the other officials. We have already seen that Christ Church, like many other monasteries of the time, engaged in trade and commerce, above all of wool and wheat. With such economic interests, it is hardly likely that the abbey despised the skills needed for their continuance.[72]

Studies of the social origins of English bishops, who 'from the Norman Conquest to the Reformation held a very important position in the social, political and administrative life of the country', show that, of the 461 prelates between c. 1070 and 1532 to hold office, the most powerful came from two classes.[73] The first was of bishops from the ducal or baronial houses, such as Jocelin of Salisbury, Robert Chesney of Lincoln, Gilbert Foliot and Henry of Winchester; each reign saw a proportion of such bishops come to office. Thus, of the 85 bishops who held office in Edward III's reign, 15 came of aristocratic families. The second class was of men who were of middle-class background, who rose to fame through their services in the king's administration, such as Nigel of Ely, Thomas of Canterbury, Hubert Walter. All were men of great administrative ability, but little spirituality. Their great contributions were of the order of secular achievements, such as establishing a system of national finance and justice.[74] The reigns of Henry II and Richard I prove this. In 1200 the bishops included 'a king's son, a justiciar's son, the nephew and protégé of another justiciar, and sons of two great marcher lords'. There were also others who came 'from every class of free men'.[75] Roger Skerning, Bishop of Norwich, was the son of a priest of poor family. The noted canonist Bartholomew of Exeter was of humble birth.[76] But in the later Middle Ages it was more difficult for saints and scholars to find their way into bishoprics. Correspondingly the proportion of members of the great comital families, after 1350, increased and continued through the fifteenth century. Between 1350 and 1480 there were 20 bishops of this type, all in key jobs and much more powerful than their numbers warranted, because they were appointed at an early age.[77]

The point about such bishops is that they were hardly likely to adopt a high-minded attitude towards the secular world. The only class of bishops that could safely do this were those who had risen because of their pastoral zeal; this was the class of saintly bishops whom we find in the period 1215–1350, especially those of the generation of Robert Grosseteste of Lincoln, such as Edmund of Canterbury, Richard of Chichester, Walter of Norwich, Roger of London, Walter Cantilupe of Worcester. These men rose by personal merit alone; they alone felt impelled to translate the doctrines of the theologians and councils into a concrete programme. But the early decades of the fourteenth century saw the last of such men in Robert Winchelsey of Canterbury and John Dalberby of Lincoln (d. 1320).[78]

The social forces generated by the great variations among the clergy of birth, office and income prevented any united action or policies on economic and social matters. Opposition was almost certain to come to any measure that proposed a return to the basic Christian teachings. This we saw in the rise of the friars, who disputed among themselves about the meaning of apostolic poverty. Even on a simple issue such as pluralism, the attempt by the Council of London 1236 to enforce the constitution of °Lateran IV 29 aroused the clerks of influential families to opposition and they threatened to resort to arms. When bishoprics and other benefices often served as provision for younger sons, impecunious relatives, or pensions for the king's officials, it seems needless to ask whether compromise had been reached.[79]

Among the leading clergy, sons of merchants acquired rich benefices. The Hundergate family of Lincoln, one of the main merchant families c. 1200, had one of their members in the church of All Saints, Torksey.[80] At Deventer the family of Gerard Groote, together with the Ockenbroecks, to whom they were related, were the main cloth-merchants and had an influential part in the city administration.[81] Again, many of the mendicants came from middle-class merchant families. Francis himself was the son of a weaver of Assisi.[82] Lastly, several of the popes had origins that helped them to appreciate the problems of their society. In the early Church, Callistus, before he became pope, had been a slave in charge of a public bank for his Christian master, Carpophorus.[83] And at the end of the Middle Ages the Venetian merchant family of Condulmaro produced the future Pope Eugenius IV. As pope, Eugenius may have suppressed his commercial background, but he did not scruple to lavish 38,000 florins on his tiara made by the Florentine Ghiberti, nor to pawn it for 40,000 florins when he needed the money.[84] The rest of the Renaissance popes need no discussion to indicate the extent to which they were the product of the very special social and economic conditions of the day. Even where a pope came from a higher social class than the merchants and professed to despise the latter, one may find that this was a product not of theological niceties, but of economic ones. A good example is Pius II, who belonged to an impecunious, noble family that had been supplanted by the Sienese bourgeoisie. Pius despised the Sienese merchants as an upstart class, but he could not do without their services as bankers.[85]

The complex machinery of administration, especially of the papal Camera, demanded a high degree of technical competence and familiarity with money and trade matters. During the height of the Camera's development, the period of Avignon, 1316–78, its personnel were almost exclusively clerks who came from merchant backgrounds. Likewise, in the provinces, the various papal collectors, such as John Amalric, collector in Sardinia, were sons of merchants.[86] Others of even more humble birth, but obvious skills, rose to power by dubious methods such as clipped coins, usury, fraudulent contracts and every manner of swindle. Such was John de Palmis, collector in southern France c. 1352–9.[87]

What these examples show is a Church intensely involved in economic matters. The consequence of this was a gradual decline in the spiritual life of the Church from the time of St Francis to Luther. Financial matters absorbed much of the energy of popes, bishops, priests, down to the simplest cleric. So far from Tawney's comment about the Church being unable to compromise with capital being true, it seems only too certain that compromise had been of little difficulty in the accomplishment, and virtually impossible to break.[88]

In secular terms, compromise brought its rewards to the whole of society. The great achievement of medieval civilization of the eleventh to the thirteenth centuries would not have been possible but for the learning, example and progressive character of the clergy and monks of the time. The Church created reserves of capital, encouraged changes in land-owning, inaugurated the system of deposits, credit and banking, 'proclaimed the wise doctrine of a stable coinage and took part in large commercial enterprises'.[89] Ecclesiastical estates of cathedral chapter, bishop and monastery were often the most important determinants of regional economy, and in parts of northern Europe a combination of traders' churches often became the nucleus of new towns.[90] Economic progress demanded political and social peace, which the Church helped to provide through its general stress on peace and in particular by such doctrines as the *Truce of God*, which first appeared in Aquitaine in the eleventh century.[91] Even out of the disasters and infamies that accompanied the crusades some may salvage credit for a Church that encouraged men to look outward and eastwards for a release to their warlike energies.[92] To labour as such the Church gave 'a sense of purpose and direction', without which the acquisitive impulses would have remained stifled and undeveloped.[93] This was not yet capitalism in the sense that Marx would have understood the term, but society was moving towards that goal. Unwittingly, perhaps, the Church had contributed to its progress.

APPENDIX

SELECTED CANONS AND CONSTITUTIONS OF THE GENERAL COUNCILS

Principle of Selection

THIS appendix consists of a translation of selected texts from the first eighteen general councils, Nicaea I (325) to Lateran V (1512–17), dealing with the history of the medieval Church and economic development. There are two reasons for confining the appendix to conciliar texts. First, the inclusion of non-conciliar documents would have made the appendix necessarily bulky, that is, if the selection of other materials were to be adequately covered. (What is clearly needed is an entirely new and separate selection of documents dealing with the Church and socio-economic activity in the Middle Ages.) Second, such an amalgam would have broken the thematic image projected by the conciliar texts. The general councils do have a unity, not necessarily a historical one, of course, which presents to the general reader an opportunity of quickly testing certain commonly held assumptions, e.g. the Church always banned usury (the decrees read through show that it did not) or treated merchants as inferior members of society. The decrees especially illustrate the Church's concern for its own economic interests and its often lack of concern for the general well-being of other associated classes. Non-conciliar documents would not enable this synoptic view to be so easily conveyed to the reader.

Not all the canons relevant to, or dealing with, economic matters have been translated. We have in the main body of the work often referred to certain texts (indicated throughout by °) that are not to be found in the appendix. As the following Chronological Index shows, these canons constitute a large part of the available material. Usually they have been excluded because they repeat or are substantially the same as a text or texts actually translated. Adequate cross-references are given at the foot of each canon and constitution to indicate such other material. Where the complete text is not translated, the omissions are indicated by ellipses.

Chronological Index to the Short Titles and Contents of the Canons and Constitutions of the General Councils Consulted*

FIRST GENERAL COUNCIL: *Nicaea I (325)*

Canons

11.°On those who have apostatized for a reason other than compulsion or threat of loss of property. [*COD* 10; Schroeder 39]

17. On clerics who take usury. [*COD* 13; Schroeder 47-8]

FOURTH GENERAL COUNCIL: *Chalcedon (451)*

Canons

2.°No bishop is to be ordained for money. [*COD* 63-4; Schroeder 86-7]

3. No bishop, cleric or monk may engage in estate management. [*COD* 64-5; Schroeder 90]

4.°On the dignity of monks. They are not to engage in secular or ecclesiastical affairs, nor shall they receive a slave without his master's consent. [*COD* 65; Schroeder 92]

5.°Bishops and clerics are not to transfer from one See to another. [*COD* 66]

8.°Clerics in poorhouses or monasteries shall remain under the jurisdiction of their bishop. [*COD* 67; Schroeder 97]

10.°No cleric may serve two churches. [*COD* 68]

11.°All poor persons are to be provided with letters of peace, but letters of commendation shall be given to persons of distinction. [*COD* 68; Schroeder 102]

22. After the death of a bishop, his clergy may not seize his property. [*COD* 73; Schroeder 120]

23.°On excommunicated clerics and monks. [*COD* 73-4; Schroeder 121]

24. Consecrated monasteries may not revert to secular dwellings. [*COD* 74; Schroeder 121]

* This index follows *COD* 45*-64*.

144

25.°On the ordination of bishops. [*COD* 74; Schroeder 122]

26. Stewards and their appointment as church administrators. [*COD* 75; Schroeder 123]

SEVENTH GENERAL COUNCIL: *Nicaea II (787)*

Canons

3. Secular rulers are not to elect bishops. [*COD* 116; Schroeder 146]

4.°Bishops are not to accept gifts. [*COD* 117–18; Schroeder 146–7]

5.°Those who despise clerics for being ordained without gifts are subject to a fine. [*COD* 118–19; Schroeder 147]

8. Jews are not to be received unless their conversion is genuine [*COD* 121–2; Schroeder 148]

10.°A cleric is not to leave his parish and go to another without the knowledge of the bishop. [*COD* 122–3; Schroeder 149]

11.°No episcopal residence or monastery should be without a steward. [*COD* 123; Schroeder 149]

12. No bishop or abbot shall alienate church property. [*COD* 123–4; Schroeder 149–50]

13.°Those who turn monasteries into common dwellings are greatly at fault. [*COD* 124–5; Schroeder 150]

15. No cleric may serve two churches. [*COD* 126; Schroeder 151]

16.°Clerics shall not wear ostentatious dress. [*COD* 126–7; Schroeder 151]

17.°No one shall undertake to build a church who does not have the means of completing it. [*COD* 127–8]

19.°The vows of intending clerics, monks, and nuns are to be made without the exaction of money. [*COD* 128–9; Schroeder 152–3]

21.°Monks may not leave their monastery for another. [*COD* 130]

EIGHTH GENERAL COUNCIL: *Constantinople IV (869–870)*

Canons

12.°Episcopal elections made with the support of the secular power are in no way to be recognized as lawful. [*COD* 151; Schroeder 168]

13.°To fill the higher ecclesiastical offices, clerics attached to the cathedral of Constantinople shall be chosen, and not strangers or outsiders. [*COD* 152; Schroeder 168]

15.°Valuables are not to be alienated, nor Church property through emphyteusis. [*COD* 153-4; Schroeder 169]

18.°Church property and privileges must be neither violated nor terminated. [*COD* 156; Schroeder 171]

19.°Archbishops and metropolitans are not to go to other churches under mere pretext of visitation and thereby burdening their suffragans with excessive expenses, when the real motive is greed. [*COD* 156-7; Schroeder 171-2]

20. No bishop shall recover estates granted by him or on his behalf without the consent of the official in charge of the particular city or region. [*COD* 157; Schroeder 172]

23.°Bishops are forbidden to dispose of properties belonging to other churches. No cleric shall celebrate divine office outside his own church. [*COD* 159; Schroeder 174]

24.°Metropolitans may not commit the administration of their see to their suffragans. [*COD* 160; Schroeder 174]

NINTH GENERAL COUNCIL: *Lateran I (1123)*

Canons

1. On simoniacal ordinations. [*COD* 166; Schroeder 178]

4.°Episcopal control of church prebends and cures of souls. [*COD* 166]

8. Laymen are not to dispose of ecclesiastical matters. [*COD* 167; Schroeder 180]

10. On those who go on a crusade to Jerusalem or Spain. [*COD* 167-8; Schroeder 186]

11.°The goods of porticani dying without heirs are not to be invaded. [*COD* 168; Schroeder 186-7]

12.°Offerings made to churches are not to be seized by laymen, nor are churches to be fortified. [*COD* 168; Schroeder 188]

13. On counterfeiting. [*COD* 168-9; Schroeder 188]

14. Pilgrims and travellers to Rome and other holy places to be safeguarded. [*COD* 169; Schroeder 188]

16.°Monks are to be subject to their bishop. [*COD* 169]

17. Military invasion of the papal state of Benevento prohibited. [*COD* 170]
18. Parish priests are to be appointed by the bishop; also on tithes. [*COD* 170; Schroeder 190]
19. On the dues owed by monasteries to the bishops, and on possession by the prescription of thirty years. [*COD* 170; Schroeder 191]
20. Church property and persons, including the workers and tools of their trade, to be unmolested. [*COD* 170; Schroeder 192]
21. Priests, deacons, sub-deacons and monks forbidden to have concubines or to marry. [*COD* 170; Schroeder 192]
22.°Alienations of church property and offices forbidden. [*COD* 170; Schroeder 193–4]

TENTH GENERAL COUNCIL: *Lateran II* (*1139*)

Canons

1.°On simoniacal ordinations. [*COD* 173; Schroeder 197]
2.°On other forms of simony. [*COD* 173; Schroeder 197]
4.°On the qualities of bishop and cleric. [*COD* 173; Schroeder 199–200]
5.°The property of a deceased bishop is to be safeguarded. [*COD* 173; Schroeder 200]
9. On monks who disregard their rule by the pursuit of law and medicine for gain. [*COD* 174–5; Schroeder 201]
10. Laymen are forbidden to possess tithes or churches. [*COD* 175; Schroeder 202]
11. All travellers, as well as rural workers and their stock, are to be secure from harm. [*COD* 175; Schroeder 202–3]
13. Usury forbidden. [*COD* 176; Schroeder 203–4]
16.°Ecclesiastical offices are forbidden to be bestowed on the plea of hereditary right. [*COD* 177; Schroeder 206]
18. Arson condemned. [*COD* 177; Schroeder 207]
19.°On bishops who fail to enforce the above decree. [*COD* 177; Schroeder 207]
24. No payment should be demanded for chrism, oil or burial. [*COD* 178; Schroeder 211]
25.°Laymen may not dispose of ecclesiastical offices. [*COD* 178; Schroeder 211]

F

ELEVENTH GENERAL COUNCIL: *Lateran III* (1179)

Canons

2.°All ordinations and acts made by antipopes are illicit. [*COD* 187-8; Schroeder 216]

4. On the type of hospitality to be given to bishops. [*COD* 189-190; Schroeder 218-19]

5. No priest is to be ordained without a title. [*COD* 190; Schroeder 220]

7.°No new taxes are to be levied on churches. [*COD* 190-1; Schroeder 221]

8.°On filling vacant benefices and offices. [*COD* 191]

9. On the violation of episcopal rights by religious Orders, especially the Templars and Hospitallers. [*COD* 191-3; Schroeder 222-3]

10.°No payment is to be demanded from one who enters a monastery. Monks are forbidden to own property. On priors. [*COD* 193; Schroeder 223-4]

11.°On clerical continence. [*COD* 193-4; Schroeder 224]

12. Clerics may not act as advocates in secular causes. [*COD* 194; Schroeder 225]

13.°On pluralism and residency. [*COD* 194; Schroeder 225]

14.°On pluralism and on lay violation of episcopal rights. Laymen are not to hold tithes or transfer them to other laymen. [*COD* 194-5; Schroeder 226]

15.°On church property and clerical wills; also on deans. [*COD* 195; Schroeder 226-7]

16.°On chapter decisions and on customs contrary to the sacred canons. [*COD* 195-6; Schroeder 227]

17.°On the presentation of clerics. [*COD* 196]

18. On provisions for the education of clerics and of the poor. [*COD* 196; Schroeder 229]

19. The laity are forbidden to impose various dues and taxes upon the clergy. [*COD* 197; Schroeder 230-1]

22. A renewal of Lateran II 11 on immunity for travellers and rural workers; also the prohibition of new tolls and impositions. [*COD* 198; Schroeder 231-2]

23. On lepers, their churches and immunity from payment of tithes. [*COD* 198-9; Schroeder 232]

46.°Clergy are not to be compelled to pay taxes. [*COD* 231; Schroeder 276]

49.°The punishment of the unjust excommunicator. [*COD* 233; Schroeder 279]

53. On those who commit their lands to others for cultivation in order to avoid paying tithes. [*COD* 235; Schroeder 282]

54. Tithes must be paid before deduction for taxes. [*COD* 236; Schroeder 282]

55. Tithes must be paid on future acquisitions of land, notwithstanding existing privileges. [*COD* 236; Schroeder 283]

56. No parish priest should lose tithes because of an agreement made by others. [*COD* 236–7; Schroeder 283–4]

59.°No religious may act as surety without consent of his abbot and monastery. [*COD* 238; Schroeder 285]

61. Religious are not to accept tithes from the laity. [*COD* 238–9; Schroeder 286]

62. Relics are not to be exhibited or new ones venerated without permission from Rome. [*COD* 239–40; Schroeder 286–7]

63.°On simony. [*COD* 240; Schroeder 288]

64.°The same: on monks and nuns. [*COD* 240–1; Schroeder 288–9]

65.°The same: on unjust extortion of money. [*COD* 241; Schroeder 289]

66.°The same: on clerical greed. [*COD* 241; Schroeder 289]

67. On Jewish usuries. [*COD* 241–2; Schroeder 289–90]

68. Jews must wear a dress that distinguishes them from Christians. [*COD* 242; Schroeder 290–1]

69. Jews are not to hold public office. [*COD* 242–3; Schroeder 291]

70. Jewish converts may not retain their former rite. [*COD* 243; Schroeder 291–2]

[71]. An expedition to recover the Holy Land. [*COD* 243–7; Schroeder 292–6]

THIRTEENTH GENERAL COUNCIL: *Lyons I (1245)*

Constitutions

[1]. On usury. [*COD* 269–71; Schroeder 306–8]

[2].°On aid for the Empire of Constantinople. [*COD* 271–2; Schroeder 308–10]

[3]. Admonition by prelates to their flock. [*COD* 272; Schroeder 310]
[4]. On the Tartars. [*COD* 273; Schroeder 311]
[5]. °On the crusade. [*COD* 273–7; Schroeder 313–17]

FOURTEENTH GENERAL COUNCIL: *Lyons II* (*1274*)

Constitutions

[1a]. °On the liberation of the Holy Land. [*COD* 285–6; Schroeder 360–1]
[1b]. °On the payment of tenths for the aid to the Holy Land. [*COD* 286–7; Schroeder 361–2]
[1c]. °On pirates and Saracens; on observing a six years' peace among Christian princes; on the crusade. [*COD* 287–8; Schroeder 362–3]
3. °On elections. [*COD* 295; Schroeder 337]
12. °On those who invade the goods and properties of churches, monasteries and other consecrated places. [*COD* 297; Schroeder 341]
14. °Grants in commendam. [*COD* 298; Schroeder 344]
17. °On the office of the judge ordinary. [*COD* 298–9; Schroeder 345]
18. °On the office of the ordinary. [*COD* 299–300; Schroeder 346–7]
19. °On the form of pleading. [*COD* 300–1; Schroeder 347–8]
21. °On prebends and offices. [*COD* 301; Schroeder 348–9]
22. °Non-alienation of church property. [*COD* 301–2; Schroeder 349–50]
23. °Religious houses are to be subject to the bishop. [*COD* 302–3; Schroeder 351–2]
24. °Provisions and Procurations. [*COD* 303; Schroeder 353]
25. Immunity of churches. [*COD* 304; Schroeder 354–5]
26–27. On usury. [*COD* 304–6; Schroeder 355–7]
28. On injuries and loss. [*COD* 306; Schroeder 358]

FIFTEENTH GENERAL COUNCIL: *Vienne* (*1311–12*)

Decrees

[4]. °On supplying the neglect of prelates. [*COD* 338–9; Schroeder 415–16]

[6]. On lawsuits. [*COD* 339; Schroeder 417–18]

[8]. On clerical occupations. [*COD* 340–1; Schroeder 421]

[9].°On clerical dress. [*COD* 341; Schroeder 423–4]

[10]. On the cure of souls for the Dominicans and Franciscans and on the rights of the secular clergy. [*COD* 341–5; Schroeder 379–82]

[11]–[12]. On tenths, first-fruits and offerings. [*COD* 345; Schroeder 424]

[14]. On the religious dress and way of life. [*COD* 346–9; Schroeder 425–8]

[15].°On the dress of nuns and way of life. [*COD* 349–50; Schroeder 387–8]

[17]. On hospitals. [*COD* 350–2; Schroeder 391–3]

[18]. On patronage; the income of priests. [*COD* 352; Schroeder 393–4]

[19]. Religious must pay their dues. [*COD* 352–3; Schroeder 429]

[20].°Against excessive procurations demanded by bishops visiting monasteries, especially of the Cistercian Order. [*COD* 353–4; Schroeder 405–6]

[21]. Excommunication and interdict of those who tax ecclesiastical persons and goods in transit. [*COD* 354; Schroeder 430]

[24].°On providing chairs of languages (Hebrew, Greek, Arabic, and Chaldaic) for instruction of the infidel. [*COD* 355–6; Schroeder 395–6]

[27].°On the office of the Inquisitor. [*COD* 358–9; Schroeder 400–1]

[29]. On usury. [*COD* 360–1; Schroeder 401]

[30]. On episcopal exactions from monasteries. [*COD* 361–3; Schroeder 431–3]

[34].°On the punishment of those who coerce ecclesiasts to resign their benefices. [*COD* 365–6; Schroeder 404]

[35].°Penalties against transgressors of various laws relating to religious orders, payment of tithes, and burial. [*COD* 366–7; Schroeder 439–40]

[38]. On the interpretation of the Rule of the Franciscans. [*COD* 368–77; Schroeder 406–13]

SIXTEENTH GENERAL COUNCIL: *Constance (1414–18)*

1417 *Session XXXIX (9 October)*
     °On spoils and procurations. [*COD* 419]

1418 *Session XLIII* (*21 March*)

Statutes promulgated on the reform of the Church. On (°exemptions, unions and incorporations, revenues during vacancy, simony, dispensations), tenths and other taxes, (°clerical decorum and propriety). [*COD* 423–6; Schroeder 453–5]

SEVENTEENTH GENERAL COUNCIL: *Basel, Ferrara, Florence, Rome* (*1431–45*)

1434 *Session XIX* (*7 September*)

Decree on Jews and converts. [*COD* 459–60]
On those who wish to be converted to the faith. [*COD* 460–1]

1435 *Session XXI* (*9 June*)

On annates. [*COD* 464–5; Schroeder 475–6]
°On peaceful possessors. [*COD* 465; Schroeder 476]
°On those who wander about the church during divine service. [*COD* 467; Schroeder 478]
°On those who pledge the divine office. [*COD* 467–8; Schroeder 478–9]
°The prohibition of public displays in churches. [*COD* 468; Schroeder 479]

EIGHTEENTH GENERAL COUNCIL: *Lateran V* (*1512–17*)

1514 *Session IX* (*5 May*)

Bull for reform of the Curia. On (°the suitability of candidates for benefices, promotions, unworthy prelates, provisional collation and commendams), poor parishes and hospitals, (°unions), pluralism. [*COD* 590–3; Schroeder 488–91]
On cardinals: modest living, (°household staff), as advocates, (°titular churches and visitation), maintenance of same, on revenues, (°commendams), style of living, (°dress, the dress of the parafrenarii, of other clerics, penalties for infringement, general application to all members of the Curia, extirpation of heresy, cardinals as legates, residence), funeral expenses, (°voting in consistory). [*COD* 593–7; Schroeder 491–5]
On reform of the Curia and other matters: (°secular and

religious instruction, fines for blasphemy, clerical incontinence, papal states, simony, pluralism), lay intrusion and control of ecclesiastical goods, revenues, and offices forbidden, lay taxation of clerics prohibited (°superstitions, apostasy). [*COD* 599–601; Schroeder 495–8]

1515 *Session X (4 May)*

On reform of the *montes pietatis*. [*COD* 601–3; Schroeder 498–500]

°Bull against exempt clergy: transgressions, papal notaries, cardinalitial households, episcopal visitation of exempt monasteries, temporary exemptions, lawsuits and appeals, patronage and lay oppression of the Church, provincial synods, impoverished cathedral churches. [*COD* 603–8; Schroeder 500–3]

Documents

FIRST GENERAL COUNCIL: NICAEA I (325)

CANON 17

On clerics who take usury
Many clerics, motivated by greed and a desire for gain, have forgotten
the scriptural injunction, 'he gave not his money to usury', and instead
demand a monthly rate of one per cent on loans they make; therefore
this holy and great council decrees that in future anyone taking interest
or in any way whatsoever dealing in usury and demanding his fifty
per cent profit or seeking some similar way of earning money is to be
deposed and removed from his order.

COD 13; Schroeder 47–8.
Cf Lateran II 13, III 25, IV 67; Lyons I [1], II 26, 27; Vienne [29].
See above, p. 63.

FOURTH GENERAL COUNCIL: CHALCEDON (451)

CANON 3

No bishop, cleric or monk may engage in estate management
It has come to the knowledge of the holy council that some members
of the clergy are administering other people's property and engaging
in secular pursuits for profit. They neglect the divine ministry, spend
their time in other people's houses, and, from motives of greed, undertake to look after their property. This holy and great council has
decreed, therefore, that in future no bishop, cleric or monk shall
supervise such estates or engage in commerce, unless it is a lawful
obligation that he cannot escape, such as the guardianship of minors,
or a God-fearing duty imposed by the bishop of the city to look after
the affairs of the Church or of orphans and widows and of such persons
not otherwise provided for, such as especially need the help of the
Church. If anyone in future goes against this statute he shall be
liable to the ecclesiastical penalties.

COD 64–5; Schroeder 90.
Cf Vienne [38].
See above, p. 54.

CANON 22

After the death of a bishop, his clergy may not seize his property
It is not lawful for clerics after the death of their bishop to seize his personal property, which has also been forbidden by the ancient canons; those who do so shall be in danger of deposition.

COD 73; Schroeder 120.
Cf °Canon 25; °Lateran II 5.
See above, p. 29.

CANON 24

Consecrated monasteries may not revert to secular dwellings
Monasteries that have once been dedicated with the consent of the bishop shall remain monasteries for good, and all the property belonging to them shall be safeguarded as such, and no longer shall they be permitted to become secular dwellings.   Those who permit this to be done shall be subject to the canonical penalties.

COD 74; Schroeder 121.
(See also °Nicaea II 13, where monasteries converted to public lodging-houses during the iconoclastic period are ordered to be restored.
Cf *COD* 124–5; Schroeder 150.)

CANON 26

Stewards and their appointment as church administrators
Since in some churches, so we have heard, the bishops manage the ecclesiastical property without stewards, it has been decided that every church having a bishop shall also have a steward chosen from its own clergy who is to administer the church property in accord with the instructions of the bishop, so that the administration of the church may

not be unattested and thereby ecclesiastical property squandered and reproach brought upon the priesthood. If he [the bishop] will not do this, he shall be subject to the holy canons.

COD 75; Schroeder 123.
Cf °Nicaea II 10 & 11; °Constantinople IV 13.
See above, pp. 29, 30.

SEVENTH GENERAL COUNCIL: NICAEA II (787)

CANON 3

Secular rulers are not to elect bishops
Every election of bishop, priest or deacon carried out by secular rulers is illicit according to the canon which says: 'If any bishop relying on secular powers obtains a church with their aid, he is to be deposed; all those who communicate with him shall be excommunicated.' A person who becomes a bishop should be elected by bishops. In this respect it was decreed by the fathers gathered at Nicaea* that 'a bishop be ordained by other bishops of his province. But if this for some reason, such as pressure of circumstances or the length of the journey involved, cannot be done, then let the ceremony of consecration be performed by three of them, and the others consent by letter. The right of confirmation of these acts belongs in every province to the metropolitan.'

  * Nicaea I 4.

COD 116; Schroeder 146, in an abbreviated form.
Cf °Constantinople IV 12; °Lateran IV 25.
See above, p. 31.

CANON 8

Jews are not to be received unless their conversion is genuine
We decree that Jews who have become Christians in appearance only, but secretly keep the Sabbath and observe other Jewish customs, shall not be permitted to join in communion or prayer or even to enter the church, but let them openly be Hebrews according to their religion. Their children shall not be baptized nor shall they purchase or possess a slave. But if any of them is truly and sincerely converted and makes

a sincere profession of faith, renouncing Jewish customs and possessions, so that others may be brought to conversion, then such a man may be received and baptized, and his children likewise . . .

COD 121-2; Schroeder 148.
Cf Lateran III 26, IV 70.
See above, p. 71.

CANON 12

No bishop or abbot shall alienate church property
If a bishop or abbot alienate or surrender any part of the revenues of the bishopric or monastery into the hands of princes or any other person, his act is invalid according to the canon of the blessed apostles, which says: 'A bishop has responsibility for all ecclesiastical property, and he must administer it as though God is his overseer. It is not lawful for him to appropriate any part of it to himself, or to give his relatives the things that belong to God. If, however, they are poor, let them be given alms, but this is not to be used as a pretext for despoiling the Church.'★ Even if they claim as an excuse that the land in question does not make a profit but a loss, it should still not be given to the local lord, but to clerics or farmers. If the ruler uses intrigue to buy the land from the farmer or cleric, the transaction is void, and the land must be restored to the bishopric or monastery. The bishop or abbot acting thus shall be put away, the bishop from his bishopric and abbot from his monastery, like one who squanders what he has not gathered.

★ Canon 38.

COD 123-4; Schroeder 149-50.
Cf °Constantinople IV 15; °Lateran I 4 & 22; °Lyons II 22.
See above, p. 29.

CANON 15

No cleric may serve two churches
In future, no cleric shall be appointed to serve two churches, for such an act hints of base business dealing and is far removed from ecclesi-

astical usage. In fact we have the words of Christ himself: 'No man can serve two masters: either he will hate the one and love the other, or love the one and hate the other.' Therefore let each one — according to the words of the apostle — serve in the church to which he is called, and remain there. In ecclesiastical matters things that are achieved through material motives are alien to God. To obtain the necessities of life there are various occupations by means of which, if one so desires, one may satisfy the bodily needs, as St Paul said.*
This rule applies in the imperial city, but in rural districts, because of the sparsity of population, exceptions may be made.

* Acts 20:34.

COD 126; Schroeder 151.
Cf °Chalcedon 10; °Lateran III 13, 14, IV 29; °Lyons II 18.

EIGHTH GENERAL COUNCIL:
CONSTANTINOPLE IV (869–70)

CANON 20

No bishop shall recover estates granted by him or on his behalf without the consent of the official in charge of the particular city or region
This holy council has learnt that in certain places some bishops have used their own authority, and without the consent of the persons properly concerned, to expel those who have taken property on lease on their estates, on pretext that the conditions of the agreement have not been fulfilled. Such action is entirely prohibited unless he who contracted the lease has first been told by suitable and proper persons, namely that he will be expelled from the land held by him if he fails to give the agreed rent for three years. If he fails for that length of time, then the bishop shall take the matter to the local or regional court and argue his case against the leaseholder in their presence, proving his contempt. Only then, with the judgement of the court, may he take possession of the property. Let no one either personally or on his own behalf seize the aforesaid property; such action is suspect, as a sign of both greed and desire for gain. If any bishop or metropolitan shall seize property from anyone in defiance of this statute, under the belief that he is defending his own property, let him

be deprived of his office for some time and let him return what he has so forcibly taken. If he persists in his action, refusing to obey the decision of this council, let him be deposed.

COD 157; Schroeder 172.
See above, p. 30.

NINTH GENERAL COUNCIL: LATERAN I (1123)

CANON 1

[On simoniacal ordinations]
Following the precepts of the holy fathers and recognizing the duty of our office, we absolutely forbid in virtue of the authority of the Apostolic See that anyone be ordained or promoted for money in the Church of God. If anyone has thus obtained ordination or promotion in the Church, he will be deprived of the rank so acquired altogether.

COD 166; Schroeder 178.
Cf °Chalcedon 2; °Nicaea II 5, 19; °Lateran II 1, 2, IV 63, 64; °Constance Sess. XLIII [4]; °Lateran V Sess. IX Reform of the Curia.
See above, p. 32.

CANON 8

[Laymen are not to dispose of ecclesiastical matters]
In accordance with the decision of the most blessed Pope Stephen, we declare that lay persons, no matter how devout they may be, have no authority to dispose of anything belonging to the Church, but according to the Apostolic canons* the supervision of all ecclesiastical affairs belongs to the bishop, who shall administer them as though God were his witness. If therefore any prince or other layman shall arrogate to himself the right of disposition, control or ownership of ecclesiastical goods or properties, let him be judged guilty of sacrilege.

* C. 39.

COD 167; Schroeder 180 (canon 4).
Cf °Lateran I 12, II 25, III 2, 14, IV 44, 45; Lateran III 9: °Lyons II 22.
See above, pp. 9, 30.

CANON 10

[*On those who go on a crusade to Jerusalem or Spain*]
To those who go to Jerusalem and give aid for the defence of the
Christians and for the extirpation of the tyrannous infidel, we grant
the remission of their sins and we take under the protection of St Peter
and of the Roman Church their homes, families and all their goods, as
was already decreed by Pope Urban.   Whoever, therefore, shall dare
distrain or seize these during the absence of their owners, shall incur
excommunication.   Those, however, who with a view to going to
Jerusalem or to Spain are known to have attached the cross to their
garments and afterward removed it, we command them in virtue of
our Apostolic authority to replace it and begin the journey within a
year from the coming Easter.   Otherwise we shall excommunicate
them and interdict within their territory all divine service except the
baptism of infants and the last rites for the dying.

COD 167–8; Schroeder 186 (=canon 11).
Cf Lateran IV [71]; Lyons I [1], [3], [5]; °Lyons II [1b]; Lateran III 27
and °Lateran IV 3 for heresy provisions; Lateran IV [71] and Lyons I
[4] for papal finances.
For converts, see Basel Sess. XXI.
See above, pp. 37, 44.

CANON 13

[*On counterfeiting*]
Whoever knowingly coins or deliberately passes counterfeit coin shall
be cut off from the communion of the faithful as one of the accursed,
as an oppressor of the poor and a disturber [of the peace] of the city.

COD 168–9; Schroeder 188 (canon 15).

CANON 14

[*Pilgrims and travellers to Rome and other holy places to be safeguarded*]
If anyone shall dare attack pilgrims and travellers going to Rome to
visit the shrines of the Apostles and the oratories of other saints and
rob them of the things they have with them or exact from merchants

new imposts and tolls, let him be excommunicated till he has made amends.

COD 169; Schroeder 188 (canon 16).
Cf Lateran IV 68 regarding Jewish travellers.   Cf Lateran II 11, III 22, 24.
See above, pp. 38, 56, 57.

CANON 17

[*Military invasion of the papal state of Benevento prohibited*]
As it is our wish to maintain the property of the Roman church, with the help of the grace of God, in a peaceful state, we decree and forbid under the penalty of anathema any military person to invade or violently seize the Beneventan state of [the patrimony of] St Peter. If anyone presumes otherwise, he is to be excommunicated.

COD 170.
See above, p. 30.

CANON 18

[*Parish priests are to be appointed by the bishop; also on tithes*]
Priests shall be appointed to parish churches by the bishops, to whom they shall be responsible for the care of souls and other matters pertaining to the bishop.   They are not permitted to receive tithes and churches from laymen without the agreed consent of the bishops.   If they act otherwise let them be subject to canonical penalties.

COD 170; Schroeder 190.
Cf Lateran II 10, III 9, IV 32, 61, 54; °Lateran III 14; Vienne [11]; °Lateran V Sess. x Bull against exempt clergy; for exemptions, see Lateran III 23, IV 55, 67; for fraud, Lateran IV 53, 56.
See above, p. 34.

CANON 19

[*On the dues owed by monasteries to the bishops, and on possession by the prescription of thirty years*]
The tax that monasteries and their churches have paid since the time

of Gregory VII shall be continued.   We absolutely forbid abbots and
monks to acquire church and episcopal property by the prescription
of thirty years.

COD 170; Schroeder 191.
Cf Lateran IV 32; Vienne [18].

CANON 20

[*Church property and persons, including the workers and tools of their trade
to be unmolested*]
Having in mind the example of our fathers and fulfilling the duty of
our pastoral office, we decree that churches and their possessions, as
well as the persons connected with them, namely, clerics and monks
and the lay brothers, also the labourers* and the tools of their trade,
shall remain safe and unmolested.   If anyone shall presume to act
contrary to this decree and, recognizing his crime, does not within
the space of thirty days make proper amends, let him be cut off from
the Church and anathematized.

   * *oratores* in COD and Gratian C. 24 q.3 c.24.

COD 170; Schroeder 192.

CANON 21

[*Priests, deacons, sub-deacons and monks forbidden to have concubines or to
marry*]
Priests, deacons, sub-deacons and monks are forbidden to have concubines or to contract marriage.   We decree in accordance with the
definitions of the sacred canons that marriages already contracted by
such persons must be dissolved, and that the persons be sentenced to
do penance.

COD 170; Schroeder 192.
Cf °Lateran III 11.
See above, p. 33.

TENTH GENERAL COUNCIL: LATERAN II (1139)

CANON 9

[On monks who disregard their rule by the pursuit of law and medicine for gain]

A vicious and detestable custom, so we understand, has arisen by which monks and canons regular, after having taken the habit and made their profession, disregard the rule of the holy masters Benedict and Augustine, by studying civil law and medicine for the sake of material gain. Instead of devoting themselves to psalmody and plain chant, they are led by the impulses of avarice to turn themselves into advocates, and, trusting in their fine delivery, they confuse by the variety of their statements what is just and unjust, right and wrong. The imperial constitutions, however, prove that it is absurd and disgraceful for clerics to want to become forensic experts. We decree, therefore, in virtue of our apostolic authority, that offenders of this kind be severely punished. . . .

COD 174–5; Schroeder 201.
Cf °Lateran IV 18.
See above, p. 54.

CANON 10

[Laymen are forbidden to possess tithes or churches]

By our apostolic authority we forbid that tithes of churches, which canonical authority shows to have been given for religious purposes, be possessed by laymen. Let them take heed that whether they have received them from bishops, kings or other persons, unless they are returned to the Church, they shall be judged guilty of sacrilege and shall incur the danger of eternal damnation. . . . Also churches are not to be committed to supply priests; every church that has sufficient means must have its own priest.

COD 175; Schroeder 202.
Cf Lateran I 18.
See above, p. 34.

CANON 11

[*All travellers, as well as rural workers and their stock, are to be secure from harm*]
We also command that priests, clerics, monks, travellers, merchants, country people, coming or going, and those engaged in agriculture, as well as the stock cattle with which they till the soil and carry seed to the field, and also their sheep, shall at all times be unharmed.

COD 175; Schroeder 202–3.
Cf Lateran I 14.
See above, pp. 38, 56.

CANON 13

[*Usury forbidden*]
We condemn that detestable, shameful and insatiable rapacity of money-lenders, which has been denounced by divine and human laws and throughout the Old and New Testaments, and we deprive them of all ecclesiastical consolation, commanding that no archbishop, no bishop, no abbot of any order, nor anyone in clerical orders, shall, except with the utmost caution, dare receive usurers; but throughout their life let them be stigmatized with the mark of infamy, and unless they repent let them be deprived of Christian burial.

COD 176; Schroeder 203–4.
Cf Nicaea I 17; Lateran III 25, IV 67; Lyons I [1], II 26, 27; Vienne [29].
See above, pp. 49, 63, 64, 66.

CANON 18

[*Arson condemned*]
By the authority of God and of the Blessed Apostles Peter and Paul we altogether condemn and prohibit that most vile, devastating, horrible and malicious work of incendiarists; for this disease, this form of hostile waste, surpasses all other forms.   There is no one who is not aware how detrimental this is to the people of God and how much it damages their minds and bodies.   For the good of the people,

every possible means must be employed and no effort spared to eradicate and exterminate such scandalous waste. Therefore, if anyone, after the promulgation of this prohibition, shall, through malice, hatred, or revenge, set fire, or cause it to be set, or knowingly participate by advice or help, let him be excommunicated. Moreover, when an incendiarist dies, he is to be denied Christian burial. Nor shall he be absolved until, as far as he is able, he has made restitution to the one injured and has sworn to set no more fires. As a penance let him spend one year in the service of God either in Jerusalem or in Spain.

COD 177; Schroeder 207.
See above, p. 47.

CANON 24

[*No payment should be demanded for chrism, oil or burial*]
We decree further that no payment shall be demanded for chrism, oil and burial.

COD 178; Schroeder 211.
Cf °Lateran III 7, IV 66; Vienne [10] (in part).
See above, p. 21.

ELEVENTH GENERAL COUNCIL: LATERAN III (1179)

CANON 4

[*On the type of hospitality to be given to bishops*]
Since the Apostle declared that he and his followers would support themselves with their own hands in order to nullify the preaching of the false apostles and not to be a burden on those to whom he preached, it is a very serious matter and one that needs to be corrected, the fact that some of our brethren and bishops make such exorbitant demands upon their subjects that the latter are at times forced to offer church ornaments for sale in order to meet those demands, and provisions that would otherwise last for a long time are consumed in one brief

hour. We therefore decree that archbishops on their diocesan visita-
tions shall have in their train not more than forty or fifty horses,
depending on the various conditions of the provinces and the resources of the churches; cardinals not more than twenty or twenty-
five; bishops not more than twenty or thirty; archdeacons five or
seven at most, and deans are to be content with two. They are not
to take with them hunting dogs and birds, but on their journey let
them seek not their own ends, but the things of Jesus Christ. They
are not to look for elaborate meals, but let them gratefully accept what
simple and wholesome food they are served. We also forbid bishops
to burden their subjects with taxes and excessive dues. However, in
cases of necessity, which sometimes arise, or in cases justified by a
reasonable cause, they may make a moderate and charitable appeal to
them for aid. For since the Apostle says: 'Children ought not to lay
up for the parents, but the parents for the children' [2 Cor. 12:14],
how much more unbecoming is it to paternal solicitude if bishops
oppress their subjects instead of helping them in time of need. Archdeacons and deans shall impose no exactions or taxes on priests or
clerics. What has been said above with reference to the number of
horses allowed refers to those places where the revenues and resources
of the church are ample. But in the poorer places we enjoin the
observance of the rule that the coming of many should not harm the
few, lest by such favour those who have previously been accustomed
to use only a few horses, should thereby believe a greater liberty
granted to them.

COD 189–90; Schroeder 218–19.
Cf °Nicaea II 4; °Constantinople IV 19; °Lateran IV 33, 34; °Lyons
II 24; °Vienne [15], [20]; Vienne [19]; °Constance Sess. xxxix.
See above, p. 267 n 105.

Canon 5

[No priest is to be ordained without a title]
If a bishop ordains anyone to the diaconate or priesthood who has not
a proper title, that is, one which provides him with a living, then he
must supply these necessities until he can assure him a suitable position
in a church, unless the cleric ordained has sufficient means of his own
or from his father.

COD 190; Schroeder 220.
Cf °Chalcedon 6.
See above, p. 54.

CANON 9

[*On the violation of episcopal rights by religious Orders, especially the Templars and Hospitallers*]

Because it is our duty not only to instil religion, but also to foster its growth in every way, we cannot do better than by the authority committed to us to cherish those things that are right and correct those that impede the progress of truth.   From the bitter complaints of our brethren and fellow bishops it has come to our knowledge that the Templars and Hospitallers and also other religious have exceeded the privileges granted them by the Apostolic See, by frequently encroaching upon episcopal authority, which action is not only a source of scandal to the people of God, but also creates grave danger to souls. We are told that they accept lay investiture, they admit to the sacraments and to Christian burial those excommunicated and under interdict, appoint and remove priests in their churches without their [bishops'] knowledge and consent, and when their brethren go out seeking alms, since it has been granted to them that on their arrival the churches may once a year be opened to them and that they may celebrate the divine offices therein, many of them from one house or different houses often enter an interdicted locality, abuse their privileges by celebrating the divine offices, and then presume to bury the dead in the aforesaid [interdicted] churches.   They also weaken episcopal authority through the fraternal societies that they established in many places, when, against their decisions and under the pretext of certain privileges, they aim to protect all who wish to become members of their fraternity.   These things are not done so much with the knowledge and counsel of the majority as from the indiscretions of a few, and we decree that all excesses and all conduct whose lawfulness may be questioned, be removed. We forbid them and all other religious to receive churches and tithes from the hands of laymen without the approval of the bishops, and those are to be given up which they have recently received contrary to this instruction; and we ordain that those who are excommunicated and those also personally under interdict be avoided by them and by all others, according to the decision of the bishops. For those churches that do not belong to them *pleno jure*, let them present to the bishops priests to be appointed, who shall be responsible to them [the bishops] for the care of the people, and to the order for satisfactory administration of the temporalities; nor must they presume to remove priests who have been appointed unless they consult the bishops. If the Templars or Hospitallers should enter an interdicted church they may not celebrate the ecclesiastical office more than once a year, nor may they bury there the bodies of the dead. Concerning the fraternal societies, we decree that if the members do not give themselves absolutely to the aforesaid brethren, but continue to retain their private possessions, they are for that reason by no means exempt from the authority of the bishops, but are subject to them as are other subjects, when they have to be corrected for their excesses. What has been said of the aforesaid brethren is to be observed also by other religious who intrude upon the rights of bishops and presume to produce our grants of privileges against their canonical decisions. If they act contrary to this decree, then the churches in which they dare do this shall be placed under interdict and what they have done shall be held null and void.

COD 191-3; Schroeder 222-3.
Cf Lateran I 18.

CANON 12

[Clerics may not act as advocates in secular causes]
Clerics of the order of subdiaconate and above, as well as those in minor orders, if they are supported from the revenues of the church, shall not act as advocates in non-spiritual affairs in the presence of a secular judge, unless such matters concern their cause or the cause of their church or that of those who are unfortunate enough not to be able to handle it themselves. Neither shall any cleric presume to accept the office of general procurator of a town or assume secular authority under princes or other seculars so as to become their justiciar. If anyone goes against this, which is the teaching of the Apostle: 'No man, who is a soldier to God, concerns himself with secular affairs' [2 Tim. 2:4] and engages in this fashion, let him be deposed from the ecclesiastical ministry, since, having neglected the clerical office, he devoted himself to secular affairs that he might please the powers of

the world. Should a religious act contrary to any of the foregoing instructions, we decree that he is to be punished more severely.

COD 194; Schroeder 225.
Cf Lateran II 9.
See above, p. 16.

CANON 18

[*On provisions for the education of clerics and of the poor*]
The Church of God as a devoted mother is bound to provide for those in need, both in the things that pertain to the body and also in those that pertain to the good of the soul. Therefore, in order that the opportunity of acquiring an education may not be denied to the poor who cannot be aided by their parents' means, let some suitable benefice be assigned in every cathedral church to a master who shall teach *gratis* the clerics of that church and the poor students, by means of which benefice the material wants of the master may be relieved, and to the students a way opened to knowledge. In other churches, also, or in monasteries, let it be restored if in times past something of this sort has therein existed. For licence to teach, no one shall demand a fee or under pretext of some custom ask something from those who teach; nor shall anyone who is qualified and seeks a licence be denied the position to teach. Whoever acts contrary to this shall be deprived of his ecclesiastical benefice. It seems only right that a person who, through greed, seeks to hinder the progress of churches by the sale of the licence to teach, should not have the fruit of his labour within the Church of God.

COD 196; Schroeder 229.
Cf °Lateran IV 11; Lateran IV 32; °Vienne [24]; Basel Sess. xix Decree on the Jews.
See above, pp. 77, 79.

CANON 19

[*The laity are forbidden to impose various dues and taxes upon the clergy*]
It must be considered a very serious matter, not less from the point of view of those who sin in committing the offence, as well as from that

of those who have to suffer its consequences, that in different parts of
the world rulers and municipal authorities as well as others in authority
frequently impose so many burdens on the churches and oppress them
with such heavy and repeated exactions, that the conditions of the
clergy in those districts is worse than it was under Pharaoh, who had
no knowledge of the divine law. He, indeed, having reduced all
others to servitude, left the priests and their possessions in their former
liberty and supplied them with food at public expense. But these
others impose upon the churches nearly all their burdens and afflict them
with so many compulsory services that to them may be applied the
words of Jeremiah: 'The prince of provinces is made tributary'
[Lam. 1:1]. Whether it be earthworks, military expeditions or whatever else they think ought to be done, they are obsessed with the idea
that the cost of all these things ought to be met from the goods intended for the use of the churches, the clergy and Christ's poor. They
so restrict the jurisdiction and authority of the bishops and other prelates that no power over their subjects seems to remain to them.
Under these circumstances the churches are to be pitied, and the rulers
also are to be pitied for they seem to have absolutely discarded the fear
of God and respect for ecclesiastical order. Therefore, we forbid under
penalty of anathema that they do such things in the future, except with
the consent of the bishop and clergy and then only in extraordinary
cases, namely, when the resources of the laity do not suffice to meet
the common necessities, the aid of the churches may be enlisted. If
magistrates and others should presume to do this in the future and
take no heed of our warning, then they and their supporters shall be
liable to excommunication; nor shall they be restored to the communion of the faithful till they have made suitable satisfaction.

COD 197; Schroeder 230–1.
Cf °Lateran IV 46; Vienne [21].
See above, pp. 4, 29, 85.

CANON 22

*[A renewal of Lateran II 11 on immunity for travellers and rural workers;
also the prohibition of new tolls and impositions]*
We renew the decree that priests, monks, clerics, lay brothers, travellers,
merchants, country-dwellers going to and from their homes, and

agricultural workers, as well as the animals that carry the seed to the field, are to enjoy suitable protection.

Nor shall anyone presume without the authority and consent of the kings and princes to impose new demands for tolls or to renew such impositions or in any way increase old ones. If anyone acts contrary to this and does not amend on being warned, let him be cut off from Christian communion till he has made satisfaction.

COD 198; Schroeder 231–2.
Cf Lateran I 14, II 11.
See above, pp. 38, 56.

Canon 23

[*On lepers, their churches and immunity from payment of tithes*]
According to the Apostle, great consideration ought to be shown toward the weaker members, yet there are some churchmen who, because they seek the things that are their own rather than those of Jesus Christ, do not permit lepers, who cannot live with those of sound body and cannot assemble with them in the church, to have their own churches and cemeteries or the ministrations of their own priest. Since this is at variance with Christian piety, we are moved by our apostolic charity to ordain that they be permitted to have without hinderance their own church wherever a number sufficient to maintain a church with a cemetery and their own priest live together the common life. Let them take care, however, that they do not prejudice the parish rights of churches already existing. For we do not desire that what is granted to them out of Christian charity should redound to the injury of others. We decree also that they shall not have to pay tithes on their garden and dairy produce.

COD 198–9; Schroeder 232.
Cf Lateran I 18 (tithes).
See above, p. 78.

Canon 24

[*On trade with the Saracens; on pirates*]
Wanton greed has so taken possession of some men that, while they glory in the name of Christian, at the same time they supply the

Saracens with arms, iron and stays for their galleys, and thus they become equal and even superior to them in malice, since they furnish them with weapons and other necessaries for attacking the Christians. There are some also who to satisfy their greed undertake to pilot the galleys and marauding ships of the Saracens. We decree, therefore, that all these are excommunicated for their wickedness, that their possessions are to be confiscated by the Catholic princes and magistrates of the cities, and that they themselves, if captured, are to be reduced to slavery by their captors. We command, furthermore, that excommunication be frequently and solemnly pronounced against them by the churches of the coastal cities.

They also are to be excommunicated who capture or despoil Latin and other Christians who are travelling by ship for business or other honest purposes. Moreover, those who are led by a spirit of avarice to rob ship-wrecked Christians instead of helping them, according to the rule of faith, are to be excommunicated if they do not restore what they have taken.

COD 199; Schroeder 232–3.
Cf Lateran I 14 (protection of merchants).
See above, pp. 35, 37, 56.

CANON 25

[On notorious usurers]
Seeing that almost everywhere the crime of usury has taken such hold that many pass over other professions to devote themselves to the business of usury, as if it were lawful, and thus disregard the strict scriptural prohibition, we decree that notorious usurers are not to be admitted to the communion of the altar, nor, if they die in that sin, to receive Christian burial. Neither shall anyone accept their offering. Anyone taking such an offering or giving them Christian burial, shall be compelled to return what he has taken. Furthermore, till he has satisfied the wishes of the bishop, let him remain suspended from office.

COD 199; Schroeder 233.
Cf Lateran II 13.
See above, pp. 49, 64, 66.

CANON 26

[*On Jews and Saracens, their servants and the right of converts to inherit*]
Jews and Saracens shall not, either under pretext of looking after
children or for service or any other reason, be permitted to have
Christian servants in their homes.   Those who presume to live with
them shall be excommunicated.   The testimony of Christians against
Jews is to be accepted in all cases, since they use their witnesses against
Christians, and we decree that they be punished with anathema who
wish that in this respect Jews be given preference to Christians, since
it is proper that they be subject to Christians and be treated by them
with kindness only.   If by the grace of God any should be converted
to the Christian faith, they shall not be disinherited, since converts
ought to be better off after than before they received the faith.   But
if it turns out otherwise, then we enjoin the princes and rulers of those
regions, under penalty of excommunication, that they ensure that
their share of the inheritance and possessions be restored to them in
full.

COD 199–200;   Schroeder 233–4.
Cf Nicaea II 8.
See above, p. 71.

CANON 27

[*On heretics*]
It was the opinion of St Leo that ecclesiastical justice, although it contents itself with spiritual judgement and does not exact punishments
that involve the shedding of blood, is, however, aided by the ordinances of Catholic princes, for men often seek a salutary remedy only
when they fear that bodily punishment will be inflicted on them.
Therefore, since in Gascony, in the district of Albi, in Toulouse and
its neighbourhood, and in other places, the perversity of the heretics,
whom some call Cathari, others Patarini, others again Publicani, and
others by various names, has assumed such proportions that they
practise their wickedness no longer in secret as some do, but preach
their error openly and thus mislead the simple and the weak, we decree
that they and all who defend and receive them are anathematized, and
under penalty of anathema we forbid anyone to take them into their

homes, to admit them to their land, or to do business with them. If anyone should die in that error, they are not to receive Christian burial, nor may offerings be made on their behalf, under pretext of privileges granted by us.

With regard to the Brabantians, Aragonians, Basques, Navarese, and others who practise such cruelty toward the Christians that they respect neither churches nor monasteries, spare neither widows nor orphans, young nor old, age nor sex, but after the manner of pagans destroy and lay waste everything, we decree likewise that those who hire, maintain or patronize them throughout the regions in which they rave so madly shall publicly be denounced in the churches on Sundays and on other solemn feast-days and shall be regarded as subject to the same punishment as the aforesaid heretics; nor shall they be restored to the communion of the Church till they have abjured that horrid society and its heresy. Those who are bound to them are hereby released from the obligation of fealty, homage, and all service so long as they [the heretics] persist in their wickedness. These and all the faithful we command in remission of their sins that they vigorously oppose such pests and defend with arms the Christian people. Let their possessions be confiscated and let the princes be allowed to reduce to slavery men of this kind. Those who in conflict with them die in true repentance need not doubt that they will receive the remission of their sins and the fruit of eternal reward. Trusting in the mercy of God and in the authority of the blessed apostles Peter and Paul, we also grant to the faithful who take up arms against them and at the advice of the bishops or other prelates undertake to conquer them, a remission of two years' penance; or if they are engaged there for a longer period, we leave it to the discretion of the bishops, to whom the execution of this affair has been committed, to grant further remission according to the type of work performed. Those who refuse to obey the bishops' injunctions in this matter are to be denied the reception of the body and blood of the Lord. In the meantime we place under the protection of the Church, as we do the crusaders to the Holy Land, those who in the ardour of faith take up this work of conquering them, and we decree that they remain secure from all disturbances in their possessions as well as in their persons. If anyone shall presume to harm them, let him be excommunicated by the bishop of the locality and let the sentence be observed by all till the things taken from them be returned and a suitable satisfaction made for the loss incurred.   Bishops and priests who do not vigorously resist the aforesaid evils shall be deprived of their office till they have obtained pardon of the Apostolic See.

COD 200-1; Schroeder 234-5.
Cf Lateran I 10.

TWELFTH GENERAL COUNCIL: LATERAN IV (1215)

CONSTITUTION 16

On clerical dress
Clerics shall not hold offices of profit or engage in secular and, above all, dishonest pursuits.   They shall not attend the performances of mimics, clowns and actors.   They shall not visit taverns except in case of necessity, namely, when on a journey.   They are forbidden to play games of chance or be present at them.   They must have a becoming crown and tonsure and apply themselves diligently to the study of the divine offices and other useful subjects.   Their garments must be worn closed at the top and neither too short nor too long. They are not to use red or green garments or gloves with fancy stitching or beak-shaped shoes or gilded bridles, saddles, pectoral trappings, spurs or anything else indicative of sumptuous dress. . . .

COD 219; Schroeder 257.
Cf °Nicaea II 16; °Vienne 9; °Constance Sess. xliii [7].
See above, pp. 54, 79.

CONSTITUTION 19

Churches are not to be used as warehouses
We do not wish to leave uncorrected the practice by which certain clerics convert their churches to warehouses for their own and other persons' household goods, so that the churches have the appearance of the houses of lay people rather than the temple of God; they disregard the fact that the Lord ' does not permit the carrying of a vessel through the temple' [Mark 11:16].   There are also others who not only leave

the churches untidy but also let the sacred vessels and liturgical vestments, altar cloths and corporals become so dirty that sometimes they create aversion in other people. Therefore, since the zeal of the house of God hath eaten us up [John 2:17], we strictly forbid that household goods be placed in the churches; unless by reason of hostile invasion, sudden fire, or other urgent reasons it should become necessary to store them there. When, however, the necessity no longer exists, let them be returned to their former location. We command also that the aforesaid churches, vessels, corporals and vestments be kept spotlessly clean. For it seems rather absurd to tolerate in sacred things a filthiness that is disdainful even in profane objects.

COD 220; Schroeder 258–9.
Cf °Lateran II 25; °Basel Sess. xxi (COD 468).
See above, p. 4.

CONSTITUTION 32

Patrons must allocate a fair share of the revenues to the clergy
In some districts a deplorable vice and custom has grown up, namely, that patrons of parish churches, and some others, practically appropriate all their revenues, leaving to the incumbent priests such a small share as to deprive them of a decent living. We learned from an unimpeachable source that in some places parish priests receive for their maintenance only a quarter of a quarter, that is, one sixteenth of the tithes. Thus it is that in these localities you scarcely ever find a parish priest who has even the rudiments of learning. Since therefore the mouth of the ox that threshes should not be muzzled, and he who serves the altar should live by the altar, we decree that, notwithstanding any custom on the part of a bishop, patron or anyone else, priests must receive a fair share of the income.

He who has a parish church must serve it himself, as is only right, and not entrust its administration to a vicar, unless it is a parish church annexed to a prebend or office. In this case we grant that he who has such a prebend or office, since it is necessary for him to serve in the major church, must arrange to have appointed for the parish church a suitable and permanent vicar, who, as we said before, shall have a fair share of the revenues of that church; otherwise by authority of this decree let him be deprived of it and let it be conferred on another who will and can fulfil the aforesaid requirements. We also absolutely forbid anyone to fraudulently grant another person a pension in the form of a benefice from the revenues of a church that ought to have its own priest.

COD 225–6; Schroeder 269–70.
Cf Lateran I 18.
See above, pp. 34, 100.

CONSTITUTION 39

On the grant of restitution against the owner of goods he did not seize
It often happens that a person who has been unjustly despoiled of his property finds that it has been transferred to a third party, against whom he has no claim for restitution, and thus he loses effective right to the property as such, for being no longer in possession, proof of ownership becomes difficult. Therefore, notwithstanding the severity of the civil law, we decree that if anyone in future shall knowingly accept such an article, thus becoming an accessory to the theft — there is little difference, especially when it is a question of danger to the soul, between the deed itself or accepting the proceeds — the one robbed is to be helped to obtain restitution from such a possessor.

COD 228–9; Schroeder 273.

CONSTITUTION 40

On rightful possession
It sometimes happens that the plantiff who, in consequence of the non-appearance of the opposing party, has been awarded possession cannot on account of the violence or deceit of the accused obtain actual possession for a whole year, which means that the malice of the defendant gains the advantage, for many jurists hold that after the lapse of a year the former is not to be regarded as the owner. Therefore, that the condition of the disobedient party may not be better than that of the obedient, we decree that in the aforesaid case even after the lapse of a year the plaintiff is the true owner.

In general we forbid that decisions in spiritual matters be referred to a layman, because it is not becoming that a layman should arbitrate in such matters.

COD 229; Schroeder 273–4.

CONSTITUTION 53

On those who commit their lands to others for cultivation in order to avoid paying tithes

In some districts there are certain people who, according to their rites, are not accustomed to pay tithes, though they are nominally Christians. To these some owners entrust the cultivation of their estates, in order to defraud the churches of tithes and thereby realize greater profits. Wishing, therefore, to safeguard the churches against loss in this matter, we decree that the owners may entrust to such people and in such a manner the cultivation of their estates, but they must without dispute pay the churches the tithes in full. Moreover, they must be compelled to do so by ecclesiastical censure, if necessary. All tithes due by reason of divine law or approved by local custom must be paid.

COD 235; Schroeder 282.
Cf Lateran I 18.

CONSTITUTION 54

Tithes must be paid before deduction for taxes

Although it is not in the power of man that the seed should yield a return to the sower, for as the Apostle said, 'Neither he that planteth is anything, nor he that watereth; but God who giveth the increase' [1 Cor. 3:7], when he spoke of the dead seed producing much fruit, yet some men are driven by avarice and strive to defraud over tithes, deducting from the profits and first-fruits taxes and other dues which sometimes thus escape the payment of the tithes. But since the Lord, as a sign of His universal dominion, formerly reserved tithes to Himself by a special title, we, wishing to protect the churches against loss and souls from danger, decree that by the prerogative of general dominion the payment of tithes precedes the payment of taxes and other dues, or at least they to whom the taxes and other dues are paid before deduction for tithes, should be compelled by ecclesiastical censure to pay the tithes to the churches to which they are rightfully due, for property passes with its obligations.

COD 236; Schroeder 282.
Cf Lateran I 18.

CONSTITUTION 55

Tithes must be paid on future acquisitions of land, notwithstanding existing privileges
Recently the abbots of the Cistercian Order met in General Chapter and, in response to our warning, wisely decreed that members of the Order should not in future buy property on which tithes were owing to other churches, unless it was for the purpose of establishing new monasteries. And if such possessions shall have been given them through the pious generosity of the faithful or bought for the purpose of founding new monasteries, they may commit their cultivation to others, by whom the tithes will be paid to the churches, lest by reason of their privileges the churches were further oppressed. We decree, therefore, that from alien property or from future acquisitions, even if they cultivate them with their own hands and at their own expense, they must pay the tithes to the churches to which they were formerly paid, unless they come to some other arrangement with those churches. We, therefore, holding this decree acceptable and accepted, wish it to be extended also to other regulars who enjoy similar privileges, and we ordain that the prelates of the churches be more willing and energetic in meting out justice to evildoers and that they strive to observe their privileges better and more perfectly.

COD 236; Schroeder 283.
See above, pp. 43, 103.

CONSTITUTION 56

No parish priest should lose tithes because of an agreement made by others
Several members, so we understand, of the regular and secular clergy, when they lease houses or grant fiefs, sometimes make a contract prejudicial to the parish churches, namely that the lessees and feudal

tenants pay the tithes to them and choose burial among them. Since such an agreement springs from greed, we condemn it absolutely. Furthermore we declare that whatever has been received by means of such a contract must be returned to the parish church.

COD 236–7; Schroeder 283–4.
Cf Lateran I 18.

CONSTITUTION 61

Religious are not to accept tithes from the laity
In the Lateran Council* regulars were forbidden to receive churches and tithes from the hands of laymen without the consent of the bishops; also under no circumstances were they to admit to the sacrament those excommunicated or interdicted by name. Since we want to curb this evil more effectively and to see to it that transgressors are suitably punished, we decree that in churches that do not belong to them with full title, they shall present to the bishops priests to be appointed in accordance with the statutes of that council, that they may be responsible to them in matters pertaining to the cure of souls. In temporal affairs, however, let them [the priests] render a satisfactory account. Once priests have been appointed, they must not remove them without the approval of the bishops. We add, moreover, that care be taken to present candidates who are noted for their way of living or who would be the likely recommendation of the bishops themselves.

 * Lateran III 10 [cf *COD* 238 n 4].

COD 238–9; Schroeder 286.
Cf Lateran I 18.

CONSTITUTION 62

Relics are not to be exhibited or new ones venerated without permission from Rome
From the fact that some people expose for sale and openly exhibit the relics of saints, great harm is done to the Christian religion. In order that this may not occur in future, we ordain by the present decree that henceforth old relics may not be exhibited outside their case or

exposed for sale.   And let no one presume to venerate new ones publicly, unless they have previously been approved by the Roman
pontiff.   In future, prelates shall not permit those who come to their
churches to venerate the relics, to be deceived by useless forgeries or
false documents as has been done in many places for the sake of gain.
We also forbid alms-seekers, some of whom misrepresent themselves
and preach certain abuses, to be admitted, unless they produce genuine
letters from either the Apostolic See or the diocesan bishop.   Even
then they may not preach anything to the people but what is contained
in those letters. . . . Those who are assigned to collect alms must be
honest and discreet, must not seek lodging for the night in taverns or
in other unbecoming places, or indulge in useless and extravagant expenditure, and above all must avoid wearing the habit of a false
religious.   Since through indiscreet and superfluous indulgences, which
some prelates of churches do not hesitate to grant, contempt is brought
on the keys of the Church, and the penitential discipline is weakened,
we decree that on the occasion of the dedication of a church an indulgence of not more than one year be granted, whether it be dedicated by one bishop only or by many, and on the anniversary of the
dedication the remission granted for penances enjoined is not to
exceed forty days.   We command also that in each case this number
of days be made the rule in issuing letters of indulgences which are
granted from time to time, since the Roman pontiff who possesses the
plenitude of power customarily observes this rule in such matters.

COD 239–40; Schroeder 286–7.
Cf Lyons I [3]; Vienne [38].

CONSTITUTION 67

On Jewish usuries
The more Christians are restrained from the practice of usury, the
more are they oppressed in this matter by the treachery of the Jews,
so that in a short time they exhaust the resources of the Christians.
Wishing, therefore, in this matter to protect the Christians against
cruel oppression by the Jews, we ordain in this decree that if in future,
under any pretext, Jews extort from Christians oppressive and excessive interest, the society of Christians shall be denied them until
they have made suitable satisfaction for their excesses.   Christians

shall also, it necessary, be compelled by ecclesiastical censure, from which there shall be no appeal, to abstain from all business dealings with them.   We command the princes not to be hostile to the Christians on this account, but rather to try to stop the Jews from practising such excesses.   Lastly, we decree that the Jews be compelled by the same penalty to compensate churches for the tithes and offerings owing to them, which the Christians were accustomed to supply from their houses and other properties before they fell into the hands of the Jews under some title or other.   In this way the churches will be protected against loss.

COD 241–2; Schroeder 289–90.
Cf Nicaea II 8; Lateran I 18, III 26, IV [71]; Lyons I [5]; Basel Sess. XIX Decree on Converts.
See above, pp. 35, 72.

CONSTITUTION 68

Jews must wear a dress that distinguishes them from Christians
In some provinces a difference of dress distinguishes Jews and Saracens from the Christians, but in others so much confusion has arisen that no difference is noticeable.   Thus it happens that sometimes by mistake Christians mingle with the women of Jews and Saracens, and, likewise, Jews and Saracens mingle with those of the Christians.   In order that such dangerous contagion, and its excesses, should not have an excuse of this sort for becoming more widespread, we decree that such people of both sexes in every Christian province and at all times be distinguished in public from other persons by a difference of dress, since even Moses enjoined this on them.   On the days of the Lamentation and on Passion Sunday they may not appear in public, because some of them, so we understand, on those days do not shame to show themselves richly attired and do not fear to amuse themselves at the expense of the Christians, who, in memory of the sacred passion, are dressed for mourning.   This we most strictly forbid, lest they should presume in some measure to burst forth suddenly in contempt of the Redeemer.   And, since we ought not to be ashamed of Him who blotted out our offences, we command that the secular princes restrain presumptuous persons of this kind by suitable punishment, lest they presume to blaspheme in some degree Him who was crucified for us.

COD 242; Schroeder 290–1.
Cf Lateran IV 69; Basel Sess XIX (*COD* 459–60).
See above, p. 57.

CONSTITUTION 69

Jews are not to hold public office
Since it is absurd that a blasphemer of Christ should exercise authority
over Christians, we renew in this general council on account of the
boldness of transgressors what the Synod of Toledo★ wisely enacted
in this matter, prohibiting Jews from being given preference in the
matter of public offices, since in such capacity they are most troublesome to the Christians.   But if anyone should commit such an office
to them, let him, after previous warning, be restrained by such punishment as seems proper by the provincial synod, which we command
to be celebrated every year.   The official, however, shall be denied
commercial and other intercourse of Christians, till in the judgement
of the bishop all that he acquired from the Christians from the time he
assumed office has been restored for the needs of the Christian poor,
and the office that he irreverently assumed let him lose with dis-
honour.   The same we extend also to unbelievers.

★ An. 589 c.14 (Mansi 9.996).

COD 242–3; Schroeder 291.
Cf Lateran IV 68.

CONSTITUTION 70

Jewish converts may not retain their former rite
Some [Jews], we understand, who voluntarily approached the waters
of holy baptism, do not entirely cast off the old man that they may
more perfectly put on the new one, because they retain the remnants
of their former rite, and thereby obscure the beauty of the Christian
religion.   But since it is written: 'Accursed is the man that goeth on
the two ways' [Ecclus. 2:14], and 'a garment that is woven together
of wool and linen' [Deut. 22:11] ought not to be put on, we decree
that such persons be in every way restrained by the prelates from the
observance of the former rite, that, having given themselves of their
own free will to the Christian religion, the right form of discipline

may preserve them in its observance, for not to know the way of the Lord is a lesser evil than once having known it to retrace one's steps!

COD 243; Schroeder 291–2.
Cf Nicaea II 8.
See above, p. 72.

CONSTITUTION [71]

An expedition to recover the Holy Land
Burning with an ardent desire to liberate the Holy Land from the hands of the ungodly, and having taken the advice of prudent men who are fully familiar with the circumstances of the times and of the places, and with the approval of the sacred council, we declare that all who have taken the cross and have decided to go by sea, hold themselves in readiness so that they may, on 1 June of the year after next, come together in the Kingdom of Sicily, some at Brindisi, others at Messina and neighbouring places, depending on which suits best, and here, God willing, we will be present personally in order that with our advice and help the Christian army may be safely ordered and receive the divine and Apostolic blessing. Those who have decided to go by land should strive to hold themselves prepared for the same time; for their aid and guidance we shall in the meantime appoint a competent legate *a latere*. Priests and other clerics who are with the Christian army, subjects as well as prelates, must be earnest in prayer and exhortation, teaching them by word and deed that they always keep before their eyes the fear and love of God, lest they say or do something that might offend the divine majesty. And should any have fallen into sin, let them quickly rise again through true repentance, practising humility both of mind and body, observing moderation in food as well as in dress, avoiding dissensions and emulations, and ridding themselves of all malice and ill will, that being thus fortified with spiritual and material arms, they may fight with greater success against the enemies of the faith, not indeed relying on their own strength, but putting their trust in God. To the clerics we grant for a period of three years as complete an enjoyment of their benefices as if they actually resided in them, and they may, if necessary, even give them as pledges during this time. Therefore, that this undertaking may not be impeded or retarded, we strictly command all prelates that each one in his own territory induce those who have laid aside the crusader's cross to resume

it, and carefully to admonish them and others who have taken the cross, as well as those who happen to be engaged for this purpose, to renew their vows to God, and, if necessary, to compel them by excommunication and interdict in their lands to cease all delay. . . .

Moreover, that nothing connected with the affairs of our Lord Jesus Christ be omitted, we wish and command that patriarchs, archbishops, bishops, abbots and others who have the care of souls, diligently explain the meaning of the crusade to those committed to them, adjuring — through the Father, Son and Holy Ghost, one, only true and eternal God — kings, dukes, princes, marquises, counts, barons and other prominent leaders, as well as cities, villages and towns, that those who cannot go personally to the Holy Land will furnish a suitable number of soldiers and, for a period of three years, in proportion to their resources, will bear the necessary expenses connected therewith, for the remission of their sins, as we have made known in the general letters already sent over the world and as will be expressed in greater detail below. In this remission we wish to participate not only those who for this purpose furnish their own ships, but those also who undertake to build ships. To those who refuse to render aid, if any should be found to be so ungrateful to God, the Apostolic See firmly protests that on the last day of the final judgement they will be held to render an account to us in the presence of a terrible Judge. Let them first consider with what conscience, with what security, they can confess in the presence of the only begotten Son of God, Jesus Christ, into whose 'hand the Father has given all things', if in this matter they refuse to serve Him who was crucified for sinners, in a matter so peculiarly His own, by whose favour they live, by whose benefits they are sustained, and by whose blood they were redeemed.

However, lest we should seem to place grave and too heavy burdens on the shoulders of the people, but refuse to lift a finger ourselves, like those who talk but do not act, we ourselves donate to the cause what we have been able to save by strict economy, that is, £30,000 besides a ship to convey the crusaders from Rome and its vicinity and 3000 marks of silver, the remnant of alms received from the faithful. The remainder we have given to the abbot of blessed memory, patriarch of Jerusalem, and to the masters of the Temple and Hospital for the necessities of the Holy Land. Desiring also that other prelates as well as all the clergy should share in the merit and the reward, we have, with the approval of the council, further decreed that absolutely all clerics, subjects as well as superiors, shall, in aid of the Holy Land, and for a period of three years, pay into the hands of those appointed by the Apostolic See for this purpose, one-twentieth part of ecclesiastical revenues; some religious orders only being excepted who rightly deserve to be exempted from pre-taxation, and those [clerics] also who take or already have taken the crusader's cross and are about to set out personally. We and our brethren, the cardinals of the Holy Roman Church, will pay one-tenth of our revenues. All are bound to the faithful observance of this under penalty of excommunication, so that those who deliberately commit fraud in this matter will incur that penalty.

Since by the just judgement of the heavenly King it is only right that those who are associated with a good cause should enjoy a special privilege, although the date of departure is at least one year hence, we exempt the crusaders from collections, taxes and other assessments. Their persons and possessions, after they have taken the cross, we take under the protection of Blessed Peter and ourselves, decreeing that they stand under the protection of the archbishops, bishops and all the prelates of the Church. Besides, special protectors will be appointed, and, till their return or till their death shall have been certified, they shall remain unmolested, and if anyone shall presume the contrary, let him be restrained by ecclesiastical censure.

In the case of crusaders who are bound under oath to pay interest, we command that their creditors be compelled by the same threat to cancel the oath given and to cease exacting interest. Should any creditor force the payment of interest, we command that he be similarly forced to make restitution. We command also that the Jews be compelled by the secular power to cancel interest, and, till they have done so, intercourse with them must be absolutely denied by all Christians under penalty of excommunication. For those who cannot before their departure pay their debts to the Jews, the secular princes shall provide such a period of remission that from the time of their departure till their return or till their death is known, they shall not be embarrassed with the inconvenience of paying interest. If a Jew has received security for such a debt, he must after deducting his own expenses, pay to the owner the income from such security. Prelates who show themselves negligent in obtaining justice for the crusaders and their servants shall be subject to severe penalty.

Since the corsairs and pirates too violently impede assistance to the

G 2

Holy Land by capturing and robbing those who go there and those returning, we excommunicate them and their principal abettors and protectors, forbidding under threat of anathema that anyone knowingly hold intercourse with them in any contract of buying and selling, and enjoin upon the rulers of cities and their localities that they check and turn them away from this iniquity.   And since an unwillingness to disturb the perverse is nothing else than to favour them, and is also an indication of secret association with them on the part of those who do not resist manifest crime, we wish and command that severe ecclesiastical punishment be imposed by the prelates on their persons and land.   We excommunicate and anathematize, moreover, those false and ungodly Christians who furnish the enemies of Christ and of the Christian people arms, iron and supports for the construction of ships; those also who sell them ships and who in the ships of the Saracens hold the post of pilot, or in machines or in any other way give them aid or advice to the detriment of the Holy Land; we decree that their possessions be confiscated and they themselves become the slaves of their captors.   We command that this sentence be publicly read out in all maritime cities on all Sundays and feast-days, and that to such people the church be not opened till they return all that they have obtained in so reprehensible a traffic and give the same amount out of their own pocket in aid of the Holy Land, so that they are punished in the precise manner that they sinned.   In case they are not able to pay, then let them be punished in other ways, so that their punishment will act as a deterrent to others who might try to do the same.

Furthermore, under penalty of anathema, we forbid all Christians for a period of four years to send their ships to Eastern countries inhabited by the Saracens, in order that a greater supply of ships may be available to those who wish to go to the aid of the Holy Land, and also so that the Saracens will be denied the benefits that they usually gain from such commercial dealings.

Although tournaments have been generally forbidden and specifically penalized by different councils, we have further decided to ban them under penalty of excommunication for a period of three years, because at this time they represent a serious obstacle to the success of the crusade.

For the success of this undertaking it is above all necessary that the leaders of the Christian world should keep peace among themselves. Therefore, with the advice of the holy council, we decree that for four years peace be observed throughout the whole of Christendom, so that through the prelates discordant elements may be brought together in a sound peace, or at least to a strict observance of the truce. Those who refuse to accept these terms must be compelled by personal excommunication and interdict of their lands unless the malice that inspired their wrongdoings was such that they ought not to enjoy such peace. But, if they should despise ecclesiastical censure, they shall have every reason to fear that by the authority of the Church the secular power will be invoked against them as disturbers of the affairs of the One crucified.

We, therefore, by the mercy of Almighty God, trusting in the authority of the Blessed Apostles Peter and Paul, in virtue of that power of binding and loosing which God has conferred on us, though unworthy, grant to all who aid in this work personally and at their own expense, a full remission of their sins provided they have sincerely repented and orally confessed, and promise them when the just shall receive their reward an increase of eternal happiness. To those who do not personally go to the Holy Land, but at their own expense send there as many suitable men as their means will permit, and to those also who go personally but at the expense of others, we grant a full remission of their sins. Participants of this remission are, moreover, all who in proportion to their means contribute to the aid of the Holy Land or, in regard to what has been said, give suitable advice and assistance. Finally, to all those who in a spirit of piety have embarked on this holy undertaking, this general council imparts the help of its prayers and blessings that they may advance worthily to salvation.

COD 243–7; Schroeder 292–6.
Cf Lateran I 10.
See above, pp. 37, 38, 44, 56, 106.

THIRTEENTH GENERAL COUNCIL: LYONS I (1245)

CONSTITUTION [1]

On usury

Our pastoral care directs our attention to churches that have fallen into neglect and it urges us to provide a suitable constitution against their going to ruin in the future. The unfathomable greed of usury has brought many churches to the verge of destruction, and some prelates are very negligent and remiss in paying off debts, especially those contracted by their predecessors, and are too much inclined to contract further debts, especially by mortgaging the properties of their churches. They are also negligent in taking care of property already acquired, preferring to make a name for themselves by undertaking new projects, rather than looking after their properties, as well as recovering those alienated, restoring ones that have been lost, and repairing those fallen to ruin. Under these circumstances, and in order that in future they may not excuse themselves on any plea however plausible and try to put the blame for their own negligence on their predecessors or others, we, with the approval of the council, decree that bishops, abbots, deans and others who exercise lawful and proper powers of administration shall within one month after entering office (notice having been given earlier to their immediate superior, so that he may be present in person or through some other reliable and competent ecclesiastical person), with those present, who have been called especially for this by the chapter or convent, see to it that an inventory is made of the things taken over by them at the beginning of their administration. A careful record shall be made of the various goods and chattels, such as books, charters, instruments, privileges, church ornaments, vestments and all other things that belong to the furnishings of an urban or rural foundation; also the debts and claims must be carefully listed so that the condition of the church when they took charge of it, the manner in which they governed it during their incumbency, and what state they have left it in at their death or in the event of removal may easily be known to their superior, if necessary, and to those who have been made responsible for the care of the churches. Archbishops, who are immediately subject to the Roman pontiff, must invite one of their suffragans, who shall appear either in person or through a deputy as mentioned above, and abbots and other minor exempt prelates must invite a neighbouring bishop, who, however, must not claim for himself any right in the exempted church. The said inventory must be provided with the seals of the new incumbent and his clerics, as well as of the representative of the archbishop or of the neighbouring bishop summoned for this purpose, and must be preserved with due care in the archives of the church. A transcript of this inventory, similarly sealed, is to be placed in the hands of the newly installed incumbent and in the hands also of the prelate invited by him. The church property at hand must be carefully guarded and its administration properly conducted, and if it can be done, known debts must be paid as soon as possible from the chattels of the church. But if this movable property is not enough for a quick settlement of the debt, then all other income, except what is needed to cover necessary expenses, must be used to pay off the debts that are usurious or excessively heavy. If, however, the debts are not burdensome or usurious, a third part of the revenues, or, on the advice of those who were summoned to make the inventory, a larger part may be set aside for this purpose. Moreover, by the authority of the same council we strictly forbid the aforesaid rulers of churches to put either themselves or the churches committed to them under obligations to others, or to contract debts that might prove a source of trouble, either in their own names or in the name of the churches. But if there is pressing need, or if some reasonable benefit of the churches should demand it, prelates with the consent and advice of their superiors, and archbishops and exempt abbots with that of the aforesaid parties summoned by them and of their colleagues, may contract debts that are not usurious, if it can be done, but never may they contract them on the open markets. In the contracts must be given the names of the debtors and creditors, and the reasons why the debt is contracted; and even where the money is used for the benefit of the church, we earnestly wish that ecclesiastical persons or churches should not be pledged for its security. Furthermore the privileges of churches are not to be given as security, but they must be properly guarded in a safe place; nor may other properties of the churches be given except for necessary and beneficial debts contracted in the aforesaid manner.

That this salutary constitution may be inviolably observed and bear fruit, which we sincerely hope, we decree that all abbots, priors, deans, and provosts of cathedrals and other churches at least once a year give a strict account of their administration to their colleagues, and that this account, written and signed, be faithfully read in the presence of the visiting superior. Archbishops and bishops, likewise, once a year must give an account to their chapters of their administration of property belonging to their own household and, over and above this, bishops must give a similar account to the metropolitans, and metropolitans to the legates of the Apostolic See or to others to whom the visitation of their churches has been committed by the Apostolic See. The written accounts must always be kept in the treasury of the Church, so that the later ones may be compared with the earlier and present ones, and thus the superior will be able to tell whether the administrator was diligent or negligent in his duties; in case of negligence, let the superior, having God before his eyes and, laying aside love, hatred or fear, impose on him such a punishment that he may not deserve to receive another on this account either from God or from the superior or from the Apostolic See. The present decree we command to be observed not only by future prelates, but also by those already so promoted.

COD 269–71; Schroeder 306–8 (=I 13).
Cf Lyons II 13.
See above, p. 108.

CONSTITUTION [3]

Admonition by prelates to their flock
The children of the Church have for a long time contributed lavishly, and many have laid down their lives, to win back the land which the Son of God consecrated with His blood, as we learn to our sorrow from the things that have previously happened to Christians fighting against the infidels across the sea. But, since it is particularly the desire of the Apostolic See that redemption of this land may with God's help be speedily brought about, we take this opportunity for procuring the favour of God to arouse through our letters your interest in the cause. We therefore earnestly beseech you in the Lord Jesus Christ, commanding that in your sermons or when in confession you impose penance, you induce the faithful committed to your care, by pious admonition as well as by the grant of a special indulgence, should you see fit, that for the remission of their sins they should leave something for the aid of the Holy Land or of the Empire of Constantinople. Moreover, we ask you to see to it that the money which they, out of respect for the One Crucified, give for assistance of this kind be carefully kept in fixed places under your seals, and that other grants bequeathed for this purpose be carefully put in writing. May your goodness execute this work of piety, in which we seek only the interests of God and the salvation of the faithful, with such

promptness that in the end you may hope for the reward of heavenly glory from the hand of the eternal Judge.

COD 272; Schroeder 310 (I 15).
Cf Lateran I 10, IV 62.

CONSTITUTION [4]

On the Tartars
Desiring above all things the spread of the Christian religion throughout the earth, we are overcome with inexpressible grief when, at times, some so oppose our desire in this matter, by employing contrary aims and actions, that they strive in every possible way to remove that religion utterly from the face of the earth. The savage race of Tartars, seeking to subjugate or rather to annihilate the Christian people, first collected its forces and then entered Poland, Russia, Hungary and other Christian regions and laid them waste. Sparing neither sex nor age it vents its rage with horrible cruelty on all without distinction and inflicts upon those countries unheard-of destruction. It does this with unbroken progress, for it knows not a sword idle in the scabbard, it carries an incessant persecution to other countries, in order that, later attacking the more powerful Christian armies, it may exercise its savagery more fully; so that once the land has lost its faithful, which God forbid, the faith itself will wither away, as it mourns its followers who were conquered by the ferocity of that race. In order, therefore, that so detestable an aim of that race may not be realized, but by the power of God may fail and terminate in the opposite direction, it must be considered seriously by all Christians, and the proper precaution taken, that its progress may be so impeded that it cannot make any further advance toward them by use of armed force, however powerful. Therefore, with the advice of the holy council, we admonish, exhort and command all the faithful to see to it that all roads and approaches by which that race can enter Christian countries be carefully inspected and so fortified with ditches, walls and other works as may appear necessary, so that any further advance may be effectively halted. But in case of an actual advance, the Apostolic See must be the first to be informed, so that the Pope may obtain for you the aid of the faithful, and you with the help of God may be safe against the exertions and insults of that race. We will contribute

abundantly toward such expenses as you may deem necessary and useful, and we will see to it that the Christians of all provinces contribute their share to meet this common danger. We will, moreover, in regard to this matter dispatch letters similar to the present one to other Christians through whose territory the aforesaid race may gain access.

COD 273; Schroeder 311 (I 16).
Cf Lateran I 10.

FOURTEENTH GENERAL COUNCIL: LYONS II (1274)

CONSTITUTION 25

Immunity of churches

'Holiness belongs to the house of God', thus it is fitting that 'His abode which has been established in peace' should have quiet worship and due respect. . . . Where the divine services are celebrated with peace and quiet, let no one create a disturbance, excite commotion or commit violence. Let all discussions, assemblies and public meetings cease. Let all idle talk and gossip and, above all, foul and profane language find no place there. Finally, whatever other things might disturb the divine offices or offend the eyes of the divine Majesty, let them be banished from the churches, lest where the forgiveness of sins is to be sought, there may be given an occasion of sinning, or sin may actually be committed. In the churches and in the cemeteries let business matters, and especially fairs and markets, be excluded, and let the racket of lay tribunals be silent in them. Let no cause, and especially no criminal cause, be conducted therein by laymen, nor let trials of laymen take place there.

COD 304; Schroeder 354-5.
Cf Lateran IV 19; °Basel Sess. xxi (*COD* 468).
See above, p. 4.

CONSTITUTION 26

On usury

Desiring to check the canker of usury which devours souls and exhausts resources, we command that the constitution of the Lateran

Council* against usurers be inviolably observed under threat of divine malediction. And since the fewer the opportunities given to usurers the more easily will the practice of usury be destroyed, we decree by this constitution that no community or association, nor any individual, whatever their office, rank or status, shall permit strangers and non-residents of their estates, who publicly practise or wish to practise usury, to rent offices for this purpose on their territory or to retain those that they already have, or permit them to dwell elsewhere, but they shall expel all known usurers from their territory within three months and shall not permit their return in the future. No one shall lease or under any other title whatsoever let them have the use of their houses for the purpose of practising usury. Those who act otherwise, if they are churchmen, patriarchs, archbishops, or bishops incur suspension; individuals of lower rank incur excommunication, and communities and other associations are placed under interdict. If, through obstinacy, they despise these censures for more than a month, their territories shall be placed and remain under interdict so long as the usurers remain there. If, however, they are laymen, then, notwithstanding any privilege, let their ordinaries restrain them from such excesses by ecclesiastical censure.

* Lateran III 25.

COD 304–5; Schroeder 355–6.
Cf Lateran II 13.
See above, pp. 106, 109–11.

CONSTITUTION 27

[On usury]

Even though notorious usurers have made definite or general provision in their wills regarding restitution in the matter of illegally charged interest, church burial shall nevertheless be denied them till full satisfaction has been made to those to whom it is due, if they are available; in case of absence, to those who are authorized to act for them. If these also are absent, it is to be made to the ordinary of the locality, or to his vicar, or to the testator's parish priest, in the presence of witnesses residing in that parish (in this case the ordinary, vicar and rector may by the authority of this constitution receive in their name and in the presence of witnesses a pledge on which legal action may be based), or at the request of the ordinary a pledge concerning the restitution to be made may be given to a competent notary. If the amount of usury received is known, this is always to be expressed in the aforesaid pledge, otherwise the amount is to be determined by him who receives the pledge. However, he may not knowingly fix this amount at a lower figure than what he believes to be the correct one, otherwise he shall be bound to make satisfaction for the remainder. All religious and others who dare in contravention of this constitution to admit notorious usurers to ecclesiastical burial, we decree that they incur the penalty prescribed by the Lateran Council* against usurers. No one may witness the wills of notorious usurers, and no one may hear their confession or give them absolution, unless they make full restitution or give a satisfactory pledge to that effect, in so far as their resources permit. Wills of notorious usurers that do not follow this injunction are *ipso jure* invalid.

* Lateran III 25.

COD 305–6; Schroeder 357.
Cf Lateran II 13.
See above, pp. 10, 49, 106, 109–11, 115.

CONSTITUTION 28

On injuries and loss

Pledges, or reprisals as they are commonly called, in which one person or party is made to bear a burden or penalty in place of another, have already been prohibited by civil law as contrary to law and natural justice. However, in order that the prohibition against applying them to churchmen may be the more feared, the more they are in a special manner checked, we strictly forbid reprisals to be granted against the aforesaid persons or their possessions, or, even where they are generally granted on the ground of custom, which we regard rather as an abuse, we forbid that these grants be carried into effect against them. Those who go against this decree, by granting and executing pledges or reprisals against such persons, unless they revoke such action within a month from the time of their concession, if they are individuals, incur the sentence of excommunication, if a community, it is subject to interdict.

COD 306; Schroeder 358.
See above, p. 47.

FIFTEENTH GENERAL COUNCIL: VIENNE (1311–12)

Decree [6]

[*On lawsuits*]
Desiring to restrict the costly delays of lawsuits in the cases mentioned
below, which experience shows arise from a too scrupulous observance
of rules of judicial procedure, we decree that in future a shorter course
of procedure be adopted in cases involving elections, postulations and
provisions; also in the matter of the various ranks and offices, canonries
and prebends and all other ecclesiastical benefices; also of tithes, even
when, after an admonition, recourse is had to ecclesiastical censure to
compel payment; lastly, in the matter of matrimony and usury, and
all other matters in any way related to these. The foregoing provisions we wish to be applied not only to future cases, but also to current
ones, and to matters that are pending appeal.

COD 339; Schroeder 417–18.
Cf °Lateran IV 37; °Lyons II 19.

Decree [8]

[*On clerical occupations*]
We strictly command local ordinaries to warn by name three times
those clerics who publicly and personally engage in the meat or
butcher's trade or inn-keeping that they abandon such trades within a
period of time to be specified by the ordinaries, and they are not to
resume them in the future. Those who, after such warning, do not
discontinue such practices or at any time resume them, if they be
married, shall lose *eo ipso* all clerical privileges; if unmarried, they
shall lose their privileges in so far as these are of a real or tangible kind,
and if in addition they dress as laymen, then they also lose *eo ipso* their
personal rights as clerics so long as they are engaged in the aforesaid
pursuits. In regard to other clerics who are engaged in secular commercial activities or in any business inconsistent with the clerical state,
and those also who carry arms, the ordinaries shall so strive to observe
the canonical statutes that the aforesaid clerics be restrained from such

excesses.   Moreover, let them see to it that they themselves are not guilty of negligence in these matters.

COD 340–1; Schroeder 421 (c.9).
Cf Chalcedon 3.
See above, pp. 54, 55.

DECREE [10]

[*On the cure of souls for the Dominicans and Franciscans and on the rights of the secular clergy*]

... For a long time past there has existed between the bishops and the parish clergy and priests throughout the various provinces of the world on the one hand, and the Friar Preachers and the Friars Minor on the other, a grave and dangerous quarrel in the matter of preaching to the people, of hearing their confessions, giving them penance, and of burying the dead who chose to be buried in the churches or the cemeteries of the friars. . . . [Therefore, we] decree and ordain that the friars of the aforesaid orders may in their churches and their other places of worship and in public places freely preach and expound to the clergy and people the word of God, except during the time that the local prelates wish to preach or have someone preach for them; during this time they shall not preach except by previous arrangement with and special permission of the prelates.   In the schools of general studies where it is customary to give a special sermon to the clergy on certain days, at funeral services and on special or particular feasts of these religious, the friars are permitted to preach, unless it is the time when it is customary to preach to the clergy in the aforesaid places, or the bishop or superior prelate should for certain and urgent reasons assemble the clergy before himself.   In the parish churches, however, the friars may not and shall not dare to preach or expound the word of God unless they shall have been called or invited by the parish clergy and with their permission sought and obtained a licence, unless the bishop or superior prelate should command them to preach. . . . If the bishops grant the permission sought for hearing confessions, let the aforesaid masters, ministers and others receive it with thanks and let the persons chosen execute the office committed to them. If, however, any bishops should be unwilling to accept for this office any one of the friars presented to them, then another may and ought to be substituted, but similarly presented to the same bishops. Should the bishops again refuse the necessary faculties of hearing confessions, then we ourselves from the plenitude of Apostolic power graciously grant it to them so that they may freely and lawfully hear the confessions of those desiring to confess to them and likewise to impose penance. By this concession, however, we do not by any means intend to bestow upon the friars chosen for such work more extensive powers in this matter than is given by law to the parish clergy, unless the prelates themselves should suggest that in this matter a larger power ought to be granted them.

To this decree and to our dispositions, we add, moreover, that the friars of the aforesaid Orders may have free burial in their churches and cemeteries wherever located, that is, they may bury all who should wish to be buried in their churches or cemeteries. However, in order that the parish churches and their clergy or rectors, who have charge of the administration of the sacraments and to whom it belongs by law to preach and expound the word of God, and to hear confessions, may not be defrauded of their due and necessary means, since labourers are worthy of their hire, we decree and ordain by the same Apostolic authority that the friars of the aforesaid Orders shall be obliged to give to the parish clergy, rectors and curates a quarter share (as now laid down by us) of the income accruing from funerals and from everything bequeathed to them in any manner whatsoever for any fixed or definite purpose, even of such bequests of which it has hitherto not been customary or by law established to give or demand the quarter or canonical portion; also of all gifts or bequests of any kind made to them directly or, indirectly, to others on their behalf, at the time of death or during the illness that caused the death of the donor. The friars must see to it that such legacies do not pass to others, from whom the fourth is by no means owing, but are put to the use and needs of the friars themselves, also that all gifts and donations made to them, likewise promised gifts and donations made in time of death or by the sick, should be put or given to the care of the donors themselves. In order to enforce the observance of these provisions, we make it on the part of the friars a matter of conscience, so that if (which God forbid) it should happen that fraud or deception has been practised in this matter, i.e. contrary to our wishes concerning the parish clergy, they will be held to a strict account on the day of judgement. Beyond the portion fixed above, the parish clergy may not demand anything, neither are the friars obliged to give more, nor can they be forced to do so by anyone. . . .

COD 341–5; Schroeder 379–82 (c.2).
Cf Lateran II 24; °Vienne II [4].
See above, p. 45.

DECREE [11]

[*On tithes, first-fruits and offerings*]
Those religious who dare to appropriate or usurp by fraud or under some dubious title, noval or other tithes belonging to the churches, and to which they have no legitimate claim; or who either do not permit or prevent a tithe being paid to the churches on animals that belong to their servants and shepherds and others whose animals intermingle with their own flocks; or who defraud the churches by buying animals in numerous places and then leave them in the care of those from whom they bought them or in the care of others; or who refuse to pay or prevent the payment of tithes on lands whose cultivation they entrust to others, if, after a just demand on the part of those whom it concerns, they do not within a month desist from such practices, or if they do not within two months make full restitution of what, contrary to the above, they have presumed to usurp or to retain, to the churches thus defrauded, are suspended from all offices and administrative duties and benefices till a just settlement has been made. If these religious hold no offices or benefices, then in place of suspension they incur excommunication from which they can be absolved only after they have made full satisfaction, any privileges to the contrary notwithstanding. The foregoing, however, we do not wish to be extended to animals that are held by the donors or benefactors of the religious, since these might have given themselves and their effects to them.

COD 345; Schroeder 424 (II 11).
Cf Lateran I 18.
See above, p. 35.

DECREE [12]

[*On tenths, first-fruits and offerings*]
If a tenth is granted to anyone, then it can and should be levied, in the region in which it was granted, according to the customary rate and

in the coinage generally current at the time.   Church chalices, books and other ornaments used in the liturgy are not to be taken or accepted by the collectors, agents or other exactors of the tenth as a pledge or pawn, nor are they to be distrained or seized in any manner whatsoever.

COD 345.

Decree [14]

[*On the religious dress and way of life*]

That nothing unbecoming, that no tares should find their way into the field of the Lord, namely into the Order of black monks, and there grow side by side with the good seed, but rather that 'flowers of worth and esteem' may produce fruit in abundance, that is, in a desire to forbid any notable excess in dress that is over-lavish or at table in food or drink, or in jousting and feasting, we decree the following:

(1) The upper garment next to the habit may be of black, brown or white colour, according to the custom of the locality in which they reside.   The quality of the material must be in keeping with monastic moderation.   Nothing expensive and fine must be used, but what is practical. . . .

(3) Hunting and fowling as well as keeping either personally or in another's charge hunting dogs and birds for such purposes, are forbidden, nor may they permit their relatives staying in the monastery to keep such dogs and birds, unless the monastery possesses a forest or an animal reserve or has the right to hunt on property belonging to others, in which case they are permitted to keep dogs and birds, provided they do not keep them in the monastery or in the houses in which they live or within the cloister, and the monks themselves do not personally take part in the hunt. . . .

(5) Some monks, so we understand, having grown weary of the sweet yoke of regular observance, have left their monasteries on the pretence that they could not safely remain there.   Giving this or some similar reason they seek the greater freedom of the secular courts, where, unless their plea for money and aid is heeded by their superiors, they conspire against them, betray them, cause them to be captured and imprisoned and their monasteries to be burned, and they sometimes presume with the help of the princes to seize the whole or part of the possessions of the monasteries. . . .

(6) Following in the footsteps of our predecessors, we strictly forbid individual monks from living alone in priories and places of which they have charge. If the revenues of such priories and the like are not sufficient to maintain two of them then, unless the abbots provide for their needs, let the local ordinaries in agreement with the abbots join such priories to others in the district belonging to the monasteries, or to the monasteries themselves, or merge several such places in one, whichever way is more convenient and practical. The monks of these places that have been united to their priories are to be recalled to their monasteries, and, for the maintenance of the clergy who are to serve the united priories, due provision is to be made from the revenues of such places. . . .

COD 346–9; Schroeder 425–8 [II c.12].
Cf Nicaea II 16; Lateran IV 12.

DECREE [17]

[On hospitals]

It sometimes happens that the rectors of pilgrim-houses, leper-houses and alms-houses or hospices neglect the care of these institutions and make no effort to recover their rights, goods and property from the hands of those who have occupied and usurped them. On the contrary, they let them become a complete loss and the houses and buildings go to ruin. Moreover, they forget that these places were founded and endowed by the generosity of the faithful in order that the poor and those afflicted with leprosy might find a home therein and be supported by the revenues. This they unfeelingly refuse to carry out. Instead they turn the revenues to their own uses, even though things that have been given by the faithful for a certain purpose ought to be applied to that purpose and to no other, except with the authority of the Apostolic See. Since we detest such negligence and abuse, we hereby decree, with the approval of the holy council, that those whose duty it is by right or by law, by legitimate custom or by privilege of the Holy See should strive to reform those places in the matters aforesaid, should recover what has been usurped, lost and alienated, and compel the rectors to receive the poor and maintain them to the extent that the revenues of those institutions will permit. Should they prove negligent in this matter, we enjoin the ordinaries of the localities that, even though the aforesaid institutions enjoy the privilege of exemption, they carry out personally or through others each and all of the aforesaid instructions and compel the rectors of those not exempt, by their own authority, of those exempt or otherwise privileged, by the authority of the Apostolic See, to observe the foregoing directions; those acting in contravention, whatever be their status or condition, and their abettors, shall be restrained by ecclesiastical censure and other legal means. In all other respects, exemptions and privileges are to stand.

That the foregoing instructions may be the more promptly observed, none of these institutions shall in the future be handed over to the secular clergy as a benefice, even though this has been the custom in the past (which we fully condemn), unless it is provided otherwise in the documents relating to their foundation or unless the office of rector is filled by election. Instead their administration shall be entrusted to prudent, competent and reputable men, whose knowledge, willingness and competence will assure a just management and protection of these institutions, their possessions and rights on behalf of the unfortunate individuals concerned and who are not likely to divert their revenues into other channels. All of these things we make a matter of conscience on the part of those to whom the appointment of administrators of such institutions belongs. Those to whom the administration or management is entrusted shall be bound by oath that they will take proper care of the institutions, make an inventory of their properties, and give an account each year of their administration to the ordinaries or to those to whom the institutions are subject or to their representatives. Any action in contravention of these instructions we declare null and void.

The foregoing instructions we do not wish to be applied to the hospitals of military orders and religious. However, we command their rectors in virtue of holy obedience that they in them exercise due hospitality and provide for the poor in accordance with the rules and ancient observance of their Orders. To carry out this provision they shall be compelled by severe disciplinary measures by their superiors, statutes and customs to the contrary notwithstanding.

Moreover, if there are hospitals having from ancient time an altar or altars and a cemetery, and priests celebrating and administering to the poor the sacraments of the Church, or if the parish rectors have been accustomed to exercise these ministries therein, it is our intention that this ancient custom be continued.

COD 350–2; Schroeder 391–3 (c.7).
See above, p. 79.

DECREE [18]

[On patronage; the income of priests]

In order that the constitution* be observed which forbids anyone (even in the presentation of exempt churches) to be admitted to some church, custom to the contrary notwithstanding, unless a share of the revenues of that church has been assigned to him in the presence of the ordinary, by which he may be able to meet his obligations to the ordinary and also have a suitable means of livelihood for himself, we, with the approval of the holy council, take occasion to explain and enlarge on it. Ordinaries are strictly forbidden to accept anyone presented by any ecclesiastical person having the right of presentation, unless within a definite and convenient period of time, to be specified by the ordinaries, the presentors in their presence have assigned to the one presented a suitable portion of the revenues of the church. If within the time specified the presentors fail to assign such a portion, then in order that their failure may not prove injurious to the individual presented, we decree that the ordinaries ought (unless another canonical obstacle stands in the way) to accept those presented, and the authority of assigning such a portion shall devolve upon them to the detriment of the presentors. We command the ordinaries, moreover, that in assigning this portion they exercise due moderation and not be knowingly influenced by personal likes and dislikes, or otherwise. In the churches of priories or in the churches of other places, regular as well as secular, in which religious or others, to whom the revenues of such places belong, have been accustomed to fulfil the aforesaid obligations, the above instructions do not apply, but all the obligations that might encumber the priests or vicars of those churches, if the said assignment had been made, the aforesaid religious or others shall be bound to bear fully, to treat in a proper fashion the priests or vicars, and to supply them with sufficient and suitable means of support. To ensure full observance of all these things, especially of what has been said with regard to the assignment of a suitable portion by the ordinaries, we wish that the aforesaid religious and all others

* VI 3.4.1.

be compelled by the ordinaries by ecclesiastical censure, exemptions or privileges or statutes notwithstanding.

COD 352; Schroeder 393-4 (c.8).
Cf Lateran I 19.
See above, p. 34.

DECREE [19]

[*Religious must pay their dues*]
Since it is only natural that those who enjoy advantages should also bear the burdens connected with them, we decree that religious who have under any title obtained churches and convents should strive to pay promptly to the papal legates the procurations due to them from these churches and convents, and also fulfil their duties towards the bishops in matters that pertain to their rights, for all these obligations rested upon the churches and convents before the religious received them, and by passing into their hands the obligations were not cancelled, but naturally passed with them, unless the religious can by Apostolic privilege, exemption or other legitimate reason excuse themselves. Such privileges and exemptions, however, we do not wish to be extended to future acquisition of churches and convents.

COD 352-3; Schroeder 429 (II c.13).
Cf Lateran III 4.

DECREE [21]

[*Excommunication and interdict of those who tax ecclesiastical persons and goods in transit*]
By the present constitution we decree that the local ordinaries, when the matter becomes known to them, publish or have published by their subjects the sentences of excommunication and interdict lawfully incurred by those who, either on their own initiative or at the behest of another, demand or extort from churches or other ecclesiastical persons while on a journey a tax or impost on goods that they carry with them or have carried by others, goods that are their own and will not be made the object of barter or sale. They do this to the danger of their own soul and to the disadvantage and loss of those from whom

such tax is demanded.   They [the ordinaries] shall continue to publish
such sentences of excommunication and interdict till restitution and
suitable satisfaction has been made.

COD 354; Schroeder 430 (II 14).
Cf Lateran III 19.
See above, p. 86.

DECREE [29]

[*On usury*]
Reliable sources inform us that certain communities in violation of
the law, both human and divine, approve the practice of usury.   By
their statutes confirmed by oath they not only permit the exaction and
payment of usury, but deliberately compel debtors to pay it.   They
also try by heavy statutory penalties and various other means and
threats to prevent recovery by individuals who demand repayment of
excessive interest.   For our part, we want to put an end to these
abuses and so we decree, with the approval of the council, that all civil
officials of these communities, that is, magistrates, rulers, consuls,
judges, lawyers and other similar officials, who in future make, write,
or draw up statutes of this kind or knowingly decide that usury may
be paid or in case of it having been paid may not be freely and fully
restored when its return is demanded, incur the sentence of excommunication.   They shall incur the same sentence if they do not within
three months remove such statutes from the books of those communities (if they have the power to do so), of if they presume in any way
to observe the said statutes or customs to the same effect.   Moreover,
since money-lenders frequently conclude loan-contracts in an occult
or fraudulent manner, which makes it difficult to convict them on a
charge of usury, we decree that they should be forced by ecclesiastical
censure to produce their books on such occasions.

Finally, if anyone falls into the error of believing and affirming that
it is not a sin to practise usury, we decree that he be punished as a
heretic, and we strictly command the ordinaries of the localities and
the inquisitors to proceed against those suspected of such errors in the
same way as they would proceed against those accused publicly or
suspected of heresy.

COD 360–1; Schroeder 401 (c.15).
See above, pp. 48, 111.

DECREE [30]

[*On episcopal exactions from monasteries*]

Complaints frequently come to us from religious that many bishops and their superiors, as well as other ecclesiastical and religious prelates, in various ways unjustly disturb their peace. Some seize and imprison exempt religious in cases not legally permitted. Others by threats of severe penalties hinder *laymen* from paying to religious the tithes and revenues due them; they even go so far as to forbid them to attend their masses. Those who work in their mills and cook their food, their vassals and domestics, in short all who in any way have dealings with them, they arbitrarily and without reasonable cause suspend, penalize with interdict and excommunication, and at times unlawfully confiscate their properties. Those who complain or with good reason have recourse to appeals against injustices, they sometimes seize or cause to be seized and cast into prison. There are prelates who, without legitimate reason, refuse to allow chaplains appointed by the religious superiors to celebrate in churches that rightfully and legally belong to the religious, or to administer the sacraments to the people of the parish. Others, without justification, suspend, excommunicate, seize and imprison exempt abbots, monks, lay brothers and even secular clerics who are in the service of the monastery, and place under interdict their churches and houses if they refuse obedience to them in those things in which they are under no obligation to obey. Moreover, in their demands for charitable aid from the exempt, and those subject to them, the prelates exceed all reasonable limits. Contrary to law they impose on them unusual and excessive exactions. They burden the parish churches in which they have right of patronage with new taxes and undue obligations. Just legal judgements or decisions made by the delegates of the Apostolic See or by the conservators in favour of the exempt monasteries are not allowed to be published, nor are the bishops allowed to withhold instructions to their subjects for their execution. They restrain public notaries from drawing up instruments, judges from doing justice, and attorneys from giving counsel and aid in legal matters of the religious. When superiors of exempt orders present their subjects for promotion to orders or benefices they [the bishops] refuse to admit them, unless in the document by which such presentation is made they pledge obedience to them. For vacant churches in which the monasteries have right of patronage, bishops reject competent persons properly presented and appoint persons who are incompetent and unworthy. Again, some churches with the cure of souls attached, which belong to the maintenance of the abbots and whose revenues are sometimes granted as a lease to secular clergy, are on the death of the latter conferred by the bishops on their own clerics, even though the churches despite the death of the clerics are not really vacant. Some bishops unjustly appropriate the rights of the religious, and so regulate matters in regard to revenues belonging to the churches that not enough remains for the livelihood of their rectors. At the order of prelates, armed bands, contrary to justice, destroy the mills and other properties of exempt religious, property they have held from time immemorial. They frequently send to the monasteries their relatives and nephews and sometimes also their animals together with the shepherds, with the demand for free maintenance. Frequently, also, prelates compel abbots and priors of monasteries to grant to their relatives and nephews monastic properties or possessions, either in perpetuity or for a limited period, concessions and payments which we wish to be considered *ipso jure* invalid. They sometimes compel the same abbots and priors to present them for vacant churches, in which they [the abbots and priors] have the right of presentation, and at times even to receive into the order, their friends, relatives or nephews. They also frequently permit and tacitly consent to the forcible seizing of movable and immovable properties of monasteries in their territory by soldiers, vassals and even their own temporal officials in cases not permitted by law, and they perpetrate various other injustices against ecclesiastical persons and the people of the monasteries. Sometimes, also, under pretext of privilege, which they claim to possess for a certain time, they collect from vacant benefices the revenues of the first year and thus unjustly deprive abbots, priors and others of revenues belonging to them. Not content with that, they unlawfully seize the horses, cattle, treasury and other properties of monasteries and vacant benefices, all of which should be reserved to the successors. Some sell for a specified time the incomes of their offices to soldiers and influential persons so that the exempt religious located in the neighbourhood may be more vigorously oppressed. Others destroy monasteries. There are even some who seize houses, hospitals and other movable and immovable properties of monasteries with no intention of restoring them. Moreover, many prelates without just cause prevent exempt religious from repairing their property. Others pass statutes that detract from the privileges of exempt religious. In general, many prelates inflict grave injuries and losses on religious, especially on those exempt and privileged, on their people and properties, and on their spiritual and temporal rights, and these things they do in violation of justice and of the privileges of the religious. . . .

Therefore, by the present decree we strictly command all prelates that they abstain absolutely, and also see to it that their subjects abstain, from giving further cause for complaints of the aforesaid nature . . .

COD 361–3; Schroeder 431–3 (II 15).
See above, pp. 46, 79.

DECREE [38]

[*On the interpretation of the Rule of the Franciscans*]
. . . The first of these points concerns the Rule which says: 'This is the Rule and Way of life of the Friars Minor, i.e. to observe the gospel of Our Lord Jesus Christ, by living in obedience, without property and in chastity', and later, 'After the year of probation they may be admitted to obedience, promising to observe that life and Rule always'; and again 'poverty and the holy gospel of Our Lord Jesus Christ we shall observe as we have faithfully sworn'. On this there was some question whether the brethren are bound by their Rule to all the precepts and counsels of the Gospel, or whether they are bound only to the three counsels, namely, to live in obedience, chastity and poverty, and to those things that are placed in the Rule as mandatory. On this matter we follow the example of our predecessors and declare that, since a vow implies something definite and limited, it follows that he who by vow subscribes to a Rule cannot be said to be bound by virtue of the vow to those evangelical counsels that are not contained in the Rule. That this was the intention of St Francis is evident from the fact that he embodied in the Rule some evangelical counsels and excluded others. Had he intended by the phrase 'This is the Rule and life' of the Friars Minor to bind them to all evangelical counsels, his inclusion in the Rule of some and his exclusion of others would be meaningless. But, since the nature of the restriction demands that everything foreign to it be excluded and everything related

to it be included, we declare explicitly that the brethren by their acceptance of the Rule are bound not only to those three vows simply and absolutely accepted, but they are also bound to fulfil all those things that are related to or implied in these three vows as the Rule itself states. For, if they were bound only to the three vows, promising to observe the Rule precisely and simply by living in obedience, chastity and poverty, and not bound also to all things contained in the Rule and which in one way or another affects the vows, then the words, 'I promise always to observe the Rule' would be pronounced invalid and useless, for no obligation is formed. However, it need not be held that St Francis intended that the followers of his Rule should be bound equally to all the things contained in it — thus altering the three vows — without distinguishing between those things that constitute explicitly a mortal sin and those that do not, since he himself applies to some things the word 'precept' or its equivalent, while in the case of others he makes use of different expressions.

Likewise, since in those things that concern the salvation of the soul, the safer course is to be pursued in order to avoid grave remorse of conscience — we declare that though the brethren are not bound to the observance of all things contained in the Rule by way of counsel, as they are bound to the observance of precepts or to the equivalents of precepts, it is, nevertheless, to their benefit, in order to observe the purity and rigour of the Rule, to know that they are bound to the things indicated below as equivalent to precepts. Therefore, that these equivalents based on content or logical interpretation may be had in a brief form, we declare that what is said in the Rule about not having more tunics than one with a capuche and another without a capuche, about not wearing shoes, not riding on horses except in case of necessity, about wearing simple dress, about the obligation of fasting 'from the feast of All Saints until Christmas' and on the six feasts that clerics say the divine office according to the Ordinal of the Holy Roman Church, that superiors be solicitous about the necessities of the sick and attentive regarding the clothing of the brethren, about the attention that the brethren owe a sick member of the community, about the brethren not preaching in a diocese where they have been forbidden to do so by the bishop, about no one attempting to preach unless he has been examined, approved and appointed to this work by his superiors, about brethren who, knowing that they cannot observe

G

the Rule specifically, ought to have recourse to their superior; also, about what is said in the Rule regarding the form of habit for the novices and the professed members, and lastly what pertains to the manner of reception and profession; all these things the brethren are bound to observe as obligatory. Furthermore, this order has traditionally held and continues to hold that whenever the term 'they are held' appears in the Rule, it has the force of a precept and must be observed by the brethren as such.

Again, since many of the brethren have doubts whether they are permitted to receive temporal goods from those entering the order, if freely given, and whether they may without fault induce them to give such goods or any portion thereof to individuals and to convents, then, in case they should be asked to give advice in regard to such distribution, we, considering that St Francis established his Order in extreme poverty and wished that his followers should entertain no desire for the worldly goods of those entering the order, declare that in future the brethren may not by any means seek to obtain such goods for themselves, nor may they act as advisers in regard to their distribution.   But, since the Rule leaves those entering the Order free to dispose of their goods according as they are moved by God, it seems permissible for the brethren, considering their necessities, to receive something of such goods if those entering wish to give it as an offering.

Although we have declared that the provisions of the Rule regarding the number of habits and the quality of material to be used for them and other garments is equivalent to a precept, yet this matter must, in a large measure, be left to the judgement of superiors and must also be dictated by the custom of each country or locality, since it is impossible to make a rule that would be applicable to every country. To the judgement of superiors we leave also the matter as to the circumstances under which the brethren may wear shoes.   Outside of the fasts from the feast of All Saints to the Nativity of Our Lord and Quadragesima the brethren are not bound to any fasts except those instituted by the Church.   For it is not likely that the author of the Rule or he who approved it intended to absolve them from observing those fasts to which other Christians are bound by the common law of the Church.   In reference to the receipt of money either personally or through a third person the brethren must be cautious and not appeal to persons for money for other reasons and by other procedures than those indicated by our predecessor, lest they become

H

transgressors of the precept and the Rule.   Where a thing is not expressly granted, it is in a general way prohibited, and so it is understood to be denied.   Therefore, any acquisition of money and the
taking of money offerings in the church or elsewhere, as well as
receptacles designed for money offerings, and any other method for
obtaining money not granted by our predecessor are absolutely forbidden.   Recourse or appeal to special friends is permitted by the
Rule in two cases only, namely, to supply the needs of the infirm and
the needs of the brethren in regard to clothing, which, as our predecessor has pointed out, may be reasonably extended to other needs
at times when alms are few or their giving should cease altogether,
but in no other cases are they permitted to appeal to such friends either
directly or through intermediaries.   Lastly, since blessed Francis himself desired that the followers of his Rule be totally divested of all
desire of and attachment to worldly things and that they be especially
detached from money and completely cut off from the use of it, it is
necessary that they be careful, that while for the above reasons they
may make appeals for money to meet their urgent needs, they should
in all things so conduct themselves as one possessing nothing.   Therefore, to command when and in what manner money is to be spent, to
demand an account of expenditures, to deposit it or cause it to be de-
posited in any manner, to place money in a chest and to carry its key,
these and similar acts we wish the brethren to know are illicit.   Thus,
when our blessed founder, giving expression to the Rule to the form
of the aforesaid poverty, said: 'the brethren shall make nothing their
own, neither house nor land nor anything else, but as pilgrims and
strangers wandering on earth and serving the Lord in poverty and
humility, shall support themselves entirely by alms', this has been
explained by our predecessors as applying both to the individual religious and to the Order as a whole; neither may possess anything;
whatever is given to them in any way or form belongs not to them,
but to the Roman Church, and they have only the use of such things.

     To our examination have also been directed things that are said to
be done in the Order and which are apparently at complete variance
with the vow of poverty and the purity of the Order (though the
brethren as a body and especially the superiors maintain that such
things, at least many of them, do not take place).   The following,
especially, call for a remedy: the brethren not only permit, but
actually cause, themselves to be made heirs; they sometimes receive

annual revenues in such large amounts that convents receiving them can subsist on them alone; when affairs of theirs, even in temporal matters, come up in court they assist the lawyers and agents and are present personally to encourage them; they act as executors of wills and interfere in the disposition and restitution to be made in matters of usury; they have extensive market-gardens and vineyards from which they receive plenty of vegetables and wine for the market; in times of harvest or vintage they gather such an abundance of grain and wine by begging and buying, and storing them away in granaries and cellars, that they can live for the remainder of the year without asking for alms; their churches and other buildings betray such lavish expenditures that they appear more like the dwellings of the rich than those of poor friars; church vestments in many places are of such quantity and quality that in these matters they outdo the great cathedrals. Even horses and weapons offered them as funeral trappings are accepted. Against this, however, the brethren as a body and especially the superiors maintain that such things, at least most of them, do not take place, and that, if they do, they are severely punished, indeed there are numerous ancient statutes that strictly prohibit such things . . . to this we reply as follows.

Since it is a truth of everyday life that what is outwardly done is but the expression of an interior disposition, it is necessary that the brethren who have freely and by vow stripped themselves of all temporal things, abstain from everything that is or appears to be contrary to that vow. Inheritance implies ownership, not just use, consequently in consideration of this vow they are incapable of inheritance, which of its very nature extends itself to money and to movables and immovables. Similarly, it is repugnant to the vow of poverty to receive the income of such inheritance or even a part of it, for it can be presumed that it was fraudulently done. The same applies to annual revenues from whatever source they come. Furthermore, since not only that which is known to be evil, but also everything that has the appearance of evil, must be avoided by the pure in heart, it is but natural that the brethren should abstain from acting as assistants to lawyers and agents in court when the matter considered reverts or may revert to their temporal interest, for in such cases people are led to believe that they are seeking something that is their own, which is not only derogatory to their vow but also a source of scandal to their neighbour. Since they are forbidden not only to receive and own money, but also the handling of it, and may not engage in court action for temporal affairs, they are forbidden also to act as executors of wills. However, their advice in such matters is not opposed to the statute, since in that case they exercise no jurisdiction. While it is lawful and consistent with reason that the brethren who devote themselves to prayer and study should have suitable gardens and fields for meditation, recreation and the cultivation of the necessary vegetables for themselves, it is, however, contrary to their Rule to dispose of such products for a monetary consideration. As has been explained by our predecessor, even if lands, vineyards and the like should be bequeathed to them to cultivate for their own use, they may not accept them, since their possession, considering the value of the produce, partakes of the nature of an income. Their holy founder wished that they, like the birds of the air, should have no granaries or cellars, but should rely on divine Providence for all things. Churches and other buildings must not exceed in number and size the requirements of the community and in future must be consistent with the vow of poverty. God, *who knows all secrets*, takes into account chiefly the intention, not the outward act, of those serving Him. He does not wish to be honoured with things that are out of harmony with the condition and state of His servants. Extravagance and excessive cost in the matter of ecclesiastical vessels and vestments partake of the nature of treasure and abundance, and are in the judgement of men manifestly inconsistent with the Rule and profession of the Friars Minor.

There has, moreover, sprung up among the brethren a troublesome question concerning the *usus pauper*, that is, whether by the profession of their Rule they are bound to the strict and simple use of things. There are some who maintain that because, as far as ownership goes they are bound by vow to an absolute non-proprietorship, so also in the matter of use are they bound to a rigid and austere use of things. Others, however, maintain that by their profession they are not bound to any *usus pauper* that is not expressed in the Rule, though by the nature of their state they are bound to moderate and proper use in the same way as, and more strictly than, the rest of Christians. Wishing to put an end to these conflicts, we declare that the Friars Minor are by the profession of their Rule in a special manner bound to strict use, that is, one of poverty, which is contained in the Rule and bound in that form of obligation in which the Rule expresses or contains such uses. But to say, as some are said to have done, that it is heresy to hold that the simple use is included or not included in the vow of evangelical poverty, we declare presumptuous and rash. . . .

COD 368-77; Schroeder 406-13.
Cf °Chalcedon 3.
See above, pp. 45, 46.

SIXTEENTH GENERAL COUNCIL:
CONSTANCE (1414-18)

SESSION XLIII

[6] *On tenths and other taxes*
We command and decree that the laws prohibiting the imposition of tenths and other taxes on churches and ecclesiastical persons by anyone inferior to the pope be strictly observed. Also, such taxes are not to be levied by us generally, and on the clergy as a whole, unless the needs of the universal Church should seriously require it, and then with the advice and consent of our brethren, the cardinals of the Holy Roman Church and of those prelates whose advice can conveniently be obtained. Nor shall we impose such taxes on the clergy of a particular country or province without first consulting the prelates of that country or province and obtaining the consent of the majority. In the latter case such taxes may only be collected by ecclesiastical persons with Apostolic authority.

COD 425; Schroeder 454.

SEVENTEENTH GENERAL COUNCIL:
BASEL, FERRARA, FLORENCE, ROME (1431-45)

SESSION XIX (7 September 1434)

[*Decree on Jews and converts*]
This holy and general council of Basel, lawfully convened under the protection of the Holy Spirit, representing the universal Church and following in the footsteps of our Saviour Jesus Christ, has long and earnestly desired that all should know the true gospel and, once they have known, that they should persevere in its teaching. In order,

therefore, that Jews and other unbelievers may be converted to the true faith, and that those who have been converted should remain unwavering in it, this council, determined to pass suitable legislation, has provided that all diocesans should annually appoint certain men learned in scripture to those places where Jews and other unbelievers dwell, that there they might preach and expound the truths of the Catholic faith, so that those unbelievers who hear the Word of God might then recognize the errors of their ways. Under penalty of prohibiting trade between themselves and Christians, as well as other suitable means, they may compel unbelievers of both sexes, who have reached the age of reason, to listen to this preaching. However, let the diocesans and the preachers so conduct themselves with charity that they win them for Christ not only by expounding the truth, but by other charitable works as well. We decree further that Christians of whatever rank or status who in any way prevent or hinder Jews from coming to this preaching shall incur the mark of one who supports unbelief. And in order that this preaching may be the more fruitful, the more skilled the preachers are in the language of their audience, we order that the constitution formerly issued at the council of Vienne* should be fully applied, namely, that two teachers of Hebrew, Arabic, Greek and Chaldaic should be appointed in the schools. Moreover, in order that this should be more effectively observed, we desire that rectors of the colleges should, among the things they promise to fulfil when assuming their office, also swear to observe this constitution. Again let the provincial councils, where studies of this kind are established, see to it that those who are going to teach these languages should receive adequate remuneration.

Finally, we renew the sacred canons and command diocesans as well as secular powers that they prohibit in every way possible Jews and other unbelievers from having Christians, men or women, as servants or nursemaids, and also to see to it that Christians do not join with them in their feasts, weddings, banquets and public baths, or even hold excessive conversation, nor that they should employ them as doctors, marriage brokers or agents in other public affairs, nor put them in charge of public offices, nor admit them to academic posts, nor lease them estates or other church properties. They are also prohibited from buying, under penalty of forfeiture, church books, chalices, crucifixes and other ornaments, nor shall they accept pledges,

* C. 24.

again under penalty of loss of the sum loaned.   They are to be forced under threat of heavy penalties to take on a form of dress by which they can be clearly distinguished from Christians.   Moreover, in order to avoid excessive social intercourse, they must be made to dwell separate from Christians in their cities and towns, in places as far distant from the churches as possible.   Nor may they on Sundays and other solemn feast days open their shops or work in public.

COD 459–60.
Cf Lateran IV 68.
See above, p. 84.

[*On those who wish to be converted to the faith*]
If any of them wish to be converted to the Catholic faith, then their goods, personal as well as real property, may remain with them intact and unharmed.   But if they have acquired such goods through usury or illicit enterprise, and the individuals are known to whom rightful restitution must be made, then such restitution must be made in full, for otherwise the sin is not forgiven.   But if the individuals are not known, then because such goods are to be put by the Church to pious uses, this holy synod, exercising authority over the universal Church, has granted as a favour that they may remain with the person who has become baptized (in a sense, this being a pious use), and it prohibits, under penalty of divine anathema, both ecclesiastical and secular persons, from inflicting, or allowing to be inflicted under any guise whatever, any harm on these persons, rather let them judge that they have gained a great deal in saving such men for Christ.   And since, as it is written, he 'who has an abundance of this world, but sees his brother in need and does not open his heart to him, how shall the charity of God remain in him' [1 John 3:17], if they at the time of conversion are in need or want, then 'through the bowels of God's mercy' [Luke 1:78], this holy council exhorts ecclesiastics as well as seculars to extend a helping hand to the converts.   Let the diocesans exhort them to help not only Christians, but also future converts, as far as the resources of the churches allow, which are set aside for the purpose of helping the poor, and let them defend these converts from hostile and malicious attacks on their integrity and loyalty.   And since through the grace of baptism they are made 'citizens of the saints and servants of God'

[1 Eph. 2:19], and since it is better to be born again in the spirit than in the flesh, we order by this edict that they enjoy all privileges, liberties and immunities of the states and places where they were born again in holy baptism such as others of native origin enjoy. Let the priests who baptize them and those who act as their sponsors both before and after baptism carefully instruct them in the articles of faith and of the new law and rites of the Catholic Church. And let them and the diocesans see to it that they do not, at least for some time, come into contact with Jews and other unbelievers, lest, like persons newly cured of some ailment, they should on the slightest contact with the disease be again infected. And since, as experience shows, common intercourse among converts tends to weaken their faith, this holy synod exhorts the ordinaries to see to it that, to the extent they shall see necessary for an increase of faith, the neophytes marry with Christians baptized in their early years. This will bring about the increase in faith. Under grave penalties neophytes are prohibited from burying their dead in the Jewish manner or observing the Sabbath and other solemn feasts and ancient rites. Rather let them come to the churches and listen to our preaching as do other Catholics, and conform themselves to Christian practices in every way. Those who despise these instructions are to be charged with the guilt of heresy to the diocesans or inquisitors by the priests in whatsoever parish they are situated or through others whose duty it is either by lay or ancient custom to enquire into such things, or by any men whatsoever. Moreover, let the secular arm be invoked, if necessary, in order that they should be punished by them and that this may be an example for others. On all these matters let there be a serious enquiry in provincial councils and synods; moreover, bishops and priests who are negligent in these matters are to be suitably punished, just as much as the neophytes and unbelievers. If any person, whatever his status or rank, defends or maintains that neophytes should not be compelled to observe Christian rites, or defends any of the propositions cited above, then he incurs the penalties directed against supporters of heretics. Neophytes, indeed, if they neglect to correct themselves after canonical admonition, and are known to have apostatized and returned to their vomit, let proceedings be instituted against them as against confirmed heretics according to the sacred canons. If any indults or privileges have been granted or shall be granted to the Jews or unbelievers by ecclesiastics or seculars of whatever status or rank, even papal or imperial, such that they inflict harm on the Catholic faith, the Christian name, or any such, then this holy council declares them null and void, all decrees as well as Apostolic and synodal constitutions on the above matters to remain in force.   And in order that the memory of this blessed constitution may be kept and that no one can claim ignorance as an excuse, this holy synod orders that it be promulgated at least once a year at divine service throughout all the cathedrals and collegiate churches and other consecrated places where the faithful usually congregate.

COD 460–1.
Cf Lateran I 10, IV 68; Lateran II 13 and IV 67 for usury.
See above, p. 38.

SESSION XXI (9 June 1435)

[*On Annates*]
In the name of the Holy Spirit this council decrees that, in future, whether in the Roman Curia or elsewhere, for the confirmation of elections, the granting of postulations, provisions, collations, presentations, even lay ones, various types of election and institutions, installations and investitures, whether it be a question of episcopal or metropolitan churches, of monasteries, dignitaries, benefices, or any ecclesiastical office whatsoever, also for the conferring of holy orders, as well as the blessing and grant of the pallium, no payment shall be demanded either before or after such act on the ground that it is payment for sealing the appropriate bull, of common annates, for various miscellaneous services, such as first-fruits and taxes, or on pretext of some title or other, or the grant of some custom, privilege or statute, in short, under no pretext whatever, whether directly or indirectly, shall payment be made.   Only the writers in the chancery office, the abbreviators and registrars of the letters and various minutes shall receive suitable remuneration for their work. . . .

COD 464–5; Schroeder 475–6.
See above, p. 94.

H 2

EIGHTEENTH GENERAL COUNCIL:
LATERAN V (1512–17)

SESSION IX (5 May 1514)

[Bull for Reform of the Curia]

[5] We decree, furthermore, that in future parish churches, major dignities and other ecclesiastical benefices whose annual revenues do not exceed the sum of 200 ducats according to general estimation, as well as hospitals, leper institutions, pilgrim houses and the like, which have been established for the poor, whatever their value, may no longer be given *in commendam* to the cardinals of the Roman Church or conferred under any title whatsoever on anybody, unless they have become vacant through the death of their staff, in which case they may be given *in commendam* to the cardinals, who, however, are bound to hand them over within six months to persons capable and agreeable to them, without prejudice to their right of reversion to these benefices. . . .

[7] Dispensations for more than two incompatible benefices may not be granted, except for serious and urgent reasons to those only who are qualified according to the form of common law.   For those persons, whatever their rank, who hold more than four parish churches or their perpetual vicariates and the larger, principal dignities, we fix henceforth a limit of two years, within which they must resign all but four of the benefices into the hands of the ordinary, who shall confer them on others, notwithstanding any reservation, even a general one, or one resulting from the status of the persons resigning. . . .

COD 590–3; Schroeder 488–91.
See above, p. 79.

On cardinals

Since the cardinals of the Holy Roman Church are the highest dignitaries after the Pope, it is right and proper that they should be, to all, examples of purity of life and of the splendour of virtue.   Therefore, we not only exhort and admonish them, but also ordain and decree that they live in accordance with the teaching of the Apostle, *soberly*, *chastely*, and *piously*, abstaining not only from evil, but also from all semblance of evil, so that their light shines among men.   They are to honour God in all their works.

[1] They are to be vigilant, attentive to the divine offices and celebration of mass, have their chapels in suitable places, as they once did, abstain from luxury and display in their houses, servants, at table and in the furnishings, and have before their eyes priestly moderation, and treat in a friendly manner prelates and all others who come to the Roman curia. Moreover, let them pursue the causes of these persons freely and liberally, both with us and our successors.

[3] Since they assist the Roman pontiff, the common father of all the faithful, they may not be personal advocates or agents for individuals. We decree, moreover, that they show no partiality, do not become defenders or promoters for princes, communities or others against anyone, except in so far as justice and equity demand, and their dignity and state require; but, having divested themselves of all prejudice and self-interest, let them earnestly strive to end disputes and bring about peace among all. Let them with pious zeal promote the just undertakings of princes and of all others, but especially those of the poor and of the religious; and, as becomes their office, and so far as their resources will permit, let them aid the oppressed and those unjustly burdened. . . .

[5] For the increase of divine worship and for the salvation of his soul, each cardinal shall donate to his titular church either during his life or by will as much as is necessary for the suitable maintenance of one priest, or, in case the church should need repairs or other help, let him make his donation for this purpose, according as his conscience may dictate.

[6] Although relatives, especially if they are poor and well-deserving, are not to be neglected, but are rather to be cared for, nevertheless they may not be provided with a host of benefices or be so enriched by means of ecclesiastical revenues that others suffer loss through such generosity, which thus gives rise to scandal. We decree, therefore, that the goods of the churches are not to be spent thoughtlessly or squandered, but applied to good and pious purposes, for the sake of which abundant and wealthy revenues were fixed and declared by the Church Fathers. . . .

[8] In regard to the number of servants and horses, the cardinals should act cautiously and with foresight, lest having a greater number than their means, rank and office will permit, they can be accused of indulging in waste and extravagance; while, on the other hand, they will be considered greedy and niggardly if, having an abundance, they

furnish food to a very few. For the house of a cardinal should be a hospitable one, a harbour and shelter for learned and honest men, for impoverished nobles and persons of high repute and esteem. Let them, therefore, act prudently in this matter, having a knowledge of the character of their servants, lest their wickedness brings them a bad name and thus furnish occasion for gossip and calumny among the people.

[17] We decree also that the total funeral expenses of the cardinals must not exceed the sum of 1500 florins, and only for a just and proper reason may the executors spend more. The solemn obsequies and the lying in state take place on the first and ninth day; during the octave the customary masses may be celebrated. . . .

COD 593-7; Schroeder 491-5.

Reform of the Curia and other matters

. . . [7] Since the plenary disposition and administration of the revenues of cathedral and metropolitan churches, of monasteries and of all other ecclesiastical benefices belong solely to the Roman pontiff and to those who canonically hold them, and secular princes may not intrude themselves and interfere in matters belonging to the said churches, monasteries, and benefices, we decree that the incomes, revenues and returns of churches, monasteries, and benefices may not be sequestrated, seized or in any manner held, nor, if held under some fancied pretext, may the respective ecclesiastical administrators be hindered in their free disposition of them by secular princes, not even by the emperor or kings or their officials and judges, nor by any other persons whether public or private. What has been confiscated or seized by the command of the above must be restored freely and fully, without exception and delay, to the prelates to whom they rightfully and lawfully belong. If anything has been dissipated or squandered and cannot be recovered, those who are responsible for the confiscations and seizures must make full satisfaction to the prelates under penalty of excommunication or interdict. Those who act contrary to these provisions shall be punished with ecclesiastical censures, with the deprivation of the fiefs and privileges that they have received from the Church, and with the punitive measures prescribed by the canons, all of which we hereby renew.

[8] Since neither human nor divine law gives laymen any authority

over ecclesiastical persons, we renew the constitutions *Felicis* of Boniface VIII, our predecessor of happy memory, and *Si quis suadente* of Clement V, and also all other Apostolic decrees issued in defence of ecclesiastical liberty and against those who seek to destroy it; also the penalties contained in the bull *In Coena Domini* against the latter are to remain in force. The decisions of the Lateran as well as the earlier general councils forbade, under penalty of excommunication, the imposition of tenths and other tax levies, by kings, rulers, dukes, counts, barons, republics and other states on clerics, prelates and other ecclesiastical persons, or even their acceptance when freely given. These are now renewed. Those who give aid or advice, openly or secretly, in this matter, or in any manner aid transgressors, incur excommunication *latae sententiae*. Cities, communities and corporations are subject to interdict. Prelates submitting to such impositions or consenting to them without the express permission of the Roman pontiff incur *ipso facto* excommunication and deposition. . . .

COD 599–601; Schroeder 495–8.
See above, p. 85.

Session x (4 May 1515)

On reform of the montes pietatis

Leo etc. . . . Some time ago there was carried on among theologians and jurists, not without scandal to the people, a controversy, which, as we have learned, has recently been renewed, regarding the relief of the poor by loans to be made to them by the public authorities, a system of relief commonly known as *montes pietatis*, which have been established in many cities of Italy by the officials of the cities and other outstanding Christians for the purpose of relieving the needs of the poor by loans of this kind and thus protecting them against the avarice of usurers. This institution has been approved by devout men and has also been praised, endorsed and confirmed by several of our predecessors, the supreme pontiffs. In regard to the legality of the institution, the opinions of theologians and jurists were divided. Some maintained that those *montes* were illicit in which something beyond or in return for the money lent was demanded by the promoters from the poor to whom the loan was given and that these promoters could not escape the crime of usury or injustice, since, as St Luke testifies, Christ expressly forbade that we should hope for anything more than we gave in return for a loan [Luke 6:35]. For usury means nothing else than gain or profit drawn from the use of a thing that is by its nature sterile, a profit that is acquired without labour, cost or risk. The same theologians and jurists maintained further that those institutions militated against commutative and distributive justice, because the expenses for their maintenance were extorted solely from the poor to whom the loans were given. Moreover, they added, they were an incentive to delinquency, incited to theft, and promoted general laxity.

On the other hand, there were many theologians and jurists, in the Italian schools, who held the opposite opinion, and both in their writings and lectures supported such an excellent system, one that was so worthwhile to the rest of society, and which, in their view, was gratuitous and not a direct cause of the interest; the custody of the object pawned, however, and consequently the space, labour and personal responsibility involved were legitimate conditions or titles upon which a moderate interest could be demanded. One of the *rules of law* states that he who enjoys advantages ought also to carry responsibility, especially if Apostolic authority acquiesces. This opinion was approved by our predecessors, the Roman pontiffs Paul II, Sixtus IV, Innocent VIII, Alexander VI and Julius II, and was defended and preached to the people by saints and men held in high esteem for their sanctity.

Therefore, wishing to make suitable provisions in this matter and commending the exertions of both parties, one for its zeal for justice against the practice of usury, the other for its love of truth and devotion that the needs of the poor may be relieved, with the approval of the holy council we declare and define that the aforesaid *montes pietatis*, established by the civil authorities and thus far approved and confirmed by the Apostolic See, in which the loan is gratuitous, but for expenses and indemnity only a moderate rate of interest is received, are not be declared a species of evil or an incentive to sin, nor are they in any manner or form to be condemned as usurious, rather they are meritorious and ought to be approved, and their benefits and spiritual utility as well as the indulgences granted by the Apostolic See in connection with them ought to be preached to the people. Other *montes* similar to the above may be established with the approval of the Apostolic See. It would indeed be much more perfect and holy if such *montes* were entirely free, that is, if those who establish them would provide some fund or revenues that would cover, if not all, at least half the salaries of officials and assistants, which would lighten the burden of the poor. For the establishment of such funds the faithful ought to be invited by means of greater indulgences. All religious and ecclesiastics, as well as secular persons, who in the future presume to preach or argue by word or in writing against the contents of this constitution incur the penalty of excommunication *latae sententiae*, privileges of any kind whatsoever notwithstanding, and this includes Apostolic constitutions and ordinances and similar contrary decrees.

COD 601-3; Schroeder 498-500.
See above, p. 115.

Abbreviations

AESC	*Annales: économies, sociétés, civilisations.*
AFH	*Archivum Franciscanum Historicum.*
AHES	*Annales d'histoire économique et sociale.*
AHR	*American Historical Review.*
Am. Eccl. R.	*American Ecclesiastical Review.*
Annuaire	*Annuaire de l'institut de philologie et d'histoire orientales et slaves.*
ASOC	*Analecta Sacri Ordinis Cisterciensis.*
BIHR	*Bulletin of the Institute of Historical Research.*
Camb. Econ. Hist.	*The Cambridge Economic History of Europe:* II *Trade and Industry in the Middle Ages,* ed. M. M. Postan and E. E. Rich (1952); III *Economic Organisation and Policies in the Middle Ages,* ed. M. M. Postan, E. E. Rich and E. Miller (1963).
CCM	*Cahiers de la civilisation médiévale.*
CH	*Church History.*
CHR	*Catholic Historical Review.*
CIC	*Codex Iuris Canonici.*
Cîteaux	*Cîteaux in de Nederlanden.*
COD	*Conciliorum Oecumenicorum Decreta* (Centro di documentazione istituto per le scienze religiose: St Louis, Mo., 1962).
Le Concile	*Le Concile et les conciles. Contribution à l'histoire de la vie conciliaire de l'Église,* ed. O. Rousseau (Chevetonge, 1960).
Congrès 1958	*Congrès de droit canonique médiéval, Louvain et Bruxelles 22–26 juillet 1958* (Bibliothèque de la Revue d'Histoire Ecclésiastique 33: Louvain, 1959).
CUA	Catholic University of America.
DDC	*Dictionnaire de droit canonique.*
Demant	V. A. Demant, *The Just Price* (1930).
DTC	*Dictionnaire de théologie catholique.*
EcHR²	*Economic History Review,* 2nd series.
EHR	*English Historical Review.*
EIC	*Ephemerides Iuris Canonici.*
gratian	*Decretum Magistri gratiani,* ed. E. Friedberg (Leipzig, 1879).
HJ	*Historisches Jahrbuch der Görres-Gesellschaft.*
IER	*Irish Ecclesiastical Record.*
Italian Renaissance Studies	*Italian Renaissance Studies,* ed. E. F. Jacob (1960).

JEcH	*Journal of Economic History.*
JEH	*Journal of Ecclesiastical History.*
JTS	*Journal of Theological Studies.*
JWH	*Journal of World History* = *Cahiers d'histoire mondiale.*
Mansi	J. D. Mansi, *Sacrorum Conciliorum nova et amplissima collectio.*
Med. Stud.	*Medieval Studies.*
MIÖGF	*Mitteilungen des Instituts für Österreichische Geschichtsforschung.*
MGH	*Monumenta Germaniae historica.*
Mundy–Loomis	*The Council of Constance*, trans. by Louise Ropes Loomis; edited and annotated by J. H. Mundy and K. M. Woody (New York, 1961).
PG	*Patrologiae Cursus Completus. Series Graeca*, ed. J. P. Migne, 162 vols (Paris, 1857–1912).
PL	*Patrologiae Cursus Completus. Series Latina*, ed. J. P. Migne, 221 vols (Paris, 1844–64).
Proc. 10th Intern. Cong.	*Proceedings of the Tenth International Congress of Historical Sciences* (Rome, 1956).
RDC	*Revue de droit canonique.*
Rev. bénéd.	*Revue bénédictine.*
RHE	*Revue d'histoire ecclésiastique.*
RHEF	*Revue d'histoire de l'Église de France.*
RHKUL	*Roczniki Humanistyczne Katol. Univ. Lubelskiego.*
RSCI	*Rivista di storia della chiesa in Italia.*
Schroeder	H. J. Schroeder, O.P., *Disciplinary Decrees of the General Councils* (St Louis, Mo., 1937).
SG	*Studi gregoriani.*
SJEcH	*The Tasks of Economic History: Supplemental Issue of the Journal of Economic History.*
Studi Sapori	*Studi in onore di Armando Sapori*, 2 vols (Istituto Editoriale Cisalpino: Milan, 1957).
Studies Gwynn	*Medieval Studies in Honour of A. Gwynn*, ed. J. A. Watt and others (Dublin, 1961).
Tawney	R. H. Tawney, *Religion and the Rise of Capitalism* (1926; Pelican, 1938).
TRG	*Tijdschrift voor Rechtsgeschiedenis* = *Revue d'histoire de droit.*
TRHS	*Transactions of the Royal Historical Society.*
Weber	Max Weber, *Die protestantische Ethik und der Geist des Kapitalismus* (1904–5; 2nd ed. 1920), translated into English by Talcott Parsons as *The Protestant Ethic and the Spirit of Capitalism* (1930).
ZKT	*Zeitschrift für Katholische Theologie.*

Bibliography

J. Absil, 'L'Absentéisme du clergé paroissial au diocèse de Liège au xve siècle et dans la première moitié du xvie', in *RHE* LVII (1962) 5–44.

H. L. Adelson, 'Early Medieval Trade Routes', in *AHR* LXV (1959–60) 271–87.
— *Medieval Commerce* (Princeton, N.J., 1962).

H. S. Alivisatos, 'Les Conciles œcuméniques v^e, vi^e, viie et viiie', in *Le Concile*, 111–23.

P. A. Amargier, 'Benoît d'Alignan, évêque de Marseille (1229–1268). Le contexte et l'esprit d'une théologie', in *Le Moyen Age*, LXXII (1966) 443–62.

H. Ammann, 'Die Anfänge des Aktivhandels und der Tucheinfuhr aus Nordwesteuropa nach dem Mittelmeergebiet', in *Studi Sapori*, I 273–310.

R. J. Aubenas, 'Quelques Réflexions sur le problème de la pénétration du droit romain dans le Midi de la France au moyen âge', in *Annales du Midi*, LXXVI (1964) 371–7.

H. Aubin, 'Der Aufbau des Abendlands im Mittelalter', in *Historische Zeitschrift*, CLXXXVII (1959) 497–520.

E. Bach, 'Études genoises: Le Minutier de Lanfranco', in *Studi Sapori*, I 373–89.

J. J. Bagley and P. B. Rowley, *A Documentary History of England*: 1 (*1066–1540*) (1966).

J. W. Baldwin, 'The Medieval Merchant before the Bar of Canon Law', in *Papers of the Michigan Academy of Science, Arts and Letters*, XLIV (1959) 287–99.
— *The Medieval Theories of the Just Price: Romanists, Canonists and Theologians in the Twelfth and Thirteenth Centuries* (Transactions Amer. Philos. Soc. NS XLIX no. 4: Philadelphia, 1959).

J. Balon, *La Structure et la gestion du domaine de l'Église au moyen âge dans l'Europe des Francs*, 2 vols: 1 *Ius Medii Aevi* (Namur, 1959).

D. Barath, 'The Just Price and the Costs of Production according to St Thomas Aquinas', in *New Scholasticism*, XXXIV (1960) 413–30.

M. W. Barley, 'Cistercian Land Clearances in Nottinghamshire: Three Deserted Villages and their Moated Ancestor', in *Nottingham Medieval Studies*, I (1957) 75–89.

J. Barry, 'The Appointment of Coarb and Erenagh', in *IER* XCIII (1960) 361–5.

E. Bartell, 'Value, Price and St Thomas', in *Thomist*, XXV (1962) 325–81.

T. Barutta, S.D.B., 'Los concilios ecuménicos I: síntesis teológico-histórico-canónica', in *Didascalia*, XIII (1959) 492–5.

C. C. Bayley (ed.), *War and Society in Renaissance Florence: the 'De Militia' of Leonardo Bruni* (Toronto, 1961).

J. M. W. Bean, 'Plague, Population and Economic Decline in England in the Later Middle Ages', in *EcHR*² xv (1963) 423–37.

M. B. Becker, 'Three Cases concerning the Restitution of Usury in Florence', in *JEcH* xvii (1957) 445–50.

— 'Florentine Politics and the Diffusion of Heresy in the Trecento. A Socio-economic Enquiry', in *Speculum*, xxxiv (1959) 60–75.

— 'Some Economic Implications of the Conflict between Church and State in "Trecento" Florence', in *Med. Stud.* xxi (1959) 1–16.

— 'La esecuzione della legislatura contro le pratiche monopolistiche delle arti fiorentine alla metà del secolo quattordicesimo', in *Archivio storico italiano*, cxvii (1959) 8–28.

— 'Church and State in Florence on the Eve of the Renaissance (1343–1382)', in *Speculum*, xxxvii (1962) 509–27.

E. E. Best, 'Max Weber and the Christian Criticism of Life', in *Theology Today*, xvi (1959) 203–14.

R. R. Betts, 'The Social Revolution in Bohemia and Moravia in the Later Middle Ages', in *Past and Present*, ii (1952) 24–31.

H. Beumann, 'Kreuzzugsgedanke und Ostpolitik im hohen Mittelalter', in *HJ* lxxii (1953) 112–32.

L. Beutin, 'Italien und Köln', in *Studi Sapori*, i 29–46.

M. Bévenot, 'The Inquisition and its Antecedents', I & II, in *Heythrop Journal*, vii (1966) 257–68, 381–93.

Lord Beveridge, *Prices and Wages in England from the Twelfth to the Nineteenth Century:* i, *Price Tables: Mercantile Era* (1939).

— 'Westminister Wages in the Manorial Era', in *EcHR*² viii (1955) 18–35.

A. Blanchet, 'La Monnaie et l'Église', in *Académie des Inscriptions et Belles-Lettres. Comptes-Rendus des Séances de l'Année 1950*, 18–26.

B. Blumenkranz, 'Deux Compilations canoniques de Florus de Lyon et l'action antijuive d'Agobard', in *Revue historique de droit français et étranger*, 4ᵉ série, xxxiii (1955) 227–54, 560–82.

F. Bogdan, 'Les Problèmes de l'exemption des cisterciens en Pologne au moyen âge', in *RHKUL* viii (1960) 123–72.

J. Boussard, 'La Vie en Anjou aux xiᵉ et xiiᵉ siècles', in *Le Moyen Age*, lvi (1950) 29–68.

— 'Les Institutions financières de l'Angleterre au xiiᵉ siècle', in *CCM* i (1958) 475–94.

R. H. Bowers, 'A Middle English Mnemonic Poem on Usury', in *Med. Stud.* xvii (1955) 226–32.

W. M. Bowsky, 'The Impact of the Black Death upon Sienese Government and Society', in *Speculum*, xxxix (1964) 1–34.

Catherine E. Boyd, *Tithes and Parishes in Medieval Italy* (Ithaca, 1952).

M. N. Boyer, 'Travel Allowances in XIV-Century France', in *JEcH* xxiii (1963) 71–85.

J. F. L. Bray, *Financial Justice* (Aquinas Papers 22: Blackfriars, 1954).

A. R. Bridbury, *England and The Salt Trade in the Later Middle Ages* (1955).
— *Economic Growth: England in the Later Middle Ages* (1962).
M. Briek, O.F.M., 'De momento conciliorum pro iuris Ecclesiae formatione', in *Antonianum*, XXXVIII (1963) 50–86.
C. N. L. Brooke, 'Canons of English Church Councils in the Early Decretal Collections', in *Traditio*, XIII (1957) 471–80.
— *Europe in the Central Middle Ages 962–1154* (1964).
R. B. Brooke, *Early Franciscan Government* (1959).
E. F. Bruck, *Kirchenväter und soziales Erbrecht* (Berlin, 1956).
G. A. Brucker, *Florentine Politics and Society 1343–1378* (Princeton Studies in History 12: Princeton, N.J., 1962).
J. A. Brundage, 'A Twelfth-century Oxford Disputation concerning the Privileges of the Knights Hospitallers', in *Med. Stud.* XXIV (1962) 153–60.
— 'The Crusade of Richard I: Two Canonical *Quaestiones*', in *Speculum*, XXXVIII (1963) 443–52.
— 'Recent Crusade Historiography: Some Observations and Suggestions', in *CHR* XLIX (1964) 493–507.
A. M. Burg, 'Les "Droits paroissiaux" dans le diocèse de Strasbourg: avant et après le concile de Vienne', in *RDC* I (1951) 300–8.
R. I. Burns, 'The Organisation of a Mediaeval Cathedral Community: the Chapter of Valencia (1238–1280)', in *CH* XXXI (1962) 14–23.
— 'A Medieval Income Tax: the Tithe in the Thirteenth-century Kingdom of Valencia', in *Speculum*, XLI (1966) 439–52.
H. E. Butler (ed.), *Chronicle of Jocelin of Brakelond* (Nelson Medieval Texts 1: 1949).
H. J. Byrne, *Investment of Church Funds* (CUA Canon Law Studies 309: Washington, D.C., 1951).
Calendar of the Plea Rolls of the Exchequer of the Jews preserved in the Public Record Office: 1 Henry III A.D. 1218–1272, ed. J. M. Rigg (1905).
J. Calmette, *The Golden Age of Burgundy* (Eng. tr. 1962).
P. T. Camelot, 'Les Conciles œcuméniques des ive et ve siècles', in *Le Concile*, 45–73.
— 'Les Conciles œcuméniques dans l'antiquité', in *Lumière et vie*, VIII 45 (1959) 3–17.
Pier Giovanni Caron, 'Asile et hospitalité dans le droit de l'Église primitive', in *Revue internationale des droits de l'antiquité*, X (1963) 187–97.
E. Carpentier, 'Autour de la peste noire: famines et épidémies dans l'histoire du xive siècle', in *AESC* XVII (1962) 1062–92.
— *Une Ville devant la peste: Orvieto et la peste noire de 1348* (1962).
M. B. Carra De Vaux Saint-Cyr, O.P., 'Les Conciles œcuméniques du second millénaire de l'histoire de l'Église', in *Lumière et vie*, VIII 45 (1959) 18–38.
E. M. Carus-Wilson, *Medieval Merchant Venturers: Collected Studies* (1954).

E. M. Carus-Wilson and Olive Coleman, *England's Export Trade 1275–1547* (1963).

M. Castaing, 'Le Prêt à intérêt à Toulouse aux xiie et xiiie siècles', in *Bulletin philologique et historique* (1953 & 1954; publ. 1955) 273–8.

F. A. Cazel, Jr, 'The Tax of 1185 in Aid of the Holy Land', in *Speculum*, xxx (1955) 385–92.

L. Charvet, 'Aux origines de la prescription de cent ans' (Cod. iur. can. 1511 §1)', in *EIC* xix (1963) 152–66.

A. Chédeville, 'Les Restitutions d'églises en faveur de l'abbaye de Saint-Vincent-du-Mans', in *CCM* iii (1960) 209–17.

C. R. Cheney, *English Synodalia of the Thirteenth Century* (Oxford, 1941).

— *Selected Letters of Pope Innocent III concerning England* (1953).

— *From Becket to Langton* (Manchester, 1956).

— 'The So-called Statutes of John Pecham and Robert Winchelsey for the Province of Canterbury', in *JEH* xii (1961) 14–34.

— 'A Letter of Pope Innocent III and the Lateran Decree on Cistercian Tithe-paying', in *Cîteaux Commentarii Cistercienses*, fasc. 2 (1962) 146–51.

M. D. Chenu, *La Théologie au douzième siècle* (Études de Philosophie Médiévale 45: 1957).

A. C. Chibnall, *Sherington: Fiefs and Fields of a Buckinghamshire Village* (Cambridge, 1965).

C. M. Cipolla, 'Currency Depreciation in Medieval Europe', in *EcHR*² xv (1963) 413–22.

— 'Per la storia delle terre della "Bassa" Lombardia', in *Studi Sapori*, i 665–72.

— R. S. Lopez and H. A. Miskimin, 'Economic Depression of the Renaissance?' in *EcHR*² xvi (1964) 519–29.

A. J. Clark, *The Natural Law and Private Property in Early Glossators of the Decretum* (CUA Canon Law Studies: Licentiate, n.p. Washington, D.C., 1962).

C. Clark, 'Medieval Economics: Some Assumptions Re-examined', in *Tablet*, ccxiv (1960) 467–8.

— *The Conditions of Economic Progress* (1940; 3rd ed. 1957).

F. Clark, 'A New Appraisal of Late-Medieval Theology', in *Gregorianum*, xlvi (1965) 733–65.

J. F. Cleary, *Canonical Limitations on the Alienation of Church Property* (CUA Canon Law Studies 100: Washington, D.C., 1936).

A. Combes, 'Facteurs dissolvants et principe unificateur au concile de Constance', in *Divinitas*, v (1961) 299–310.

Y. Congar, 'La Primauté des quatre premiers conciles œcuméniques', in *Le Concile*, 75–109.

— 'Aspects ecclésiologiques de la querelle entre mendiants et séculiers dans la seconde moitié du xiiie siècle et le début du xive', in *Archives d'histoire doctrinale et littéraire du moyen âge*, xxviii (1961, appeared 1962) 35–151.

— *Power and Poverty in the Church* (1964).

G. Coniglio, 'L'usura a Lucca ed una bolla di Niccolò V del 1452', in *RSCI* VI (1952) 259-64.

G. Constable, 'The Second Crusade as seen by Contemporaries', in *Traditio*, IX (1953) 213-79.

— 'Cluniac Tithes and the Controversy between Gigny and Le Miroir', in *Rev. bénéd.* LXX (1960) 591-624.

— 'Nona et Decima: an Aspect of Carolingian Economy', in *Speculum*, XXXV (1960) 224-50.

— 'Resistance to Tithes in the Middle Ages', in *JEH* XIII (1962) 172-85.

— *Monastic Tithes from their Origin to the Twelfth Century* (Cambridge Studies in Medieval Life and Thought 10: 1964).

J. D. Conway, *Times of Decision* (Notre Dame, Indiana, 1962).

J. E. Coogan, 'Lea, Coulton and Anti-Catholicism', in *Am. Eccl. R.* CXXXV (1956) 171-82, 231-43.

E. Coornaert, 'Caractères et mouvement des foires internationales au moyen âge et au XVIe siècle', in *Studi Sapori*, I 355-71.

P. J. Corish, 'The Church and the Councils', in *IER* XCVIII (1962) 203-12.

N. Coulet, 'Le Monde bénédictin et la crise du XIVe siècle', in *AESC* XVII (1962) 1001-5. Review of A. D'Haenens book (q.v.).

H. E. J. Cowdrey, 'Archbishop Aribert II of Milan', in *History*, LI (1966) 1-15.

O. C. Cox, *The Foundations of Capitalism* (New York, 1959).

A. C. Crombie, *Augustine to Galileo: I Science in The Middle Ages: V-XIII Centuries; II Science in the Early Middle Ages and Early Modern Times: XIII to XVII Centuries* (first publ. 1952; 2nd ed. 1959, 1961).

C. M. D. Crowder, 'Le Concile de Constance et l'édition de von der Hardt', in *RHE* LVII (1962) 409-45.

H. Dallmayr, *Die Grossen vier Konzilien* (Munich, 1961).

W. M. Daly, 'Christian Fraternity, The Crusaders and the Security of Constantinople, 1097-1204; the Precarious Survival of an Ideal', in *Med. Stud.* XXII (1960) 43-91.

H. C. Darby, *The Medieval Fenland* (1940).

J. G. Davies, *Daily Life of the Early Church* (1952).

— *Social Life of Early Christians* (1954).

— *The Early Christian Church* (1965).

C. H. Dawson, *Medieval Essays* (1954).

J. F. Dede, 'Business Pursuits of Clerics and Religious: Further Considerations', in *Jurist*, XXIII (1963) 50-62.

A. D'Haenens, 'La Crise des abbayes bénédictines au bas moyen âge: Saint-Martin-de-Tournai de 1290 à 1350', in *Le Moyen Age*, LXV (1959) 75-95.

— *L'Abbaye Saint-Martin-de-Tournai de 1290 à 1350: origines, évolution et V. dénouement d'une crise* (Université de Louvain, Recueil de Travaux d'Histoire et de Philologie, 4e série, fasc. 23: Louvain, 1961).

A. Demant (ed.), *The Just Price* (1930).

— 'The Problem of the Just Price in the Modern World', in *The Just Price*, 111–30.

Bernard W. Dempsey, S.J., *Interest and Usury* (Washington, D.C., 1943).

Florence Edler De Roover, 'Restitution in Renaissance Florence', in *Studi Sapori*, II 773–89.

Raymond De Roover, 'Money, Banking, and Credit in Medieval Bruges', in *SJEcH²* (1942) 52–65.

— *Money, Banking and Credit in Medieval Bruges: Bankers, Lombards and Money Changers* (Medieval Academy of America: 1948).

— 'New Interpretations of the History of Banking', in *JWH* II (1954) 38–76.

— 'Cambium ad Venetias: Contribution to the History of Foreign Exchange', in *Studi Sapori*, I 629–48.

— 'Joseph A. Schumpeter and Scholastic Economics', in *Kylos*, X (1957) 115–46.

— 'The Concept of the Just Price: Theory and Economic Policy', in *JEcH* XVIII (1958) 418–34, to 438.

— 'La Doctrine scolastique en matière de monopole et son application à la politique économique des communes italiennes', in *Studi in onore di Amintore Fanfani*, I (Milan, 1962) 151–79.

— *The Rise and Decline of the Medici Bank 1397–1494* (Cambridge, Mass., 1963).

— 'Gli antecedenti del Banco Mediceo e l'azienda bancaria di messer Vieri di Cambio de' Medici', in *Archivio storico italiano*, CXXIII (1965) 3–13.

P. De Vooght, 'Le Conciliarisme aux conciles de Constance et de Bâle', in *Le Concile*, 143–81.

E. L. Dietrich, 'Das Judentum im Zeitalter der Kreuzzüge', in *Saeculum*, III (1952) 94–131.

Digesto religioso, V (1959) 34–5.

H. Dilcher, *Die Theorie der Leistungsstörungen bei Glossatoren, Kommentatoren und Kanonisten* (Frankfurter Wissenschaftliche Beiträge, Rechts- und Wirtschaftswissenschaftliche Reihe 21: Frankfurt, 1960).

T. F. Divine, *Interest: A Historical and Analytical Study in Economics and Modern Ethics* (Milwaukee, 1959). (Substantially author's doctoral thesis of 1938.)

R. Doehaerd, 'Méditerranée et économie occidentale pendant le haut moyen âge', in *JWH* I (1953) 571–93.

W. J. Doheny, *Church Property: Modes of Acquisition* (CUA Canon Law Studies 41: Washington, D.C., 1927).

R. A. Donkin, 'Localisation, situation économique et rôle parlementaire des abbés cisterciens anglais (1295–1341)', in *RHE* LII (1957) 832–41.

— 'The Disposal of Cistercian Wool in England and Wales during the Twelfth and Thirteenth Centuries: I', in *Cîteaux*, VIII (1957) 109–31.

— 'The Urban Property of the Cistercians in Mediaeval England', in *ASOC* XV (1959) 104–31.

R. A. Donkin, 'Settlement and Depopulation on Cistercian Estates during the Twelfth and Thirteenth Centuries, especially in Yorkshire', in *BIHR* XXXIII (1960) 141–65.

— 'The English Cistercians and Assarting *c*. 1128–*c*. 1350', in *ASOC* xx (1964) 49–75.

J. S. Donnelly, 'Changes in the Grange Economy of English and Welsh Cistercian Abbeys, 1300–1540', in *Traditio*, x (1954) 399–458.

J. T. Donovan, *The Clerical Obligations of Canons 138 and 140* (CUA Canon Law Studies 272: Washington, D.C., 1948).

D. L. Douie, *The Conflict between the Seculars and the Mendicants at the University of Paris in the Thirteenth Century* (Aquinas papers 23: Blackfriars, 1954).

D. F. Dowd, 'The Economic Expansion of Lombardy, 1300–1500: A Study in Political Stimuli to Economic Change', in *JEcH* xxi (1961) 139–60.

H. Dubled, 'Aspects de l'économie cistercienne en Alsace au xiie siècle', in *RHE* liv (1959) 765–82.

F. R. H. Du Boulay, 'The Quarrel between the Carmelite Friars and the Secular Clergy of London, 1464–1468', in *JEH* vi (1955) 156–74.

G. Duby, 'Le Budget de l'abbaye de Cluny entre 1080 et 1155', in *AESC* vii (1952) 155–71.

C. Du Cange, *Glossarium mediae et infimae latinitatis* (Niort, 1885).

C. Duggan, *Twelfth-century Decretal Collections* (1963).

P. J. Dunning, 'Irish Representatives and Irish Ecclesiastical Affairs at the Fourth Lateran Council', in *Studies Gwynn*, 90–113.

F. Dvornik, *The General Councils of the Church* (Faith and Fact Books 83: 1961).

K. Eder, 'Die zwanzig allgemeinen Konzilien in historischer Schau', in *Theologische Praktische Quartalschrift*, CIX (1961) 193–208.

R. D. Edwards, 'The Kings of England and Papal Provisions in Fifteenth-century Ireland', in *Studies Gwynn*, 265–80.

L. E. Elliott-Binns, *Medieval Cornwall* (1955).

R. W. Emery, 'The Second Council of Lyons and the Mendicant Orders', in *CHR* xxxix (1953–4) 257–71.

— *The Jews of Perpignan in the Thirteenth Century* (New York, 1959).

H. O. Evenett, 'The Last Stages of Medieval Monasticism in England', in *Studia monastica*, ii (1960) 387–419.

R. D. Face, 'The *Vectuarii* in the Overland Commerce between Champagne and Southern Europe', in *EcHR*² xii (1959) 239–46.

A. Fanfani, *Catholicism, Protestantism and Capitalism* (1938; New York, 1955).

A. E. Feaveryear, *The Pound Sterling: A History of English Money* (1931).

H. E. Feine, 'Kirchleihe und kirchliches Benefizium nach italienischen Rechtsquellen des frühen Mittelalters', in *HJ* lxxii (1953) 101–11.

W. K. Ferguson, *The Renaissance* (Berkshire Studies in European History: New York, 1940).

R. Fossier, 'Les Granges de Clairvaux et la règle cistercienne', in *Cîteaux*, vi (1955) 259–66.

K. Foster, O.P., 'A Note on St Thomas's Teaching on Charity', in *Downside Review*, LXXVII (1959) 271–6.

G. Fourquin, *Les Campagnes de la région parisienne à la fin du moyen âge* (Publications de la Faculté des Lettres et Sciences Humaines de Paris, Série 'Recherches' 10: 1964).

G. Fransen, *Le Dol dans la conclusion des actes juridiques* (Gembloux, 1946).

— 'L'Ecclésiologie des conciles médiévaux', in *Le Concile*, 125–41.

A. Frolow, *Recherches sur la déviation de la IVᵉ croisade vers Constantinople* (1955).

H. Fuhrmann, 'Das ökumenische Konzil und seine historischen Grundlagen', in *Geschichte im Wissenschaft und Unterricht*, XI (1961) 672–95.

G. Fussenegger, 'Relatio commissionis in concilio Viennensi institutae ad decretalem "Exivi de paradiso" praeparandam', in *AFH* I (1957) 145–77.

L. C. Gabel (ed.), *Memoirs of a Renaissance Pope: the Commentaries of Pius II*, trans. F. A. Gragg (1959).

A. L. Gabriel, 'The Practice of Charity at the University of Paris during the Middle Ages: Ave Maria College', in *Traditio*, V (1947) 335–9.

M. P. Gaffney, 'Social Security in the Middle Ages', in *Irish Monthly*, LXXVIII (1950) 206–13.

P. Antonio García García, 'El concilio IV de Letrán (1215) y sus comentarios', in *Bulletin, Traditio*, XIV (1958) 484–502.

— 'Los comentarios de los canonistas a las constituciones del concilio IV de Letrán (1215)', in *Congrès 1958*, 151–61.

P. Gasnault, 'La Perception dans le royaume de France du subside sollicité par Jean XXII "contra haereticos et rebelles partium Italiae"', in *Mélanges d'archéologie et d'histoire*, LXIX (1957) 273–319.

J. Gaudemet, *La Formation du droit séculier et du droit de l'Église aux ivᵉ et vᵉ siècles* (Institut de Droit Romain de l'Université de Paris 15: Sirey, 1957).

— 'Aspects de la législation conciliaire française au xiiiᵉ siècle', in *RDC* IX (1959) 319–40.

L. Génicot, 'Sur les témoignages d'accroissement de la population en occident du xiᵉ au xiiiᵉ siècle', in *JWH* I (1953) 446–62.

— 'Clercs et laïques au diocèse de Liège à la fin du moyen âge', in *TRG* XXIII (1955) 42–52.

R. C. Gerest, 'Concile et réforme de l'Église, de la fin du xiiiᵉ siècle au concile de Trente', in *Lumière et vie*, XI no. 59 (1962) 21–56.

A. Ghinato, *Monte di pietà e monti frumentari di Amelia: origine e 'antichi statuti'* (Studi e Testi Francescani 9: Rome, 1956).

— 'Un propagatore dei monti di pietà del '400. P. Fortunato Coppoli da Perugia O.F.M. († 1477)', in *RSCI* X (1956) 193–211.

— 'A chi si deve attribuire la rivelazione profetica dei monti di pietà?' in *AFH* L (1957) 231–6.

— 'I francescani e il monte di pietà di Terni dal 1490 al 1515', in *AFH* LII (1959) 204–89.

M. Gibbs and J. Lang, *Bishops and Reform, 1215–1272* (Oxford, 1934; reprint 1962).

J. Gilchrist, 'The Interpretation of the Renaissance', in *Manna*, VI (1963) 4–20.

— 'The Reformation and the Historians: I — The Background; III — Continuity and Change in England', in *Twentieth Century* (Melbourne) XV (1961) 114–26, 313–28.

— 'Proprietary Churches', in *New Catholic Encyclopedia* (New York, 1967) XI 874–5.

— 'Laity in the Middle Ages', in *The New Catholic Encyclopedia* (New York, 1967) VII 331–5.

J. Gill, *The Council of Florence* (1959).

— *Eugenius IV: Pope of Christian Union* (Westminster, Md, 1961).

B. Gille, 'Les Développements technologiques en Europe de 1100 à 1400', in *JWH* III (1956–7) 63–108.

I. Giordani, *The Social Message of the Early Church Fathers*, trans. from Italian by A. I. Zizzamia (Paterson, N.J., 1944).

C. J. Godfrey, 'Pluralists in the Province of Canterbury in 1366', in *JEH* XI (1960) 23–40.

E. H. Gombrich, 'The Early Medici as Patrons of Art: A Survey of Primary Sources', in *Italian Renaissance Studies*, 279–311.

N. S. B. Gras, 'Stages in Business History', in *Studi Sapori*, I 5–27.

C. V. Graves, 'The Economic Activities of the Cistercians in Medieval England 1128–1307', in *ASOC* XIII (1957) 3–60.

P. Grierson, 'Commerce in the Dark Ages. A Critique of the Evidence', in *TRHS*[5] IX (1959) 123–40.

A. Gwynn, 'The Medieval Councils: Lateran I to Vienne (1123–1311)', in *IER* XCIX (1963) 147–56.

J. H. Hackett, 'State of the Church: A Concept of the Medieval Canonists', in *Jurist*, XXIII (1963) 259–90.

H. E. Hallam, 'Some Thirteenth Century Censuses', in *EcHR*[2] X (1957) 340–61.

— 'Population Density in Medieval Fenland', in *EcHR*[2] XIV (1961–2) 71–81.

P. Hamell, 'First Four Councils', in *IER* XCVIII (1962) 275–87.

G. L. Harriss, 'Aids, Loans and Benevolences', in *Historical Journal*, VI (1963) 1–19.

W. O. Hassall, *How They Lived: an Anthology of Original Accounts written before 1485* (Oxford, 1962).

F. A. Hayek, *Capitalism and the Historians* (Univ. of Chicago Press, 1954, 3rd impression 1957).

C. J. Hefele, *Histoire des conciles d'après les documents originaux*, trad. J. Leclerq (1907–21) 16 vols.

D. Herlihy, 'Treasure Hoards in the Italian Economy, 960–1139', in *EcHR*[2] X (1957) 1–14.

— 'The Agrarian Revolution in Southern France and Italy, 801–1150', in *Speculum*, XXXIII (1958) 23–41.

— 'Church Property on the European Continent, 701–1200', in *Speculum*, XXXVI (1961) 81–105.

— 'Land, Family and Women in Continental Europe, 701–1200', in *Traditio*, XVIII (1962) 89–113.

A. B. Hibbert, 'The Origins of the Medieval Town Patriciate', in *Past and Present*, III (1953) 15–27.

J. R. L. Highfield, 'The English Hierarchy in the reign of Edward III', *TRHS*5 VI (1956) 115–38.

F. Hill, *Medieval Lincoln* (1948; reprinted 1965).

R. H. Hilton, *The Economic Development of some Leicestershire Estates in the 14th and 15th Centuries* (1947).

— 'A Study in the Pre-History of English Enclosure in the Fifteenth Century', in *Studi Sapori*, I 673–85.

B. Hinchcliff, 'Church and Society before Nicea', in *Church Quarterly Review* (Jan.–March 1964) 39–51.

W. A. Hinnebusch, 'Poverty in the Order of Preachers', in *CHR* XLV (1959–60) 436–53.

E. E. Hirshler, 'Medieval Economic Competition', in *JEcH* XIV (1954) 52–8.

L. Hödl, 'Zum Streit um die Bussprivilegien der Mendikantenordern in Wien im 14. und beginnenden 15. Jahrhundert', in *ZKT* LXXIX (1957) 170–89.

C. Hollis, *Christianity and Economics* (New York, 1961).

G. A. Holmes, 'Florentine Merchants in England, 1346–1436', in *EcHR*2 XIII (1960) 193–208.

W. Holtzmann, 'Sozial- und Wirtschaftsgeschichtliches aus Dekretalen', in *Rheinische Vierteljahrs-Blätter*, XIV–XVI (1949–51) 258–66.

W. G. Hoskins, *Essays in Leicestershire History* (Liverpool, 1950).

— *The Midland Peasant: the Economic and Social History of a Leicestershire Village* (1957).

J. Imbert, *Les Hôpitaux en droit canonique* (1947).

E. F. Jacob, 'A Note on the English Concordat of 1418', in *Studies Gwynn* 349–58.

L. Jaeger, *The Ecumenical Council, the Church and Christendom* (1961; trans. from the German).

M. K. James, 'A London Merchant of the Fourteenth Century', in *EcHR*2 VIII (1955–6) 364–76.

H. F. Janssens, 'Les Juifs au haut moyen âge', in *Le Moyen Age*, LXVII (1961) 535–51.

H. Jedin, 'Nouvelles Données sur l'histoire des conciles généraux', in *JWH* I (1953) 164–78.

— *Ecumenical Councils of the Catholic Church: An Historical Outline*, trans. E. Graf (1960).

P. Johansen, 'Die Kaufmannskirche im Ostseegebiet', in *Studi Sapori*, I 311–26.

E. John, 'A Note on the Preliminaries of the Fourth Crusade', in *Byzantion*, XXVIII (1958) 95–103.

— 'The Imposition of the Common Burdens upon the Lands of the English Church', in *BIHR* XXXI (1958) 117–29.

A. H. M. Jones, 'Church Finance in the Fifth and Sixth Centuries', in *JTS* NS XI (1960) 84–94.

P. J. Jones, 'A Tuscan Monastic Lordship in the Later Middle Ages: Camaldoli', in *JEH* V (1954) 168–83.

— 'Le finanze della badia cistercense di Settimo nel xiv sec.', in *RSCI* X(1956) 90–122.

— 'Per la storia agraria italiana nel medio evo: lineamenti e problemi', in *Rivista storica italiana*, LXXVI (1964) 287–348.

Bertrand de Jouvenel, 'The Treatment of Capitalism by Continental Intellectuals', in Hayek, 93–123.

E. W. Kemp, *An Introduction to Canon Law in the Church of England* (1957).

— *Counsel and Consent: Aspects of the Government of the Church as exemplified in the History of English Provincial Synods*(Bampton Lectures for 1960: 1961).

R. M. Kingdon, 'Economic Behaviour of Ministers in Geneva in the Middle of the Sixteenth Century', in *Archiv für Reformationsgeschichte*, L (1959) 33–9.

G. Kisch, 'The Yellow Badge in History', in *Historia Judaica*, XIX (1957) 89–146.

— 'Relations between Jewish and Christian Courts in the Middle Ages', in *Historia Judaica*, XXI (1959) 81–108.

M. D. Knowles, *The Episcopal Colleagues of Archbishop Thomas Becket* (Cambridge, 1951).

— *The Religious Orders in England: III The Tudor Age* (Cambridge, 1959).

— 'The English Bishops, 1070–1532', in *Studies Gwynn*, 283–96.

E. A. Kosminsky, *Studies in the Agrarian History of England in the Thirteenth Century* (Oxford, 1956).

— 'Peut-on considérer le xive et le xve siècles comme l'époque de la décadence de l'économie européenne?' in *Studi Sapori*, I 551–69.

H. C. Krijeger, 'Genoese Merchants, their Partnerships and Investments, 1155 to 1164', in *Studi Sapori*, I 255–71.

S. Kuttner, 'Die Konstitutionen des ersten allgemeinen Konzils von Lyon', in *Studia et documenta historiae et juris*, VI (1940) 70–131.

— 'The Father of the Science of Canon Law', in *Jurist*, I (1941) 2–19.

— 'Bernardus Compostellanus Antiquus: A Study in the Glossators of the Canon Law', in *Traditio*, I (1943) 277–340.

— 'Conciliar Law in the Making. The Lyonese Constitutions (1274) of Gregory X in a Manuscript at Washington', in *Miscellanea Pio Paschini*, II (Rome, 1949) 39–81.

— 'Brief Notes. Concerning the Canons of the Third Lateran Council', in *Bulletin, Traditio*, XIII (1957) 505–6.

— 'Dat Galienus opes et sanctio Justiniana', in *Linguistic and Literary Studies in honor of H. A. Hatzfeld*, ed. A. S. Crisafulli (Washington, D.C., 1964) 237–46.

José M. Lacarra, 'Les Villes frontières dans l'Espagne des xiᵉ et xiiᵉ siècles', in *Le Moyen Age*, LXIX (1963) 205–22.

G. de Lagarde, *La Naissance de l'esprit laïque au déclin du moyen âge:* 1 Bilan du *xiiiᵉᵐᵉ siècle* (3rd ed. Louvain–Paris, 1956).

M. D. Lambert, *Franciscan Poverty* (1961).

Luca Landucci, *A Florentine Diary from 1450 to 1516, continued by an Anonymous Writer till 1542*, ed. Iodoco del Badia; trans. A. de Rosen Jervis (1927).

F. C. Lane, 'Recent Studies on the Economic History of Venice', in *JEcH* XXIII (1963) 312–34.

— 'Venetian Merchant Galleys, 1300–1334: Private and Communal Operation', in *Speculum*, XXXVIII (1963) 179–205.

— 'At the Roots of Republicanism', in *AHR* LXXI (1966) 403–20.

G. Langmuir, ' "Judei Nostri" and the Beginning of Capetian Legislation', in *Traditio*, XVI (1960) 203–39.

— 'The Jews and Archives of Angevin England: Reflections on Medieval Anti-semitism', in *Traditio*, XIX (1963) 183–244.

G. Lapiana, 'The Church and the Jews', in *Historia Judaica*, XI (1949) 117–44.

G. Lavergne, 'La Persécution et la spoliation des lépreux à Périgueux en 1321', in *Recueil de travaux offert à M. Clovis Brunel* II (1955) 107–13.

G. Le Bras, 'L'Invasion de l'Église dans la cité', in *Mélanges Lavedan* (1954) 187–98.

— 'La Part du monachisme dans le droit et l'économie du moyen âge', in *RHEF* XLVII (1961, appeared 1962) 199–213.

— 'Conception of Economy and Society', in *Camb. Econ. Hist.* III (1963) 554–75.

— *Institutions ecclésiastiques de la chrétienté médiévale*, Iᵉʳᵉ partie, livres I à VI (Histoire de l'Église 12: 1964).

— 'Usure', in *Dictionnaire de théologie catholique*.

J. Leclercq, 'Épîtres d'Alexandre III sur les cisterciens', in *Rev. bénéd.* LXIV (1954) 68–82.

— *Christianity and Money*, trans. from French by E. Earnshaw Smith (New York, 1959).

Ch. Lefebvre, 'Une Décrétale d'Alexandre III en matière de simonie et le chapitre de Saint-Pierre à Lille', in *Mélanges de science religieuse*, XIV (1957) 21–38.

J. A. Lefèvre, 'Que savons-nous du Cîteaux primitif?', in *RHE* LI (1956) 5–41.

H. J. Légier, 'L'Église et l'économie médiévale. Un exemple: la monnaie ecclésiastique de Lyon et ses vicissitudes', in *AESC* XII (1957) 561–72.

J. Le Goff, *Marchands et banquiers du moyen âge* (1956).

J. Lestocquoy, 'Inhonesta mercimonia', in *Mélanges Louis Halphen* (1951) 411–15.

J. Lestocquoy, 'Note sur certains voyages en xie siècle', in *Studi Sapori*, I 179–86.

A. R. Lewis, 'The Closing of the Mediaeval Frontier', in *Speculum*, XXXIII (1958) 475–83.

A. L. Lilley, 'The Secularization of Economic Justice', in Demant, 76–91.

E. Lio, 'Le obbligazioni verso i poveri in un testo di S. Cesario riportato da Graziano (can. 66, C. XVI q. I) con falsa attribuzione a S. Agostino', in *SG* III (1955) 51–81.

A. G. Little and E. Stone, 'Corrodies at the Carmelite Friary of Lynn', in *JEH* IX (1958) 8–29.

A. Lodolini, 'Le finanze pontificie e i "monti" ', in *Rassegna storica del Risorgimento*, XLIV (1957) 421–8.

R. S. Lopez, 'Italian Leadership in the Medieval Business World', in *SJEcH*² VIII (1948) 63–8.

— 'Still Another Renaissance', in *AHR* LVII (1951) 1–21.

— 'The Unexplored Wealth of the Notarial Archives in Pisa and Lucca', in *Mélanges Louis Halphen* (1951) 417–32.

— 'Les Influences orientales et l'éveil économique de l'occident', in *JWH* I (1953) 594–622.

— 'An Aristocracy of Money in the Early Middle Ages', in *Speculum*, XXVIII (1953) 1–43.

— 'East and West in the Early Middle Ages; Economic Relations', in *Proc. 10th Intern. Cong.* III (1956) 113–63.

— 'I primi cento anni di storia documentata della banca a Genova', in *Studi Sapori*, I 215–53.

— 'L'Extrême Frontière du commerce de L'Europe médiévale', in *Le Moyen Age*, LXIX (1963) 470–90.

— and I. W. Raymond, *Medieval Trade in the Mediterranean World* (Records of Civilisation, Sources and Studies 52, ed. A. P. Evans: New York, 1955).

— and H. A. Miskimin, 'The Economic Depression of the Renaissance', in *EcHR*² XIV (1961–2) 408–26.

W. E. Lunt, *Papal Revenues in the Middle Ages*, 2 vols (New York, 1934).

— *Financial Relations of the Papacy with England 1327–1534* (*Studies in Anglo-Papal Relations during the Middle Ages*, II; Medieval Academy of America Cambridge, Mass. 1962).

A. Luttrell, 'Intrigue, Schism, and Violence among the Hospitallers of Rhodes: 1377–1384', in *Speculum*, XLI (1966) 30–48.

G. Luzzatto, 'Les Noblesses: les activités économiques du patriciat vénitien (x^e–xive siècles)', in *AHES* IX (1937) 25–7.

— 'Tasso d'interesse e usura a Venezia nei secoli xiii–xv', in *Miscellanea in onore di Roberto Cessi* (1958) I 191–202.

— *An Economic History of Italy*, trans. P. Jones (New York, 1961).

— 'Storia economica di Venezia dall'xi al xvi secolo (Centro internazionale delle Arti e del Costume: Venice, 1961).

B. Lyon, 'Medieval Real Estate Developments and Freedom', in *AHR* LXIII (1957-8) 47-61.

M. Maccarrone, 'Il IV Concilio Lateranense', in *Divinitas: Pontificiae Academiae Theologicae Romanae Commentarii*, V (1961) 270-98.

J. F. McCarthy, 'The Genius of Concord in Gratian's Decree', in *EIC* XIX (1963) 105-51, 259-95.

J. J. McCusker, 'The Wine Prise and Mediaeval Mercantile Shipping', in *Speculum*, XLI (1966) 279-96.

W. J. McDonald (ed.), *The General Council* (Washington, D.C., 1962).

L. McFarlane, 'Papal Finance and the Papal State', in *Month*, NS XXIX (1963) 107-9.

M. McGuire, 'The History of the Church from Pentecost to 604. A Survey of Research, 1954-1958', in *Theological Studies*, XX (1959) 82-107.

T. P. McLaughlin, C.S.B., 'The Teaching of the Canonists on Usury (xii, xiii & xiv centuries)', in *Med. Stud.* I (1939) 81-147, II (1940) 1-22.

R. E. McNally, 'The History of the Medieval Papacy: a Survey of Research 1954-1959', in *Theological Studies*, XXI (1960) 92-132.

J. T. McNeill, 'Thirty Years of Calvin Study', in *CH* XVII (1948) 207-40.

— *Medieval Handbooks of Penance* (1938; reprint New York, 1965).

E. D. McShane, 'The History of the Church from 1300 to 1648, A Survey of Research, 1955-1960', in *Theological Studies*, XXII (1961) 59-85.

Sr James Eugene Madden, C.S.J., 'Business Monks, Banker Monks, Bankrupt Monks: the English Cistercians in the Thirteenth Century', in *CHR* XLIX (1963) 341-64.

H. Maisonneuve, *Études sur les origines de l'inquisition*, 2nd ed. (1960).

— 'La Morale d'après les conciles des xe et xie siècles', in *Mélanges de science religieuse*, XVIII (1961) 1-46.

Kathleen Major, 'Finances of the Dean and Chapter of Lincoln from the Twelfth to the Fourteenth Century: a Preliminary Survey', in *JEH* v (1954) 149-67.

Marian Malowist, 'L'Évolution industrielle en Pologne du xive au xviie siècle', in *Studi Sapori*, I 571-603.

— 'Les Mouvements d'expansion en Europe aux xve et xvie siècles', in *AESC* XVII (1962) 923-9.

R. Manselli, 'Onorio III e Federico II (revisione d'un giudizio?)', in *Studi romani*, XI (1963) 142-59.

J. D. Mansi, *Sacrorum conciliorum nova et amplissima collectio* (Florence, 1759 and following).

MS Florence, Laurenziana S. Croce III sin 6.

MS Washington, Catholic University of America 183.

L. F. Marks, 'The Financial Oligarchy in Florence under Lorenzo', in *Italian Renaissance Studies*, 123-47.

L. Martines, *The Social World of the Florentine Humanists 1390-1460* (1963).

P. Michaud-Quantin, 'Aspects de la vie sociale chez les moralistes', in *Miscellanea Mediaevalia,* III (1964) 30–43.

E. Miller, 'The English Economy in the Thirteenth Century', in *Past and Present,* XXVIII (1964) 21–40.

H. A. Miskimin, 'Le Problème de l'argent au moyen âge', in *AESC* XVII (1962) 1125–30.

— *Money, Prices and Foreign Exchange in Fourteenth-century France* (Yale Studies in Economics 15: New Haven, 1963).

G. Mollat, *The Popes at Avignon 1305–1378* (1963; New York, 1965).

J. R. H. Moorman, *Church Life in England in the Thirteenth Century* (1945).

J. B. Morrall, 'Papacy and Council in the Century before the Reformation', in *IER* XCIX (1963) 217–26.

J. H. Mundy, *Liberty and Political Power in Toulouse 1050–1230* (New York, 1954).

— 'Hospitals and Leprosaries in Twelfth- and Early Thirteenth-century Toulouse', in *Essays in Medieval Life and Thought,* ed. J. H. Mundy *et al.* (New York, 1955) 181–205.

— 'Un Usurier malheureux', in *Annales du Midi,* LXVIII no. 33 (1965) 217–25.

J. H. Mundy and K. M. Woody (ed.), *The Council of Constance,* trans. by Louise Ropes Loomis (New York, 1961).

B. N. Nelson, 'The Legend of the Divine Surety and the Jewish Moneylender', in *Annuaire de l'institut de philologie et d'histoire orientales et slaves,* VII (1939–44) 289–338.

— *The Idea of Usury* (Princeton, N.J., 1949).

— 'The Usurer and the Merchant Prince: Italian Businessmen and the Ecclesiastical Law of Restitution, 1100–1550', in *SJEcH²* VII (1947) 104–22.

F. J. Niederer, 'Early Medieval Charity', in *CH* XXI (1952) 285–95.

John T. Noonan, *The Scholastic Analysis of Usury* (Cambridge, Mass., 1957).

J. W. O'Brien, 'Christianity and Economics', in *Am. Eccl. R.* CXXXIII (1955) 162–70, 253–7.

W. Onclin, 'Le Statut des étrangers dans la doctrine canonique médiévale', in *Recueils da la Soc. Jean Bodin,* X: 'L'étranger', 2nd part (Brussels, 1958) 37–64.

I. Origo, *The Merchant of Prato: Francesco di Marco Datini* (1957).

— *The World of San Bernardino* (New York, 1962).

D. Oschinsky, 'Medieval Treatises on Estate Management', in *EcHR²* VIII (1955) 296–309.

M. D. O'Sullivan, *Italian Merchant Bankers in Ireland in the Thirteenth Century* (Dublin, 1962).

Jocelyn Otway-Ruthven, 'The Medieval Church Lands of County Dublin', in *Studies Gwynn,* 54–73.

P. Ourliac, 'La Théorie canonique des rentes au XVe siècle', in *Études historiques* à *la mémoire de Noël Didier* (Fac. de droit et des sciences économiques de Grenoble: 1960) 231–43.

M. Pacant, 'Saint Bernardin de Sienne et l'usure', in *Le Moyen Age*, LXIX (1963) 743–52.

W. A. Pantin, *The English Church in the Fourteenth Century* (Cambridge, 1955).

T. W. Parker, *The Knights Templars in England* (Tucson, Ariz., 1963).

P. D. Partner, 'Camera papae: Problems of Papal Finance in the Later Middle Ages', in *JEH* IV (1953) 55–68.

— 'Papal Finance and the Papal State', in *History Today*, VII (1957) 766–74.

— *The Papal State under Martin V* (British School at Rome: 1958).

— 'The "Budget" of the Roman Church in the Renaissance Period', in *Italian Renaissance Studies*, 256–78.

F. Pegues, 'Ecclesiastical Provisions for the Support of Students in the Thirteenth Century', in *CH* XXVI (1957) 307–18.

S. Pejovich, 'The Transition of Medieval Man into the Modern Man', in *Soc. Order*, XII (1962) 474–8.

C. E. Perrin, 'Le Servage en France et en Allemagne', in *Proc. 10th Intern. Cong.* 213–45.

V. Pfaff, 'Aufgaben und Probleme der päpstlichen Finanzverwaltung am Ende des 12. Jhts', in *MIÖGF* LXIV (1956) 1–24.

Gaines Post, 'The Medieval Heritage of a Humanistic Ideal: "Scientia donum dei est, unde vendi non potest"', in *Traditio* XI (1955) 195–234.

M. M. Postan, 'Italy and Economic Development of England in the Middle Ages', in *JEcH* XI (1951) 339–46.

— *The Famulus. The Estate Labourer in the XIIth and the XIIIth Centuries* (Econ. Hist. Rev. Suppl. 2: 1954).

— 'Partnership in English Medieval Commerce', in *Studi Sapori*, I 519–49.

— 'The Costs of the Hundred Years War', in *Past and Present*, XXVII (1964) 34–53.

J. Prawer, 'Étude de quelques problèmes agraires et sociaux d'une seigneurie croisée au xiiie siècle', in *Byzantion*, XXII (1962) 5–61, XXIII (1963) 143–69.

C. Raab, O.F.M., *The Twenty Ecumenical Councils of the Catholic Church* (Westminster, Md, 1959).

J. A. Raftis, *The Estates of Ramsey Abbey. A Study in Economic Growth and Organisation* (Studies and Texts 3, Toronto Pont. Inst. of Med. Studies: 1957).

— 'Rent and Capital at St Ives', in *Med. Stud.* XX (1958) 79–92.

Yves Renouard, *Les Relations des papes d'Avignon et des compagnies commerciales et bancaires de 1316 à 1378* (1941).

— *Les Hommes d'affaires italiens du moyen âge* (1949).

— 'Les Hommes d'affaires italiens à Rochelle au moyen âge', in *Studi Sapori*, I 401–16.

Report of the Archbishops' Commission on Canon Law, *The Canon Law of the Church of England* (1947).

I

R. L. Reynolds, 'Origins of Modern Business Enterprise: Medieval Italy', in *JEcH* XII (1952) 350–77.

W. C. Robinson, 'Money, Population and Economic Change in Late Medieval Europe', in *EcHR*² XII (1959–60) 63–82.

C. Roth, 'The Economic History of the Jews', in *EcHR*² XIV (1961–2) 131–5.

— *A History of the Jews in England* (1940; 3rd ed. 1964).

C. Roth and I. H. Levine, *The World History of the Jewish People:* XI (2nd Series: *Medieval Period:* II *The Dark Ages: Jews in Christian Europe*) (1966).

P. Rousset, 'L'Idée de croisade chez les chroniqueurs d'occident', in *Proc. 10th Intern. Cong.* III 547–63.

S. Runciman, 'The Decline of the Crusading Idea', in *Proc. 10th Intern. Cong.* III 637–52.

J. C. Russell, *Late Ancient and Medieval Population* (Trans. of the Am. Phil. Soc. NS XLVIII part 3: Philadelphia, 1958).

— 'A Quantitative Approach to Medieval Population Change', in *JEcH* XXIV (1964) 1–21.

A. Sapori, *Studi di storia economica medievale*, 2 vols, 2nd ed. (Florence, 1955).

— 'Economia e morale alla fine del trecento', in *Studi senesi*, LXIV (1952) 44–76.

— *Le Marchand italien au moyen âge* (1952).

— 'L'usura nel dugento a Pistoia', in *Studi medievale*, I 181–9.

— *Studi in onore di Armando Sapori* (Istituto Editoriale Cisalpino: Milan, 1957).

V. Saxer, 'Le Statut juridique de Vézelay des origines à la fin du xiie siècle. Contribution à l'histoire des privilèges monastiques d'immunité et d'exemption', in *RDC* VI (1956) 225–62.

J. J. Scarisbrick, 'Clerical Taxation in England, 1485–1547', in *JEH* XI (1960) 41–54.

B. Schnapper, 'Les Baux à vie (xe au xvie siècle)', in *RHE* XXXIV (1957) 347–75.

H. J. Schroeder, O.P., *Disciplinary Decrees of the General Councils* (St Louis, Mo, 1937).

A. T. Sheedy, *Bartolus on Social Conditions in the Fourteenth Century* (New York, 1942).

M. P. Sheehy, 'The Later Eastern Councils: the 5th through 8th Ecumenical Councils', in *IER* XCIX (1963) 1–11.

A. Sifoniou, 'Les Fondements juridiques de l'aumône et de la charité chez Jean Chrysostome', in *RDC* XIV (1964) 247–69.

R. A. L. Smith, *Canterbury Cathedral Priory: a Study in Monastic Administration* (Cambridge, 1943).

J. Soudek, 'Aristotle's Theory of Exchange: an Inquiry into the Origin of Economic Analysis', *Proc. Amer. Philos. Soc.* XCVI (1952) 45–75.

R. W. Southern, *Western Views of Islam in the Middle Ages* (Cambridge, Mass., 1962).

W. Stark, *The Contained Economy* (Aquinas Paper 26: Blackfriars, 1956).

S. Stein, 'The Development of the Jewish Law on Interest from the Biblical

Period to the Expulsion of the Jews from England', in *Historia Judaica*, XVII (1955) 3–40.
— 'Interest taken by Jews from Gentiles', in *Journal of Semitic Studies*, I (1956) 141–64.
— 'A Disputation on Money Lending between Jews and Gentiles in Me'ir b. Simeon's Milhemeth Miswah (Narbonne, 13th century)', in *Journal of Jewish Studies*, X (1959) 45–61.
C. Stephenson, 'In Praise of Medieval Tinkers', in *SJEcH* VIII (1948) 26–42.
P. Daniel Stiernon, A.A., 'L'unione greco-latina al concilio di Firenze ed il problema ecumenico nel prossimo concilio', in *Divinitas*, V (1961) 311–23.
Ulrich Stutz, *Geschichte des kirchlichen Benefizialwesens* (Aalen, 1961).
C. H. Talbot, 'Cîteaux and Scarborough', in *Studia monastica*, II (1960) 95–158.
— 'A Cistercian Account Book', in *The Listener*, LIV (1955) 177–9.
— 'The Account Book of Beaulieu Abbey', in *Cîteaux*, IX (1958) 189–210.
R. H. Tawney, *Religion and the Rise of Capitalism* (1926; Pelican ed. 1938).
P. R. Teetor, 'England's Earliest Treatise on the Law Merchant; an Essay on the *Lex Mercatoria* from the Little Red Book of Bristol (*circa* A.D. 1280)', in *American Journal of Legal History*, VI (1962) 178–210.
J. L. Teicher, 'The Mediaeval Mind', in *Journal of Jewish Studies*, VI (1955) 1–13.
F. Thiriet, 'Les Vénitiens à Thessalonique dans la première moitié du xive siècle', in *Byzantion*, XXII (1952) 323–32.
S. L. Thrupp, *The Merchant Class of Medieval London* [1300–1500] (Chicago, 1948).
B. Tierney, 'The Decretists and the "Deserving Poor"', in *Comparative Studies in Society and History*, I (1958–9) 360–73.
— *Medieval Poor Law: a Sketch of Canonical Theory and its Application in England* (Berkeley, California, 1959).
J. Z. Titow, 'Some Evidence of the Thirteenth-century Population Increase', in *EcHR*[2] XIV (1961–2) 218–23.
P. Toubert, 'Les Déviations de la croisade au milieu du xiiie siècle: Alexandre IV contre Manfred', in *Le Moyen Age*, LXIX (1963) 391–9.
E. Troeltsch, *The Social Teaching of the Christian Churches*, 2 vols, trans. by Olive Wyon (New York, 1956).
A. E. Trugenberger, *San Bernardino da Siena; considerazioni sullo sviluppo dell'etica economica cristiana nel primo rinascimento* (Staatswissenschaftliche Studien, ed. L. V. Furlan and E. Salin, NF 9: Bern, 1951).
R. E. Turner, 'Economic Discontent in Medieval Western Europe', in *JEcH* VIII (1948) 85–100.
A. L. Udovitch, 'At the Origins of the Western *Commenda*: Islam, Israel, Byzantium', in *Speculum*, XXXVII (1962) 198–207.
T. Urdánoz, 'El concilio ecuménico y la reforma de la Iglesia, según Francisco de Vitoria', in *Miscellanea Comillas*, XXXIV–XXXV (1960) 119–49.
D. Cipriano Vagaggini, O.S.B., 'Osservazioni interno al concetto di concilio ecumenico', in *Divinitas*, V (1961) 411–30.

J. B. Van Damme, O.C.R., 'La Constitution cistercienne de 1165', in *ASOC* XIX (1963) 51–104.

C. Van de Kieft, 'Une Église privée de l'abbaye de la Trinité de Vendôme au xie siècle', in *Le Moyen Age*, LXIX (1963) 157–68.

T. P. Van Zijl, *Gerard Groote, Ascetic and Reformer (1340–1384)* (CUA Studies in Mediaeval History NS 18: Washington, D.C., 1963).

C. Verlinden, *L'Esclavage dans l'Europe médiévale: I Péninsule ibérique-France* (Rijksuniversiteit te Gent. Werken unitg. door de Fac. v.d. letteren en wijsbegeerte, 119: Bruges, 1955).

— 'La Grande Peste de 1348 en Espagne', in *Revue belge de philologie et d'histoire*, XVII (1938) 103–46.

A. Vetulani, 'The Jews in Medieval Poland', in *Jewish Journal of Sociology*, IV (1962) 274–94.

M. Villey, 'L'Idée de la croisade chez les juristes du moyen-âge' (Comitato Internazionale di Scienze Storiche: X Congresso Internazionale di scienze storiche Roma 4–11 settembre 1955; Relazioni: III Storia del medioevo, 567–94).

T. de Vio (Cajetan), *Scripta philosophica, opuscula oeconomico-socialia*, ed. P. P. Zammit (Rome, 1934).

C. Violante, 'Les Prêts sur gage foncier dans la vie économique et sociale de Milan au xie siècle', in *CCM* v (1962) 147–68, 437–59.

B. Waites, 'The Monasteries and the Medieval Development of North-east Yorkshire', in *BIHR* XXXI (1958) 231–3 (summary of thesis).

— 'The Monastic Settlement of North-East Yorkshire', *Yorkshire Archaeological Journal*, XL (1962) 478–95.

D. P. Waley, 'An Account Book of the Patrimony of St Peter in Tuscany, 1304–1306', in *JEH* VI (1955) 18–25.

— 'Papal Armies in the XIIIth century', in *EHR* LXXII (1957) 1–30.

— 'A Register of Boniface VIII's Chamberlain, Theoderic of Orvieto', in *JEH* VIII (1957) 141–52.

— *The Papal State in the Thirteenth Century* (1961).

E. I. Watkin, *The Church in Council* (1960).

J. A. Watt, 'The Theory of Papal Monarchy in the Thirteenth Century: the Contribution of the Canonists', in *Traditio* XX (1964) 179–317.

L. Watt, 'The Theory behind the Historical Conception of the Just Price', in Demant, 60–75.

Max Weber, *The Protestant Ethic and the Spirit of Capitalism* (German orig. 1904–5; 2nd ed. 1920; trans. Talcott Parsons, 1930; 2nd imp. 1948).

F. Weigle, 'Ratherius von Verona im Kampf um das Kirchengut 961–968', in *Quellen und Forschungen*, XXVIII (1937–8) 1–35.

Hans van Werweke, 'Le Mortgage et son rôle économique en Flandre et en Lotharingie', in *Revue belge de philologie et d'histoire*, VIII (1929) 53–91, esp. 64 ff.

M. J. Wilks, 'The Problem of Private Ownership in Patristic Thought and an

Augustinian Solution of the Fourteenth Century', in *Studia Patristica*, VI (Texte und Untersuchungen 81, ed. F. L. Cross; Berlin, 1962) 533–42.

G. A. Williams, *Medieval London: from Commune to Capital* (1963).

P. Wolff, 'Quidam homo nomine Roberto negociatore', in *Le Moyen Age*, LXIX (1963) 129–39.

— *Commerces et marchands de Toulouse (vers 1350–vers 1450)* (1954).

— 'Trois Études de démographie médiévale en France méridionale', in *Studi Sapori*, I 493–503.

H. Wolter et H. Holstein, *Lyon I et Lyon II* (Histoire des conciles œcuméniques 7: 1966).

S. Wood, *English Monasteries and their Patrons in the Thirteenth Century* (1955).

C. R. Young, 'King John of England: an Illustration of the Medieval Practice of Charity', in *CH* XXIX (1960) 264–74.

D. B. Zema, 'Reform Legislation in the Eleventh Century and its Economic Import', in *CHR* XXVII (1941) 16–38.

— 'The Houses of Tuscany and of Pierleone in the Crisis of Rome in the Eleventh Century', in *Traditio*, II (1944) 155–75.

— 'Economic Reorganisation of the Roman See during the Gregorian Reform', in *SG* I (1947) 137–68.

Notes

NOTE. Publication details are given *only* when reference is not included in the Bibliography.

CHAPTER I

1. For bibliography, see B. N. Nelson, *The Idea of Usury*, 165–220; J. W. Baldwin, *The Medieval Theories of the Just Price: Romanists, Canonists and Theologians in the Twelfth and Thirteenth Centuries*, 89–90; *Camb. Econ. Hist.* III, 605–74.

2. Baldwin, *Just Price*, 5–6.

3. J. M. W. Bean, 'Plague, Population and Economic Decline in England in the Later Middle Ages', in *EcHR²* xv (1963) 423–37, here 436; G. A. Holmes, in *EcHR²* xv 539.

4. J. T. Noonan, *The Scholastic Analysis of Usury*; Baldwin is cited above, n. 1; B. Tierney, *Medieval Poor Law: A Sketch of Canonical Theory and its Application in England*.

5. A. Sapori, *Le Marchand italien au moyen âge* (1952) p. xxxix, describes the medieval Church as 'le plus grand institut économique et politique de l'époque'. For statistics of the extent of ecclesiastical property, see the following table given by D. Herlihy in 'Church Property on the European Continent, 701–1200', in *Speculum*, XXXVI (1961) 81–105, here 86:

	8th	9th	10th	11th	12th
Italy	14	31	25	20	16
Germany	17	35	—	—	—
Northern France	19	44	51	39	32
Southern France	—	31	31	31	13
Spain	—	5	7	15	13

which are percentages of the total cultivated lands. Ownership tripled over the seventy-five years from 751 to 825, which was the Carolingian period of reform and restoration. The peak was 876–900, when the Church owned approximately one-third of the land. Then came a downward trend, with a slight upturn in the eleventh-century Gregorian Reform movement. By the twelfth century the Church had about 15 per cent of the land. The decline continued into the thirteenth century (ibid. 87, 92). However, the Church's share of the total wealth did not diminish, for its income from the tithe correspondingly increased.

6. O. C. Cox, *The Foundations of Capitalism*, 141, 165, where the author links the proximity of Florence to Rome, which enabled the city to get control of papal finances, as the main factor in the success of Florentine capitalism. The condition of papal finances affected the rest of the money-market;

compare the following note by a Venetian merchant about the middle of the fifteenth century: 'At Genoa, money is dear in September, January and April, because of the ships leaving . . . at Rome or wherever the pope is to be found, the price of money varies according to the number of vacant benefices and the pope's allocations, which send up the price of money, wherever he is located . . . at Valencia it is dear in July and August because of the wheat and rice . . . at Montpellier there are three fairs which cause a large dearness of money' (J. Le Goff, *Marchands et banquiers du moyen âge*, 30). These fluctuations were the basis of exchange banking, for they provided the means by which the bankers could take interest legitimately. See p. 73. Also R. De Roover, *The Rise and Decline of the Medici Bank 1397–1494*, 124, 194 ff.

7. Tierney, *Poor Law*, 2.

8. P. Johansen, 'Die Kaufmannskirche im Ostseegebiet', in *Studi Sapori*, I 311–26; here 314–16, 320.

9. *Calendar of the Plea Rolls of the Exchequer of the Jews preserved in the Public Record Office:* I Henry III A.D. *1218–1272*, ed. J. M. Rigg, 133.

10. C. Roth, *A History of the Jews in England*, 109. The practice of using the church for secular functions was an ancient one, cf J. G. Davies, *Daily Life in the Early Church*, 112. On the Templars, see T. W. Parker, *The Knights Templars in England*, 82.

11. In 1307, at Lincoln, the Abbot of Barlings tried to acquire a vacant site, but the jury of inquisition reported that this would hurt the town because the abbot and canons intended to pull down the church on the site and there to erect a warehouse in which to store their tanned hides, wool, corn and other products until they could sell at a profit like common merchants (F. Hill, *Medieval Lincoln*, 151). I. Origo, *The World of San Bernardino*, 88, cites the saint's condemnations of trade in cloister, church or consecrated cemetery.

12. E. Troeltsch, *The Social Teaching of the Christian Churches*; R. H. Tawney, *Religion and the Rise of Capitalism*; C. Hollis, *Christianity and Economics*. Cf W. Stark, *The Contained Economy*, e.g. 5: 'medieval man did not like the idea of competition'; 'Prices did change over the centuries, but they changed so slowly in the normal course of events that people were hardly aware of the changes.' See p. 24 and ch. 7 for the Weber–Tawney theses.

13. Noonan, *Usury*, 2. The medieval merchant sought to keep his affairs secret, and he went to extraordinary lengths to do so; cf Le Goff, *Marchands et banquiers*, 84–5.

14. W. Onclin, 'Le Statut des étrangers dans la doctrine canonique médiévale', in *Recueils de la Société Jean Bodin*: x *L'Étranger*, 2nd part, 37–64, here 38.

15. Cf C. V. Graves, 'The Economic Activities of the Cistercians in Medieval England, 1128–1307', in *ASOC* XIII (1957) 3–60, here 10.

16. I. Giordani, *The Social Message of the Early Church Fathers*, 259.

17. W. J. Doheny, *Church Property: Modes of Acquisition*, passim. See also p. 29.

18. Doheny, *Church Property*, 69. Also L. Charvet, 'Aux origines de la

prescription de cent ans (Cod. iur. can. *c.* 1511 §1)', in *EIC* XIX (1963) 152–66, here 152–3. The author considers Chalcedon 17 was not well observed in the East.

19. Against this, see A. J. Clark, *The Natural Law and Private Property in Early Glossators of the Decretum,* 51, that the glossators were 'perhaps, all too well acquainted with the inequalities within private ownership to admit it in its entirety to full standing in the natural law'.

20. In *DDC* II (1937) 336–41, 'Biens ecclésiastiques'; see also J. F. Dede, 'Business Pursuits of Clerics and Religious: Further Considerations', in *Jurist* XXIII (1963) 50–62, especially 51.

21. H. J. Byrne, *Investment of Church Funds,* 5.

22. M. J. Wilks, 'The Problem of Private Ownership in Patristic Thought and an Augustinian Solution of the Fourteenth Century', in *Studia Patristica,* VI 533–42, here 537.

23. D. Waley, *The Papal State in the Thirteenth Century,* here 301, 302.

24. J. Gill, *Eugenius IV: Pope of Christian Union,* 179.

25. See p. 93. Also D. P. Waley, 'Papal Armies in the XIIIth Century', in *EHR* LXXII (1957) 1–30, especially 11, 15, 19, 21. In the end its Angevin ally, not the papacy, was the victor. The papacy had meanwhile lost spiritual prestige by its use of temporal strength (ibid. 30).

26. Baldwin, *Just Price,* 12 and 7. See also R. S. Lopez, 'Les Influences orientales et l'éveil économique de l'occident', in *JWH* I (1953) 594–622, especially 617. See p. 24.

27. Cf R. S. Lopez, 'East and West in the Early Middle Ages: Economic Relations', in *Proc. 10th Intern. Cong.* III (1956) 113–63, especially 118, where he gives statistics of town areas, e.g. in the early Middle Ages Paris was barely 8 hectares, Tournai was 12; Cologne was abnormally large with 96 hectares. Constantinople had 1420 hectares and 100,000 inhabitants (ibid. 120). But this was not as large as Venice, Milan and Florence in their later medieval prime.

28. R. S. Lopez, 'L'Extrême Frontière du commerce de l'Europe médiévale', in *Le Moyen Age,* LXIX (1963) 479–90, cites (484) the figure for the export of silk cloth from Lucca between 1335 and 1341 as on average 40 tons a year. The profit margin was small for a pound of raw silk purchased in China for 8 sous, sold in Genoa for 23–25 sous.

29. On agricultural improvements cf A. C. Crombie, *Augustine to Galileo:* I *Science in the Middle Ages: V–XIII Centuries* (1952) 189–96.

30. In general, see G. Le Bras, *Institutions ecclésiastiques de la chrétienté médiévale,* Ière partie, Livres II à VI (in *Histoire de l'Église* 12: 1964) 529–64.

31. Roth, *History of the Jews,* 104, that the Church claimed jurisdiction over Jews in certain cases, such as sacrilege, blasphemy, illicit association with a Christian woman and striking a cleric.

32. On church property, see J. F. Cleary, *Canonical Limitations on the Alienation of Church Property,* passim.

33. Running counter to this was the example of monastic property, where, if the monks were to be prevented from living outside the monasteries, some form of lay management was necessary; thus, at the end of the thirteenth century in England the Benedictine estates began to appoint lay stewards and wardens in order to fulfil the injunctions of Archbishop Pecham; cf D. Oschinsky, 'Medieval Treatises on Estate Management', in *EcHR²* vɪɪɪ (1955) 296–309, here 304.

34. This, of course, did not eliminate abuses; compare, in the case of England, J. R. H. Moorman, *Church Life in England in the Thirteenth Century*, passim, but especially 6–11, 28–34, 38–43.

35. J. Gilchrist, 'Laity in the Middle Ages', in *New Catholic Encyclopedia* (New York, 1967) vɪɪ 331–5.

CHAPTER 2

1. For the general history of canonical development, see *The Canon Law of the Church of England* (1947) 7–44. Also E. W. Kemp, *An Introduction to Canon Law in the Church of England*, 11–32. The standard work is A. M. Stickler, *Historia iuris canonici latini*: ɪ *Historia fontium* (Turin, 1950).

2. C. Duggan, *Twelfth-century Decretal Collections*, 13.

3. J. R. Palanque, G. Bardy et P. de Labriolle, *De la paix constantinienne à la mort de Théodose* (*Histoire de l'Église*, ed. A. Fliche et V. Martin 3: 1950) 22.

4. J. Gaudemet, *La Formation du droit séculier et du droit de l'Église au ivᵉ et vᵉ siècles*, 156. Also M. Briek, 'De momento conciliorum pro iuris Ecclesiae formatione', in *Antonianum*, xxxvɪɪɪ (1963) 50–86, especially 62, that some 1086 of the 3945 texts found in Gratian belong to the early fifth century. Cf Gratian D.15 c.2.

5. Gaudemet, *La Formation*, 160; Stickler, *Historia*, ɪ 48–50.

6. The *Hispana* or *Codex canonum ecclesiae Hispanae* was one of the products of the Third Council of Toledo (589). The collection first appeared with its decrees in a chronological form, but this was later altered to give us the *Collectio Hispana systematica*. Cf Stickler, *Historia*, ɪ 78–84.

7. Stickler, *Historia*, ɪ 131–42.

8. Ibid. 154–9. Books ɪɪɪ and xv deal with economic matters.

9. Ibid. 166–88.

10. P. Fournier et G. Le Bras, *Histoire des collections canoniques en occident*, 2 vols (1932) ɪɪ 352.

11. Cf Baldwin, *Just Price*, 31; J. T. Donovan, *The Clerical Obligations of Canons 138 and 140*, 23. The most significant of the early papal pronouncements relating to their authority over general councils was Gregory VII's *Dictatus pape* 16: 'No synod may be described as a general synod without his decision'; cf J. Gilchrist, 'Canon Law Aspects of the Eleventh Century Gregorian Reform Programme', in *JEH* xɪɪɪ (1962) 21–38; here 30–1.

12

12. S. Kuttner, 'The Father of the Science of Canon Law', in *Jurist*, I (1941) 2–19. The chaotic state of the canon law — even after the pre-Gratian reforms — was basically a matter of the huge accumulation of material over a thousand years or so. Courage was needed to separate the useful from the superfluous; Tierney, *Poor Law*, 7.

13. Stickler, *Historia*, I 200; also Baldwin, in *Papers Michigan Academy*, XLIV 290–1. On the title of Gratian's collection, cf J. M. McCarthy, 'The Genius of Concord in Gratian's Decree', in *EIC* XIX (1963) 105–51, 259–95; here 136–7.

14. McCarthy, in *EIC* XIX passim.

15. Baldwin, *Just Price*, 35.

16. Cf McCarthy, in *EIC* XIX 151. A. Gwynn, 'The Medieval Council: Lateran I to Vienne (1123–1311)', in *IER* XCIX (1963) 147–56; here 151. Innocent III received his training in canon law from Huguccio and subsequently held the chair of canon law at Bologna.

17. Stickler, *Historia*, I 218; Baldwin, *Just Price*, 41. For the twelfth century some 1100 decretals are known, cf S. Kuttner, *Traditio*, XX (1964) 493. Then with the advent of the series of papal registers the number grows enormously.

18. Stickler, *Historia*, I 240; cf Noonan, *Usury*, 44. The designation of this collection by the symbol 'X' represents its title, *Liber Extra*.

19. The text, although purporting to be the *sixth* book of the *Decretals* of Gregory IX — hence the symbol 'VI' — was in fact divided into five books, and the internal arrangement was the same as that in the *Decretals*. John XXII promulgated a seventh book in 1317 (it included 30 decrees of the council of Vienne) and it took its name, the *Clementines*, from his predecessor Clement V. The *Extravagantes* of John XXII consist of 20 bulls of John in the form of one book with 14 titles. The *Extravagantes Communes* contain decretals of various popes from the latter part of John XXII's reign to Sixtus IV. It consists of five books divided into titles, containing in all 73 capp. The term *Extravagantes* refers to the title *Corpus iuris canonici* given in the thirteenth century to Gratian's *Decretum*. Hence collections of decrees *outside* the *Corpus* were known as *Extra (Corpus iuris) vagantes*, cf McCarthy, in *EIC* XIX 36.

20. In 1500 Jean Chappuis published the six parts under this title.

21. Baldwin, *Just Price*, 41.

22. Stickler, *Historia*, I 270; also Tierney, *Poor Law*, 12.

23. The main decretist commentaries were *Paucapalea*, *Summa Rolandi*, Rufinus, *Summa* (1157–9); *Summa Parisiensis* (*c.* 1160), Stephanus Tornacensis, *Summa Elegantius in iure divino* (*c.* 1169), all three of the French school; Johannes Faventinus (*c.* 1171) at Bologna; various French *summe* in the 1170s, e.g. *Summa Inperatorie maiestati*; works of the Anglo-Norman school, e.g. *Summa omnis qui iuste* (*c.* 1186, at Oxford?); and then back to the Bolognese school, e.g. *Summa Tractaturus magister*, until Huguccio eclipsed them all.

24. Cf S. Kuttner, 'Bernardus Compostellanus Antiquus: a Study in the

Glossators of the Canon Law', in *Traditio*, I (1943) 277–340, here 284; also Baldwin, *Just Price*, 47.

25. Hostiensis is an outstanding but typical example of the thirteenth-century canonists: he studied Roman Law at Bologna and canon law at Paris. In 1244 he was ambassador of Henry III of England to Innocent IV; created bishop in 1244 and in 1262 Cardinal and Archbishop of Ostia. He published his *Summa* 1250–61, the *Commentaria super libros decretalium* until his death in 1271; cf Noonan, *Usury*, 49. Also Baldwin, *Just Price*, 42; R. Kay, 'Hostiensis and some Embrun Provincial Councils', in *Traditio*, xx (1964) 503–13.

26. Tierney, *Poor Law*, 12.

27. McCarthy, in *EIC* xix 145. As already indicated, canonists were often trained in both kinds of law, which accounts for the easy transition of ideas and principles between the two systems. Rufinus and Stephen of Tournai were students of Bulgarus at Bologna, Johannes Bassianus was one of the first teachers of both laws; Johannes Teutonicus and Tancredus (d. 1235) studied Roman Law under Azo; likewise Vincentius Hispanus (d. 1248) under Accursius. Goffredus of Trani (d. 1245) and Innocent IV (d. 1254) were both experts in Roman Law. Hostiensis was the *iuris utrius monarcha*; cf Baldwin, *Just Price*, 43. The *Corpus iuris civilis* known to these lawyers from the twelfth century onwards consisted of the four books that contain the legislative work of the Emperor Justinian, i.e. the *Code*, originally issued in 529, but now surviving in the second edition of 534; *Digest* (or *Pandects*) 533, a collection of extracts from famous Roman lawyers, who were themselves codifying current jurisprudence; *Institutes* designed as an introduction to the principles of law; *Novels*, the constitutions of Justinian that appeared after the second edition of the Code, which were privately collected. Christianity, in its turn, had influenced Roman Law: cf Gaudemet, *La Formation*, 197, 203.

28. Baldwin, *Just Price*, 10.

29. It was not, however, afraid to speak out against what it regarded as unjust or immoral laws, cf Vienne [29].

30. J. F. Cleary, *Canonical Limitations*, 16–18.

31. On fraud and sale, see Baldwin, *Just Price*, 55; G. Le Bras discusses the *nudum pactum* in *Camb. Econ. Hist.* III 561.

32. For a brief but adequate survey of the bibliography available for the history of the councils, see H. Jedin, 'Nouvelles Données sur l'histoire des conciles généraux', in *JWH* I (1953) 164–78, and especially, by the same author, *Ecumenical Councils of the Catholic Church: an Historial Outline*, 240–50.

33. The basis of the documents translated in the Appendix is the text of the councils edited by the Centro di documentazione istituto per le scienze religiose, *Conciliorum Oecumenicorum Decreta (COD)*.

34. General councils were not absolutely necessary for the life of the Church, cf L. Jaeger, *The Ecumenical Council, the Church and Christendom*, p. xiii.

35. E. W. Kemp, *Counsel and Consent: Aspects of the Government of the Church as exemplified in the History of English Provincial Synods*, 18.

36. Baldwin, Noonan and Tierney touch on this matter, but only indirectly and as part of a larger treatment of their main topic.

37. C. J. Hefele, *Histoire des conciles*, here v, Ier partie 724.

38. C. R. Cheney, *From Becket to Langton*, 141.

39. C. R. Cheney, 'The So-called Statutes of John Pecham and Robert Winchelsey for the Province of Canterbury', in *JEH* XII (1961) 14–34, here 20.

40. Factors that complicate the issue still further are (*a*) lack of authentic texts for several of the councils, e.g. for Lateran I; cf Jedin, *Ecumenical Councils*, 67, and (*b*) the occasional disparity between the promulgated and published texts of the same council.   On the latter, see the brilliant reconstruction of Lyons I by S. Kuttner, 'Die Konstitutionen des ersten allgemeinen Konzils von Lyon', in *Studia et documenta historiae et juris*, VI (1940) 70–131, and by the same author, 'Conciliar Law in the making.   The Lyonese Constitutions (1274) of Gregory X in a Manuscript at Washington', in *Miscellanea Pio Paschini II* (Rome, 1949) 39–81.

41. Cheney, *Becket to Langton*, 23.

42. Cf L. Génicot, 'Clercs et laïques au diocèse de Liège à la fin du moyen âge', in *TRG* XXIII (1955) 42–52.

43. For a modern definition, see P. J. Corish, 'The Church and the Councils', in *IER* XCVIII (1962) 203–12, here 209–10.

44. Cf H. Fuhrmann, 'Das ökumenische Konzil und seine historischen Grundlagen', in *Geschichte im Wissenschaft und Unterricht*, XI (1961) 672–95, here 676.

45. Jedin, *Ecumenical Councils*, 24, and in *JWH* I 170; also Fuhrmann, *op. cit.* 679.

46. Jedin, *Ecumenical Councils*, 39, comments that we are better informed about this council (surviving lists, letters, etc.) than about any other council of Christian antiquity.   The number of bishops was not 600, but smaller.

47. In *IER* XCVIII 209–10.   See also H. S. Alivisatos, 'Les Conciles œcuméniques v^e, vi^e, viie et viiie', in *Le Concile*, 111–23, especially 117; Fuhrmann, 686, remarks that not until the eleventh century was the decision of Rome made that 'Eine Synode ist allgemein durch Beteiligung Roms'.

48. P. J. Dunning, 'Irish Representatives and Irish Ecclesiastical Affairs at the Fourth Lateran Council', in *Studies Gwynn*, 90–113, here 93–94.   See also M. Gibbs and J. Lang, *Bishops and Reform 1215–1272*, 170, on °Lateran IV 29 and Lateran IV 32.

49. Gibbs and Lang, *Bishops and Reform*, 134.

50. M. D. O'Sullivan, *Italian Merchant Bankers in Ireland in the Thirteenth Century*, 54.

51. Gill, *Eugenius IV*, 61.

52. Mundy–Loomis, 30–1.

53. [Sess. X] 'Cardinal of St Mark . . . reported the substance . . . that Pope John XXIII . . . still had his gang of go-betweens and assistants, merchants and money-changers, who wielded more influence in these affairs than cardinals

and men of honor. Many of them were his own familiars. Almost every
thing he owned was for sale. These were notorious facts. In addition, it was
generally understood that he had alienated much of the patrimony of the
Roman Church, such as the fortress of Radicofani to the Sienese; likewise
property belonging to the cardinals, titular churches and other churches of the
city of Rome, as well as outside churches, monasteries, and ecclesiastical
institutions. All this property, it was widely said, was for sale in his hands.'
Mundy–Loomis, 243–4.

54. Gill (*Eugenius IV*, 14) cites the speech of the German delegate (Mansi,
XXVII 1156C): 'avaritia, quae est idolorum servitus, ambitio ecclesiasticarum
dignitatum, haeresis, et simonia, et periculosissima schismata . . . fastusque et
pompae surrexerunt et creverunt in clero. Ita ut ex his studia litteratorum
et literatos defecisse, ecclesiarum, monasteriorum, dignitatum, et beneficiorum
aedificia solemnia corruisse et immobilia bona inculta permansisse, pretiosaque
mobilia distracta, solos pecuniosos, nummularios, quondam expulsos de
templo, leves et vagabundos, ignaros, vitiolos, et minus idoneos . . . praelatos
fuisse. . . .'

55. On the early councils, see P. T. Camelot, O.P., 'Les Conciles œcuméni-
ques des ive et ve siècles', in *Le Concile*, 45–73, and 'Les Conciles œcuméniques
dans l'antiquité', in *Lumière et vie*, VIII no. 45 (1959) 3–17, especially 8 ff. The
idea of such a council was not a novelty in A.D. 325.

56. Cf Camelot, in *Lumière et vie*, VIII 9; Gaudemet, *La Formation*, 137. In
the East the eighth general council (Constantinople IV (869–70)) is not recognized as ecumenical; cf Alivisatos, in *Le Concile*, 120. The so-called *Pseudo-
synodus Photiana* takes its place. For the Imperial sanction of the councils'
decisions, see the following: F. Dvornik, *The General Councils of the Church*,
27; Jedin, in *JWH* I 168–9; Fuhrmann, in *Geschichte im Wissenschaft und
Unterricht*, XI 678: 'Die Beschlüsse sind von Kaiser bestätigt und als Reich-
erlasse verbreitet worden'.

57. The Greeks considered that a general council needed both Churches,
hence there were no more after the first eight; cf Fuhrmann, *op. cit.* 679.

58. R. C. Gerest, O.P., 'Concile et réforme de l'Église, de la fin du xiii^e
siècle au concile de Trente', in *Lumière et vie*, XI no. 59 (1962) 21–56, here
21.

59. For example, Nicaea I 17 was directed against usury (see p. 63) and was
frequently renewed by later councils; cf Jedin, *Ecumenical Councils*, 20.

60. On the special status accorded the first four councils, cf Yves Congar,
'La Primauté des quatre premiers conciles œcuméniques', in *Le Concile*, 75–
109; here 89, where he cites Gratian D.15 c.1. Also P. Hamell, 'First Four
Councils', in *IER* XCVIII (1962) 275–87.

61. On the Latin councils, cf M. B. Carra De Vaux Saint-Cyr, O.P., 'Les
Conciles œcuméniques du second millénaire de l'histoire de l'Église', in
Lumière et vie, VIII no. 45 (1959) 18–38. Of the reform synods from 1049 to
1122 at least 100 such councils were held; cf D. B. Zema, 'Reform legislation

in the Eleventh Century and its Economic Import', in *CHR* XXVII (1941) 16–38, here 22.

62. Gwynn, in *IER* XCIX 147, remarks that the absence of the Eastern bishops and patriarchs from the Latin general councils was one reason why the latter were less concerned with dogma and doctrine.

63. All the councils were concerned with secular affairs; Jaeger, *Ecumenical Council*, 21, cites the example of Lateran IV which dealt with crusades, the foundation of the Latin Empire of Constantinople, Magna Carta extorted from King John of England, succession to the dukedom of Toulouse, and the conflict over the succession of Frederick II as Emperor.

64. The regular Roman synods gradually disappeared — their functions being taken over by the papal consistory — and this disappearance strengthened the importance of the general councils; Dvornik, *General Councils*, 53.

65. There is a large bibliography on Lateran IV: cf Antonio García García, O.F.M., 'El Concilio IV de Letrán (1215) y sus comentarios', in *Traditio*, XIV (1958) 484–502, especially 484, for a list of contemporary commentaries on the decrees of the council, and 'Los comentarios de los canonistas a las constituciones del concilio IV de Letrán (1215)', in *Congrès 1958*, 151–61; M. Maccarrone, 'Il IV Concilio Lateranense', in *Divinitas*, V (1961) 270–98. Other historians agree that the council was 'the greatest representative assembly of medieval Christendom', Tierney, *Poor Law*, 83; cf C. R. Cheney, 'A Letter of Pope Innocent III and the Lateran Decree on Cistercian Tithe-paying', in *Cîteaux Commentarii Cistercienses*, fasc. 2 (1962) 146–51, especially 146, where the author concludes that 'the decrees mark the culmination of a period of speculation and experiment in matters of doctrine and Church government which can be traced uninterrupted from at least the pontificate of Alexander III; on several matters they indeed only reiterate Alexander's decrees in the Third Lateran Council'. The council met in three sessions on 11, 20 and 30 November 1215. It was attended by some 412 bishops, 800 abbots and priors, and numerous representatives of prelates and chapters, and deputies of almost all the secular rulers. In all some 2000 representatives! Cf Dvornik, *General Councils*, 54. Except for c.42 and the constitution *Ad liberandam terram sanctam* the rest of the 70 [71] canons passed into *Compilatio IV* and the same except for c.49 into the *Decretals* of Gregory IX; García, in *Traditio*, XIV 485.

66. Cf P. Toubert, 'Les Déviations de la croisade au milieu du xiiie siècle: Alexandre IV contre Manfred', in *Le Moyen Age*, LXIX (1963) 391–9, especially 391 n (2) for the bibliography. The Hohenstaufen threatened the papacy, not dogmatically, but in its temporal power. Manfred was accused not of heresy, as had been the case in previous deviations, but of an *impium foedus*, i.e. collusion with the Saracens of South Italy (ibid. 392, 394). Cf Waley, in *EHR* LXXII 25, that a crusade was often a sign that the papacy could not pay or could not get soldiers.

67. Cf the gloss of Damasus on *Lateran IV c.3* '*De haereticis*'. v. '*occupandam*' (= *COD* 210. 7): 'Et ita catholici possunt occupare res hereticorum, nec

facient contra precepta Decalogi: "Non concupisces rem proximi tui" De hac materia dic ut xxiii. q.vi. notatur', MS Florence, Laurenziana S. Croce III sin 6 fo. 96ra.

68. Cf R. Manselli, 'Onorio III e Federico II (revisione d'un giudizio?)', in *Studi romani*, XI (1963) 142–59, especially 148. The severe measure of Lyons I [*COD* 254–9 for the Bull of Deposition of Frederick II] contains, among the several charges brought against the Emperor, one of invasion, despoliation and illegal taxation of the Church and religious Orders; cf *COD* 257. 31–42. Frederick's dealings with the Saracens are dealt with *COD* 258. 18–31. Cf Dvornik, *General Councils*, 57; Gwynn, in *IER* XCIX 154; Gerest, in *Lumière et vie*, XI 23. This council also concerned itself with the invasion of Hungary by the Tartars, aid for the Holy Land and the Latin Empire of Constantinople.

69. For Lyons II, cf Gerest, in *Lumière et vie*, XI. Significantly, at Vienne for the first time procurators appeared as representatives of those bishops unable to attend in person; Jaeger, *Ecumenical Council*, 30. The decrees of these councils were modified without reference to the participants, cf Jedin, in *JWH* I 170–2.

70. Gerest, in *Lumière et vie*, XI 51, commenting on Lateran V, concludes that the Holy Spirit does nothing when men want to do nothing. J. D. Conway sums up the working of the council as leisurely, lethargic, listless, lax (*Times of Decision*, 251).

71. Gill, *Eugenius IV*, 207. At his election Eugenius had to agree to the *Capitulations* that 'the half of all and every census, right, revenue, income and emolument whatsoever of the Roman Church' was to go to the College of Cardinals (ibid. 208).

72. Ibid. 185–6.

73. Cf Dunning, in *Studies Gwynn* 94 n 22.

74. Gwynn, in *IER* XCIX 149; see also Jaeger, *Ecumenical Council*, 18, and Maccarrone, in *Divinitas*, V 272.

75. Cf S. Kuttner, 'Dat Galienus opes et sanctio Justiniana', in *Linguistic and Literary Studies in honor of H. A. Hatzfeld*, 237–46, also 238 n 5 where he points out that Lateran II 9 = Clermont c.5 (Mansi, XXI 438).

76. For the complicated procedure of the fifteenth-century councils, see E. F. Jacob, 'A Note on the English Concordat of 1418', in *Studies Gwynn*, 349–58, especially 350 for the Council of Constance in 1418.

77. Nor should one disregard the warning so often given that 'In any age, and the Middle Ages was hardly an exception, theory is no guarantee of practice. . . .' (Baldwin, *Just Price*, 10).

78. Cf Zema, in *CHR* XXVII 23, where he estimates that of the 151 decrees as many as 105 relate to the safeguarding and canonical use of ecclesiastical estates and revenues.

CHAPTER 3

1. Byrne, *Investment of Church Funds*, 8.

2. For bibliography, cf *Camb. Econ. Hist.* II 531–56.

3. R. S. Lopez and I. W. Raymond, *Medieval Trade in the Mediterranean World*, 36.

4. Cf C. Roth and I. H. Levine, *The World History of the Jewish People*, XI (2nd Series: *Medieval Period:* II *The Dark Ages: Jews in Christian Europe*) 129, for Jewish trade and settlement in the Rhineland and Meuse valley, which 'came to acquire world-wide importance'.

5. H. L. Adelson, *Medieval Commerce*, 53–4.

6. Lopez argues that the tenth century was the originating period of the Renaissance: he points to the population rise, land reclamation, Viking expansion and settlement, contracts of *commenda*, new types of ships, the use and spread of the horseshoe and collar, beginning of guilds, growth of communes in Italy, e.g. in 897 the citizens of Turin ousted the bishop: cf 'Still another Renaissance', in *AHR* LVII (1951) 1–21, especially 2–5. But *contra*, see P. Grierson, 'Commerce in the Dark Ages. A Critique of the Evidence', in *TRHS*⁵ IX (1959) 123–40. Grierson hardly deals with the arguments of Lopez, who cites *inter alia* the following villages that became towns during the tenth century: going through the alphabet, Algiers, Antwerp, Bolgher, Bremen, Kiev, Itil, Magdeburg, Prague . . . etc. (*AHR* LVII 7).

7. There are many detailed studies of individual towns that must be the basis of any judgement we make concerning the economic revolution, e.g. J. H. Mundy, *Liberty and Political Power in Toulouse 1050–1250*, in discussing the town's expansion cites forest clearance, population growth, physical growth of the town, trade and industry (ibid. 4, 5, 8, 44 ff).

8. C. M. Cipolla, 'Currency Depreciation in Medieval Europe', in *EcHR*² XV (1963) 413–22, and 419 for the Italian communes controlled by merchants from the eleventh century onwards.

9. R. L. Reynolds, 'Origins of Modern Business Enterprises; Medieval Italy', in *JEcH* XII (1952) 350–77, here 363. Also Lopez and Raymond, *Medieval Trade*, 51, where they stress the rise of the town, and not the grant of market rights, as of the greatest significance. A market channels goods, but does not create trade.

10. On the availability of money and its use from the time 'when documented history began', see H. A. Miskimin, *Money, Prices and Foreign Exchange in Fourteenth-Century France*, 20–1. For Venice, see Adelson, *Medieval Commerce*, 58, and F. C. Lane, 'Recent Studies on the Economic History of Venice', in *JEcH* XXIII (1963) 312–34, especially 312. More technically, as De Roover argues, adopting the position of Schumpeter, 'capitalism is as old as credit creation, which would carry us back to 1200 or thereabouts'. — R. De Roover, *Money, Banking and Credit in Medieval Bruges*, 354.

11. Lopez, in *AHR* LVII 8. Cf P. J. Jones, 'Per la storia agraria italiana nel medio evo: lineamenti e problemi', in *Rivista storica italiana*, LXXVI (1964) 287–348, especially 335.

12. B. Waites, 'The Monastic Settlement of North-East Yorkshire', in *Yorkshire Archaeological Journal*, XL (1962) 478–95, here 482–3. Not all the abbeys flourished; Rievaulx was taken into royal custody in 1276 and again in 1288, because the abbey could not pay its debts to the Italian merchants. Whitby and Guisborough were also in a state of collapse.

13. For a detailed bibliography, see H. E. Hallam, 'Population Density in Medieval Fenland', in *EcHR²* XIV (1961–2) 71–81, here 79–80.

14. A. C. Chibnall, *Sherington: Fiefs and Fields of a Buckinghamshire Village*, 100.

15. G. A. Williams, *Medieval London: from Commune to Capital*, 15.

16. On the *commenda*, see A. L. Udovitch, 'At the Origins of the Western Commenda: Islam, Israel, Byzantium', in *Speculum*, XXXVII (1962) 198–207. Also Lopez, in *AHR* LVII 8; Le Goff, *Marchands et banquiers*, 20; B. N. Nelson, 'The Legend of the Divine Surety and the Jewish Moneylender', in *Annuaire de l'institut de philologie et d'histoire orientales et slaves*, VII (1939–44) 289–338, here 296.

17. H. C. Krijeger, 'Genoese Merchants, their Partnerships and Investments, 1155 to 1164', in *Studi Sapori*, I 255–71, here 258, 263. For the period 1202–1226, see E. Bach, 'Études genoises: Le Minutier de Lanfranco', in *Studi Sapori*, I 373–89.

18. Yves Renouard, *Les Hommes d'affaires italiens du moyen âge*, 14; also G. Luzzatto, *An Economic History of Italy*, 51–3.

19. Luzzatto, *Economic History*, 117. Marco Datini da Prato left a fortune of 75,000 florins, mostly to charity: Le Goff, *Marchands et banquiers*, 89.

20. Y. Renouard, *Les Relations des papes d'Avignon et des compagnies commerciales et bancaires de 1316 à 1378*, 585. When the banks did go bankrupt the efficient machinery of the papacy usually succeeded in recovering most of its debts (ibid. 601).

21. Cf B. Lyon, 'Medieval Real Estate Developments and Freedom', in *AHR* LXIII (1957–8) 47–61, especially 58, for land reclamation in maritime Flanders. For England, see M. M. Postan, 'Italy and the Economic Development of England in the Middle Ages', in *JEcH* XI (1951) 339–46, where he rejects the argument that English expansion depended for its model and inspiration on Italy. Also Adelson, *Medieval Commerce*, 59.

22. O'Sullivan, *Italian Merchant Bankers*, 11.

23. Krijeger, in *Studi Sapori*, I 269; also H. Ammann, 'Die Anfänge des Aktivhandels und der Tucheinfuhr aus Nordwesteuropa nach dem Mittelmeergebiet', in *Studi Sapori*, I 273–310, especially 283, 300, 306.

24. See J. C. Russell, *Late Ancient and Medieval Population*, 140, and 'A Quantitative Approach to Medieval Population Change', in *JEcH* XXIV (1964) 1–21. Also P. J. Jones, in *Riv. stor. ital.* LXXVI 311.

25. England in 1086, using the evidence of Domesday Book, had a population of about one million, with a density of about 9 inhabitants to the square kilometre: Lopez, *Proc. 10th Intern. Cong.* III 121.

26. Cipolla, in *EcHR*² xv 417; also L. Génicot, 'Sur les témoignages d'accroissement de la population en occident du xi⁰ au xiii⁰ siècle', in *JWH* I (1953) 446–62. According to Russell, *Medieval Population*, 137, ecclesiastical policies favoured increasing population, but his arguments seem specious. Miskimin, *Money, Prices and Foreign Exchange*, 15, summarizes the argument thus: 'The consensus of historians would have two centuries of population growth, until the end of the thirteenth or early fourteenth centuries, a levelling off until the Black Death of 1348–49, and thereafter a sharp decline. England had a population of 3 millions before the plague and 2,073,279 thereafter.' (Also ibid. 16.) For examples of particular population increases, cf H. E. Hallam, 'Some Thirteenth-century Censuses', in *EcHR*² x (1957) 340–61, especially 340–1. Cf Jones, in *Riv. stor. ital.* LXXVI 290, that, in Italy, population 'si raddoppiò, raggiungendo un totale variamente stabilito fra 7 e 9 milioni'.

27. J. Z. Titow, 'Some Evidence of the Thirteenth-century Population Increase', in *EcHR*² xiv (1961–2) 218–23, here 220. In 1311 the population of Taunton in Somerset, England, was about 4160 persons, with arable land at a ratio of 2·5 acres per person. In 1248 the average had been 3·3 acres because of the smaller population (ibid. 223). For London, Williams, *Medieval London*, 315, but see also S. L. Thrupp, *The Merchant Class of Medieval London [1300–1500]*, 186, where the figure is set at 30,000–40,000 'maintained by a steady stream of immigration'. For the Fenland, see Hallam, in *EcHR*² xiv 72. As in Taunton, the population increases did not cease when land reclamation ceased, but continued, thus creating pressure on resources. In the next two centuries the balance was upset, no new techniques were evolved to deal with the problem, and 'five centuries lapsed before the Lincolnshire Fenland supported as many people again' (ibid. 79). On town population, van Werweke, 'Le Mortgage et son rôle économique en Flandre et en Lotharingie', in *Camb. Econ. Hist.* III 38–9.

28. On technology, see Lopez, in *JWH* I 598. Also the joint symposium by C. M. Cipolla, R. S. Lopez and H. A. Miskimin, 'Economic Depression of the Renaissance', in *EcHR*² xvi (1964) 519–29. Lopez (525 n 1) cites S. Lilley, *Men, Machines and History* (1951), who assigns twelve capital innovations and a 69-point score to the period 1200–1350, but only six innovations and a 34-point score to the period between 1350 and 1550. Further details of inventions given by B. Gille, 'Les Développements technologiques en Europe de 1100 à 1400', in *JWH* III (1956–7) 63–108, especially 67, where the author lists 5624 water-mills as mentioned by Domesday Book.

29. W. O. Hassall, *How They Lived: an Anthology of Original Accounts written before 1485*, 18. For shipping, see J. J. McCusker, 'The Wine Prise and Mediaeval Mercantile Shipping', in *Speculum*, xli (1966) 279–96, especially 283.

30. E. M. Carus-Wilson, 'An Industrial Revolution of the Thirteenth Century', in *Medieval Merchant Venturers: Collected Studies*, 183–210, here 208.

31. Gille, in *JWH* III 91.

32. O'Sullivan, *Italian Merchant Bankers*, 98.

33. Cf N. S. B. Gras, 'Stages in Business History', in *Studi Sapori* I 5–27, here 9; also Baldwin, *Just Price*, 7.

34. Le Goff, *Marchands et banquiers*, 49–51, gives details of Sire Jehan Boine-broke, merchant-draper of Douai, at the end of the thirteenth century, who exploited his workers and other merchants who dealt with him; ibid. 18–19 for the fairs of Champagne.

35. O'Sullivan, *Italian Merchant Bankers*, 10, 12. Also Verlinden in *Camb. Econ. Hist.* III 130, 133.

36. In the end the gulf was bridged by merchants' sons entering the Church. Le Goff, *Marchands et banquiers*, 88, cites Bernardo Tolomei, great banker of Siena, who founded the Olivetans. Godric de Finchale was canonized; also Homebon, merchant of Cremona, one of the *humiliati*, the worker-monks, powerful in the wool industry, was canonized by Innocent III in 1197. Ibid. 64 for the list of families.

37. Baldwin, *Just Price*, 36. For example, the total acreage of Dublin county was 222,710 acres, of which the Church, at the end of the Middle Ages, held 104,000 acres; J. Otway-Ruthven, 'The Medieval Church Lands of County Dublin', in *Studies Gwynn*, 54–73, here 56. In London the Church owned more than half the flour-mills *c.* 1300; Thrupp, *Merchant Class*, 119. At Lincoln half the arable near the city had become mortmain; Hill, *Medieval Lincoln*, 334.

38. D. Herlihy, 'Land, Family and Women in Continental Europe, 701–1200', in *Traditio*, XVIII (1962) 89–113, especially 111; also Luzzatto, *Economic History*, 20–1. The same applies to the period of the crusades; cf G. Duby, 'Le Budget de l'abbaye de Cluny entre 1080 et 1155', in *AESC* VII (1952) 155–71, here 161.

39. Cf Doheny, *Church Property*, 10, where he comments on Nicaea II 12; also Byrne, *Investment*, 3; Cleary, *Canonical Limitations*, 34.

40. E. John, 'The Imposition of the Common Burdens upon the Lands of the English Church', in *BIHR* XXXI (1958) 117–29, especially 127. For the Arras example of merchants taking minor vows, see J. Lestocquoy, 'Inhonesta mercimonia', in *Mélanges Louis Halphen*, 411–15, here 411. Le Goff gives further details of such families as the Hucquedieu and Crespin, who served the monastery of Saint-Vaast at Arras (*Marchands et banquiers*, 76, 88).

41. These included the *pallium*, the payment made by archbishops on receiving this insignia of their authority; the *quindennia* payable every five years by holders; cf G. de Lagarde, *La Naissance de l'esprit laïque au déclin du moyen âge: I Bilan du xiiie siècle*, 56–7. See also Renouard, *Les Relations*, 23; O'Sullivan, *Italian Merchant Bankers*, 28.

42. P. Partner, 'Papal Finance and the Papal State', in *History Today*, VII (1957) 766–74, here 766, stresses the increasing importance of the papal patrimony as the source of the papacy's income. He describes the patrimony as 'a loosely knit state, which in the west included Rome and its district, the ancient Latium as far south as Terracina and Ceprano, and as far north as the river Pescia, running inland along the Sienese border into Umbria, to Città delle Pieve, Perugia and Città di Castello. On the Adriatic it extended from Ravenna and Bologna in the north (with suzerainty over Ferrara and some neighbouring areas) south down to the coast to Ascoli Piceno, and eastwards into the mountainous interior to the Duchy of Spoleto'. For the history of the state and its revenues, see D. Waley, *The Papal State in the Thirteenth Century*, especially 1–29, 252–75. At the end of the thirteenth century the income from the papal states was still not significant, and it 'probably accounted for only about one-tenth of the papacy's total revenues' (ibid. 275). Waley estimates the revenue from the state at about 30,000 florins (1 florin = 35s of Ravenna, 32s 6d papal currency c. 1300) (ibid. 272). On the census from exempt monasteries in England cf. Lunt: 'in 1327 . . . there were twelve monasteries which owed annual payment of census in return either for being exempted from episcopal jurisdiction and being under the immediate jurisdiction of St Peter and the pope, or for being under the protection of the apostolic see. They were Anglesey, Bodmin, Bury St Edmunds, Carlisle, Chacombe, Chertsey, Faversham, Malmesbury, St Albans, St Mary without Aldgate, Scarborough and Tonbridge' (*Financial Relations*, II 55). Peter's Pence during most of the period before 1327 was treated as temporal income, but it gradually came to be regarded as spiritual, and in 1328 it was definitely decided that 'the due belonged to the jurisdiction of the ecclesiastical courts' (ibid. 52).

43. W. E. Lunt, *Papal Revenues in the Middle Ages*, I 51, 52.

44. P. D. Partner, *The Papal State under Martin V*, 137.

45. G. Constable, *Monastic Tithes*, 2.

46. Numerous provincial councils had forbidden and continued to prohibit this practice, e.g. Antioch 24 and Arles III 5, Toledo IV 33, Arles V 13; Doheny, *Church Property*, 9.

47. Byrne, *Investment*, 3–5, 9. Strictly, *emphyteusis* granted 'ownership of an immovable thing regarding its use only, while the direct ownership is retained, under the obligation of some payment to the direct proprietor, either perpetually or during the lifetime of one or more persons, or for a specified time, which may not be less than ten years'; cf. B. W. Dempsey, *Interest and Usury*, 141. Also Sheedy, *Bartolus*, 169 that the period was 'usually to the third generation'. See also Luzzatto, *Economic History*, 64–5, where he cites the edict of Otto III in 998 that no lease of church land, whether by *emphyteusis* or by *libellus*, should be for longer than one life. Full commentary in Byrne, *Investment*, 10–11, and Cleary, *Canonical Limitations*, 34.

48. Cf Lib. Sext. gloss. 1.6.5 ad *oeconomatus* 'Oeconomus, cui res ecclesiastica gubernanda mandatur . . .'=Lyons II 4. Bartolus cites the grant of a

lease in which five years was specified as the period for payment of overdue rent; Sheedy, *Bartolus*, 169.

49. Cf Le Bras, *Institutions ecclésiastiques*, Ière partie, 254.

50. Catherine E. Boyd, *Tithes and Parishes in Medieval Italy*, 56–7.

51. J. Gilchrist, 'Proprietary Churches', in *New Catholic Encyclopedia*, XI 874–5.

52. R. W. Southern, *The Making of the Middle Ages* (1953) 168, describes the monastery as expected to be a centre of activity, for it was, after all, an investment by the lay lord.

53. J. Gilchrist, 'The Reformation and the Historians: I — The Background; III — Continuity and Change in England', in *Twentieth Century*, XV (1961) 114–26, 313–28, here 122, 314.

54. Luzzatto, *Economic History*, 64.

55. *Adversus Simmiacos*, II 20 (*MGH: Libelli de lite*, I 163.36–164.9) II 35 (ibid. 184.11–24).

56. Cf D. Herlihy, 'Treasure Hoards in the Italian Economy, 960–1139', in *EcHR*^{2} X (1957) 1–14, especially 4. Recovery of church lands was brought about not only by gift, but also by purchase, which meant that capital in the form of treasure was converted into real estate (ibid. 5). Also see Zema, in *CHR* XXVII 18.

57. Cf Schroeder, 87.

58. J. Gilchrist, '*Simoniaca haeresis* and the Concept of Orders from Leo IX to Gratian', in *Proceedings of the Second International Congress of Medieval Canon Law* (Boston, 1963) (E Civitate Vaticana, 1965) 209–35, especially 214.

59. In *Traditio*, XVIII 98 and 110.

60. Cf D. B. Zema, 'Economic Reorganisation of the Roman See during the Gregorian Reform', in *SG* I (1947) 137–68.

61. Constable, *Monastic Tithes*, 57.

62. Ibid. ch. 2, 'Monastic possession of tithes', 57–83, especially 63–5.

63. Cf Gregory VII autumn synod of 1078 c. 7 (Reg. VI. 5b ed. Caspar 404); C. Violante, 'Les Prêts sur gage foncier dans la vie économique et sociale de Milan au xie siècle', in *CCM* V (1962) 147–68, 437–59. The author brings out very well the expansion of credit in this period and the part played by the Gregorian Reform's need for ready cash. Matilda of Tuscany's support of Gregory VII and his successors subsequently led to conflict between Pope and Emperor for possession of Matilda's lands. The conflict lasted for a century, but in the end both parties lost to the communes and other local interests; cf Partner, *Martin V*, 11. In 1079 Matilda had willed her entire allodial possessions to the Church; she died in 1115. On the Pierleoni, cf D. B. Zema, 'The Houses of Tuscany and of Pierleone in the Crisis of Rome in the Eleventh Century', in *Traditio*, II (1944) 155–75. Cf Conway, *Times of Decision*, 129.

64. A. Chédeville, 'Les Restitutions d'églises en faveur de l'abbaye de Saint-Vincent-du-Mans', in *CCM* III (1960) 209–17, here 211; C. Van de

Kieft, 'Une Église privée de l'abbaye de la Trinité de Vendôme au xie siècle', in *Le Moyen Age*, LXIX (1963) 157–68; Constable, in *Rev. bénéd.* LXX 591.

65. W. G. Hoskins, *The Midland Peasant: the Economic and Social History of a Leicestershire Village*, 19–20, gives details of the history of the Church of Wigston given by Robert, Earl of Meulan, and Earl of Leicestershire, to the Cluniac priory of Lenton *c.* 1109–18. The priory was content to take an annual payment of 100s from the rectorial revenues that were worth about 56 marks (£37 6s 8d). The living passed to a lay lord at the Reformation. In 1766 the Duke of St Albans 'as compensation for the great tithe got one-seventh of the enclosure award'.

66. Constable, *Monastic Tithes*, 89, 98.

67. On °Lateran III 14, see Boyd, *Tithes and Parishes*, 126, 165, 265.

68. Cheney, *Becket to Langton*, 132–6.

69. For the development of the canonical doctrine of the resident vicar 'permanent and irremoveable except by formal judicial process and endowed with a portion of the income to be fixed by the bishop', see Tierney, *Poor Law*, 83; also Cleary, *Canonical Limitations*, 43–4. Herlihy, in *Speculum*, XXXVI 98, concludes that by the late twelfth century the tithe was 'coming to rival if not to surpass direct ownership as the Church's chief economic support'.

70. Tierney, *Poor Law*, 83.

71. Ibid. 92, 96; Cheney, *Becket to Langton*, 139; L. E. Elliott-Binns, *Medieval Cornwall*, 332, gives figures 5 marks for 1222; 60 shillings for 1287; 7 marks for 1353, and 8 marks for 1378. An agricultural labourer and his family needed about £3 p.a.

72. Constable, *Monastic Tithes*, 2.

73. Constable, in *JEH* XIII 175, and *Monastic Tithes*, 130, limits this to small tithes 'from vegetables, poultry and the like'. On the later period, see J. A. F. Thomson, 'Tithe disputes in later medieval London', in *EHR* LXXVIII (1963) 1–17.

74. Noonan, *Usury*, 35; Nelson, *Usury*, 16.

75. Constable, *Monastic Tithes*, 267–8, 287–8.

76. Tierney, *Poor Law*, 83; Le Bras, *Institutions ecclésiastiques*, Ière partie, 256. Lateran V renewed former legislation on tithes in Sess. X Bull *against Exempt Persons*, COD 607. 4–5, 15; Elliott-Binns, *Medieval Cornwall*, 324.

77. Gilchrist, in *JEH* XIII 23–4.

78. Cf Cleary, *Canonical Limitations*, 49.

79. Zema, in *CHR* XXVII 27.

80. Cf Lestocquoy, 'le clergé n'a connu une véritable séparation de monde du commerce qu'au moment de la législation élaborée au concile de Trente' (*Mélanges Halphen*, 411).

81. De Roover, *Medici Bank*, 135–7, for letters of credit.

82. R. S. Lopez, 'An Aristocracy of Money in the Early Middle Ages', in *Speculum*, XXVIII (1953) 1–43, here 41.

83. Renouard, *Les Relations*, 16–17. Several of the popes came from the

great merchant families of Italy, e.g. Innocent IV was a member of the leading Genoese family of Fieschi, cf. Le Goff, *Marchands et banquiers*, 94. He adds that the entry of merchants' sons into the Church has not been sufficiently stressed as a bridge for the change of attitude that occurred towards commerce in the thirteenth century. See p. 129.

84. On the crusades, see J. A. Brundage, 'Recent Crusade Historiography: Some observations and Suggestions', in *CHR* XLIX (1964) 493–507, especially 500 n 18 for economic aspects and 505 where he says that little work has been done on the economic background to the crusades and of the men who took part.

85. M. Villey, 'L'Idée de la croisade chez les juristes du moyen-âge', in *Proc. 10th Intern. Cong.* III 587–8. Innocent III based his canonical theory of the crusades on Lateran III 27. Also H. Maisonneuve, *Études sur les origines de l'inquisition*, 94–5.

86. Ibid. 177–9. The papacy's grant of financial privileges to the crusaders often brought the popes into conflict with the policy of the secular rulers. Thus Innocent III tried to persuade Philip Augustus, who had recalled the Jews to his realm despite strong opposition on the part of the clergy, to abide by the terms of the crusade indulgence formulated in the decree *Post miserabile* of 15 August 1198, 'which called for remission by Jews of all interest payments owed them by crusaders' (Nelson, in *Annuaire*, VII 331). On the other hand the papal decree against usury was enforced in England, even for those who had made a money-grant, but did not actually go; cf Roth, *A History of the Jews*, 52.

87. Even so licences to trade were still granted, cf Adelson, *Medieval Commerce*, 171–2, Reading no. 35, a licence for Venetians to trade with the Saracens, 3 December 1198, granted by Innocent III. The licence forbade the Venetians to take war supplies, which included 'iron, flax, pitch, sharpened stakes, ropes, arms, galleys, ships and timbers, finished or unfinished'. Clerics, who were normally tax exempt, sometimes engaged in illicit trade and this roused the anger of the merchants. Worse still, they even traded with the Saracens, acting on behalf of lay merchants. Cf Renouard, *Les Relations*, 16. Among the goods exported to the Saracen regions were slaves, which 'constituait un des plus grands trafics des marchands chrétiens médiévaux' (Le Goff, *Marchands et banquiers*, 74–5); also cf Lopez, in *Proc. 10th Intern. Cong.* III 144, that as the local supply of slaves in Catholic Europe ceased, the merchants 'turned to the heathens beyond the northern and eastern pale of the Carolingian and Ottoman empire' (ibid. 144). The ban on trade with the Saracens was not always fortunate in its effect. When it was kept, it tended to worsen the balance of payments position between East and West; cf Adelson, *Medieval Commerce*, 76–7. The papacy charged heavy fees for the grants of licence to trade. For interesting details of a merchant's store of arms, cf I. Origo, *The Merchant of Prato*, 36–7.

88. Lopez, in *JWH* I 613 stresses the amount of booty taken in the first and

fourth crusades. The commercial importance of the crusades may be illustrated in the case of the Venetians, who *c.* 1200 were in danger of expulsion from the Aegean. The success of the attack on Constantinople and the creation of a Latin Empire of the East (1204) restored Venetian supremacy all along the coasts of the Empire; in turn this ruined the Byzantine merchants. Cf Luzzatto, *Economic History*, 77.   See also J. M. Lacarra, 'Les Villes frontières dans l'Espagne des xie et xiie siècles', in *Le Moyen Age*, LXIX (1963) 205–22, especially 220; also P. Rousset, 'L'Idée de croisade chez les chroniqueurs d'occident', in *Proc. 10th Intern. Cong.* III 547–63.

89. Adelson, *Medieval Commerce*, 66; also Cox, *Capitalism*, 37.

90. F. C. Lane, 'Venetian Merchant Galleys, 1300–1334: Private and Communal Operation', in *Speculum*, XXXVIII (1963) 179–205, especially 184.

91. Dvornik, *General Councils*, 55.

92. Kuttner, in *Miscellanea Pio Paschini*, II 47.

93. Le Bras, *Institutions ecclésiastiques*, Ière partie, 253.

94. Ibid. 254–5.

95. Lopez, in *AHR* LVII 19; Maisonneuve, *Études sur les origines*, 76; Pacaut, in *CCM* VIII (1959) 8.   The late medieval heresies were regarded as not only against the faith, but also as detrimental to the well-being of society; Jaeger, *Ecumenical Council*, 21.   The heretics preached apostolic poverty and attacked the growing luxury and political activities of the Church; cf S. Runciman, *Medieval Manichee* (Cambridge, 1947) 116, 125.

96. M. Bévenot, 'The Inquisition and its Antecedents', in *Heythrop Journal*, VII (1966) 257–68, 381–93, here 392.

97. Cf Maisonneuve, *Études sur les origines*, 33–4.   Lay pressure forced the Church to accept the death penalty for heresy; likewise, Innocent III to change his mind in 1208 and organize the Albigensian crusade; cf Runciman, *Medieval Manichee*, 131.

98. MS Flor. Laur. S. Croce III sin. 6 fo. 97ra [*COD* 210. 7].   See also the gloss of Damasus on '*oblationes*' (= *COD* 210. 34) 'they [the clergy] can demand due offerings because a like debt is taken from excommunicates, as shown below.   Thus it is agreed that tithes and first-fruits can be taken from them, because the same are taken from Jews, as shown above *De decimis*.   *De terris*, bk 1' (ibid fo. 97rb).

99. On anti-semitism and Innocent III, see A. Vetulani, 'The Jews in Medieval Poland', in *Jewish Journal of Sociology*, IV (1962) 274–94.   The author argues that the rising anti-semitism was inspired by territorial rulers in France and Germany, 'who, by exploiting the religious fanaticism of the people, tried to destroy their Jewish creditors'.   Thus the universal canonical legislation was an attempt to bring about a *modus vivendi*, on the assumption that by separating the Jews from Christians the ill-will would be reduced and this would enable the Jews to continue in their chosen trades (ibid. 288).   For the secular authority's treatment of the Jews in England, see Roth, *History of the Jews*, e.g. 69, where he cites Edward I's Statute of Jews (1275), which for-

bade Jews from charging interest.   The same statute allowed the Jews to become merchants and artisans, but with no practical effect, for it did not free them from social oppression (ibid. 72).

100. Le Bras, *Institutions ecclésiastiques*, Ière partie, 258–9.

101. S. Runciman, 'The Decline of the Crusading Idea', in *Proc. 10th Intern. Cong.* III 637–52, especially 646–7.

102. Ibid. 648.

103. On monasticism and economic development, see G. Le Bras, 'La Part du monachisme dans le droit et l'économie du moyen âge', in *RHEF* XLVII (1961, appeared 1962) 199–213, where the over-all conclusion is that the monks had a dominant role in the medieval economy until the twelfth century.   Our present approach is one that historians of monasticism sometimes overlook, but see A. D'Haenens, 'La Crise des abbayes bénédictines au bas moyen âge: Saint-Martin-de-Tournai de 1290 à 1350', in *Le Moyen Age*, LXV (1959) 75–95, and N. Coulet, 'Le Monde bénédictin et la crise du xive siècle', in *AESC* XVII (1962) 1001–5, which reviews D'Haenens work;   Coulet cites D'Haenens 'rule', i.e. 'la nécessité de considérer une institution religieuse sous le double point de vue de sa structure sociale-religieuse et de sa structure économique' (ibid. 1003).

104. The earliest example of exemption is that of Bobbio in northern Italy in 628.

105. Episcopal visitation often imposed a severe economic burden on monasteries.   There are frequent complaints of the abuses of procurations, hence the relevance of such canons as Lateran III 4, which restricted the size of the retinues of archbishops and bishops on canonical visitation; cf Russell, in *JEcH* XXIV 8.   A well-run monastery kept an exact accounting of what visitors should get by way of food and drink; cf C. H. Talbot, 'The Account-book of Beaulieu Abbey', in *Cîteaux*, IX (1958) 189–210, especially 195. Beaulieu in Hampshire, England, was founded 1204–5; its account-book is 'the only one of its kind known to exist': Talbot, 'A Cistercian Account-book', in *The Listener*, LIV (1955) 177–9.   Contrary to modern opinion, but in line with sound economic principles, no medieval monastery, however desirous it was of fulfilling the precept of charity, could afford to dispense charity indiscriminately, otherwise it would have quickly gone bankrupt.   See p. 120.

106. Bertrand de Jouvenel, 'The Treatment of Capitalism by Continental Intellectuals', in *Capitalism and the Historians*, ed. F. A. Hayek, 93–123, especially 107.

107. Noonan, *Usury*, 14.

108. O'Sullivan, *Italian Merchant Bankers*, 19.   By 1152 the Cistercian Order had 340 foundations, 51 of which were in England and Wales.   At the end of the thirteenth century the figures had risen to 700 and 75 respectively; see R. A. Donkin, 'The English Cistercians and Assarting *c.* 1128–*c.* 1350', in *ASOC* XX (1964) 49–75, here 49, 51.

109. R. A. L. Smith, *Canterbury Cathedral Priory: A Study in Monastic*

Administration, pp. vii, 116–17, 131–2. Surplus corn was shipped abroad as early as 1207, also corn was sold at home. Monkton returned £74 6s 0d for sale of corn in 1230–1, and Adesham £50 9s 3d. Although most labour services had been commuted for rent by the late thirteenth century, carrying services were retained (ibid. 122).

110. Lopez, in *Speculum*, XXVIII 41, and A. Blanchet, 'La Monnaie et l'Église', in *Académie des Inscriptions et Belles-Lettres, Comptes-Rendus des Séances de l'Année 1950*, 18–26, here 20.

111. Ibid. 23.

112. Lopez, in *Speculum*, XXVIII 41.

113. Duby, in *AESC* VII 162, 163.

114. Ibid. 166, 168.

115. Cf R. A. Donkin, 'Localisation, situation économique et rôle parlementaire des abbés cisterciens anglais, (1295–1341)', in *RHE* LII (1957) 832–41. On the Jews, see pp. 111–12. Gilbert Crispin, Abbot of Westminster, had business dealings with the Jews: cf *PL* CLIX 1034 ff, cited by Roth, *History of the Jews*, 5.

116. J. M. Rigg, 21.

117. Tithes were a tenth part of all fruits and profits paid to the ministers of the Church in recognition of God's authority over men. There were three types of tithe: predial paid on annual crops; personal on the profits of one's industry or occupation; and mixed, i.e. on the produce of animal husbandry, such as milk, wool and meat. The predial tithe was the greater tithe, the other two lesser tithes. Strictly speaking, therefore, the tithe fell on everything agricultural and non-agricultural, even on a prostitute's earnings, said Raymond of Peñaforte. However, 'as custom hardened into law ... non-agricultural revenues often came to be regarded as free from tithes ...' Cf G. Constable, 'Resistance to Tithes in the Middle Ages', in *JEH* XIII (1962) 172–85, here 177; 'Cluniac Tithes and the Controversy between Gigny and Le Miroir', in *Rev. bénéd.* LXX (1960) 591–624, here 611–12; and *Monastic Tithes*, 16–19. Commutation of tithes for a money payment became common from the eleventh century onwards. Note that fixity of receipts in the case of the greater tithe had become the rule by the twelfth century.

118. Le Bras, *Institutions ecclésiastiques*, Iᵉʳᵉ partie, 256.

119. Constable, in *Rev. bénéd.* LXX 606–7, and *Monastic Tithes* 220, 232. Initially this freedom 'applied only to demesne lands and to goods produced by the monks themselves or for their own use' (*Rev. bénéd.* LXX 607).

120. Constable, *Monastic Tithes*, 241–2, 254, 270. The Order enjoyed this privilege from 1132 to 1215, except for the period of Hadrian IV (1154–9), when the exemption applied only to their noval land so cultivated; cf J. S. Donnelly, 'Changes in the Grange Economy of English and Welsh Cistercian Abbeys, 1300–1540', in *Traditio*, X (1954) 399–458, here 409. Hadrian's restriction applied, of course, to all monasteries so that he 'anticipated the solution worked out by Alexander III ... and finally adopted by the Lateran

Council in 1216' (Constable, in *Rev. bénéd.* LXX 623, and *Monastic Tithes,* 279). The *novalia* were new lands from which tithes had never been paid. See Boyd, *Tithes and Parishes,* 264–6. On the Cistercian ownership of tithes 'of other men', which the Order at first rejected, see Constable, *Monastic Tithes,* 190–7. Notice that after Hadrian's withdrawal of the exemption Alexander III restored full exemption only to the Cistercians and the military Orders; Constable, *Monastic Tithes,* 304.

121. J. B. Van Damme, 'La Constitution cistercienne de 1165', in *ASOC* XIX (1963) 51–104, here 64.

122. Graves, in *ASOC* XIII 20 associates wool production in England, and certainly in Yorkshire, with the arrival of the Cistercians. Eventually, other producers outstripped them, so that in the thirteenth century the total monastic production was less than one-sixth of the national output.

123. It is commonly assumed that all or most of Cistercian expansion took place in 'waste' lands and so did not affect existing settlements. See pp. 102–3. Taking England as an example, recent studies suggests some modification, cf M. W. Barley, 'Cistercian Land Clearances in Nottinghamshire: Three Deserted Villages and their Moated Ancestor', in *Nottingham Mediaeval Studies* I (1957) 75–89, where the establishment of the abbey of Rufford in the mid-twelfth century led to the disappearance of three villages and the growth of a new settlement. Also C. R. Cheney, 'A Letter of Pope Innocent III and the Lateran Decree on Cistercian Tithe-paying', in *Cîteaux Commentarii Cistercienses,* II (1962) 146–51, suggests that the 'Cistercian method of exploiting the land had led to expropriations and the decay of villages' (ibid. 149). The dispute over the parish church of Scarborough, given by King Richard II to Cîteaux in 1189, provides a good example of the legal and spiritual difficulties that the breach of the original constitution of the Order gave rise to. See also Graves, in *ASOC* XIII 10.

124. Waites, in *Yorks. Arch. J.* XL 627, 629.

125. Ibid. 652.

126. Cheney, in *Cîteaux Commentarii Cistercienses,* II 150. Graves, in *ASOC* XIII 13 concludes: 'In this survey of practices one major conclusion stands out. The economic ideal as set forth in the *Exordium Parvum* was a failure. Serfs and mills were owned and exploited, the advowson of churches was normal, and secular involvement in commerce was a wide-spread fact.'

127. Departures from the *instituta* in respect of poverty and ownership of property occurred as early as the pontificate of Alexander III, cf J. Leclercq, 'Épîtres d'Alexandre III sur les cisterciens', in *Rev. bénéd.* LXIV (1954) 68–82, especially 73. The Cîteaux Chapter tried to follow Alexander's advice by passing statutes, but these met with resistance as the offending passages were later cut from his decretals (ibid. 81). On the 1189 Chapter, cf Madden, in *CHR* XLIX 347.

128. Madden, in *CHR* XLIX 349–53; Constable, *Monastic Tithes,* 303–4.

129. Constable, *Monastic Tithes,* 306; Donnelly, in *Traditio,* X 409. Cf

H. Dubled, 'Aspects de l'économie cistercienne en Alsace au xiie siècle', in *RHE* LIV (1959) 765–82, especially 777, 781. The author examines the records of the monasteries of Lucelle, Baumgarten and Neubourg to see how much of their land development consisted of new cultivation or old lands and their existing cultivators. Most of their donated lands were uncultivated when given. See also Cheney, in *Cîteaux Commentarii Cistercienses*, II 146, and Le Bras, *Institutions ecclésiastiques*, Ière partie, 256–7.

130. Madden, in *CHR* XLIX 355. The decree of Lateran IV 55 permitted the religious to come to some arrangement with the parish clergy in lieu of tithe; many did so by substituting a fixed rent in money or in animals or in produce for the variable sum that accrued from the tithe; cf Boyd, *Tithes and Parishes*, 264.

131. The explanation is, of course, that the religious Orders, once involved in business activities — and could they have avoided this? — could not escape the prevailing economic principles without suffering bankruptcy, and even loss of their spiritual effectiveness. Sometimes, because of the special privileges they enjoyed, the religious houses went further than the laity in pursuing competitive methods. The textile guilds had to cope with non-guild operators located in monasteries, convents and Beguine houses in the thirteenth century, who were often laymen hired for wages; cf E. E. Hirshler, 'Medieval Economic Competition', in *JEcH* XIV (1954) 52–8, here 56.

132. Taxation of clergy constituted 'the most frequent *casus belli*' between the papacy and Frederick II of Germany; Waley, *Papal State*, 134, 143.

133. Graves, in *ASOC* XIII 39–40; similar examples of levies in 1225, 1233, 1258, 1275, 1282 and 1290 (ibid. 41).

134. Roth, *History of the Jews*, 40; Madden, in *CHR* XLIX 345.

135. Madden, in *CHR* XLIX 345.

136. Graves, in *ASOC* XIII 23.

137. O'Sullivan, *Italian Merchant Bankers*, 125.

138. Cf Graves, in *ASOC* XIII 35. The author cites other examples, such as Bruerne, which between 1286 and 1290 owed over 2000 marks to a family of English merchants, the Ludlaws, and subsequently over 1000 marks to Florentine merchants. The General Chapter permitted the community to disperse in 1293 on the grounds of poverty. Likewise in 1280 Meaux had a debt of £3678, which by 1286 had been reduced to £1443; in 1310 the debt was £1169. In the same period the stock of the abbey varied from 11,000 sheep and 1000 cattle in 1280; 1320 sheep and 477 cattle in 1286; 5406 sheep, 606 cattle and 120 horses in 1310. Among the Cistercians, at least, poor management of income seems to have been a major cause of financial difficulties.

139. One of the commonest inroads on capital resources, in the case of monasteries, especially when held in custody in vacancy, was the selling of the woodland, cf S. Wood, *English Monasteries and their Patrons in the Thirteenth Century*, 93–4.

140. Madden, in *CHR* XLIX 360.

141. Cf the remark of R. Fossier, 'Les Granges de Clairvaux et la règle cistercienne', in *Cîteaux*, VI (1955) 259–66, 'C'est de cette opposition entre les principes et les réalités que l'Ordre dès la mort de Bernard, a tiré à la fois tout son prestige économique, et plus tard, tout son affaisement religieux' (ibid. 266).

142. J. A. Brundage, 'A Twelfth-century Oxford Disputation concerning the Privileges of the Knights Hospitallers', in *Med. Stud.* XXIV (1962) 153–60, here 153.

143. Miskimin, *Money, Prices and Foreign Exchange*, 8.

144. Sr James Eugene Madden, 'Business Monks, Banker Monks, Bankrupt Monks; the English Cistercians in the Thirteenth Century', in *CHR* XLIX (1963) 341–64, here 358.

145. Especially in regard to the mendicant orders; see M. D. Lambert, *Franciscan Poverty*, which deals with the rise and fall of the doctrine of the absolute poverty of Christ and His apostles within the Franciscan Order, from 1210 to 1323. On the Dominicans, see W. A. Hinnebusch, 'Poverty in the Order of Preachers', in *CHR* XLV (1959–60) 436–53, especially 448.

146. Cf D. L. Douie, *The Conflict between the Seculars and the Mendicants at the University of Paris in the Thirteenth Century*, which is an excellent summary of the dispute.

147. Lambert, *Franciscan Poverty*, 38, 58, and see 41 for the argument that the early followers of St Francis took on irregular jobs such as grave-digging and water-carrying that gave no security in time of dearth.

148. Hinnebusch, in *CHR* XLV 448.

149. Lambert, *Franciscan Poverty*, 91, 93.

150. Douie, *Conflict*, 11.

151. For John XXII's bull *Quorumdam exigit*, see Lambert, *Franciscan Poverty*, 208, 215, 245. The bull *Exivi de paradiso* of Vienne [38] illustrates the casuistry of the solution; cf Lambert, 185–90.

152. L. Hödl, 'Zum Streit um die Bussprivilegien der Mendikantenorden in Wien im 14. und beginnenden 15. Jahrhundert', in *ZKT* LXXIX (1957) 170–89, especially 170; Douie, *Conflict*, 4.

153. Similar complaints had been made at Lyons I. Both the Rule of St Francis and the Dominican Constitutions of 1228 had prohibited the friars from preaching in any diocese without the consent of the ordinary. In fact the papacy had encouraged them to undertake such activities.

154. Douie, *Conflict*, 6–8.

155. Lambert, *Franciscan Poverty*, 199–201, 208.

156. A. M. Burg, 'Les "Droits paroissiaux" dans le diocèse de Strasbourg avant et après le concile de Vienne', in *RDC* I (1951) 300–8, especially 302.

157. Constable, *Monastic Tithes*, 274, 276.

158. For those who passed the age of 20 years or so the life expectation was not much less than it is today; cf C. Brooke, *Europe in the Central Middle Ages 962–1154*, 93; Russell, in *Trans. Amer. Phil. Soc.* XLVIII 31.

159. e.g. the political violence in Florence, cf Dino Compagni, *Chronicle* III 8 (tr. Benecke 179) speaking of June 1304 'it is said that more than 1900 dwellings were burnt, and no remedy could be applied'.

160. Cf de Lagarde, *La Naissance*, I 179 ff, where, in the lay *v.* cleric struggle in Italy and in the towns of northern France, reprisals were used to force the clergy to submit. Reprisals were an important element in commerce, 'by which any merchant in a foreign land might be held responsible for the debts of a defaulting fellow-citizen', cf Origo, *Merchant of Prato*, 40.

161. Lopez, in *Proc. 10th Intern. Cong.* III 131. The high cost of the transport of goods (20–25 per cent of the original price in the case of luxury items; 100–150 per cent for heavy goods, such as grains, wine and salt, by land transport; but a range of 2–33 per cent if sea transport was possible) kept them out of reach of the masses; Le Goff, *Marchands et banquiers*, 13–14.

162. J. Gilchrist, 'The Interpretation of the Renaissance', in *Manna*, VI (1963) 4–20, here 17.

CHAPTER 4

1. For the theologians, see Baldwin, *Just Price*, 57–80.

2. In Clem. 5.5. *cap. unic.* (ed. Rome 1582 col. 280) cited by Schroeder.

3. Baldwin, *Just Price*, 57.

4. B. N. Nelson, 'The Usurer and the Merchant Prince: Italian Businessmen and the Ecclesiastical Law of Restitution, 1100–1550', in *SJEcH* VII (1947) 104–22, takes a pessimistic view of the influence of the confessional as a means of bringing about restitution of usurious profits (ibid. 111).

5. Cf A. E. Trugenberger, *San Bernardino da Siena*, 82–5, 93–100; also Origo, *San Bernardino*, 77, that he preached three sermons in Italian on dishonest trade to the Florentines in 1424 and 1425, and three to the Sienese in the same year on restitution.

6. R. De Roover, 'La Doctrine scolastique en matière de monopole', in *Studi Fanfani* I (Milan, 1962) 151–79, here 177: 'L'histoire évidemment s'arrête au seuil du confessionnal, mais ce serait une grave erreur que de vouloir dénier toute influence au sacrement de la pénitence.'

7. Cf Lateran II 13.

8. Lopez and Raymond, *Medieval Trade*, 408.

9. Cf Baldwin, *Just Price*, 8, that 'the approach of the medieval thinkers was essentially normative'; also E. Bartell, 'Value, Price and St Thomas', in *Thomist*, XXV (1962) 325–81, here 348.

10. Baldwin gives most of these examples, *Just Price*, 13.

11. Also Matthew 25:14–30. Cf S. Stein, 'The Development of the Jewish Law on Interest from the Biblical Period to the Expulsion of the Jews from England', in *Historia Judaica*, XVII (1955) 3–40, where the author observes 'The parable of the ten talents in Matthew seems to imply the general practice of charging interest in the case of commercial loans' (ibid. 7–8).

12. For church society before Nicaea I (325) cf P. Hinchcliff, 'Church and Society before Nicaea', in *Church Quarterly Review* (Jan–March 1964) 39–51.

13. Bartell, in *Thomist*, XXV 327–8; J. F. L. Bray, *Financial Justice*, 21.

14. Oratio 43 §34, *PG* XXXVI 541–4.

15. Leo I, *PL* LIV 1206, ep. 167; quoted by Baldwin, *Just Price*, 14: cf Baldwin, 'The Medieval Merchant before the Bar of Canon Law', in *Papers of the Michigan Academy of Science, Arts and Letters*, XLIV (1959) 287–99, here 289. Cf R. S. Lopez, 'East and West in the Early Middle Ages: Economic Relations', in *Proc. 10th Intern. Cong.* III (1956) 113–63, especially 158, where he points out that in the West the merchant suffered from the 'Roman bias against non-agricultural callings, the German contempt for unwarlike occupations, and the Christian mistrust of professions seeking for worldly riches earned without painful toil'.

16. On slavery, cf C. Verlinden, *L'Esclavage dans l'Europe médiévale:* I *Péninsule ibérique-France*, 100–1, for early church laws that recognized slavery.

17. J. G. Davies, *Early Christian Church*, 277.

18. Giordani, *Social Message*, 287, also 279, 283.

19. Noonan, *Usury*, 29. Dempsey, *Interest and Usury*, 131: 'The institution of private property was regarded by every scholastic moralist as incontestably of natural right.'

20. Cf G. Le Bras, in *Camb. Econ. Hist.* III 557; also Giordani, *Social Message*, 320; Bartell, in *Thomist*, XXV 337.

21. Lane, in *Speculum*, XXXVIII 181, 202, 203, gives examples of Venetian state monopoly of the galleys, which 'replaced all the privately-owned licensed fleets', but which were let by auction for private operation. This development was intended to furnish a satisfactory fleet in time of war, which it did. The Genoese acted differently. They gave everything over to private enterprise, i.e. both the building and running of the vessels. In war the state rented the ships from the merchants.

22. Davies, *Early Christian Church*, 156–7.

23. On *Eiciens*, see Noonan, *Usury*, 38–9; Baldwin, in *Papers Michigan Academy*, XLIV 292–3, and *Just Price*, 36, 38–9. Cf Gratian, *De poen*. D.5 c.2.

24. Baldwin, in *Papers Michigan Academy*, XLIV 293; Nelson, in *SJEcH* VII 104; Noonan, *Usury*, 132, 153.

25. For Rufinus, cf Baldwin, *Just Price*, 39; also in *Papers Michigan Academy*, XLIV 299.

26. Baldwin, *Just Price*, 40–1, 47.

27. Baldwin, in *Papers Michigan Academy*, XLIV 294–5.

28. Schroeder, 91.

29. Baldwin, *Just Price*, 34. Cf Cheney, *Becket*, 21–2.

30. The canonists' commentaries on Lateran III 18 and °Lateran IV 11, which provide for the re-establishment of cathedral schools, illustrate the difficulties that faced the medieval mind in determining whether a master could legitimately charge a fee for his work. The consensus of opinion was that a master

can take money for his teaching as compensation for his time and labour.   See Gaines Post, 'The Medieval Heritage of a Humanistic Ideal: "Scientia donum dei est, unde vendi non potest"', in *Traditio*, XI (1955) 195–234, especially 200–1.   Despite the recommendation of the Lateran decrees that sufficient income be provided in the form of a prebend or other means, very few of the chapters did so; thus the question of charging fees was not an academic one. See Tierney, *Poor Law*, 19–21.   Damasus, in his gloss on °Lateran IV 11 'perstiterit in docendo', considers whether a master who falls ill can continue to draw the income of his benefice: the answer is yes.   MS Flor. Laur. S. Croce III sin. 6 fol. 99ra.

31. *Regesta Pontificum Romanorum*, ed. P. Jaffé, 2nd ed. (Leipzig, 1885) 16572 (=I 6.15) cited by W. Holtzmann, 'Sozial- und Wirtschaftsgeschichtliches aus Dekretalen', in *Rheinische Vierteljahrs-Blätter*, XIV–XVI (1949–51) 258–66; here 260.

32. Le Goff, *Marchands et banquiers*, 59, 311;   also Crombie, *Augustine to Galileo*, I 223 and 235;   S. Kuttner, *Studies Hatzfeld*, 238.

33. Le Bras, in *Camb. Econ. Hist.* III 574.

34. Lambert, *Franciscan Poverty*, 91.

35. Baldwin, *Just Price*, 47.   Graves, in *ASOC* XIII 14, observes that the Cistercian 'raising of swine must have been for trade because neither meat nor lard was allowed monks', and so the importance they attached to acquiring pasture rights.

36. Baldwin, *Just Price*, 36, 38, 39.

37. In Italy various municipal decrees, e.g. Padua 1221, Pavia 1243, Pisa 1246, Perugia 1248, Treviso 1267, Bergamo 1272, Modena 1278, reinforced canonical prohibitions against clerics engaging in trade; cf de Lagarde, *La Naissance*, I 179.

38. Baldwin, *Just Price*, 40–1.

39. Ibid.

40. De Roover, *Money, Banking and Credit*, 144.

41. Baldwin, *Just Price*, 296.

42. Ibid. 48.   On monopoly, see p. 61.

43. Bray, *Financial Justice*, 22, cites the following text from Thomas Aquinas: 'Trading considered in itself has a certain debasement attached thereto, in so far as by its very nature it does not imply a virtuous or necessary end.   Nevertheless, gain, which is the end of trading, though not implying by its nature anything virtuous or necessary, does not in itself connote anything sinful or contrary to nature; wherefore nothing prevents gain from being directed to some necessary or even virtuous end, and thus trading becomes lawful.   Thus, for instance, a man may intend the moderate gain which he seeks to acquire by trading for the upkeep of his household or for the assistance of the needy.'

44. O'Sullivan, *Italian Merchant Bankers*, 13.

45. G. Luzzatto, 'Les Noblesses: les activités économiques du patriciat vénitien (xe–xive siècles)', in *AHES* IX (1937) 25–57, here 39–40.

46. Le Goff, *Marchands et banquiers*, 75.

47. F. Thiriet, 'Les Vénitiens à Thessalonique dans la première moitié du xivᵉ siècle', in *Byzantion*, XXII (1952) 323-32; especially 332.

48. Lopez, in *Proc. 10th Intern. Cong.* III 127.

49. Contemporary literature took a different view from that of the Church, cf Nelson, in *Annuaire*, VII 329.

50. Lopez and Raymond, *Medieval Trade*, 341; see also Lestocquoy, in *Mélanges Halphen*, 412, and Le Goff, *Marchands et banquiers*, 76. On the significance of Lateran III 22, see J. Lestocquoy, 'Note sur certains voyages au xiᵉ siècle', in *Studi Sapori*, I 179-86, especially 185.

51. A large bibliography exists on the famous decree of Lateran IV 68, which helped to transform the Jewish dress into a badge of shame and contributed to the social degradation of medieval Jewry; cf G. Kisch, 'The Yellow Badge in History', in *Historia Judaica*, XIX (1957) 89-146, especially 131-40, for documents, and 140-6 for bibliography; also 98-9, 119. Innocent III did not initiate any really new legislation against the Jews, but in the end the 1215 decree went everywhere (ibid. 103). It was imposed in England in 1217, in Sicily 1221, in Aragon 1228, Navarre 1234, in France in 1269, but it took a century or two for it to take firm hold (ibid. 105). Cf G. Lapiana, 'The Church and the Jews', in *Historia Judaica*, XI (1949) 117-44, especially 129. G. I. Langmuir, 'The Jews and the Archives of Angevin England: Reflections on Medieval Anti-semitism', in *Traditio*, XIX (1963) 183-244, gives a balanced summary of the political and social status of the Jews in the Middle Ages; on Lateran IV 68 he concludes that it had horrible consequences for the Jews (ibid. 235). In Castile the Jews threatened to leave, so in 1219 Honorius III had to suspend the decree (Kisch, in *Historia Judaica*, XIX 105) Jedin, *Ecumenical Councils*, 80, adds that the decree was not inspired by racial prejudice because Mohammedans living in Christian communities were subject to the same regulations, but for all that it was so much toll paid to contemporary sentiment. On Lateran I 14 see a precedent in Gregory VII Reg. II 5 (Caspar, 130. 21-32).

52. Kisch, in *Historia Judaica*, XIX 112; See Lopez and Raymond, *Medieval Trade*, 103. Lopez, in *Le Moyen Age*, LXIX 480-1, describes how, by 1330, land travel, despite the great risks involved, had reached the limits of Europe and Asia. In the tenth century an adventurous voyage was for the Venetian merchant to take the road to Pavia; by the thirteenth century the merchant had reached Trebizond, Tabriz, Astrakhan, Tana (Azof), and by the fourteenth he moved across Asia without emotion (ibid. 480-1). Cf Le Goff, *Marchands et banquiers*, 25. An as yet largely unexplored field is the extent to which heresy followed the trade routes; cf R. A. Knox, *Enthusiasm* (Oxford, 1950) 78.

53. Cf M. F. Gaffney, 'Social Security in the Middle Ages', in *Irish Monthly*, LXXVIII (1950) 206-13, especially 213, for his view of medieval society: 'We get the impression of order, simplicity, industry, security, confidence, goodfellowship.' V. A. Demant, *The Just Price*, was more perceptive and

K

analytical. See especially L. Watt, 'The Theory behind the Historical Conception of the Just Price', in Demant, 60–75; the author corrects the traditional concept, see especially 65–6, that Langenstein's theory is 'a practical rule for merchants selling something for which there is no *communis aestimatio*, not a general rule for fixing of prices'.

54. R. De Roover, 'The Concept of the Just Price: Theory and Economic Policy', in *JEcH* xviii (1958) 418–34, especially 421, and in *Studi Fanfani*, 1 151, 156. Wilhelm Roscher (1817–94) first put Langenstein's text into circulation, thence it passed into Sombart, Weber, Pesch and many others; De Roover, in *Kylos*, x 138.

55. Troeltsch, *Social Teaching*, 1 128.

56. Baldwin, *Just Price*, 7.

57. Hirshler, in *JEcH* xiv 55–7, on the extent of competition among the various trades in the Middle Ages, especially in the textile industry where, e.g. in the fifteenth century, the use of cotton came to take the place formerly held by linens and woollens; cabinet-makers competed with carpenters in house building; the needlemakers of Cologne in 1397 forbade use of a machine to punch eyes into needles and to press wire into pinheads on the ground that this would create redundancy.

58. Watt, in Demant, 60–1, rejected the conclusions of Ashley, Tawney and others; A. Sapori, 'Il giusto prezzo nella dottrina di San Tommaso e nella pratica del suo tempo', in *Studi medievale*, 1 265–303; Dempsey, *Interest*, 149–50.

59. Baldwin's is the definitive work.

60. Baldwin, *Just Price*, 17.

61. Ibid, 35, which cites Gratian C.14 q.4 c.5, in which the term refers to an exact equivalent of goods returned for money lent. See also Le Bras, in *DTC* xv 2346.

62. Baldwin, *Just Price*, 21.

63. Ibid. 29. See p. 116.

64. Ibid. 53. See Le Bras, in *Camb. Econ. Hist.* iii 563–4.

65. De Roover, in *Studi Fanfani*, 1 152, adds that Accursius (1182–1260) modified the ancient Roman Law principle 'res tantum valet quantum vendi potest' by adding the words 'sed communiter'; thus the seller cannot fix his own price arbitrarily or take advantage of the buyer's lack of knowledge of the market price, e.g. a pilgrim or a traveller, to get more than the fair and ruling price for his goods. This applies to the seller who finds himself at a disadvantage in regard to the buyer.

66. Noonan, *Usury*, 90; Baldwin, *Just Price* 49.

67. Cf Dempsey, *Interest*, 155; also 160 'anticipated or postponed payment is an implicit or virtual loan'. The decretal *Naviganti* from a letter of Gregory IX (x.5.19.19) permitted over-evaluation of goods in a loan or sale with deferred payment (representing a credit charge) as long as there was some doubt about the future market price, for this involved some risk to the seller. Cf

Noonan, *Usury*, 137; Baldwin, *Just Price*, 50; McLaughlin, in *Med. Stud.* 1 119.

68. Baldwin, *Just Price*, 80. See the later summary of this doctrine by Molina in Dempsey, *Interest*, 137. Durandus and San Antonino accepted *laesio enormis*.

69. De Roover, in *Kylos*, x 124–5, and in *Studi Fanfani*, 1 152.

70. Baldwin, *Just Price*, 68.

71. Watt, in Demant, 66.

72. Noonan, *Usury*, 82–99.

73. D. Barath, 'The Just Price and the Costs of Production according to St Thomas Aquinas', in *New Scholasticism*, xxxiv (1960) 413–30, here 413.

74. De Roover, in *JEcH* xviii 422 cites St 2.2. q.77 a.3 ad 4.

75. De Roover, in *Kylos*, x 131. The minority tradition was the nominalist one, cf De Roover, in *Studi Fanfani*, 1 155, that Jean Gerson (1362–1428) was the most radical of the nominalists in insisting that the *Legislator* should fix almost all prices. Langenstein was a nominalist (ibid. 156).

76. De Roover, 'utility according to Jean Buridan (d. 1358) is based on the market price based on the estimation by the mass of buyers and sellers', in *Studi Fanfani*, 1 153. See also Bartell, in *Thomist*, xxv 358.

77. Hirschler, in *JEcH* xiv 58.

78. Ibid.

79. Bartell, in *Thomist*, xxv 379.

80. Ibid. 373. On San Antonino, cf De Roover, in *Kylos*, x 117.

81. De Roover, in *JEcH* xviii 423.

82. Baldwin, *Just Price*, 80.

83. De Roover, in *JEcH* xviii 426, in *Studi Fanfani*, 1 161–3, and *Medici Bank*, 155; Baldwin, *Just Price*, 76. Forestallers were those who bought up goods before they reached the open market; regrators, those who bought even in the open market to sell at a higher price; engrossers, those who got such a share of the goods on the market that they could control the price; cf Demant, 28; Dempsey, *Interest*, 139. Cf Binns, *Medieval Cornwall*, 183.

84. De Roover, in *Studi Fanfani*, 1 160; cf Cod. 4.59.1, 2.

85. De Roover, in *JEcH* xviii 425; Baldwin, *Just Price*, 80.

86. Baldwin, *Just Price*, 33, gives examples of attempts by Carolingian legislation to fix certain maximum prices; p. 34 he concludes that in the Carolingian period we can discern most of the twelfth-century canonist elements of the just price; ibid. 36, where De Roover cites as example Gratian C.14 q.4. c.9. (cf in *Studi Fanfani*, 1 166–7, 171).

87. De Roover, in *JEcH* xviii 426.

88. Baldwin, in *Papers Michigan Academy*, xliv 298–9, 288. At the end of the thirteenth century the notion that the merchant serves the common good comes in; Le Goff, *Marchands et banquiers*, 80–1.

89. The term *usura* usually applied to profits from loans 'to be distinguished from immoral profits derived from sale, which were called *turpe lucrum*',

Baldwin, *Just Price*, 38.   But it could include the latter, and this became a source of confusion in the doctrine.

90. S. Stein, 'Interest taken by Jews from Gentiles', in *J of Semitic Studies*, I (1956) 141–64, comments, 'The Pentateuchal commandments on usury presuppose simple agricultural conditions' (ibid. 141), and 'from the eleventh century onwards, economic tendencies shift generally from agriculture and barter to trade, industry, guild formation and town building' (ibid. 142).   For the concept of money as sterile, see Stark, *Contained Economy*, 10.

91. See p. 24.   See also Lopez and Raymond, *Medieval Trade*, 157, and M. M. Postan, 'Partnership in English Medieval Commerce', in *Studi Sapori*, I 519–49, here 523, where he says that dividend not interest was the product of the various forms of the *societas*.

92. Baldwin, *Just Price*, 37, and in *Papers Michigan Academy*, XLIV 293 'the *Decretum* supplemented by Patristic *paleae* formed the legal frame of reference in which later canonists were to work.   Usury was defined with such breadth that it could be interpreted as implicating all commercial profits.'

93. Cf T. F. Divine, *Interest: an Historical and Analytical Study in Economics and Modern Ethics*, 52.

94. Le Goff, *Marchands et banquiers*, 72; Schroeder, 499, comments on Luke 6:34 that it is not to be understood as a condemnation of interest; it is only an exhortation to general and generous behaviour.   Nelson, *Usury*, 3–28, examines the medieval exegesis of the deuteronomic commandment on usury. Divine, *Interest*, 35, gives the provincial decrees cited in the text, and others. Cf Stein, in *Historia Judaica*, XVII 4.

95. Noonan, *Usury*, 15; Baldwin, *Just Price*, 32.   Cf T. P. McLaughlin, 'The Teaching of the Canonists on Usury (XII, XIII and XIV Centuries)', in *Med. Stud.* I (1939) 81–147, II (1940) 1–22; here I 84.   Nelson, in *Annuaire*, VII 299 and 301, for permitted legal rates of interest in Byzantium, i.e. land loans at 8 per cent and sea loans at 12 per cent.

96. Baldwin, *Just Price*, 32.

97. Noonan, *Usury*, 15; Baldwin, *Just Price*, 32.

98. Divine, *Interest*, 34; Noonan, *Usury*, 15; Baldwin, *Just Price*, 32, states that 'the extension of the prohibition of usury to the laity had antecedents prior to the eighth century', and he cites Elvira (306) c.20, Carthage I, Leo I ep. 4.3 (*PL* LIV 613), and the council of Clichy in Gaul in the seventh century (*MGH: Concilia*, 197).   For the penitentials, see J. T. McNeill, *Medieval Handbooks of Penance*, 174, 292, 307.

99. Noonan, *Usury*, 15.   See Gratian C.14 q.3 cc. 2–4; C.14 q.4 c.9. Also Baldwin, in *Papers Michigan Academy*, XLIV 291.

100. Noonan, *Usury*, 16–17, that usury in the period 750–1050 was badly defined, being treated as *turpe lucrum* and not as a sin against justice.

101. Anselm of Lucca is the first medieval author to treat usury as specifically a sin against the Seventh Commandment; Noonan, *Usury*, 17.   R. De Roover, in *Studi Fanfani*, I 160–1, brings out the distinction between *usura* as a sin of

theft (*usura est rapina facere*) and mere *turpe lucrum*; where possible the profits of theft must be restored to the individual or his heirs, but *turpe lucrum* could be expiated by charitable donations.

102. Noonan, *Usury*, 18; Divine, *Interest*, 59.

103. Noonan, *Usury*, 14.

104. The Lombards of Bruges were forbidden to lend on church ornaments and vestments, in Louvain pawnbrokers were forbidden to lend money on school texts to students of the university; in Troyes loans on agricultural implements were illegal (De Roover, *Money, Banking and Credit*, 134). Church councils also extended the idea of sacrilegious theft to protect merchants' goods, e.g. at Council of Puy in 990, at Verdun-sur-les-Doubs in 1016; cf Maisonneuve, in *Mélanges*, XVIII 34–5.

105. De Roover, *Money, Banking and Credit*, 105.

106. Baldwin, *Just Price*, 35–6, cites the appropriate texts in Gratian; Baldwin, in *Papers Michigan Academy*, XLIV 292, for the *palea* D.88 c.11 *Eiciens*, c.12 *Quoniam* and c.13 *Quid est*.

107. In fifteenth-century Bruges the maximum rate of interest was fixed at 43.5 per cent; De Roover, *Money, Banking and Credit*, 105. The Jews in England had the same maximum rate; cf Roth, *History of the Jews*, 53. These high rates applied to 'distress-borrowing'; commercial rates ranged around 10–16 per cent, with a low at 5 per cent and a high at 24 per cent (Divine, *Interest*, 39).

108. Violante, in *CCM* v 150.

109. Roth, *History of the Jews*, 107; Renouard, *Les Relations*, 69.

110. Noonan, *Usury*, 34.

111. Renouard, *Les Relations*, 69.

112. De Roover, *Money, Banking and Credit*, 306.

113. De Roover, in *SJEcH* II 56–7, and *Medici Bank*, 272–3, 268. The English kings did not pay interest, but exempted the company's goods from customs duty. Cf O'Sullivan, *Italian Merchant Bankers*, 23–4.

114. R. De Roover, 'Joseph A. Schumpeter and Scholastic Economics', in *Kylos*, x (1957) 115–46, especially 140, where he puts the distinction: 'In scholastic doctrine, moreover, *all* interest was usury, but it was strictly confined to *borrowed* money, that is, to any increment beyond the principal of a loan or *mutuum*. The dictum was *solum in mutuo cadit usura*. In other words usury occurred only in a loan, whether straight (open usury) or concealed under the form of another contract (palliate usury). The scholastic approach, therefore, was entirely legal and assumed as a premise that the loan or *mutuum* was a gratuitous contract. Canon law still clings to this principle today.' Cf Mataralli, in *Studi e testi*, CCXIX (1962) 149.

115. The word *interesse* seems to have been coined by Azo and introduced into canonical terminology by his pupil, Laurentius Hispanus, whence it passed into the *Glossa ordinaria*. Cf Le Bras, in *Camb. Econ. Hist.* III 567. The canonists excluded exchange from the charge of usury: *cambium non est*

K 2

mutuum. However, it was permitted by the canonists even where it was being used as a method of charging interest.

116. Cf S. Stein, 'A Disputation on Moneylending between Jews and Gentiles in Me'ir b. Simeon's Milhemeth Miswah (Narbonne, 13th cent.)', in *Journal of Jewish Studies,* x (1959) 45–61, for the exegesis of Deut. 23:21, and 'The Development of the Jewish Law on Interest from the Biblical Period to the Expulsion of the Jews from England', in *Historia Judaica,* XVII (1955) 3–40, here 32; G. Kisch, 'Relations between Jewish and Christian Courts in the Middle Ages', in *Historia Judaica,* XXI (1959) 81–108, especially 102. Nelson, *Usury,* 7, cites the text of Ambrose (*PL* XIV 779).

117. 'Inter-Jewish moneylending on interest . . . was forbidden or only possible by the use of various legal fictions', Stein, in *J of Semitic Studies,* I 143. In some cases, the Jew was the tool of a Christian lord who provided the capital, e.g. in eleventh-century Provence: *World History Jewish People,* ed. Roth, XI 159.

118. Stein, in *J of Jewish Studies,* x 58–9; Noonan, *Usury,* 101. The theologians (but not the canonists) rejected the deuteronomic double-standard; cf Nelson, *Usury,* 14–15. Cf Ambrose, *De Tobia Liber Unus* (*PL* XIV 779) on usuries for unbelievers.

119. X.5.19.6.

120. Noonan, *Usury,* 34. These were the professional lenders who 'made loans for consumption purposes to the poor at high rates'. Cf Divine, *Interest,* 61, where he cites X.5.19.3. Urban III confirmed Lateran III 25 and it passed into the decretals with the confirmation *Consuluit* (X.5.19.10). Cf Noonan, *Usury,* 19.

121. Nelson, in *Annuaire,* VII 329.

122. McLaughlin, in *Med. Stud.* II 4, 12. The usurer was easily identified, cf A. Sapori, 'L'usura nel dugento a Pistoia', in *Studi di storia economica medievale,* 2nd ed. (Florence, 1955) I 188: 'Esteriorménte l'usuraio si riconesceva dal banco col tappeto dietro il quale se ne stava seduto bene in vista di tutti . . . e dal quaderno in cui faceva i calcoli degli interessi.' See Dante's description in *Divina Commedia,* XVII 55–75.

123. Nelson, in *Annuaire,* VII 329.

124. In the external forum an agreement is necessary; in the internal, the intention is enough: cf Le Bras, in *DTC* xv 2348.

125. Latin text, McLaughlin, in *Med. Stud.* I 125 = Hostiensis, *Summa, de usuris,* n 8, fo. 374ᵛ. Commentaria ad X.5.19.16 *computandos,* 3.21.6 *canonicas*; explanation of terms in *Med. Stud.* I 129–44. On the mortgage, see Madden, in *CHR* XLIX 348; also Violante, in *CCM* v 168, whose examples include priests as creditors.

126. Aubenas, in *Annales du Midi,* LXXVI (1964) 371–7, here 371.

127. Le Bras, in *DTC* xv 2349, where he cites Innocent III (*PL* CCXV 766).

128. P. Wolff, *Commerces et marchands de Toulouse (vers 1350–vers 1450),* 360–1, on sale with right of repurchase within a specified time; on 363 he lists

several loans made *racione amicabilis mutui*, but even these were often disguised usury. The *poena conventionalis* is justified by several canonists, including Johannes Teutonicus and Raymond of Peñaforte, provided it was not invoked in order to conceal usury; Nelson, in *Annuaire*, VII 327 n 43.

129. Divine, *Interest*, 42–4.

130. Noonan, *Usury*, 49.

131. McLaughlin, in *Med. Stud.* I 145–7; Divine, *Interest*, 56; De Roover, in *Kylos*, X 141. Where the lender risked the loss of all or part of his capital, he was more of 'a stockholder than a bondholder'. See Le Goff, *Marchands et banquiers*, 78.

132. Divine, *Interest*, 52; Dempsey, *Interest*, 172.

133. Noonan, *Usury*, 115.

134. Ibid. 118.

135. McLaughlin, in *Med. Stud.* I 122–3.

136. Noonan, *Usury*, 32. The author stresses that there 'was no single scholastic doctrine' (80–1).

137. Ibid. 41. On Thomas Aquinas, see Stark, *Contained Economy*, 11–16.

138. Nelson, *Usury*, 10, and in *Annuaire*, VII 327 n 43, where Peter the Chanter, *PL* CCV 157, is cited in support. The theologians' *poena nec in fraudem* is the *poena conventionalis* of the canonists.

139. Noonan, *Usury*, 54.

140. Ibid. 52, 66.

141. De Roover, *Money, Banking and Credit*, 124 'even in the light of the most orthodox economic theory. There is no doubt that money devoted to consumption is barren and cannot be used without being spent. The result of a loan to a consumer is merely a transfer of purchasing power from the lender to the borrower. This is the theory which is at the bottom of the canonist doctrine, but confusedly expressed and only dimly perceived.'

142. Ibid. 125, and 'Money, Banking and Credit in Medieval Bruges', in *SJEcH* II (1942) 52–65, where he indicates the high overheads incurred by the money-lenders (ibid. 58). Iris Origo leaves the cost factor out of account, and thus she fails to ask the right questions of her subject when she leaves him with the doctrine that every loan should be gratuitous (*San Bernardino*, 89). See pp. 70, 113.

143. M. Pacaut, 'Saint Bernardin de Sienne et l'usure', in *Le Moyen Age* LXIX (1963) 743–52, examines the teaching of Sermo 38 *Quod lege naturae, scripturae et sanctae Ecclesiae prohibetur usura*. The rubric seems absolute enough, but, as Pacaut concludes, it has nuances of meaning of which the essential fact is the intention of the lender — whether or not he intends to respect charity (ibid. 744). Thus, Bernardino accepts the work of the money-changer, loans made *damnum emergens*, *lucrum cessans* and *necessitas publica*; and investments in commerce (ibid. 748). See also Stark, *Contained Economy*, 17.

144. The sixteenth-century scholastics developed the doctrine in full, cf Dempsey, *Interest*, 163.

145. De Roover, in *SJEcH* II 52. Bruges in the period 1350–1450 had a population of about 40,000 and some 15 or 16 money-changers; cf De Roover, *Money, Banking and Credit*, 250–1. Florence had a somewhat similar group: in 1338 there were 80 *banchi grossi* in Florence; cf De Roover, *Medici Bank*, 16. In 1460 only 33; and in 1516 only 8.

146. Cf Langmuir, in *Traditio*, XVI 207.

147. Lopez, in *Speculum*, XXVIII 1, 25, 28.

148. The debtors of Aaron of Lincoln (see p. 43) included the Archbishop of Canterbury, bishops of Bangor and Lincoln, Abbot of Westminster, and the Prior of the Knights Hospitallers; Roth, *History of the Jews*, 16.

149. Roth, *History of the Jews*, 109; Langmuir, in *Traditio*, XIX 219–21, and '"Judei nostri" and the beginning of Capetian legislation', in *Traditio*, XVI (1960) 203–39. See also Stein, in *Journal of Jewish Studies*, X 48 for Jewish freedom in Narbonne before the legislation of Innocent III in 1215 and Louis the Pious in 1230 (and other years).

150. Divine, *Interest*, 61. The first reference to *Jewish* usury in decrees of general councils was Lateran IV 67, which was the culmination of other papal measures in 1198, 1205 and 1208. Subsequently, Raymond of Peñaforte and other canonists denied the Jews the right to take usury from Christians, and held that they should restore the profits. Roth, *History of the Jews*, 39–40, cites Wilkins, *Concilia Magna Britanniae*, I 570–1, for the prohibition in 1219 by William de Blois, Bishop of Worcester, against Jews employing Christian nurses or servants, and from taking sacred objects in pledge; the decree was repeated in 1229, and again in 1240 in much the same form by William's successor, Walter de Cantelupe. But Jews could buy non-Christian slaves, cf Vetulani, in *Jewish J Sociology*, IV 276.

151. Lateran IV [71], see p. 265 n. 86.

152. Council of Basel, Sess. XIX 'On those who wish to be converted' (*COD* 460. 8–18). See also the prohibition of the same council 'Decree on Jews and Neophytes' against all social mingling of Jews and Christians; it even prohibited the former from opening their shops on Sundays and feast-days (*COD* 460. 3–5). Langmuir, in *Traditio*, XIX 230 and 237–8 deals with Richardson and others who blame the Church for the fate of the Jews by pointing out that 'the effective power over society attributed to the Church by historians of this persuasion might have surprised Innocent III'. It is true that the Church after 1215 propagated a hostile doctrine, but the ill-treatment of the Jews worsened as the Church itself lost power.

153. Noonan, *Usury*, 35; also Vetulani, in *Jewish J Sociology*, IV 282. Even the oppressive restrictions were turned to financial advantage by some churchmen and princes, for Jewish physicians, financiers and scholars paid for exemption from the decree of Lateran IV 68; Kisch, in *Historia Judaica*, XIX 115. The glossators of Lateran IV 67 and °Lyons I [5] refused to concede that the Jews could exact moderate usury on the argument that the canons condemned immoderate charges only. However, examples exist throughout the thir-

teenth century to prove that Jewish usury was tacitly condoned whenever it suited the interest of the secular rulers and, at times, the Church; *Divine Interest*, 62. Thus, Vetulani, *Jewish J Sociology*, IV 290, cites the synod of 1285 art. 33, which prohibited the pawning of 'res sacras et libros' with the Jews 'nisi de gravi necessitate de licentia prelatorum'.

154. Roth, *History of the Jews*, 3; also Lopez and Raymond, *Medieval Trade*, 103.

155. Nelson, *Usury*, 7–8. One feature that distinguished pawnbrokers from bankers was that the former used their own capital, whereas the latter relied a great deal on borrowed money; cf De Roover, *Money, Banking and Credit*, 117. The Cahorsins took their name from Cahors in Gascony, but they included others from southern France and Italy; the Lombards 'consisted mainly of Piedmontese from Asti and Chieri, merchants from Piacenza, and Tuscans from Siena, Florence and Pistoia'; cf Luzzatto, *Economic History*, 133; also R. De Roover, 'New Interpretations of the History of Banking', in *JWH* II (1954) 38–76, especially 51; Divine, *Interest*, 40. Aaron of Lincoln is a good example of a powerful money-lender; when he died, some time before 1186, he was owed £15,000 by 430 debtors. The Exchequer created a special branch, the *scaccarium Aaronis*, to deal with the collection of the debts, which had escheated to the crown. In 1205 half the debts were still owing; cf Roth, *History of the Jews*, 16.

156. Stein, in *Historia Judaica*, XVII 40, mentions that some 16,000 Jews were expelled in 1290.

157. e.g. Philip the Fair ordered a general seizure of Jewish property in 1306. In 1315 they were allowed to return to France. In 1321 a heavy tax was imposed on them and maximum interest rates fixed at 43.3 per cent p.a.; cf Wolff, *Commerces et marchands*, 398. The Jews finally disappeared, e.g. from the Toulouse region, towards the end of the fourteenth century.

158. Divine, *Interest*, 40; Lopez and Raymond, *Medieval Trade*, 105, cites the Jews as charging 30 per cent p.a. In Nuremberg it was 43 per cent. In this period emerged the 'Shylock' concept of the Jew contrasted with the 'noble Christian merchant'; cf Nelson, in *Annuaire*, VII 330.

159. De Roover, *Money, Banking and Credit*, 127–8; Stein, in *Jewish J Sociology*, I 149: 'the establishment of Jewish loan-banks was subject to a licence of the papal administration or of the local rulers or both'. At the time and place of writing (Adelaide, May 1967) one pawnbroker advertises his rate as 5 per cent per month.

160. De Roover, *Money, Banking and Credit*, 157; Cox, *Foundations of Capitalism*, 168, mentions that the Jews had to wear the yellow badge, were confined to the Via dei Giudei, denied citizenship, could not carry arms and were excluded from the wholesale trade. The Jews began to arrive in Florence in 1436. The next year the *Signoria* banned all Christian money-lenders.

161. Cox, *Foundations of Capitalism*, 168.

162. In Perpignan the crown fixed the rates of interest at a maximum of

20 per cent for less than a year and 16 per cent for more than a year; R. W. Emery, *The Jews of Perpignan in the Thirteenth Century*, 84. A rate of 20 per cent was probably too low because of the costs of running the business and covering bad debts (ibid. 86). The clergy formed only a small part of the Jews' clientele, and of the clergy the religious were the main borrowers. However, the clergy were a debtor class, but to the Christian money-lenders (ibid. 46). In the fourteenth century the Jewish community in Perpignan declined.

163. De Roover, *Money, Banking and Credit*, 205. The money-changers who confined their 'exchange' activities to local exchange, must be distinguished from the merchant-bankers, whose range of business was much wider: 'Trade came first, banking was next, commission and agency were often scarcely less important, and shipping and underwriting were usually a poor fourth' (ibid. 89). Often the merchants did 'exchange' on the side, thus the distinction was a narrow one. On the other hand, the Bruges money-changers in the fourteenth century were 'bankers who combined dealings in exchange (not in bills of exchange) with deposit banking'; De Roover, in *SJEcH* II 60.

164. In exchange the *instrumentum* recorded the loan of money in one currency and specified its repayment in another at a definite time and place. Indemnity clauses to cover possible change in the value of the coin or delay in repayment were included; cf Parker, *Knights Templars*, 76.

165. G. Mollat, *The Popes at Avignon 1305–1378*, 280.

166. R. S. Lopez, 'I primi cento anni di storia documentata della banca a Genova', in *Studi Sapori*, I 215–53, here 220.

167. Renouard, *Les Relations*, 91, states that the thirteenth-century popes received interest on vast sums left with the merchant companies, using the pretext, common at that time, of a delay in repayment of the deposits; see also ibid. 59–60. See De Roover, *Money, Banking and Credit*, 250, 305. The first records of deposit banking are in the Genoese notarial archives of the twelfth and thirteenth centuries; De Roover, in *JWH* II 38. On time deposits the Florentine branch of the Medici Bank paid 6–7 per cent; cf. De Roover, *Medici Bank*, 237.

168. O'Sullivan, *Italian Merchant Bankers*, 14.

169. Renouard, *Les Relations*, 60.

170. Cheques were first used in the fourteenth century; De Roover, in *JWH* II 54. The earliest extant ones relate to Pisa in 1374; De Roover, *Medici Bank*, 18. Deposit banking provided for increasing the flow of specie by substituting book values and book transfers of currency from one merchant to another, or from city to city. Without it the commercial expansion would have suffered.

171. The bankers operated on a fractional reserve system; they thus created new money as surely as if they could have printed banknotes. In Bruges the exchange-bankers did not operate outside the city and rarely undertook to make payments outside of Bruges; bills of exchange were the province of the

merchant-bankers; De Roover, *Money, Banking and Credit*, 350, in *JWH* II 52, and *Medici Bank*, 228.

172. Cox, *Foundations*, 167.

173. Ibid. Also De Roover, *Money, Banking and Credit*, 31. The Francesi failed in 1304, the Macci in 1312, and the Cerchi Bianchi in 1320. For the debts of the English kings, see O'Sullivan, *Italian Merchant Bankers*, 22.

174. De Roover, in *JWH* II 44. These companies consisted in fact of a series of successive groups or partnerships, trading as a unit: thus the four successive groups of the Peruzzi from 1300 to 1324 declared dividends of 15·4, 20, 14·5 and 16 per cent p.a. on capital employed; cf Renouard, *Les Relations*, 58. In 1335 it had a loss of 15·5 per cent; the last 'company' went bankrupt in 1343. For fourteenth- and fifteenth-century developments, see pp. 89, 91.

175. Renouard, *Les Relations*, 85. Although the partners in the companies invested their own capital, as well as having their profits retained for the duration of the particular agreement, and being able to invest additional funds if they wished, successful operations depended on the deposit capital that earned an interest of about 7–8 per cent for the depositors. See p. 25. News that Edward III of England had failed to meet his debts caused a rush on the banks that they could not meet.

176. Ibid. 83.

177. Noonan, *Usury*, 172; De Roover, *Medici Bank*, 101.

178. De Roover, *Medici Bank*, 101–2.

179. Ibid. Cf Renouard, *Les Relations*, 85.

180. De Roover, *Medici Bank*, 11. Cf Baldwin, *Just Price*, 49, 51. More than 5000 bills of exchange have survived among the papers of the Merchant of Prato, cf Origo, *Merchant of Prato*, 147.

181. De Roover, *Medici Bank*, 111; see also Le Goff, *Marchands et banquiers*, 31–2.

182. De Roover, in *Studi Sapori*, I 634 and in *Camb. Econ. Hist.*, III 67, 68.

183. Spurious exchange transactions as a means of avoiding usury charges involved exchange and re-exchange (*cambium* and *recambium*). In dry exchange the correspondent abroad received the bill and re-drew it when it fell due. In fictitious exchange the bill was pure formality and remained in the office where it was drawn; cf De Roover, *Money, Banking and Credit*, 82.

184. Ibid. 83.

185. V. Pfaff, 'Aufgaben und Probleme der päpstlichen Finanzverwaltung am Ende des 12. Jhts', in *MIÖGF* LXIV (1956) 1–24, especially 22–3.

186. Parker, *Knights Templars*, 89 ff.

187. Ibid. 26–7. Abuse of their exemptions and other episcopal rights was severely censured by Lateran III 9.

188. Lopez and Raymond, *Medieval Trade*, 101; Runciman, in *Proc. 10th Intern. Cong.* III 648.

189. Parker, *Knights Templars*, 62, 63, 72.

190. Cf Runciman, *Manichee*, 179.

191. Giordani, *Social Message*, 299, 305, 307-8.   See also R. R. Betts, 'The Social Revolution in Bohemia and Moravia in the Later Middle Ages', in *Past and Present*, II (1952) 24-31, especially 27, where he defines the poor of Prague as those who 'owned nothing except their labour and who were at the mercy of the employer who paid their wages', and he lists these as the unemployed, unskilled, most journeymen, many master craftsmen, prostitutes, street entertainers, rogues, beggars' (ibid. 28-9).

192. Cf P. G. Caron, 'Asile et hospitalité dans le droit de l'Église primitive', in *Revue internationale des droits de l'antiquité*, X (1963) 187-97, especially 187-9.

193. Wilks, in *Studia Patristica*, VI 533-5.   The author also cites Gratian D.8 *ante* c.2; D.1 c.7 and D.8 c.1.   On communal living, see Acts 2:44-6; 4:32-7.

194. Cf Wilks, in *Studia Patristica*, VI 536.

195. Cf B. Tierney, 'The Decretists and the "Deserving Poor"', in *Comparative Studies in Society and History*, I (1958-9) 360-73, and *Poor Law*, 62, 27.

196. Wilks, in *Studia Patristica*, VI 536.

197. Cf de Jouvenel, in Hayek, *Capitalism and the Historians*, 106; Tierney, *Poor Law*, 24.

198. Cf E. Lio, 'Le obbligazioni verso i poveri in un testo di S. Cesario riportato da Graziano (can. 66, C.XVI q.I) con falsa attribuzione à S. Agostino', in *SG* III (1955) 51-81, especially 66, 72-80; also Le Goff, *Marchands et banquiers*, 87.

199. On the duration and length of the pilgrims' voyages, cf Lestocquoy, in *Studi Sapori*, I 179-86 passim.

200. Tierney, *Poor Law*, 39.

201. Ibid.   Cf Innocent III, *Liber de eleemosyna* (PL CCXVII 759).

202. Tierney, *Poor Law*, 70-1.   On the *quartese* for charity, cf A. H. M. Jones, 'Church Finances in the Fifth and Sixth Centuries', in *JTS* NS XI (1960) 84-94, here 91.

203. On °Chalcedon 8, cf J. Imbert, *Les Hôpitaux en droit canonique*, 29.

204. See p. 31; also Tierney, *Poor Law*, 71.

205. Tierney, *Poor Law*, 78-9.

206. Constable, *Monastic Tithes*, 226.

207. Tierney, *Poor Law*, 39.   Cf Gaffney, in *Irish Monthly*, LXXVIII 207; A. L. Gabriel, 'The Practice of Charity at the University of Paris during the Middle Ages: Ave Maria College', in *Traditio*, V (1947) 335-9, where, on certain days, e.g. Founder's Day, the young students had to feed the poor, clothe and shoe them, visit the sick and the imprisoned (ibid. 339).

208. On the *xenodochia*, cf Lopez, in *JWH* I 603.

209. Caron, in *Revue internationale*, X 193-4 points to the distinction between public (= religious) and private hospitals.

210. Tierney, *Poor Law*, 23.

211. C. R. Young, 'King John of England: an Illustration of the Medieval Practice of Charity', in *CH* XXIX 29 (1960) 264–74, here 265.

212. Ibid. 267, 268.

213. Cf Tierney, *Poor Law*, 50; Young, in *CH* XXIX 268.

214. Cf Graves, in *ASOC* XIII 24, and above, p. 120. Tierney, *Poor Law*, 80.

215. Lopez, in *Proc. 10th Intern. Cong.* III 138.

216. Ibid. 138, 139, 143.

217. Cf Trugenberger, *San Bernardino*, 9; on the tithe question Giles Constable deals with modern objections and concludes that there was little resistance to tithes in the Middle Ages before the thirteenth century and that when resistance did occur it was to specific instances, where an explanation can be given. Moreover, 'too great an emphasis on resistance to tithes at any time in the Middle Ages tends to obscure their real importance in the ecclesiastical, economic, and social history of Europe', in *JEH* XIII 172–3, 175, 176–7, 184, 185. Many heretics rejected tithes, but on the whole they objected to the misuse not to the institution as such (ibid. 180).

218. See especially A. R. Bridbury, *Economic Growth*, 84, who weights his argument with such phrases as 'horrifying glimpses of a thirteenth-century countryside choked with people' or 'In the later Middle Ages, loss of population, by requiting land-hunger of the survivors of the Black Death, undoubtedly improved out of all recognition the lot of the mass of the inhabitants of England.' Likewise E. Miller, 'The English Economy in the Thirteenth Century', in *Past and Present*, XXVIII (1964) 21–40, especially 38: 'the people increased more rapidly than capacity to produce'.

219. Tierney, *Poor Law*, 130, 132.

220. On the conflicting texts in Gratian, cf D.42 *post* c.1 and D.86 *post* c.6.

221. Tierney, in *Comparative Studies in Society and History*, I 370.

222. Talbot, in *Cîteaux*, IX 195.

223. Tierney, *Poor Law*, 61.

224. Ibid. 62, where he cites the *gloss. ord. ad* C.13 q.2 c.19.

225. Violante, in the two articles in *CCM* (see p. 263 n 63), brings out very well the part played by the Church in solving the medieval equivalents to old age insurance, temporary indebtedness, lack of ready cash to meet some immediate need.

226. Tierney, *Poor Law*, 85; Crombie, *Augustine to Galileo*, I 235 ff; J. H. Mundy, 'Hospitals and Leprosaries in Twelfth and early Thirteenth Century Toulouse', in *Essays in Medieval Life and Thought*, ed. J. H. Mundy, 181–205, especially 199. Cf Caron, in *Revue internationale*, X 189.

227. Mundy, in *Essays*, 200, 202–3.

228. Tierney, *Poor Law*, 85.

229. Lopez and Raymond, *Medieval Trade*, 72.

230. Origo, *San Bernardino*, 104, details Siena where the great hospital of Santa Maria della Scala had been founded in the eleventh century.

231. Cf G. Lavergne, 'La Persécution et la spoliation des lépreux à Périgueux en 1321', in *Recueil de travaux offert à M. Clovis Brunel* II 107–13, especially 108; also E. Carpentier, 'Autour de la peste noire: famines et épidémies dans l'histoire du xive siècle', in *AESC* XVII (1962) 1062–92, especially 1080.

232. Tierney, *Poor Law*, 109.

Chapter 5

1. Cf Gilchrist, in *Manna*, VI 13. For moral theology, see Michaud-Quantin, in *Miscellanea Mediaevalia*, III 32–4. Against the 'disintegration' theory, see now F. Clark, 'A New Appraisal of Late Medieval Theology', in *Gregorianum*, XLVI (1965) 733–65, where the author deals with H. A. Oberman, *The Harvest of Medieval Theology* (Cambridge, Mass., 1962) especially 737, 740.

2. Cf Lambert, *Franciscan Poverty*, 225, that Ockham 'was led into his radical criticisms of the medieval Church from his conviction that in the poverty of Christ controversy the Pope had imposed heresy on the Church'.

3. De Roover, *Money, Banking and Credit*, 162.

4. Miskimin, *Money, Prices and Foreign Exchange*, 8–9.

5. A. Fanfani, *Catholicism, Protestantism and Capitalism*, 42; De Roover, *Medici Bank*, 152–5.

6. T. P. Van Zijl, *Gerard Groote, Ascetic and Reformer (1340–1384)*, 35.

7. Ibid. 218–19.

8. Ibid. 296–8, 300, 302–3.

9. E. Carpentier, *Une Ville devant la peste: Orvieto et la peste noire de 1348*, 221. London seems to have had a general improvement in the intellectual level of instruction in the Church during the fifteenth century; see Thrupp, *Merchant Class*, 181. Doctors of divinity, instead of mere bachelors, were appointed to parishes under the patronage of the city or merchant companies.

10. Mundy–Loomis, 29–30.

11. L. C. Gabel (ed.), *Memoirs of a Renaissance Pope: the Commentaries of Pius II*, 364.

12. Cf Gill, *Eugenius IV*, 49.

13. Miskimin, *Money, Prices and Foreign Exchange*, 9.

14. M. M. Postan, 'The Costs of the Hundred Years War', in *Past and Present*, XXVII (1964) 34–53, especially 41–2. Cf A. E. Feaveryear, *The Pound Sterling: A History of English Money*, 13–14. G. L. Harriss, 'Aids, Loans and Benevolences', in *Historical Journal*, VI (1963) 1–19, argues that the royal policy of forced loans, dues, etc. at interest-free terms must replace the conventional picture of fourteenth-century England of innumerable subjects enriching themselves at the expense of the crown (19).

15. De Roover, *Medici Bank*, 23.

16. C. C. Bayley (ed.), *War and Society in Renaissance Florence: the 'De Militia' of Leonardo Bruni*, 87.

17. Bartolus of Sassoferrato (1314–57), the leading civilist of his age, held that a commune could tax future acquisitions by statutory enactment; A. T. Sheedy, *Bartolus*, 171. The clergy usually consented to make grants to the crown in order to protect their fixed revenues, for the crown could always indirectly tax land-owners by debasing the coinage and so reducing the real value of income from rents. In France, in the period 1285–1328, the clergy granted a tenth every year, and between 1328 and 1350 at least twenty were given; Miskimin, *Money, Prices and Foreign Exchange*, 45–6.

18. Cf J. H. Hackett, 'State of the Church: a Concept of the Medieval Canonists', in *Jurist*, XXIII (1963) 259–90, here 283.

19. *COD* 600. 20 – 601. 1. Innocent III threatened the York diocese with interdict when John taxed the churches without papal consent; cf C. R. Cheney, *Selected Letters of Pope Innocent III concerning England*, 104–5 = Potthast 3418. For Boniface, see Potthast 24291 (ref. Hackett, in *Jurist*, XXIII 284).

20. Clement VII had to pay 'over 140,000 ducats or 32 per cent of the revenue . . . for payment of interest on the papal debt', mostly under the form of salaries for officials; cf Partner, in *Italian Renaissance Studies*, 269.

21. E. W. Kemp, *Counsel and Consent: Aspects of the Government of the Church as exemplified in the History of English Provincial Synods*, 58.

22. In many cases wages rose after the Black Death of 1348; cf Russell, in *Trans. Amer. Phil. Soc.* NS XLVIII 140. On the other hand, Betts, in *Past and Present*, II 28, paints a very black picture of the poor in Prague during the period 1346–1419 when there was a rise in the price of basic commodities such as barley, charcoal, boots, salt-fish, beer and wine; wages did not increase correspondingly, and there was even devaluation of the coinage in the reign of Václav IV. Bridbury, *Economic Growth*, 24, mentions that wages doubled in England between 1348 and Agincourt, but he does not examine the relationship with prices.

23. R. S. Lopez and H. A. Miskimin, 'The Economic Depression of the Renaissance', in *EcHR*² XIV (1961–2) 408–26, here 411.

24. Cf Tierney, *Poor Law*, 264. In Bohemia, King Václav II in the last years of the thirteenth century brought in Italian miners to work the mines of Kutná Hora. The Prague groschen became one of the main coins of international exchange in Europe: Betts, in *Past and Present*, II 31.

25. The great famine of 1315–17 decimated the population of Europe, according to Verlinden, in *Revue belge*, XVII 103. Miskimin argues that in England and France during the fourteenth century the poor 'of both the town and the country, were probably living close enough to the subsistence level to expend almost all their income on grain': *Money, Prices and Foreign Exchange*, 24. The fifteenth-century *montes pietatis* made loans of corn as well as of money to the poor. See p. 121.

26. Generalization is impossible other than for the economically advanced regions of Europe. Adelson, who speaks of the flight of capital from business and the latter being put into a strait-jacket until the sixteenth century, expresses

a commonly held view: *Medieval Commerce*, 91.

27. Equal pay was not uncommon in the eleventh and twelfth centuries; cf Lord Beveridge, 'Westminster Wages in the Manorial Era', in *EcHR*[2] VIII (1955) 18–35, especially 34.

28. On the sumptuary laws of the general councils, see Lateran IV 16.

29. M. Malowist, 'Les Mouvements d'expansion en Europe aux xve et xvie siècles', in *AESC* XVII (1962) 923–9 exemplifies this tendency in England, Scandinavia, Denmark, Germany, Spain, Poland and Hungary (ibid. 924).

30. Elliott-Binns, *Medieval Cornwall*, 182.

31. Luca Landucci, *A Florentine Diary from 1450 to 1516 . . . continued by an Anonymous Writer till 1542*, 124.

32. Ibid. 116 (25 Jan 1496). The author mentions other deaths.

33. De Roover, *Money, Banking and Credit*, 139: 'The amazing volume of literature on the subject of usury and the numerous pronouncements of the Church show clearly that consumers' credit constituted a social problem of major importance and that it was foremost in the public mind.'

34. De Roover, *Money, Banking and Credit*, 150–1.

35. W. K. Ferguson, *The Renaissance*, 46: 'During the 14th and 15th centuries, as Italian business expanded to unprecedented proportions, capital played a predominant part in the economic life of Italy, having spread from commerce to export industry, banking and agriculture' — a view hardly tenable today.

36. L. Martines, *The Social World of the Florentine Humanists 1390–1460*, 23.

37. Ibid. 290.

38. Ibid. 291; also De Roover, *Medici Bank*, 48.

39. De Roover, *Medici Bank*, 372–3.

40. Cf Renouard, *Les Hommes d'affaires*, 93: 'une stagnation qu'un recul'; De Roover, *Medici Bank*, 5: 'stagnation, if not regression'; Bridbury, *Economic Growth*, 100, reverses the statement in the case of England, but detailed studies do not support his thesis, e.g. Hoskins, *The Midland Peasant*, 84–8, describes the depressed state of Wigston Magna in the early fifteenth century. In general, see A. R. Lewis, 'The Closing of the Mediaeval Frontier', in *Speculum*, XXXIII (1958) 475–83; F. C. Lane, 'At the Roots of Republicanism', in *AHR* LXXI (1966) 403–20, here 404.

41. In *EcHR*[2] XIV 409–10.

42. E. A. Kosminsky, 'Peut-on considérer le xive et le xve siècles comme l'époque de la décadence de l'économie européenne?' in *Studi Sapori*, I 551–69, here 568.

43. Ibid. 560.

44. Ibid, 567.

45. Lopez, in *EcHR*[2] XIV 413.

46. G. Fourquin, *Les Campagnes de la région parisienne à la fin du moyen âge*, 117. See also Kosminsky, 'La dépression et le déclin en France ne font pas de doute', in *Studi Sapori*, I 562.

47. C. M. Cipolla, 'Per la storia delle terre della "Bassa" Lombardia', in *Studi Sapori*, I 665–72, here 667–8.

48. A. R. Bridbury, *England and the Salt Trade in the Later Middle Ages*, 68.

49. J. Calmette, *The Golden Age of Burgundy*, 250–1, 254.

50. Lopez, in *EcHR*[2] XIV 412.

51. Waites, in *Yorks. Arch. J*, XL 482.

52. M. Malowist, 'L'Évolution industrielle en Pologne du xive au xviie siècle', in *Studi Sapori*, I 571–603, here 574.

53. Malowist, in *Studi Sapori*, I 583, 585–7, 588.

54. Bridbury, *Salt Trade*. 109.   The local ecclesiastical corporations such as the abbeys of Buzay and Fontenelles and the Cordeliers of Bourgneuf quickly became involved in the new and booming enterprise at the Bay (ibid. 71).

55. Ibid. 41.   Also Carus-Wilson, *Medieval Merchant*, 245–6, 248–9, 254, 255, 259, for the various fluctuations in the export of wine from Gascony during the fourteenth century.

56. Smith, *Canterbury Cathedral Priory*, 155–6.   The decline in sheep farming continued generally in England through the fourteenth century; there were severe murrains in 1348, 1363, 1369, and 1386; the monopoly by the Merchant Staplers also served to limit wool production.

57. Kosminsky, in *Studi Sapori*, I 561–2.

58. *EcHR*[2] XIV 420.

59. Ibid. 424–5.   In 1336 the Peruzzi had 90 employees, in 1341 the Acciaiuoli had 53, and in 1469 the Medici 60.   The banking capital of the Peruzzi in 1310 was 108,000 florins, the Medici in 1451 was 72,000 florins.   See De Roover, *Medici Bank*, 50, 61–2, 68, 77, for exact figures in the comparison of the earlier (and larger) banks with the Medici.

60. De Roover, *Medici Bank*, 85–6, 95.

61. De Roover, *Medici Bank*, 16.

62. J. H. Mundy and P. Riesenberg, *The Medieval Town* (Princeton, N.J., 1958) 70–1.   Cf Van Werveke, in *Camb. Econ. Hist.* III 21, 34; Van Zijl, *Gerard Groote*, 35, for Deventer, where the senate of twelve magistrates and twelve councillors, 'who belonged exclusively to a few noble and rich families ... elected each other every year'.   For tax exemptions due to poverty and the physical contraction of the city of Lincoln in the later Middle Ages, see Hill, *Medieval Lincoln*, 272, 286–7, 312.   There are frequent references to empty shops and houses in ruins; even the Fossdyke, which connected with the River Trent, was allowed to silt up, so affecting trade.   See J. H. Mundy and P. Riesenberg, *Medieval Town*, 70–1.

63. W. G. Hoskins, *Essays in Leicestershire History*, especially 67–107, 'The Deserted Villages of Leicestershire', where the author shows that some sixty villages disappeared, mostly before 1500, which is about one-sixth of the medieval total of 370 (ibid. 101).   See also Chibnall, *Sherington*, 131–3, and 138–9 for 'the slow worsening of the free peasants as the century progressed'.

64. Mundy, *Medieval Town*, 72–3; Hibbert, in *Camb. Econ. Hist.* III 180,

181, that there was more economic freedom in the thirteenth than in the fourteenth and fifteenth centuries, and 197 for the growth of restrictions of all kinds in the later period. For London, see Williams, *Medieval London*, 88; on Cologne, see L. Beutin, 'Italien und Köln', in *Studi Sapori*, I 29–46, especially 41–2. On Venice, see Pius II's description in his *Commentaries* (ed. Gabel, 135–6): 'Merchandise is shipped here from almost the entire world and there is no more famous trading center in all Europe. Merchants from all over the West bring their wares here and carry away the wares of the East. They have an armoury and a magnificent dockyard called the Arsenal protected by all sorts of engines where they are ceaselessly building galleys and other craft. It is thought that at a moment's notice they could at pleasure equip 100 galleys and as a matter of fact they have sometimes done so.'

65. Lopez, in *EcHR*² XIV 414.

66. Mundy, *Medieval Town*, 70; Hibbert, in *Camb. Econ. Hist.* III 207.

67. Crombie, *Augustine to Galileo*, II 109–10.

68. Tierney, *Poor Law*, 111–13.

69. Bridbury, *Economic Growth*, 23, says the decline in England began with the famine of 1315–17. However, Russell, in *Trans. Amer. Phil. Soc.* NS XLVIII 113, concludes that the populations continued to rise till the Black Death. In 1348 the population of England was 3,757,500, in 1400 only 2,000,000; the upturn began about 1430 and by 1545 the population had reached 3,220,000 (ibid. 118). The pre-Plague figure for Italy was 9,200,000; post-Plague 5,500,000. There was a recurrence of Plague in 1361–2, 1367, 1375, 1390, 1407, 1413, 1434, 1464 and 1471; cf Bean, in *EcHR*² XV 424 for the effect in England. On Germany, see Carpentier, in *AESC* XVII 1065, that the Plague which struck in 1350 took 50 per cent of the population of Magdeburg, 50 to 66 per cent of Hamburg, 70 per cent of Bremen, but only 25 per cent of Lübeck; rural mortality was probably as high as the urban rate.

70. P. Wolff, 'Trois Études de démographie médiévale en France méridionale', in *Studi Sapori*, I 493–503, here 496, 499, 502.

71. Hoskins, in *Essays Leicestershire*, 105.

72. W. M. Bowsky, 'The Impact of the Black Death upon Sienese Government and Society', in *Speculum*, XXXIX (1964) 1–34, here 14, 18.

73. Ibid. 21; Carpentier, in *AESC* XVII 1074; Lopez, in *EcHR*² XVI 526. Cf. De Roover, *Money, Banking and Credit*, 349, for the decline of Bruges and rise of Antwerp in its place.

74. Carpentier, *Une Ville*, 213, 215.

75. Jones, in *RSCI* LXXVI 305. Cf W. C. Robinson, 'Money, Population and Economic Change in late Medieval Europe', in *EcHR*² XII (1959–60) 63–82, which rejects the Malthusian view (75).

76. Carpentier, *Une Ville*, 53.

77. Ibid. 163.

78. Lopez, in *EcHR*² XIV 423. In Genoa and Marseilles population decline was 40 per cent after the Black Death, but trade fell by 70 per cent. See

Bowsky, in *Speculum*, XXXIX 21. For the reaction of the large cities, see Lopez, in *EcHR*² XVI 526, that the Italians as soon as they realized that the mass market was contracting 'turned to the production of luxury items, such as silks instead of woollens'. Even if *per capita* output remained the same much of it was channelled into the production of war materials. Thus, the Hundred Years War constituted a heavy drain on the English economic resources. The armies took between 10 and 15 per cent of the total male population between 18 and 45 years of age; as well, there was the indirect commitment of the clothiers, munitions makers and others; Postan, in *Past and Present*, XXVII 35–6. France was better off, except that the 'provision of weapons put a strain on industrial capacity' (Miskimin, *Money, Prices and Foreign Exchange*, 3).

79. Verlinden, in *Revue belge*, XVII 140, shows this for Spain; subsequently the crown insisted on return of such lands to their previous owners or their heirs. In Siena the plague legacies to the Church were so great that the government suspended its charitable payments to the formerly needy religious and other ecclesiastical institutions (Bowsky, in *Speculum*, XXXIX 16).

80. Carpentier, *Une Ville*, 155, 156.

81. D. F. Dowd, 'The Economic Expansion of Lombardy, 1300–1500: a Study in Political Stimuli to Economic Change', in *JEcH* XXI (1961) 139–60, especially 147, 153.

82. Postan, in *JEcH* XI 345. For growth of restrictive legislation, see E. M. Carus-Wilson and Olive Coleman, *England's Export Trade 1275–1547*, 2.

83. Lopez, in *EcHR*² XVI 529, and in *EcHR*² XIV 410–11.

84. For the fluctuations in papal finances in the early fourteenth century, see D. P. Waley, 'An Account Book of the Patrimony of St Peter in Tuscany, 1304–1306', in *JEH* VI (1955) 18–25.

85. Cf Wood, *English Monasteries*, 118–19. For thirteenth-century England some 425 monastic patrons have been traced, which accounts for over half the religious houses, and the remainder, some 300 or so, were probably in the advowson of their mother house (ibid. 7, 18).

86. Ibid. 101–21.

87. D'Haenens, *Le Moyen Age*, LXV 90.

88. At this time when papal finances entered a difficult phase, it may seem strange that Augustus Triumphus expressed what was probably the most absolute form of papal supremacy over temporal possessions, e.g. 'He alone, we may say, exercises an absolute property right, whilst private rights of possession are nothing but gifts or grants made *gratia papae* to the individual members of the society.' According to Augustus, it follows that a king must look to the pope for all his possessions — *omne quod habet* — so that the power to levy taxes depends on papal consent, for the king is only a steward of the pope; text and commentary in Wilks, *Studia Patristica*, VI 541–2.

89. Decline in real value of rents was part of the cyclic process of medieval economic development, e.g. in the twelfth century, with the result that 'the secular clergy became land poor'; cf Mundy, *Liberty and Political Power*, 81;

Herlihy, in *Speculum*, xxxvi 92. For the fourteenth century, see Bridbury, *Economic Growth*, 93.

90. Partner, *History Today*, vii 770.

91. Renouard, *Les Relations*, 3; Gill, *Eugenius IV*, 64–5.

92. Partner, in *JEH* iv 67.

93. Gill, *Eugenius IV*, 13.

94. Cf Lewis, in *Speculum*, xxxiii 482. If the Avignonese papacy was less wasteful than its predecessors, why then the outcry? Lewis argues that firstly there was increasing criticism of papal sources of income such as annates, led by the Spiritual Franciscans, and, secondly, in a less prosperous Europe, with a diminished gross product the popes had to vie with the secular princes for a share in terms of taxation. For John XXII, see P. Gasnault, 'La Perception dans le royaume de France du subside sollicité par Jean XXII "contra haereticos et rebelles partium Italiae"', in *Mélanges d'archéologie et d'histoire*, lxix (1957) 273–319; also Lambert, *Franciscan Poverty*, 224.

95. Renouard, *Les Relations*, 516; Partner, in *History Today*, vii 771.

96. 'the Schism was the great crisis of papal finance, a crisis more severe and decisive than the Reformation' (Partner, *History Today*, vii 772). See also Partner, in *Italian Renaissance Studies*, 256.

97. Mundy–Loomis, 6.

98. Ibid. 4–5.

99. Lunt, *Financial Relations*, ii 66–7; Partner, in *History Today*, vii 772.

100. Lunt, *Financial Relations*, ii 168, 118, 124. The English monarchs had also shared in the income of the tenths, which is one reason why the last successful mandatory tenth had been in 1336, because Edward III was 'able to persuade the clergy to make such frequent grants of income taxes that they were paying a tenth in every year except two until 1360' (ibid. 88). For the history of Provisors, see R. Dudley Edwards, 'The Kings of England and Papal Provisions in Fifteenth Century Ireland', in *Studies Gwynn*, 265–80, especially 266.

101. Partner, *Papal State*, 44–51, and in *History Today*, vii 768; Lunt, *Financial Relations*, ii 124–5, 130. On procurations, see Lunt, ii 716. Papal procurations were in fact a percentage levied on episcopal procurations, especially when the popes granted the right to visit by deputy; cf ibid. ii 714. John XXII was the first to levy them. For the text of Constance, see p. 215.

102. Gill, *Eugenius IV*, 77. Cf J. B. Morrall, 'Papacy and Council in the Century before the Reformation', in *IER* xcix (1963) 217–26, here 218 and 223, where the author suggests that the financial proposals of Basel 'struck at the roots of Papal financial independence and would have put the Papacy completely at the Council's mercy'.

103. Gill, *Eugenius IV*, 77.

104. Partner, *Papal State*, 193; Lunt, *Financial Relations*, ii 445. For the text of Basel, see p. 219.

105. Cf Lateran IV 62, which had legislated against abuses of the system of indulgences.

106. Cf P. Ourliac, 'La Théorie canonique des rentes au xvᵉ siècle', in *Études historiques à la mémoire de Noël Didier* (1960) 231–43. The purchase and sale of annuities was a means of avoiding the usury laws (ibid. 233, 241). During the fifteenth century the papacy created a large number of such offices, mostly sinecures, under titles as the 'Cavalieri di San Pietro', 'Presidenti di Ripa', 'Archivisti', 'Scudieri' and so on. Individuals invested their capital by purchasing the offices, and received a salary (in fact, this was the interest) at an average rate of 11 per cent of purchase price. In some offices, with fees attached, part of the 'interest' came from the clients and not from the papacy; even so, the papacy had to find a large sum of money annually out of current income to pay the remainder. In 1521, according to Partner, 'over 2000 offices were venal, representing an invested capital of about two and a half million gold florins, and an annual interest of about 300,000 gold florins' (in *Italian Renaissance Studies*, 258).

107. Lunt, *Financial Relations*, I 135–6.

108. Cf J. Gill, *The Council of Florence*, 347.

109. Partner, in *JEH* IV 63.

110. Partner, in *Italian Renaissance Studies*, 257.

111. Partner, in *Italian Renaissance Studies*, 259, says that the 'income of Gregory XI (1370–8) varied between 200,000 and 300,000 gold cameral florins annually of which not more than a quarter came from the papal states. That of Martin V (1417–31) was in 1426–7 about 170,000 gold cameral florins, of which 80,000 florins, or rather less than half, came from the Papal State.'

112. Trugenberger, *San Bernardino*, 77, describes the paradox of a Church so deeply involved in temporal affairs that 'Tutto cio insieme contribuisce a fomentare una practica finanziaria della Chiesa che e ben lontana dalla doctrina ... a seguire quello spirito capitalistico che in teoria era cosi decisamente combattuto.'

113. De Roover, *Medici Bank*, 200. The papacy could also bring the bankers into line by threatening to free their debtors from the liability of repayment, as Urban IV had succeeded in doing in 1262–3 with many of the Tuscan bankers; cf Waley, *Papal State*, 274–5.

114. D. P. Waley, 'A Register of Boniface VIII's Chamberlain, Theoderic of Orvieto', in *JEH* VIII (1957) 141–52 comments that 'Theoderic's letters indicate that the bankers could not operate successfully as the pope's financial agents unless the heavy artillery of ecclesiastical commination and condemnation was used as support ... against defaulting ecclesiasts' (ibid. 146). For example, John XXII forced the Hospitallers to raise money on security of their possessions (which was strictly uncanonical) in order to repay the Bardi 133,000 florins and the Peruzzi 191,000. Renouard, *Les Relations*, 542.

115. P. Partner, 'The "Budget" of the Roman Church in the Renaissance Period', in *Italian Renaissance Studies*, 256–79, here 256. These generalizations

are subject to the proviso that the financial state of the papacy could change quite rapidly, as indeed could that of any medieval secular power; cf Waley, in *JEH* VII 270-1.

116. Unless these interests coincided with its own, e.g. the Medici monopoly of the alum mines on the papal estates at Tolfa; cf Le Goff, *Marchands et banquiers*, 24.

117. Thrupp, *Merchant Class*, 184.

118. Zijl, *Gerard Groote*, 263-4.

119. Cf C. J. Godfrey, 'Pluralists in the Province of Canterbury in 1366', in *JEH* XI (1960) 23-40. The abuse had a long history, cf °Chalcedon 10, °Lateran III 13 and 14, IV 29, and °Vienne II 4. Cf F. Pegues, 'Ecclesiastical Provisions for the Support of Students in the Thirteenth Century', in *CH* XXVI (1957) 307-18, here 313; E. I. Watkin, *The Church in Council*, 117, for Lateran IV 29.

120. Pantin, *English Church*, 37.

121. Godfrey, in *JEH* XI 27. See M. D. Knowles, 'The English Bishops, 1070-1532', in *Studies Gwynn*, 283-96, here 285.

122. Zijl, *Gerard Groote*, 262-3. In Cornwall by the close of the Middle Ages some 125 out of 212 parishes were appropriated. Elliott-Binns, *Medieval Cornwall*, 327.

123. Gasnault, in *Mélanges d'archéologie et d'histoire*, LXIX 274.

124. C. H. Talbot, 'Cîteaux and Scarborough', in *Studia Monastica*, II (1960) 95-158, especially 109-10.

125. A. Luttrell, 'Intrigue, Schism and Violence among the Hospitallers of Rhodes: 1377-1384', in *Speculum*, XLI (1966) 30-48, here 33.

126. F. R. H. Du Boulay, 'The Quarrel between the Carmelite Friars and the Secular Clergy of London, 1464-1468', in *JEH* VI (1955) 156-74, especially 165-6.

127. Cf °Lateran V Sess. IX 'Reform of the Curia' [2].

128. Cf Lunt, *Financial Relations*, II 82, 88; Partner, in *History Today*, VII 774 'from a financial point of view the Reformation is therefore a paradox ...'

129. See A. D'Haenens, 'La Crise des abbayes bénédictines au bas moyen âge: Saint-Martin-de-Tournai de 1290 à 1350', in *Le Moyen Age*, LXV (1959) 75-95, especially 89-90 dealing with the recovery of the Abbey in the period 1330-50; and *L'Abbaye Saint-Martin-de-Tournai de 1290 à 1350: origines, évolution et dénouement d'une crise*, reviewed by N. Coulet, 'Le Monde bénédictin et la crise du xive siècle', in *AESC* XVII (1962) 1001-5, especially 1003, where he points out that, despite the economic recovery after 1330, the abbey never regained the great position it had enjoyed *c.* 1289. Two-thirds of the lands remained alienated. More significantly, perhaps, there was no corresponding spiritual regain, for the monastic mentality had been harmed in the previous period of decline.

130. H. O. Evenett, 'The Last Stages of Medieval Monasticism in England', in *Studia Monastica*, II (1960) 387-419, especially 393; M. D. Knowles, *The*

Religious Orders in England: III *The Tudor Age,* passim. Cf Gilchrist, in *Twentieth Century,* XV 314.

131. Smith, *Canterbury Cathedral Priory,* 12–13.

132. Ibid. 203.

133. R. H. Hilton, *The Economic Development of some Leicestershire Estates in the 14th and 15th centuries,* 79, 87.

134. Smith, *Canterbury Cathedral Priory,* 111.

135. Evenett, in *Studia Monastica,* II 396.

136. Cf Le Goff, *Marchands et banquiers,* 104, that the growth of capitalism led to laicization so that 'les rythmes de l'existence n'obéissaient plus à l'Église'.

CHAPTER 6

1. Cf D. Herlihy, 'The Agrarian Revolution in Southern France and Italy, 801–1150', in *Speculum,* XXXIII (1958) 23–41, here 32, and in *Speculum,* XXXVI 83.

2. Herlihy, in *Speculum,* XXXIII 32–3.

3. Cf Herlihy, in *EcHR* X 1–14, especially 4, where he examines some 3497 contracts dealing with transfer of land in Italy and the type of compensation offered for it.

4. Herlihy, in *Speculum,* XXXIII 36.

5. Generally, cf G. Le Bras, 'L'Invasion de l'Église dans la cité', in *Mélanges Lavedan* (1954) 187–98, especially 190–1 for urban growth of parishes.

6. Russell, in *Trans. Amer. Phil. Soc.* NS XLVIII 133.

7. Cf C. E. Perrin, 'Le Servage en France et en Allemagne', in *Proc. 10th Intern. Cong.* III 213–45; Lopez, in *AHR* LVII 15.

8. Boyd, *Tithes and Parishes,* 171, 143.

9. Ibid. 165.

10. Cf P. A. Amargier, 'Benoît d'Alignan, évêque de Marseille (1229–1268). Le contexte et l'esprit d'une théologie', in *Le Moyen Age,* LXXII (1966) 443–62, here 452–4.

11. Thrupp, *Merchant Class,* 185.

12. Chédeville, in *CCM* III 215.

13. Cf Lateran V 'Reform of the Curia' [7] and [8] (see p. 85).

14. Cf J. J. Scarisbrick, 'Clerical Taxation in England, 1485–1547', in *JEH* XI (1960) 41–54. In the period 1446–1532 the average sum paid p.a. to the papacy was £4816; in the same period the Crown took £12,500 p.a. After the Reformation the figure paid to the crown greatly increased (ibid. 45). Partner, in *History Today,* VII 771.

15. Partner, *Papal State,* 169.

16. *Commentaries,* ed. Gabel, 199, referring to Diether of Mainz's refusal to repay the bank 'that advanced the money' for the papal dues, so that the banker has been 'on your account … reduced to beggary'; see also ibid. 180, 181.

17. Partner, *Papal State*, 147, that the salt monopoly returned about 20,000–34,500 florins. For an account of the alum discovery, see Pius II, *Commentaries*, ed. Gabel, 233. Cosimo dei Medici invested 75,000 ducats (ibid. 234).

18. Partner, *Papal State*, 156. Martin V stopped the assignments.

19. Lopez, in *AHR* LVII 17; Le Bras, in *Mélanges Lavedan*, 187, 189.

20. Kemp, *Counsel and Consent*, 67; de Lagarde, *La Naissance*, I 55.

21. Cf B. Schnapper, 'Les Baux à vie (xᵉ au xviᵉ siècle)', in *RHE* XXXIV (1957) 347–75, especially 358.

22. Cf R. A. Donkin, 'Settlement and Depopulation on Cistercian Estates during the Twelfth and Thirteenth Centuries, especially in Yorkshire', in *BIHR* XXXIII (1960) 141–64, and 'The Urban Property of the Cistercians in Mediaeval England', in *ASOC* XV (1959) 104–31.

23. Cf Adelson, *Medieval Commerce*, 44.

24. Cf B. Waites, 'The Monasteries and the Medieval Development of North-East Yorkshire', in *BIHR* XXXI (1958) 231–4, here 231.

25. Ibid. 232.

26. Cf Donkin, in *Cîteaux*, VIII 110 for the work of the Umiliati (founded 1140), especially in Florence. In general, clerics were to the forefront in agricultural development: Miller, in *Past and Present*, XXVIII 25, cites William de Colerne of Malmesbury and Henry of Eastry of Christ Church, Canterbury, as examples of improving landlords.

27. Donkin, in *Cîteaux*, VIII 114.

28. Cf Graves, in *ASOC* XIII 48, 50, 51.

29. Donkin, in *Cîteaux*, VIII 114, explains that the 'height of the export trade in wool was, however, from about 1275–1325 and the Cistercians were intent upon meeting the demand. Their contracts were many and of long standing, and their obligations often compromised their freedom of action. Many sold wool in advance and were periodically in great debt', for they often had to buy wool themselves in order to meet their contracts.

30. Donkin, in *Cîteaux*, VII 120; Hill, *Medieval Lincoln*, 320. Cf Graves, in *ASOC* XIII 27–8, for issue of royal mandates to the Cistercian abbots and others in Lincoln to desist from buying wool for resale.

31. Graves, in *ASOC* XIII 23.

32. The account-book of Beaulieu shows that the early simplicity of the Order had been lost; Talbot, in *The Listener*, LIV 177. The book lists a number of officials associated with the monastic economy, including even a furrier. In 1167 Rievaulx had 140 monks and 500–600 *conversi*. In 1187 Waverley had 70 monks and 120 *conversi*; Connelly, in *Traditio*, X 413.

33. Smith, *Canterbury Cathedral Priory*, 49, 51–2.

34. Ibid. 44. The monks, however, began to buy English cloth in the fifteenth century.

35. Graves, in *ASOC* XIII 11–12; Madden, in *CHR* XLIX 344, 355–6; Talbot, in *Cîteaux*, IX 196.

36. Graves, in *ASOC* XIII 44. Debts do not necessarily indicate poverty; thus Graves, 'Lending money to poor monasteries was not good business; and the Cistercians did not want for creditors' (ibid. 44–5).

37. R. A. Donkin, 'The Disposal of Cistercian Wool in England and Wales during the XIIth and XIIIth Centuries', in *Cîteaux*, VIII (1957) 109–31, 181–202, here 119–20.

38. Smith, *Canterbury Cathedral Priory*, 61, 62, 134, 135, 138.

39. Lopez and Raymond, *Medieval Trade*, 101.

40. For the Templars, cf Conway, *Time of Decision*, 200–1; Jedin, *Ecumenical Councils*, 99–100; Kemp, *Counsel and Consent*, 89.

41. G. A. Holmes, 'Florentine Merchants in England, 1346–1436', in *EcHR²* XIII (1960) 193–208, especially 203.

42. Ibid. 193, 194, 198. See also De Roover, *Medici Bank*, 3, 116, and Renouard, *Les Relations*, 585.

43. Sapori, *Le Marchand italien*, 21, e.g. Nicholas III (1277–80) gave the German concession to the Frescobaldi and Alfoni of Florence; the Sardinian, Portuguese and Corsican to Lucquois Battosi and Caccianimici; and the English to Ricciardi of Lucca.

44. Renouard, *Les Relations*, 117; De Roover, *Medici Bank*, 195.

45. Smith, *Canterbury Cathedral Priory*, 18.

46. Ibid. 18, 26. Thus, in 1336, Richard Spycer of Fordwich and William Pynere of Sandwich were two of the priory's creditors.

47. Duby, in *AESC* VII 169.

48. *Chronicle of Jocelin of Brakelond*, ed. H. E. Butler, 1–3.

49. Hill, *Medieval Lincoln*, 218–19.

50. In 1264 Urban IV supported the claims of the Florentine firms of De Burgo, Simonetti Octaviani, Bonaveti, Bacorelli, Baramonti, and Ardhinghi against archbishops of Dublin, Armagh, Tuam and Cashel and their suffragans: O'Sullivan, *Italian Merchant Bankers*, 49–50.

51. De Roover, *Medici Bank*, 10.

52. Nelson, in *SJEcH* VII (1947) 7.

53. Cf M. Maccarrone, 'Il IV concilio lateranense', in *Divinitas*, V (1961) 270–98, especially 290.

54. J. Gaudemet, 'Aspects de la législation conciliaire française au xiiie siècle', in *RDC* IX (1959) 319–40, especially 337–8. See also Langmuir, in *Traditio*, XVI 226, that Louis IX's *Ordinance on the Jews* (1230) contained the first royal enactment that reinforced canonical sanctions against Christian usurers.

55. Gaudemet, in *RDC* IX 328.

56. Cf M. Castaing, 'Le Prêt à intérêt à Toulouse aux xiie et xiiie siècles', in *Bulletin philologique et historique*, 273–8, especially 274.

57. Ibid. 275, where Castaing points out that in the mortgage system the rate of interest could be as low as 5 per cent. On straightout loans it was between 15 and 38 per cent.

L

58. Ibid. 274.

59. Mundy, *Liberty and Political Power*, 82.

60. J. H. Mundy, 'Un Usurier malheureux', in *Annales du Midi*, LXVIII (1956) 217–25, here 217.

61. Castaing, in *Bulletin philologique et historique*, 277.

62. Wolff, *Commerces et marchands*, 179–80.

63. O'Sullivan, *Italian Merchant Bankers*, 37–8.

64. Ibid. 48.

65. Williams, *Medieval London*, 146, 147.

66. Ibid. 126.

67. Renouard, *Les Relations*, 536.

68. Ibid. 537.

69. Cf McLaughlin, in *Med. Stud.* I 109–10.

70. L. Beutin, 'Italien und Köln', in *Studi Sapori*, I 39.

71. This decree seems to distinguish between usurious and non-usurious debts, by which one may assume that loans at reasonable rates of interest are meant. The distinction fits in with what is known of the practice in other states, e.g. Venice. However, more evidence is needed, especially a study of the glosses on the text of Lyons I [I].

72. A practice frequently condemned by the popes as reprehensible was the action of individual clergy and religious or communities standing as guarantors for other persons' debts. The consequences of such an act could be harmful, e.g. in March 1206 the consuls of Toulouse ordered the prior of the Hospital of St John of Jerusalem to lease or sell the house in order to reimburse the creditors of one who had defaulted on a debt that he (the prior) had guaranteed against his order's property; Mundy, in *Annales du Midi*, LXVIII 219–20.

73. Cf Roth, *History of the Jews*, 105; also Nelson, in *Annuaire*, VII 334–5, where the prohibition against the pawning of sacred objects is linked with the medieval propaganda that the Jews desecrated such objects.

74. Cf Nelson, in *SJEcH* VII 113. De Roover, *Medici Bank*, 13, 410 n 19 overlooks the distinction.

75. Cf Noonan, *Usury*, 34.

76. Nelson, in *SJEcH* VII 117.

77. See p. 49; also Nelson, in *SJEcH* VII 106.

78. Origo, *Merchant of Prato*, 12–13.

79. Nelson, in *SJEcH* VII 113. Gaudemet, in *RDC* IX 336, comments that numerous enactments in the local church councils concern respect for last wills and the role of the clergy in execution.

80. Lopez and Raymond, *Medieval Trade*, 159, document 67. Cf Lateran III 25.

81. Nelson, in *SJEcH* VII 114.

82. Ibid. 110.

83. Cf McLaughlin, in *Med. Stud.* II 3.

84. S. Kuttner, 'Conciliar Law in the Making. The Lyonese Constitutions

(1274) of Gregory X in a Manuscript at Washington', in *Miscellanea Pio Paschini*, II 39–81.

85. Ibid. 71.

86. fo. 7ra; cf *COD* 305. 3.

87. *COD* 306. 7–9.

88. Nelson, in *SJEcH* VII 107.

89. Kuttner, in *Misc. Paschini*, II 71–2; cf *Gloss. ord.* (1588 ed.) col. 711.

90. Hill, *Medieval Lincoln*, 322.

91. On the word 'alienigenas' (*COD* 305. 3); col. 713 (1588 ed.).

92. Cf Luzzatto, in *Misc. Cessi*, I 195, where he cites a Venetian prohibition of 1281 against foreigners (Tuscans, in this instance) carrying on money-lending activities in Venice. Luzzatto, in *AHES* IX 41, that most of the lenders had been foreigners: Paduans, Veronese, and especially Tuscans.

93. Kuttner, *Misc. Paschini*, II 73.

94. Cf McLaughlin, in *Med. Stud.* II 7.

95. Noonan, *Usury*, 34.

96. Nelson, in *SJEcH* VII 117.

97. Emery, *Jews of Perpignan*, 88.

98. C. Roth, 'The Economic History of the Jews', in *EcHR*² XIV (1961–2) 131–5, here 132.

99. Carpentier, *Une Ville*, 61, 206.

100. Ibid. 93–4. The Jews paid dearly for secular protection, which often failed to do its job; cf the massacre of some 2000 Jews in Strasbourg and the surrounding region on 14 February 1349. Popular ill-feeling against Jewish usuries was one of the causes. In the Middle Ages the frustration of the lower classes over the lack of adequate consumer-credit played a large part in popular risings and movements; cf Carpentier, in *AESC* XVII 1068.

101. Nelson, *Usury*, 22–3, 114.

102. G. Coniglio, 'L'usura a Lucca ed una bolla di Niccolò V del 1452', in *RSCI* VI (1952) 259–64, here 262. At Lucca loans at interest were first recorded in 1304 and in 1372 a statute fixed the maximum rate at 40 per cent. Another example of the practical working of the usury prohibitions is from England, where in the thirteenth century the crown claimed the right to confiscate on death the property and goods of Jewish and non-Jewish usurers. Such profits, it was argued, were the fruits of sin. However, total confiscation would have left the family without capital to carry on the business. Usually, therefore, the crown took a fine; thus, the family of Hamo of Hereford (d. 1232) paid 6000 marks on his death.

103. A. Sapori, 'Economia e morale alla fine del trecento', in *Studi senesi*, LXIV (1952) 44–76, here 51. The decline should not be exaggerated, e.g. Cosimo de' Medici and Francesco di Marco Datini, the Merchant of Prato, were still concerned to make satisfaction for their wealth. Cf E. H. Gombrich, 'The Early Medici as Patrons of Art: A Survey of Primary Sources', in *Italian Renaissance Studies*, 279–311, especially 284.

104. Cf M. B. Becker, 'Some Economic Implications of the Conflict between Church and State in "Trecento" Florence', in *Med. Stud.* XXI (1959) 1–16. The author makes the interesting point that the 'Signoria was willing to make concessions to Christian economic doctrine, even at the linguistic level', that is, the pawnbrokers were fined for having 'sinned' (ibid. 8). Usurers were actually tried in the church courts and then passed to the lay tribunals for the fines to be imposed.

105. Becker, in *Med. Stud.* XXI 5.

106. M. B. Becker, 'Florentine Politics and the Diffusion of Heresy in the Trecento: A Socio-economic Enquiry', in *Speculum*, XXXIV (1959) 60–75, here 62–4.

107. Ibid. 64.

108. Becker, in *Med. Stud.* XXI 10.

109. M. B. Becker, 'Church and State in Florence on the Eve of the Renaissance (1343–1382)', in *Speculum*, XXXVII (1962) 509–27.

110. M. B. Becker, 'Three Cases concerning the Restitution of Usury in Florence', in *JEcH* XVII (1957) 445–50, especially 444–6. Becker concludes that 'the investigation of Florentine legislation concerning the practice of usury in the fourteenth century leads the researcher to the conclusion that a general theory cannot be constructed unless more facts are made known', and he points to such difficulties as the fact that the judicial records for *ante* 1343 were burned in the revolution of that year. This conclusion applies to the problem of usury generally; the usage varied from state to state, so no generalization can be made to cover all the cases.

111. Becker, in *Speculum*, XXXIV 71.

112. De Roover, *Medici Bank*, 16.

113. Cf G. A. Brucker, *Florentine Politics and Society 1343–1378*, 294–335, for the years 1375–8, and especially 314–19 for the economic costs and consequences of the conflict. 'One-fourth of this expenditure was raised from forced loans: sixteen of these *prestanze*, totaling 570,000 florins, were levied from June 1375 through June 1378. This constituted a *per capita* assessment of ten florins upon every resident of the city, an amount equal to one-third of the yearly salary of an unskilled labourer, or the annual rent of a large shop. By any standard, this was an imposing burden' (ibid. 315). In 1376 the communal leadership ordered the confiscation of church property to the sum of 100,000 florins (ibid. 318).

114. Origo, *San Bernardino*, 90.

115. De Roover, in *Kylos*, X 134, and in *Studi Fanfani*, I 156, that Bernardino's main treatise, *De contractibus et usuris*, forms 'un vrai traité d'économie politique qui se distingue par le sens des réalités et la pénétration de l'analyse'.

116. Origo, *San Bernardino*, 90, and *Merchant of Prato*, 144–5. See also Trugenberger, *San Bernardino*, 62. For the *monte*, see L. F. Marks, 'The Financial Oligarchy in Florence under Lorenzo', in *Italian Renaissance Studies*, 123–47, here 127.

117. De Roover, in *Studi Sapori*, I 639.

118. Ibid. 632.

119. Ibid. 641, 642.

120. Lane, in *JEcH* xxIII 315. See also Luzzatto, in *AHES* IX 27-8 for state borrowings.

121. G. Luzzatto, 'Tasso d'interesse e usura a Venezia nei secoli xiii-xv', in *Miscellanea in onore di Roberto Cessi* (1958) I 191-202, here 191, 194, where he cites the example of two religious who claimed a loan of 50 gold ducats from the guarantor of the debt. The court granted this sum plus 10 ducats of interest covering the period of the loan of two years. Luzzatto, in *AHES* IX 42.

122. Ibid. 201.

123. Ibid. 202. See Florence Edler De Roover, 'Restitution in Renaissance Florence', in *Studi Sapori*, II 773-89, a study of business loans at interest made by Giuliano de' Medici between 1448 and 1454. However, he had absolute security so there was no risk. In his will he ordered restitution (ibid. 779). In 1312 the Statute of the Mercanzia, as later statutes, ordered payment of interest, even if entered in the books as a gift.

124. De Roover, *Money, Banking and Credit*, 306.

125. De Roover, in *SJEcH* II (1942) 57, 58.

126. Sapori, in *Studi medievale*, I 181.

127. Thrupp, *Merchant Class*, 175.

128. Ibid. 107.

129. Lane, in *JEcH* xxIII 316, where he cites G. Luzzatto, *Storia economica di Venezia dall'xi al xvi secolo*, 81-9, 104-5.

130. For the *cambium maritimum*, see De Roover, in *Camb. Econ. Hist.* III 55.

131. Cf Lane, in *JEcH* xxIII 315. See *CIC* c. 2354, which classes usury among the grave crimes of injustice, i.e. murder, rape, arson and traffic in slavery.

132. Dempsey, *Interest and Usury*, 175-6.

133. Noonan, *Usury*, 36. The author considers it an unfair criticism that the usury prohibition was meaningless because it was not enforced by the state, and plenty of evasions existed. The real force of the law was its hold on men's souls.

134. R. Ghinato, *Monte di pietà e monti frumentari di Amelia: origine e 'antichi statuti'*, and 'Un propagatore dei monti di pietà del '400. P. Fortunato Cappoli da Perugia, O.F.M. (d. 1477)', in *RSCI* x (1956) 193-211, and 'I francescani e il monte di pietà di Terni dal 1490 al 1515', in *AFH* LII (1959) 204-89.

135. De Roover, *Money, Banking and Credit*, 145; Ghinato, in *RSCI* x 193; Tierney, *Poor Law*, 159, compares them to the present-day credit unions; Divine, *Interest*, 57.

136. Nelson, *Usury*, 19, states that the interest on petty loans ranged from 20 to 50 per cent.

137. For Cajetan (Thomas de Vio 1468-1534) and his opposition, see De Roover, in *Kylos*, x 118.   Also Nelson, *Usury*, 19.

138. Nelson, *Usury*, 19-20.

139. The Franciscans agitated for the expulsion of the licensed — mostly Jewish — money-lenders because they stood for competition; cf Nelson, in *SJEcH* VII 120.   Stein, in *J of Semitic Studies*, I 150.

140. Michaud-Quantin, in *Misc. Med.* III 34, that moralists of the fourteenth century insist on the economic role of public power, e.g. to fix prices, repair works, destroy monopolies (ibid. 35).

141. De Roover, in *JEcH* XVIII 428.

142. Ibid.

143. Ibid. 429, and in *Studi Fanfani*, I 166-9, 171, that the towns pursued 'a policy of abundance and low prices'.

144. Mundy, *Liberty and Political Power*, 64.   Cf Sheedy, *Bartolus*, 83, for the right of priors delegated by the General Assembly of Perugia to fix the amount and price of grain daily.

145. Hibbert, in *Camb. Econ. Hist.* III 176, 177, 179.

146. De Roover, in *JEcH* XVIII 430-1.

147. C. Verlinden, 'La Grande Peste de 1348 en Espagne', in *Revue belge de philologie et d'histoire*, XVII (1938) 103-46, especially 120, presents an excellent summary of wage and price regulations by the Cortès of Saragossa and of Valladolid after the plague.   The English *Statute of Labourers* (1349) provides another example.   Cf Demant, 37-9, and Miskimin, *Money, Prices and Foreign Exchange*, 21, 23, where he points out that 'grain prices were market prices in the modern sense. . . .   In contrast to grain, prices and conditions of output of most manufactured goods and many other agricultural commodities were regulated either by the guilds or the King.   Salt was a monopoly in France; retail wine prices were set in England.'

148. Thrupp, *Merchant Class*, 93, 94, 95.   The Mayor also fixed the market price of salt, cf Bridbury, *Salt Trade*, 139.

149. Hibbert, in *Camb. Econ. Hist.* III 179.

150. De Roover, in *JEcH* XVIII 433, and in *Studi Fanfani*, I 177.   Cf Thrupp, *Merchant Class*, 74.

151. De Roover, in *Studi Fanfani*, I 178-9.

152. Luzzatto, in *AHES* IX 41-2.

153. M. Becker, 'La esecuzione della legislatura contro le pratiche monopolistiche delle arti fiorentine alla metà del secolo quattordicesimo', in *Archivio storico italiano*, CXVII (1959) 8-28, here 21.

154. Bayley (ed.), *War and Society*, 98.

155. De Roover, in *JEcH* XVIII 431.

156. De Roover, in *Studi Fanfani*, I 179.   Papal monopolies also broke the scholastic bans.   Cf De Roover, *Medici Bank*, 155-6; Lunt, *Papal Revenues*, I 60.

157. Hirschler, in *JEcH* XIV 52.   Cf A. L. Lilley, 'The Secularization of

Economic Justice', in Demant, 76–91, here 85, that the German reformers had 'all the medieval hatred of usury and of the luxury to which it ministered'.

158. Mundy-Loomis, 98–9.

159. Cf de Lagarde, *La Naissance*, I 180; for Florence, in particular, see Brucker, *Florentine Politics*, 137–8.

160. de Lagarde, *La Naissance*, 180.

161. Giordani, *Social Message*, 310.

162. Ibid. 313. But Hermas and Chrysostom urged the giver not to worry about the merit of the recipient. Alms-giving is a beautiful thing in itself (ibid. 315–16).

163. Tierney, *Poor Law*, 110.

164. Text in J. J. Bagley and P. B. Rowley, *A Documentary History of England*: I (*1066–1540*) 207–21, here 212. Thrupp, *Merchant Class*, 180.

165. Tierney, *Poor Law*, 117–19. Also Betts, in *Past and Present*, II 28, for the large number and variety of classes of debtors in medieval Prague. Brucker *Florentine Politics*, 316, for the effect of the war of 1375–8 on the poorer classes in Florence. Hallam, in *EcHR* x 361, for the effect of impartible inheritance in England.

166. Cf Thrupp, *Merchant Class*, 177. De Roover, in *Camb. Econ. Hist.* III 77.

167. Bayley, *War and Society*, 26, 54, 65, 66.

168. *Commentaries*, ed. Gabel, 143.

169. Tierney, *Poor Law*, 12.

170. Cf Mundy, *Liberty and Political Power*, 77. The discontented elements in Toulouse were the poor, i.e. the ordinary artisans, the perennial enemies of usury. Most heretics were 'either declining patricians or oppressed artisans. Great businessmen like a Poncius de Capitedenario remained faithful catholics' (ibid. 79). This tells us a great deal about the so-called adverse effect of the Church's economic doctrine on big business. Florence had become a great heresy centre during the twelfth century, cf Runciman, *Manichee*, 127.

171. Martines, *Social World*, 100.

172. F. J. Niederer, 'Early Medieval Charity', in *CH* XXI (1952) 285–93, here 286–7.

173. Ibid. 289, 294.

174. Chenu, *Théologie*, 254.

175. Smith, *Canterbury Cathedral Priory*, 47–8, 200.

176. Mundy-Loomis, 32.

177. Mollat, *Popes at Avignon*, 318.

178. Gill, *Eugenius IV*, 192–3. See also Elliott-Binns, *Medieval Cornwall*, 366, where the author refers to 'thirty-nine leper hospitals'.

179. Carpentier, *Une Ville*, 73, 118–19. The medical services at the Hospital of Santa Maria, Orvieto, were sufficient. What was lacking was, of course, proper knowledge of hygiene.

180. The council was attended almost exclusively by Italian prelates. The

scheme was the traditional one — condemnation of heresy, extirpation of schism, reform of the Church, peace among Christian princes, a crusade against the Turk.

CHAPTER 7

1. Max Weber, *The Protestant Ethic and the Spirit of Capitalism* (*Die protestantische Ethik und der Geist des Kapitalismus*); R. H. Tawney, *Religion and the Rise of Capitalism*.
2. Weber, 91, 166, 170.
3. Ibid. 172, 114–15.
4. Tawney, 21.
5. Tawney, 23–4.
6. Tawney, 68.
7. Tawney, 90.
8. Weber, 6–9, which consists of an Introduction to the English translation by Tawney. Also Tawney, 311–13. Weber's impressions of the medieval world were highly coloured. Thus he wrote of the gulf that 'separated the monk of the Middle Ages from the rest of the world about him' (Weber, 121–2). Even on seventeenth-century England his picture is, to say the least, exaggerated when referring to the 'conflict between the squirearchy, the representatives of "merrie old England", and the Puritan circles of widely varying social influence' (Weber, 173).
9. Tawney, 312–13.
10. Tawney, 313.
11. Niederer, in *CH* xxi 285.
12. Zijl, *Gerard Groote*, 220, 222 and 229.
13. Waites, in *Yorks. Arch. J*, xl 632, 634.
14. Hilton, *Economic Development*, 33.
15. *Canterbury Cathedral Priory*, 142.
16. Hilton, *Economic Development*, 33.
17. De Roover, *Medici Bank*, 195, 217.
18. See p. 1. Also Duby, in *AESC* vii 163, for an increase in peasant prosperity in the region of Cluny in the late eleventh and twelfth centuries; Smith, *Canterbury Cathedral Priory*, 126, for the beginning of economic restrictions from about 1314 onwards; and Carpentier, *Une Ville*, 187, 196, for effects of the Black Death on Orvieto.
19. Tawney, 32, 35, 36.
20. Tawney, 181.
21. Tawney, 140, 141.
22. Tawney, 84.
23. Tawney, 85, 88.
24. See p. 26. Also Postan, in *Studi Sapori*, i 547, on the joint stock

company that he calls 'another distinction recently fabricated'. Tawney, 34; also 188 that 'the social teaching of the Church had ceased to count, because the Church itself had ceased to think'. This could apply to the fourteenth century as much as to sixteenth-century England.

25. Tawney, 37.

26. Tawney, 38. Thus Weber, 58, comments that 'the practical action of the average man of pre-capitalistic times, pre-capitalistic in the sense that the rational utilization of capital in a permanent enterprise and the rational capitalistic organisation of labour had not yet become dominant forces in the determination of economic activity'.

27. See p. 90; also Carus-Wilson, *Medieval Merchant Venturers*, 270, 274–5.

28. Cf M. M. Postan, 'The Chronology of Labour Services', in *TRHS*[4] xx (1937) 169–93, cited by Smith, *Canterbury Cathedral Priory*, 113.

29. 'Even at the Conquest manorial economy in Kent was characterized by reliance in the main on money rents', Smith, *Canterbury Cathedral Priory*, 113, where he cites the *Victoria County History: Kent* III 342.

30. Ibid. 114, 124, 125.

31. Ibid. 126.

32. P. D. A. Harvey, *A Medieval Oxfordshire Village, Cuxham, 1240 to 1400*, (Oxford, 1965) cited by G. C. Homans, in *Speculum*, XLI 143.

33. Weber, 73.

34. Tawney, 46.

35. Tawney, 114.

36. Tawney, 115.

37. Weber, 17. He continued: 'The important fact is always that a calculation of capital in terms of money is made, whether by modern bookkeeping methods or in any other way, however primitive and crude. Everything is done in terms of balances' (18), which must, however, be associated with 'the rational capitalistic organisation of (formally) free labour' (21).

38. *Medici Bank*, 7.

39. Thrupp, *Merchant Class*, 166–7.

40. Martines, *Social World*, 19–20.

41. Cited by Le Goff, *Marchands et banquiers*, 81, 82.

42. See p. 25; cf Thrupp, *Merchant Class*, 108–9, 177. Gerard Groote complained that, in the matter of leasing churches to clerics, deals could be made without an actual contract, therefore canon law provisions to prevent such leases could not apply. The solution was to get at the parties through the confessional; Zijl, *Gerard Groote*, 267.

43. Thrupp, *Merchant Class*, 35.

44. Weber, 75.

45. *JEcH* XVIII 427–8.

46. Tawney, 52, 53, 53–4.

47. Tawney, 50.

48. Tawney, 50, 180.

49. Tawney, 157–8.

50. Tawney, 56–7. See p. 75. Also De Roover, *Medici Bank*, 10, in *Studi Sapori*, I 645, and in *Camb. Econ. Hist.* III 55. What was ruled out was the discounting of bills (in *Studi Sapori*, I 632).

51. *Medici Bank*, 374.

52. Tawney, 180.

53. R. M. Kingdon, 'Economic Behaviour of Ministers in Geneva in the Middle of the Sixteenth Century', in *Archiv für Reformationsgeschichte*, L (1959) 33–9, here 37. See p. 114.

54. In *J of Semitic Studies*, I 156.

55. In Demant, 86, 87.

56. Le Goff, *Marchands et banquiers*, 120–1.

57. Martines, *Social World*, 37, 132, 288, where he also cites F. Catalano, 'La crisi italiana alla fine del secolo xv', in *Belfagor*, XI (1956) 393–414, 505–27.

58. Marks, in *Italian Renaissance Studies*, 132, 140, 146.

59. Weber, 17; Tawney, 84–5.

60. Weber, 170–2; Tawney, 122–3.

61. Tawney, 259–60, 262, 263.

62. Thrupp, *Merchant Class*, 174–5.

63. Ibid. 123.

64. Elliott-Binns, *Medieval Cornwall*, 192.

65. Elliott-Binns, *Medieval Cornwall*, 323–4.

66. Gill, *Eugenius IV*, 208.

67. Tawney, 42.

68. Pius II, *Commentaries*, ed. Gabel, 357.

69. Tawney, 280.

70. Smith, *Canterbury Cathedral Priory*, 44.

71. Ibid. 30, 31.

72. An establishment whose numbers varied from a maximum of 150 monks in 1125 to a minimum of 46 in 1376, several of whom had their own households, together with large numbers of *famuli* and wage labourers was an expensive undertaking that needed extreme care to balance the annual budget (ibid. 3). See p. 41.

73. Knowles, in *Studies Gwynn*, 282, 285–6.

74. M. D. Knowles, *The Episcopal Colleagues of Archbishop Thomas Becket*, 7, 14–15, 17–18, 38, and in *Studies Gwynn*, 289; also Cheney, *Becket to Langton*, 27; J. R. L. Highfield, 'The English Hierarchy in the Reign of Edward III', in *TRHS*5 VI (1956) 115–38, here 115, 120.

75. Cheney, *Becket to Langton*, 104.

76. Gibbs and Lang, *Bishops and Reform*, 8; Elliott-Binns, *Medieval Cornwall*, 287. On promotion of sons of priests, see Cheney, *Becket to Langton*, 14–15.

77. Pantin, *English Church*, 15, 22–3.

78. Knowles, in *Studies Gwynn*, 290, 291.

79. Gibbs and Lang, *Bishops and Reform*, 15–16.

80. Hill, *Medieval Lincoln*, 310.

81. Zijl, *Gerard Groote*, 35.

82. Chenu, *La Théologie*, 255.

83. Giordani, *Social Message*, 290–1; also Davies, *Early Christian Church*, 110.

84. Gill, *Eugenius IV*, 15, 200.

85. Pius II, *Commentaries*, ed. Gabel, 21.

86. Renouard, *Les Relations*, 15–16.

87. Lunt, *Papal Revenues*, I 49.

88. Cf Waley, *Papal State*, 298.

89. O'Sullivan, *Italian Merchant Bankers*, 13.

90. Hilton, *Economic Development*, 5, also 7, where he makes an exception for Leicestershire in England; Johansen, in *Studi Sapori*, I 324–5.

91. Maisonneuve, in *Mélanges*, XVIII 25.

92. In Spain the Church granted tithes to lay conquerors of former Moslem-held territories; this was a stimulus to secular settlement, so that Burns concludes: 'In short, the tithe would seem to have been a not inconsiderable boon to medieval colonialism, and a not unimportant aspect of the history of the mediaeval frontier' (in *Speculum*, XLI 452).

93. Davies, *Early Christian Church*, 66. The problem of feudal serfdom is more difficult to solve, cf Tawney, 70, that 'the disappearance of serfdom ... was part of a general economic movement, with which the Church had little to do ...'

Index

Aaron of Lincoln, 43, 282 n 148, 283 n 155; debtors, 105
Aaron of Sidingham, 3
Abbeys, *see under individual titles*
Abbots, (Nicaea II 12) 158. *See also* Monasteries)
Abortion, 100
Acciaiuoli, 74, 91, 105, 112, 291 n 59
Account-books and usury, (Vienne [29]) 206
Accounting: by heads of religious houses, (Lyons I [1]) 189–92; of poor houses, (Vienne [17]) 202–4
Accursius (1182–1260), 253 n 27, 276 n 65
Agriculture, 8, 23, 24; Church, 103, 298 n 26; protection of stock and workers, (Lateran II 11) 165, (Lateran III 22) 171–2; scripture, 51. *See also* Farming, Wool
Aix-la-Chapelle, Council of, 63
Alberti, 74, 105
Albi, 92
Albigensians, (Lateran III 27) 174
Alexander III, pope, 59, 66, 256 n 65
Alms, 305 n 162; Benedictine, 120; monastic, 79; municipal, 121; papal, 120–1; royal, 79, 120. *See also* Poor
Almshouses, 78, (Vienne [17]) 202
Alms-seekers and relics, (Lateran IV 62) 182; Franciscans, (Vienne [38]) 209–15 passim
Alum, 296 n 116, 298 n 17
Ambrosius, 108
Amsterdam, 89
Animals: protection of, (Lateran II 11) 165, (Lateran III 22) 171–2; tithe, (Vienne [11]) 200. *See also* Farming
Annates, (Basel, Session XXI) 219; opposition to, 294 n 94
Annuities, 107; usury, 295 n 106
Anselm, bishop of Lucca, and usury, 278 n 101

Anti-clericalism, 20. *See also* Clergy
Anti-semitism, 38, 266 n 99. *See also* Jews
Antwerp, 126
Apostolic poverty, 7
Aquinas, St Thomas: gain, 274, n 43; just price, 60, 130; usury, 69
Aquitaine, 139
Archives, (Lyons I [1]) 189–92 passim
Aristotle, 69
Armagh, 107
Arras, 261 n 40
Arsenal (Venice), 291 n 64
Arson, *see* Incendiarism
Astesanus, 69
Augsburg, 116
Augustine, St, 51
Augustus Triumphus, 293 n 88
Avarice, (Lateran II 9) 164, (Lateran III 24) 172–3, (Lateran IV 56) 180–1
Avignon, 73; papacy, 73, 94, 107, 112, 294 n 94
Azo, 253 n 27, 279 n 115

Banchi a minuto, 112
Banchi di pegno, 111, 112
Baldwin, J. W., 2, 53, 58–60
Bankers, 261 n 36, 283 n 155, 284 n 163; England, 73; Florence, 73; general councils, 125–6; Genoa, 73; papal, 295 n 113, 299 n 50
Banking, 105, 131, 284 n 171, 291 n 59; exchange, 248 n 6; Jews, 111
Bankruptcy, 259 n 20, 285 n 173; Cistercian, 43; Florentine, 285 n 174; papacy, 297 n 16
Bardi, 25, 27, 73, 74, 91, 105, 295 n 114
Bartell, E., 60–1
Bartholomew, bishop of Exeter, 136
Bartolus of Sassoferrato (1314–57), 262 n 48, 289 n 17
Basel, Council of (1434), 18, 21, 94, 125, 134, 215–19, 294 n 102; Session XIX, 38, 84, 282 n 152

311